KING OF HUNTERS, WARRIORS, AND SHEPHERDS: ESSAYS ON KHAṆḌOBĀ

King of Hunters, Warriors, and Shepherds

Essays on Khaṇḍobā

by

GÜNTHER-DIETZ SONTHEIMER

Edited by

ANNE FELDHAUS

ADITYA MALIK

HEIDRUN BRÜCKNER

INDIRA GANDHI NATIONAL CENTRE FOR THE ARTS

NEW DELHI

MANOHAR

2026

The editors gratefully acknowledge the permission of the following copyright holders to reprint the articles in this volume:

—CNRS, Paris, for "Some Incidents in the History of the God Khandoba" (© 1979);

—The South Asia Institute, University of Heidelberg, for "The Mallāri/Khaṇḍobā Myth as Reflected in Folk Art and Ritual" (© 1983), "Dasarā at Devaraguḍḍa: Ritual and Play in the Cult of Mailār/Khaṇḍobā" (© 1984), and "King Khaṇḍobā's Hunt and His Encounter with Bāṇāī, the Shepherdess" (© 1993);

—The Centre for South Asian Studies, University of Toronto, for "Rudra and Khaṇḍobā: Continuity in Folk Religion" (© 1987);

—The State University of New York Press, Albany, for "Between Ghost and God: A Folk Deity of the Deccan" (© 1989) and "All the God's Wives" (© 1996);

—Harrassowitz Verlag, Wiesbaden, for "The Myth of the God and His Two Wives: Two Pastoral Versions from Maharashtra" (© 1989);

—E. J. Brill, Leiden, for "God as the King for All: The Sanskrit *Mallari Mahatmya* and Its Context" (© 1990); and

—Egbert Forsten, Groningen, for "Bhakti in Khaṇḍobā Cult" (© 1991)

First published 1997
Reprinted 2025, 2026
First eBook edition 2025

ISBN 978-81-7304-018-4 (hardbound)
ISBN 978-93-6080-300-1 (eBook)

Published by
Indira Gandhi National Centre for the Arts,
Janpath, New Delhi - 110001
in association with
Ajay Kumar Jain *for*
Manohar Publishers & Distributors
4753/23 Ansari Road, Daryaganj,
New Delhi 110 002

Printed and bound in India

Contents

Foreword

I WRITE THIS foreword with great pleasure and an equal measure of grief. I am happy that a book which will or should make a substantial difference in understanding the especial dynamics of Indian culture is being published. I mourn the sudden and untimely passing away of this rare and sensitive human being who was an unconventional scholar here and there.

Impeccably trained as an Indologist, Professor G.-D. Sontheimer's range of scholarship was very deep and widespread, covering a large geographic area in India, attempting to work out a morphology of the folk level of Hinduism in relation to its other layers, simultaneously in its regional and subregional variations. He worked on the description and analysis of rituals and oral texts in a ritual context. For him the folk level of cultures encompassed folk religion, folk literature and folk performances. His approach was to cut across narrow compartmentalization of disciplines in order to do justice to the continuity of Indian culture and civilization. Professor Sontheimer's overall context of this open approach to Hinduism has been well stated in his contribution to *Hinduism Reconsidered*. The notion is that of the 'five components' of Hinduism, namely: (1) the work and teachings of the Brahmans; (2) asceticism and renunciation; (3) tribal religion; (4) folk religion; and (5) bhakti. He stressed that these components are not to be viewed as 'watertight compartments, but rather as presenting a continuum and as interacting among themselves in a fluctuating process'.

Taking the Khaṇḍobā cult of Maharashtra as an example of 'folk religion', Professor Sontheimer shows how other components are integrated into the culture and thus make it 'a mirror of Hinduism'. There is a special need to work out such categories of description and analysis, he thought, because religion does not explain itself, and various traits overlap. The study of Khaṇḍobā combines scriptural, historical and oral literary sources with a detailed documentation of the folk deity. Professor Sontheimer not only describes events in their immediate context, but also analyses typical features of folk religions, characterized by apparently antagonistic rituals—e.g. a perception of god as king and the notion that the annual renewal of fertility is the task of the kingly god who recreates life out of death.

While the rituals of folk religion, Professor Sontheimer points out, are distinguished by pomp, festivity, drama, and play form in contrast to Vedic śrauta ritual, at the same time there are other elements in them that have parallels with Vedic rituals such as the Aśvamedha Yajña. It seems that there is a constant interaction between these two realms—between the scriptural texts and oral folk literature—and it may not be advisable to generalize about the Khaṇḍobā cult on the basis of either point of view, but to try to inquire contextually when, how, and where one or the other realm overlaps or is distinct. For instance, in folk perception Khaṇḍoba is not just viewed as an *avatāra*, but he is Śiva himself, as king on earth—'here and now'—in order to look after the welfare of his followers or devotees. It is pre-eminently a cult of bhakti, associated with local culture with its dramatic performances and oral literature. Nevertheless, the local Mahatmya—i.e. the written text—tends to explain or devalue these typical dramatically performed folk rites and oral myths, by hierarchization within the framework of the brahminical system, or even ignoring them. However, oral myths are not only important in the cult but complementary to the scriptural texts. Today, oral texts and their interaction with ritual expressions and scriptural texts tend to become evanescent; as literacy increases, proliferation of temple pamphlets and booklets is widespread and generally modern change has an accelerating effect. In the long run the communicative and performative circumstances that characterize folk culture are threatened in their existence by the general technicalization of culture which has been going on for quite some time now and will gain in intensity in the future. All this has been well elaborated by Professor Sontheimer.

Professor Sontheimer's valuable contribution to the understanding of Indian civilization is indeed tremendous not only in detail but also in its approach. It was indeed very fortunate for us that he was associated with the programmes and projects of the IGNCA for many years. We shared questioning narrow compartmentalization, as also recognizing the need for evolving fresh critical tools for analysis of not only what could be termed the broad area of folk culture but also the texts. The IGNCA has, through several of its programmes in the Lok Parampara and Kshetra Sampadā, identified this constant movement of flux between the past and the present, the written and the oral, the structural and the unstructured, the universal perennial and the specific and temporal. The papers in the volumes on *Concepts of Space* and *Concepts of Time* further confirm the efficacy of adopting fresh multidisciplinary approaches. Contours of the journey, the paths and directions are as important as fixed milestones. The collection of Professor Sontheimer's essays lends further support to this approach.

Thus it is only appropriate that IGNCA should publish this volume, which has been so ably and painstakingly edited by Anne Feldhaus, Heidrun Brückner, and Aditya Malik, Professor Sontheimer's colleagues and/or students, who are themselves well known and acknowledged for their multidisciplinary and holistic approaches to the study of Indian culture. I thank the three editors singly and together. I hope this approach will be adopted by a larger number of scholars and institutions in many other areas of the live traditions of India.

Also I thank my colleague Dr Lalit M. Gujral and the co-publisher, Manohar, for seeing the book through the press.

New Delhi KAPILA VATSYAYAN
12 September 1996

Introduction

A TRADITIONAL Indian idea about people who die with their wishes unfulfilled is that they are hard to put to rest. They hover about on earth, troubling the living and seeking in vain to satisfy themselves. When Günther Sontheimer died, he left several academic wishes unfulfilled. One of these was to write a book entitled *A History of the God Khaṇḍobā*. For his colleagues, one of the haunting things about his death is the fact that now he can never write such a book. The present volume does not pretend to replace that book, nor does it pretend to fulfil any wish of his—he would certainly have pooh-poohed our efforts in bringing together his scattered writings on Khaṇḍobā—but it is the best we can do to assuage our own disappointment that his "History of Khaṇḍobā" cannot be written.

The papers collected here span nearly two decades, beginning two years after the publication of Sontheimer's *Birobā, Mhaskobā und Khaṇḍobā: Ursprung, Geschichte und Umwelt von pastoralen Gottheiten in Mahārāṣṭra* (Wiesbaden: Franz Steiner Verlag, 1976) and extending to posthumous works published as late as four years after his death in 1992. All these papers were originally written in English, but they first appeared in books and journals published in various places: Canada, France, Germany, India, the Netherlands, and the United States of America. We have presented the articles in more-or-less chronological order, allowing for the vagaries of their many original editors and publishers and for the fact that many of the articles were presented as lectures or conference papers long before they reached their published form. We have consolidated the bibliographies and lists of abbreviations, we have edited the English, and we have standardized the references, but otherwise we have left the papers as they were originally published.

Taken together, these articles not only show us how Sontheimer's thoughts about Khaṇḍobā developed but also give us some idea of the lines along which he would have written his "History". From the very first article in this volume to the last one, some of his most basic ideas about the god and his cult are found repeated again and again. Thus, an idea that forms the central thesis of one article—like the idea of Khaṇḍobā's relationship with Rudra and the Vrātyas, for example, in "Rudra and Khaṇḍobā"—is also mentioned in all or most of the other articles, and a component of the cult that is studied in depth in one article—as is the *Mallāri Māhātmya*, for instance, in "God as the King for All"—cannot be left out of the others. It is as if Sontheimer could not focus on any one aspect of this multi-faceted god and cult without also drawing our attention to the other aspects.

Thus, we can tell that the history of Khaṇḍobā that Sontheimer might have written would have been comprehensive. It would have taken into account, as these articles do, the different traditions of the wide variety of castes and tribes for whose members Khaṇḍobā is an important god. It would have extended beyond Maharashtra, as these articles do, to include the related gods Mallanna of Andhra Pradesh and Mailār of Karnataka. And it would have made use, as these articles do, of the various *kinds* of source materials that Sontheimer had gathered—*ovīs*, oral epics, of the Dhangar shepherds; narratives, comments, and statements made by people belonging to different castes and tribes; the songs (*padeṃ*) of the Vāghyās and Muraḷīs, Khaṇḍobā's "bards" and "courtesans;" the Sanskrit and Marathi Māhātmyas composed by Brāhmaṇs; descriptions and remarks searched out in the literature of the Mahānubhāvs, the Vārkarīs, and other medieval saints; and stray references culled from published and unpublished historical documents.

Even the first article in this anthology, "Some Incidents in the History of the God Khaṇḍobā", which was first published in 1978, already contains many of Sontheimer's basic ideas about the god and the cult: the connection with Mailār and Mallanna, the similarities to Rudra and Murukaṉ, the importance of the mountain and the anthill, the "fusion" of Śiva and Sūrya in Mārtaṇḍa Bhairava, the pattern represented by the god's two wives, the heroic and royal aspects of the cult, and more. Like this first article, the second, "The Mallāri/Khaṇḍobā Myth as Reflected in Folk Art and Ritual" (first published in 1984) is rather general in nature, but in addition it includes a detailed discussion of the various *vāhanas* and other animals associated with the god.[1]

"Dasarā at Devaraguḍḍa" (1981; appeared 1984) contains Sontheimer's first detailed description of a festival of Mailār, the god in Karnataka who corresponds to Khaṇḍobā in Maharashtra. This article is also the first in which Sontheimer presented in some detail his arguments for a continuity from the Vrātyas of the Vedic period and their god Rudra to the Vaggayyas or Vāghyās and their god Mailār or Khaṇḍobā. Each of the next two articles takes up one of these two themes of "Dasarā". "Rudra and Khaṇḍobā" (1987) further elaborates and refines the argument about Rudra, and "Between Ghost and God" (1989) continues the discussion of Mailār, extending it to include Mallanna, the corresponding god in Andhra Pradesh, as well.

"The Myth of the God and his Two Wives" (1989) and "God as the King for All" (1990) present samples of the two most widely divergent types of primary sources that Sontheimer used for his study of the cult of Khaṇḍobā. "The Myth of the God and his Two Wives" gives translations of two oral versions of the story, one sung and the other narrated in prose, both by Hāṭkar Dhangar shepherds whom Sontheimer knew very well. This article also provides a discussion of the Hāṭkar Dhangars' oral literature, especially their *ovīs*. "God as the King for All: the Sanskrit *Mallāri Māhātmya* and Its Context" includes a summary of the principal Māhātmya of Khaṇḍobā, and interprets this text in the light of the cult's history and current practices. "All the God's Wives" (1996) provides a large number of samples of another type of literature from the cult, a type that Sontheimer was especially actively engaged in collecting and translating during the last years of his life: the traditional songs of the Vāghyās and Muraḷīs. These songs are also illustrated in "Bhakti in the Khaṇḍobā Cult" (1991) and "King Khaṇḍobā's Hunt" (1994).

For Sontheimer, the cult of Khaṇḍobā included all five of the "components" that he considered to be the defining elements in the diversity of Hinduism. In his article "Hinduism: The Five Components and Their Interaction",[2] Sontheimer identified the components as "(1) The work and the teaching of the Brāhmaṇs; (2) Asceticism and renunciation; (3) Tribal religion; (4) Folk religion; [and] (5) Bhakti". In explicating these components, he illustrated them by means of the cult of Khaṇḍobā, calling the cult a "mirror" of Hinduism. If "The Myth of the God and his Two

Wives" and "God as the King for All", both of which were published at about the same time as "The Five Components", illustrate, respectively, tribal religion and the work of Brāhmaṇs, "All the God's Wives" illustrates an aspect of the folk religious component that Sontheimer saw as central to the cult.

"Bhakti in the Khaṇḍobā Cult" was also, clearly, written with the five components in mind. Not only does this article attempt to show the presence of the fifth component in the cult; it also illustrates the "dynamic interrelationship" between bhakti and other components. Thus, Sontheimer finds bhakti in the Māhātmya texts and in the folk-religious songs of the Vāghyās and Muraḷīs, and he examines reflections of the folk religion of the cult in the work of Vaiṣṇava bhakti poets.

Finally, in "King Khaṇḍobā's Hunt" we find Sontheimer's most mature, most complete treatment of the cult in all its aspects, but especially as an example of folk religion. The article focuses on the celebration of the Somvatī Amāvāsyā (no-moon Monday) festival in Jejuri. In contrast to what he saw as the essentially Brāhmaṇical interpretation of the festival by Stanley (1977), Sontheimer brings out an interpretation that is more prominent in the traditions of the Dhangars and the folk literature of the Vāghyās and Muraḷīs. In the course of this interpretation, he presents a rich exploration of folk traditions about hunting, heroism, kingship, eroticism, and the wilderness.[3]

Günther Sontheimer died soon after completing "King Khaṇḍobā's Hunt". He died in Germany, late on Sunday night or early on Monday morning, the first day of June 1992. That Monday was the no-moon day, and in Jejuri the Somvatī Amāvāsyā festival was being celebrated. When Sakharam Babu Lakade, one of Sontheimer's best informants and closest friends among the Dhangars, heard of his death, he said, "His soul must have traveled to Jejuri, to be here for the Somvatī festival."

NOTES

1. The editors wish to thank Frau Edeltraud Bienek for her help in finding the illustrations for this article and those for "Between Ghost and God".
2. *Hinduism Reconsidered*, edited by Günther D. Sontheimer and Hermann Kulke (New Delhi: Manohar, 1989), pp. 197-212.
3. These same themes are also central to "King Khaṇḍobā's Hunting Expedition", an 81-minute film that Sontheimer made with Henning Stegmüller. The film,

which uses for its text extracts from the *ovīs* of the Dhangars and the *padeṃ* of the Vāghyās and Muraḷīs, was completed in 1992, and exists in a German and an English version. Videocassettes of the film can be purchased from Adanos Film GmbH, Clemensstrasse 80, D-80796 München, Germany, or, in India, rented from the Indira Gandhi National Centre for the Arts, New Delhi, or the Sontheimer Cultural Association, Pune.

Abbreviations

A.	Arabic
AV	*Atharva Veda*
BŚS	*Baudhāyana Śrauta Sūtra*
ca.	circa
Cal.	Calcutta
cent.	century
crit.	critical
DED	*Dravidian Etymological Dictionary*
Dt.	District
ed., edn.	edition
HGS	*Hiraṇyakeśīgṛhyasūtra*
JB	*Jaiminīya Brāhmaṇa*
JM	*Jayādri Māhātmya*
JUB	*Jaiminīya Upaniṣad Brāhmaṇa*
Ka.	Kannada
Kh. Ā.	*Khaṇḍerāyācī Ādī* (by Jagjivan)
LS	Limbā's story
Ma., Mar.	Marathi
Mbh	*Mahābhārata*
MM, M.Māh.	*Mallāri Māhātmya* (by Siddhapāl Kesarī)
MMKh	Mallanna/Mailāra/Khaṇḍobā
MMRā	*Mallāri Māhātmya* (by Rāmdās, "Sadāśiva's servant", 1857)
MMŚ	*Mallāri Māhātmya* (by Śrīdharasvāmī Nājharekar)
MMVi	*Mallāri Māhātmya* (by Vināyaka, 1871)
Molesw.	Molesworth's Marathi-English Dictionary
MS	*Maitrāyaṇī Saṃhitā*
MV	*Mārtaṇḍa Vijaya* (Mar., 1821)
P.	Persian
PB	*Pañcaviṃśa Brāhmaṇa*
ṚV	*Ṛgveda*

Śat.	*Śatarudrīya (Taittirīya Saṃhitā)*
ŚB	*Śatapatha Brāhmaṇa*
Skt.	Sanskrit
(S)M	(Spoken Standard) Marathi
SR	Second recording of Liṃbā's story
ŚŚS	*Śaṅkhāyana Śrauta Sūtra*
TA	*Taittirīya Āraṇyaka*
TB	*Taittirīya Brāhmaṇa*
Tel.	Telugu
Tk.	Taluka
TS	*Taittirīya Saṃhitā*
VS	*Vājasaneyī Saṃhitā*
WZKS	*Wiener Zeitschrift für die Kunde Südasiens*
WZKSO	*Wiener Zeitschrift für die Kunde Süd- und Ostasiens*

Some Incidents in the History of the God Khaṇḍobā

THE STUDY of a god and his cult in historical or diachronic perspective is not only a part of the history of religion, but also throws much light on the social, cultural, philosophical, and even political history of a locality, an area, or a region, and possibly on the history of India in general. A historical approach to the study of a cult has, of course, limitations in India; one may also study a cult as an agglutination of layers and present it as the incorporation of "different aspects or levels in Hinduism" (Dumont, 1957: 40ff.). Some incidents of the very popular Khaṇḍobā cult of Maharashtra are discussed here in a summary form with a view to elaborating this point.

At the outset it must be said that the study of Khaṇḍobā ought to involve a comparison with other deities of the Deccan who all suggest a basic identity. The same god is called Mailār in Karnataka and Mallaṇṇa in Andhra. We are fortunate in having early evidence of this god in the Caṅkam literature, where he is called Murukaṉ. Khaṇḍobā may actually be traced to a prototype of a god found all over the Deccan from very early times. Literary research combined with field research shows us that certain processes in the development of this god repeated themselves in different regions of the Deccan. Such processes may be initiated anew even today, and, though not all the links of the process may be discernible, the prototype of the god or some stage of—or the emphasis on some aspects of a stage in—the process may be detected in the field. Thus from comparison a fairly consistent picture of the history of the cult emerges. Moreover, it is a common truth that the various stages in the evolution of groups as well as their spatial or social separateness are—though this becomes increasingly difficult to observe today—reflected in their beliefs and attitudes and give an idea of historical, if not prehistoric events. The oral traditions of various groups are an invaluable source of information. Many of these traditions are the rough material for, and the precursors of, the written text. Basically the cult did not change through the ages; rather, we may say that the history of the god provided endless regional and local variations of certain basic themes. These variations were contributed by various groups involved in the cult and each new group contributed new religious interpretations, new rituals, and new additions or changes of the basic myth. But as the natural habitat and the social conditions of new groups worshipping Khaṇḍobā did not vary basically from those of their predecessors, the new layers of belief, rites, attitudes, and myth did not radically alter the original god. Or, we may say, the newcomers were able to identify their beliefs and their deities with the existing cult and add to it without destroying the original one (see also Dumont, 1957: 45).

One thing we can be sure of is that the origins of the god cannot be found in the rice area, in the cultivated "nuclear agricultural areas" (Stein, 1963: 188) of the Deccan, which tend to be the civilized "*kṣetra*", with regular cultivation, peaceful, with a settled society, a rigid caste system and governed by concepts of law and order for which the Brāhmaṇical Dharmaśāstras ultimately were the guide.

The origins of this outlandish god have, in fact, to be sought at the door of this society—similarly to the Vedic Rudra, who was beyond the settlement. Like Bhairava, who has protective functions and is the *kotvāl* of Benares, and is terrible in some aspects, Khaṇḍobā has protective functions. The capacity of the Indian religious outlook would make Khaṇḍobā a god who protected the hermitage of Brāhmaṇs, the protective spirit of the realm or town, and would claim that he was a deified hero (Dhere, 1961: 14, citing the 12th cent. Jain *Samayaparīkṣā*)—the distinction between a human being and a *dev* (deity) can disappear with the passing of time. Much of Khaṇḍobā would recur in the human *daṇḍanāyaka* who protects the borders of the kingdom. He would be identified with Bhairava, who often protects temple entrances, the *devī*, or the village. But the origin was in the hilly regions and forested tracts. The ancient Tamil poets of the Caṅkam age—ca. 3rd or 4th cent. A.D.—had seen this god first worshipped in the forested mountains, in the regions called *kuriñci* after a flower that blossoms there. They called the god Cēyoṉ or Cēyyōṉ, meaning "the red one", and the red colour of the god reminded the poets of the rising sun (Zvelebil, 1977: 11). Popular etymology and love for puns often contribute to the identification of gods, and Cēyyōṉ may mean also "the young one"—which made him acceptable to the *devī* and identifiable as Skanda and Kārtikeyya, the son of Śiva. Murukaṉ, like Khaṇḍobā, originally resides on the hills: he is called in Old Tamil *malaikilavōn*, the "Lord of the Hills" (Sontheimer, 1976: 20, 92). The inhabitants of the hilly, forested region were tribal food-gatherers and hunters. They experienced the god in the form of the hill and the rising sun, but also as a hunter, and they equipped him with a spear and provided an elephant and the peacock as his *vāhana.* He was called *velāṉ,* the "carrier of the spear", like his priests who performed an ecstatic dance. He was worshipped in the form of a pillar (*kantu*), for example, and under the *kaṭambu* tree (*Tirumurukāṟṟuppaṭai*, 6.225f.).

The predominant element in the origin of Murukaṉ *and* Khaṇḍobā is the worship of the mountain in the forested tracts by hill tribes or pastoralists. In fact this is the origin of many gods before development and accretions begin. Thus in the Kolhāpūr area Khaṇḍobā is called Mallaya, which may be derived from Ka. *male + ayya,* the "Lord of the Mountain". From inscriptions of the 12th cent. we come to know that the Vīrabanañjas, a merchant guild in Kolhāpūr and Miraj associated with the Vīraśaivas or Liṅgāyats, depicted their god in the form of a mountain in their banner (Sontheimer, 1976: 91ff.). Similarly, the name of Mallaṇṇa, the god corresponding to Khaṇḍobā in Andhra, may also be derived etymologically the same way. Even today the god may be sighted on a mountain, e.g. in an unhewn stone which is then worshipped.

This may be illustrated with two references. The first is chosen at random from oral texts collected in the field. The informant is a Koḷī—the traditional tribal and then boatsman and watercarrier in Maharashtra:

In Koṅkan, in the middle of the villages Cilhure, Kusumbal and Sāle in the Tk. Māṇgāv, Dt. Kolābā, there is a mountain. On this mountain there is a temple of Khaṇḍobā. Cilhure is inhabited by Gavlīs [the pastoral caste]. One Gavlī used to graze his cows and buffaloes on the mountain. At the same time he used to cut grass with his sickle. One cow always went to a certain spot, kept standing there licking a stone. The Gavlī wondered: "Why does the cow come there daily to lick this stone?" One day when he came near the cow which was licking the stone, he hit on the stone with the sickle. *Bhaṇḍār* [turmeric powder—identifiable with Khaṇḍobā] emerged—and the more he hit the more *bhaṇḍār* emerged. Then he realized: "It must be a god". He asked the other people in the village [the identifiers]. They decided: "It is Khaṇḍobā". Later they built a temple for this god and worshipped him. Even today the Gavlīs are devotees of this Khaṇḍobā.

The other reference comes from Professor G.H. Khare's book *Maharashtrācīṃ cār daivateṃ*. Khare cites an account of the year 1750 on the origin of the famous Khaṇḍobā cult at Jejurī, one of the most important centres of Khaṇḍobā worship in Maharashtra (Khare, 1958: 90). I quote in translation:

> ... one day when the cowherd boys were sitting on the Kaḍe Paṭhār [that is, the high stony hill plateau at Jejurī and the site of the "older" Khaṇḍobā], the god Khaṇḍobā assumed form seated on a *horse* and holding a *spear*. And he sat down with them on their woolen blankets....

The origins of the god may also be found in the worship of the anthill, the seat of snakes, in which form the god may also appear. The anthill is characteristic of the forest. It should not be ploughed by farmers lest they would suffer great harm. For the forest tribes and the pastoral communities it was not only the seat of snakes, but the seat of wealth and thus the origin of sheep; and it is for some the seat of gold. It is associated with the sun and, for instance, the Kharias worship the sun with offerings on an anthill (Crooke, 1968: 9f.). Today one may still find an anthill worshipped with *bhaṇḍār* at e.g. the Somvatī Amāvasyā *jatrā* for Khaṇḍobā at Jejurī.

Khaṇḍobā has close connections with the equivalent god Mailār of Karnataka; the god Mailār at Ādimailār had, according to local traditions, his origins in an anthill inhabited by snakes. The cows of a certain Gomuni used to give milk (which again suggests a pastoral, forest background rather than an agricultural context) into the holes of that anthill. Kapila Muni, who was practising *tapas* at the anthill, advised him to spread the glory of Mārtaṇḍa Bhairav. Gomuni changed the hill into a form of Mārtaṇḍa Bhairav. The *mūrti* was called *maṇṇāppā* (Skt. *mṛṇamaya*) *dev* or *Mṛṇmaya* Mallārī, "the Mallārī formed of clay or mud".

As we can see, the origins of the gods are not only found in the worship of the mountain and the anthill, but the god is also associated with the sun. Mārtaṇḍa is the son of Aditi; Mārtaṇḍa is given as a name of the sun in Molesworth's Marāṭhī Dictionary and in Kittel's Kannaḍa Dictionary; and Allchin mentions a Mārtaṇḍeśvar temple of presumably the 12th or 13th cent. with *mūrtis* of Sūrya probably of the same period (Allchin, 1963: 10). Dr. Dhere, however, derives Mārtaṇḍa quite plausibly from a double word, namely from Ka. *māri* = *mukhavṭā*, and Mar. *toṇḍ* = head. He shows with references from a *vacana* of Basaveśvar (12th cent.) and from a passage in the work *Yogasaṃgrāma* by Śekh Mahaṃmad Śrīgondekar (16th/17th cent.) that there was a custom of painting the face of the god on cloth which was worshipped as a *mukhavṭā;* the worship of Khaṇḍobā in the form of the *liṅg* or a *mūrti* has become familiar later (Dhere, 1961: 40ff.). But could the face of the god on a piece of cloth have been on a banner (*dhvaja*), as the above-mentioned Vīraśaivas of Kolhāpūr and Miraj had it and as it is still occasionally seen on the *kāṭhīs* (flag-staffs of the god) at *jatrās* (e.g. in the Mhaskobā cult of Vīr in Purandar Tk. of Puṇe Dt.)? Dhere is of the opinion that there is originally no connection between Khaṇḍobā and Sūrya/Mārtaṇḍa (Dhere, 1963: 42). Yet the tribal and folk worship of the sun may have contributed to the identification of Khaṇḍobā with "Mārtaṇḍa Bhairava". The yellow turmeric powder which is characteristic of this god all over the Deccan, and is also considered to be gold, suggests this. Birobā or Birappa, the exclusive god of many pastoral communities like the Dhangars of Maharashtra, the Kurubas of Karnataka, and the Kurumas of Andhra, is another god of the hill who is connected with the sun. According to the traditions of the Dhangars, the splendour of Birobā's mother Sūravantī or Sūryavantī was like that of the sun, and it is said of her in one of the legends:

> Twelve years she stood on the thorns of a Khair-Tree and worshipped the sun. Then Sūrya produced water from his splendour and poured it in her *thālī.* She drank it.... [And about Birobā, who is no doubt closely associated with Śiva, having been sent by Śiva to the human continent, it is also said:] When Birobā was born from the side of his mother his splendour was even greater than the sun....

The fusion of the cults of Śiva and Sūrya into Mārtaṇḍa-Bhairava is also reflected in the Purāṇas (*Agnipurāṇa* and *Matsyapurāṇa,* referred to by von Stietencron, 1966: 252 and fn.). Khaṇḍobā is specially worshipped on Sundays, like another famous god, the Siddhanāth of Mhasvaḍ, who is Kālbhairava (Sontheimer, 1976: 27, 160). Each Sunday, however, the god (the *mūrti*) is seated on a horse dressed like a Marāṭhā Sardār in order to enable him to ride out. Monday is the special day of Śiva. Although Khaṇḍobā receives no special worship on Monday, one of the greatest festivals of Khaṇḍobā is on Somvatī Amāvāsyā, a Monday on which there is a conjunction of the *sun* and the *moon.* It is rather a festival "based on usage" than one based on *nibandhas* (Kane, 1974: 454). Khaṇḍobā's palanquin is carried from the mountain in Jejurī to the river Karhā and he has his bath in the river. Around the palanquin there is a circular yellow patch consisting of *mānkarīs* (devotees having a special right in the ritual) and others trying to touch the palanquin. They are fully covered with turmeric powder—as if the sun is descending to join the moon in the form of the river Gaṅgā or Candrabhāgā, as the Gangā is called at Kāśī and at Paṇḍharpūr. Rivers in the South tend to be identified with the Gaṅgā. In Kannaḍa Liṅgāyat folklore Gaṅgā does not become the shepherdess Bāṇāī as in Maharashtra but is the beloved mistress (Ramanujan, 1973: 181) of Śiva and she is a member of the fisher and ferrymen caste. A survival of this belief may continue in the fact that Koḷī women are the priestesses of Bāṇāī in Jejurī. Moreover, especially the Son Koḷīs, the fishermen of the seacoast who are devotees of Khaṇḍobā and have their ancestor shrines and memorial slabs in Jejurī, assemble in large numbers on Somvatī Amāvāsyā for the ritual bath in the river. For the Dhangar shepherds the procession is a hunting excursion of the god culminating in the ritual bath. The Dhangars thus continue the hunting traditions of the god. They accompany him in large numbers with their "spears" (*kāṭhīs*) and finally join the god in the ritual bathing.

Again we find two original elements combined: the association of Khaṇḍobā with the sun and the worship by castes with a tribal, pastoral, hunting and fishing background. In a medieval Telugu work called *Kṛḍābhirāmam* (v. 145) from Warangal, composed at the time of the Kākatīya dynasty, that is, in approximately the 14th cent., we read in the description of the god Mailār, who corresponds to Khaṇḍobā:

> He offers boons on Saturday and that is also the day he likes to receive offerings; he enjoys ornamentation (*śṛṅgāra*) only on *Sundays*.... He is a great *hunter, leader* of those who find happiness in *hunting with spears* [italics mine].

The tree was rarely identified with Khaṇḍobā, though we read in the Caṅkam literature of Murukaṉ being the Kaṭampa-tree, or living in or under the Kaṭampa-tree. Of course, we hear quite frequently in Maharashtra that *rakṣasīs* live in the trunks of trees and at least we can say that the leaves of the Bilvā or Bel tree were sacred to Khaṇḍobā as they are to Śiva. The origin of Khaṇḍobā must be looked for in the world of spirits amongst the tribals of the forest and the pastoral communities. He resided on the hill, and manifested himself in the form of a hill, lived in an anthill, and had some connection with the sun.

From the time of the Caṅkam literature we come across a very important phenomenon which is characteristic of the cult of

Khaṇḍobā and all other equivalent gods of the Deccan: the two "wives" of the god. The Deccan was divided basically into two ecological areas populated by two essentially different communities. On the one hand we have the forest tracts inhabited by forest tribes like the Ceñcūs or the Koḷīs and by pastoral tribes like the Kāḍū Kurubas and Kāḍū Gollas who would live in or migrate into the forest for seasonal grazing. In the other area pastoral life dominated. In the Caṅkam literature this area was called *mullai.* But there were also farmers in the pastoral region, though agriculture was still very mixed with a cattle economy. Actually this is an ecological and social situation which persisted from prehistory into very recent times. Around the 3rd millennium B.C. we have a food producing system with a rather sedentary village system. But even after the introduction of this pastoral-and-agricultural system into the area, the mesolithic cultural system based on hunting and food gathering continued side by side with it. Into the ecosystem of mesolithic groups splinters of the neolithic groups intruded, but often this resulted in the development of the sheep pastoral system rather than in drawing the mesolithic tribes as well as the branched-off neolithic groups into the pastoral agricultural fold. There are many legends in Andhra and Karnataka as well as Maharashtra which tell that generally the youngest son of a pastoral-and-agricultural family finds sheep in an anthill and starts a nomadic or semi-nomadic life better suited than regular agriculture to a semi-arid climate. We have a basic division, a basic dichotomy between two ecosystems and between two cultural groups which has found its reflection in the two wives of the god. In the case of Murukaṉ we have Valli, Murukaṉ's favourite wife, who comes from the Kuruvar hill tribe. His first wife is Teyvayānai, the pure one, who comes from the settled, upper communities. In Śrīśailam Mallikārjuna's first wife is Pārvatī. The second one, whom he meets in the forest, comes from the Ceñcū tribe. Near Sultānābād, at Odela, to the northeast of Karimnagar in Andhra, the first wife, Medaladevī, comes from the Baligas, a dominant agricultural Liṅgāyat caste, which is also associated with trade. The second wife, Ketamma, comes from the pastoral Golla community. This pattern is the same in all Mailār temples in northern Andhra. In the *Kṛḍābhirāmam* from Warangal, Mailār's first wife is called Mālavi, but he is also the husband of Pallemma (v. 145). *Palli* or *halli* originally means a tribal hamlet in the forest. In Ādimailār and Devaraguḍḍa in Karnataka the first wife is again Liṅgāyat and the second wife is "Kurubattyavva", who comes from the Kuruba shepherd community. Khaṇḍobā's first wife, of course, is Mhāḷsā, the daughter of a Liṅgāyat merchant (*vāṇī*). The Liṅgāyats were the great agricultural community of the Deccan and had a strong leaning towards a cattle economy, as, e.g. their special worship of the bull reflects. But among them were also many merchant communities. They were primarily worshippers of the *liṅgam*, but they *accepted* Mailār in the form of a *liṅgam*, and Mhāḷsā was worshipped wearing the casket containing the *liṅgam*, as, for instance, in Vadapuri, where I found old *mūrtis* of Khaṇḍobā and Mhāḷsā. Bāṇāī or Bālāi, the second wife of Khaṇḍobā, is said to have come from the Dhangars or Gavlīs, though her temple in Jejurī is served by Koḷīs. The story of Bāṇāī is found in the oral traditions of the Gavlīs and Dhangars. The way Khaṇḍobā obtains Bāṇāī, who is the leader of a big shepherd camp, resembles a *rakṣasa* marriage, a marriage by abduction, and from a brāhmaṇical point of view she is not really a legally married wife, but rather a mistress. There are beautiful legends about how Khaṇḍobā obtained Bāṇāī. In the view of the Dhangars or other tribes she has a fully accepted and respectable position which reflects the tribal marriage conventions of love and abduction, though the morality of the brāhmaṇical *śāstra* has entered the legends:

> When Khaṇḍobā married Bāṇāī there was no Brāhmaṇ. There was no marriage band to play. They threw sheep droppings instead of rice. They decided that the bleating of the sheep coming home in the evening and the bleating of the lambs who had stayed back in the camp in the morning should serve as marriage music. On this evening the shepherds assembled, said the *maṅgalāṣṭaka* verses and married them. It was rather a marriage by abduction than a marriage corresponding to rules. They, Khaṇḍobā and Bāṇāī, presented all the sheep to the shepherds, and then Khaṇḍobā and Bāṇāī came to Jejurī....

This prototype Deccan god was eminently suitable to combine various heterogeneous tribes and social groups under his royal umbrella. This is one distinctive feature of the god. The further we go to the north the more this dichotomy expressed by the two goddesses with the various social groups they represent merges into the unity of Pārvatī. Here the second wife rather becomes an illusion, *māyā*, in fact the disguised Pārvatī. In the Deccan Mhālsā may be identified with Pārvatī, but nobody will maintain that Bāṇāī and Pārvatī are identical. In Pañcmaḍhi in Madhya Pradesh we find a Śiva cult on the Cauragaḍh mountain. Here the devotees of Śiva have erected thousands of iron *triśūlas* for Śiva. The second wife, according to the local legends of the Korkūs, is a Korkū by name Girjā. She comes from a village near Cauragaḍh. But the priest or *sādhus* on Cauragaḍh maintain that Girjā and Pārvatī are one. This reminds us of the story told by the 18th cent. Marāṭhī poet Śrīdhara in his adaptation of the *Kāśīkhaṇḍa*, in which Pārvatī in the disguise of a Bhil woman searches for the angry Śiva. Śiva falls in love with her before he recognizes the disguised Pārvatī.

Khaṇḍobā attracted numerous communities into his fold and assumed protective functions for them. Of course, he also demands tributes and offerings from his devotees. The earliest reference to Khaṇḍobā in this capacity is probably found in the *Mahāmāyūrī Mantra*, where Khaṇḍobā is said to be the patron *yakṣa* of Paiṭhaṇ or Pratiṣṭhāna. Very early this god of the Deccan was invested with attributes of a chieftain, a local ruler, a *daṇḍanāyaka*, a Mahāmaṇḍaleśvar or even a king. It was the task of the king to combine, balance, and protect many heterogeneous groups—a function which was also assigned to the god of the Deccan. This expresses itself in the iconography of the god, in his *vāhanas*, and in the paraphernalia needed in his worship, the *bāvan birudeṃ*. Already in his earliest stage Murukaṉ—like Khaṇḍobā—was given a spear similar to that of a tribal chieftain, and Murukaṉ was called eventually *velaṉ*, the "carrier of the spear". And then the god rides an elephant or a peacock—*vāhanas* in whose form he might have been actually worshipped originally, and he wears the *mukuṭa* of a king. Khaṇḍobā is also Bhairav and acquires the attributes of a roving Śaivite Gosāvī who is the personification of Bhairav or Kālbhairav—the first one to come in contact with the tribes. He acquires a *triśūl* and a *ḍamaru*, along with the *kapāla* or *paral*.

On the local level Bhairav becomes the Aṣṭabhairav or *kṣetrapāl*, the protector of the field and the settled village. Another version of the "God of the Deccan" is the Tamil Aiyaṇār, who has two wives and protects the village, for which purpose the villagers keep numerous clay horses ready at his shrine. Another god is Bhramappa, a god especially found in Karnataka, who—as the origin of the name suggests—roves on a horse around the village in the night to protect the villagers with his wild hunt. He should not be seen by the villagers and they are supposed to be at home in their houses when he rides out. There is consequently not much of an iconography and actually his shrine in the village is empty. But this god has also entered the

Jain pantheon in Karnataka, where he is depicted with sword and *phala,* riding a horse (Settar, 1961: 17, 34ff.).

Khaṇḍobā as a royal protector, as the hero, *vīra, par excellence,* protecting the *kṣetra,* cattle, and brāhmaṇs, was also given the elephant, the parasol, the *pālkhi,* the horse, the shield, and—most typical—the sword. Retaining the aspects of Bhairava, he acquires in the Marāṭhā period the typical dress and outfit of a ruler of the Marāṭhā and Peśvā period; e.g. the turbans worn around the *mukuṭa* are often changed in Jejurī: sometimes they resemble the red turban of the Dhangar Sardārs. The *mūrti* of Mārtaṇḍa Bhairav has the turban of the Śindes. And in the *sabhāmaṇḍapa* of the temple Khaṇḍobā is riding a horse and is dressed like a Marāṭhā Sardār or Śiledār. Khaṇḍobā became the tutelary deity of many of the reigning Marāṭhā families who came from a pastoral background, such as the Holkars, the Gāikvāḍs or the Śindes.

It is during the time of the Yādavas of Devgiri that we find a proliferation of popular gods like Kālbhairav and Khaṇḍobā—or rather his Kannada equivalent Mairāl/Mailār, and the Andhra Mallaṇṇa, who was the family god of the Kākatīyas. There is a very pertinent passage in the *Uttarārdha* part of the 13th cent. Marāṭhī work *Līḷācaritra* (*līḷā* 298 in Tulpule's edn.) of the Mahānubhāv sect of Maharashtra. Śrīcakradhara, the founder of the sect, says in the 12th cent., obviously speaking of the conditions in his time:

> At the end of the Kaliyuga the Śiva and Viṣṇu temples disappear and Mairāla-Kṣetrapālas get established.

I think that from this time Khaṇḍobā emerges from the realm of spirits and *yakṣas* and takes the form of a god. With the establishment of local rulers during the Muslim and Marāṭhā period we find the rise of gods like Khaṇḍobā, Mairāl/Mailār, and Kālbhairav. Often this was brought about by reconstructing old Śiva or Devī temples which had been built under the Yādavas and by installing Khaṇḍobā or Kālbhairav. A typical case is the Kālbhairav of Bilūr in Jath Taluka of Sangli District. The huge Śiva temple of the Yādava period is still intact; it is not Śiva who receives most attention and is primarily worshipped, however, but the Kālbhairav to the right inside the temple before the *sabhāmaṇḍapa.* Kalbhairav, who is holding a *triśūl* and *ḍamaru,* is also worshipped in the form of an equestrian statue of a Marāṭhā Sardār. And, incidentally, Kālbhairav is worshipped with Yogeśvarī at this place. She is his first wife, whereas his second wife, the local goddess, lives appropriately in a grove outside the village. She is called Bālubāī. Here the professional guardian Kālbhairav, who is to watch the entrance to the temple of Śiva, who often acts on behalf of Śiva and who is so similar to the *daṇḍanāyaka,* protecting the borders of the kingdom, has established his independent rule, or rather is now worshipped independently. Perhaps we should say that this reflects the fall of the great empire of the Yādavas and the decentralization of power.

A further step in the career of the god is the acquisition of *asuras* or *daityas* whom he has to defeat. Murukaṉ also eventually acquired *asuras* whom he defeats with his spear and drum. Śiva becomes an *avatār* to fight the two *daityas* Maṇi and Malla, who have destroyed the *āśram* of the *ṛṣis.* In Jejurī, facing the main temple, there is only *one* huge *mūrti* of a *daitya,* and not *two.* But this is easily explained. Maṇi was killed, but Malla was spared by the god and became his devotee. Malla may be reminiscent of one of the tribal chieftains or deified heroes who were outside the brāhmaṇical fold, ruling in the pastoral or forested area. *Malla* is, of course, also a wrestler, and in Karnataka it is a Kuruba who is the chief wrestler of the village. In Tamil *mallaṉ* means "wrestler" or a "great, famous man". *Malla* is also a frequent epithet of rulers, like the Kalacuri king Someśvara Sovideva, who had the *biruda bhujabalamalla,* "the strong wrestler". Several medieval dynasties—e.g. the Yādavas and Kakātīyas—had a simple origin in the pastoral and forested area, rising on account of their prowess from the position of local chieftains, *daṇḍanāyakas,* generals, to a royal position. I suggest that this meaning of *malla* has coalesced with the meaning of "mountain" in Marathi *māl,* Kannada *male* and so on. But if it is said that one of the origins of Khaṇḍobā is the *mountain* or the miniature mountain of the anthill in the pastoral and forested area, then why should Khaṇḍobā-Mallārī, which means "the enemy of Malla", fight *malla?*

Dr. Dhere has pointed out that Khaṇḍobā's name should actually be Maṇimallāri. He shows that in Karnataka, in Hadigalli-Ballārī, the temple of Mailār is called Maṇmailār or Maṇṇumailār. *Mannu* means "mud, clay", and the local explanation is that the *mūrti* of the god is of clay. Thus the explanation is that there was originally no *daitya* by name *Maṇi* and the god should be called there the "enemy of Malla who has a *mūrti* of clay" (Dhere, 1961: 39). We can also suspect that pastoral people or somebody else already worshipped an anthill; as indicated above, the anthill was worshipped first in

Ādimailār. Mārtaṇḍa is the name of a Dhangar Gavḍā who had a daughter Baṇāī, according to oral traditions in Naldurg—before Khaṇḍobā appeared on the scene. The intruding new god is sometimes seen and presented as fighting *asuras, daityas*, or *rakṣasas*. This may show some initial tension between the original worshippers and the new ones who were associating themselves with the cult. But more so, and mostly this happened peacefully, this simply reflects the absorption and identification of primeval cults into and with the newly arriving cult and the religious beliefs coming along with it. The old cult is not eliminated, but absorbed, transformed. We can take as an example Malla himself, who becomes the ardent devotee of Khaṇḍobā and yet still receives nearly separate worship.

The case of Malla also prompts two other remarks. Firstly, much in the traditional polity of the Hindu *rājā* towards the tribes reminds us of the attitude of the god who intrudes into the forest and pastoral area: the defeated *asura* recurs in the name of the god, Mallāri. The *asura* might be killed, but continues to exist somewhat surprisingly in an independent cult or is identified with the intruding god. Similarly, again and again the traditional policy towards, for instance, the Koḷīs, who were feared warriors and robbers, was to invade their territory and to incorporate them into the imperial fold without annihilating them, which might not have been possible anyway. They were often given police functions after their defeat.

The second remark relates to the horse of Khaṇḍobā. From the *Mallāri Māhātmya* and the *Jejurīmāhātmya* it is clear that the horse has come from Maṇimalla (Sontheimer, 1976: 189). The tremendous importance of the horse in the cult of Khaṇḍobā and all the equivalent gods in the Deccan reflects the high esteem and reverence amongst the martial or potentially martial pastoral and tribal communities of the Deccan from prehistoric times. The high regard of the horse was certainly strengthened by the influence of Muslims and Rājputs. In the Deccan hardly any depiction of a god in bronze is more frequent than the equestrian god representing Mallikārjuna, Khaṇḍobā, or any other basically identical god. In some places like Candā, or amongst the Bhils, the god tends to be worshipped in the form of a horse. The Govārīs, a pastoral caste in the northeast of Maharashtra, place a clay horse near an anthill, which is said to be Dudhera, the protector of cattle.

Khaṇḍobā is not only the god who defeats demons, but he is also a god who fulfills the functions of a protector of cattle; in fact, he may be considered as Paśupati realized in popular religious belief. Much of the protective function in respect of cattle has now been transferred to Bāṇāī, yet in out-of-the-way places we can find numerous votive cattle figurines in front of an aniconic Khaṇḍobā. The special devotees of the god, the Vāghyās, who have been dedicated to the god's service in fulfilment of a vow for a child, consider themselves the dogs of the god. This is reflected in a widespread custom amongst the pastoral groups in the Deccan. For instance at Devaraguḍḍa near Rāṇebennūr in Karnataka some of the devotees eat offerings of milk without touching the wooden bowls with their hands. The custom is also found in the cult of Birappa, the tutelary god of the Kurubas in Andhra. Khaṇḍobā's dog, the Dhangars would maintain, naturally came along with Bāṇāī. The "knowledgeable" would maintain that it is Bhairava's dog and point to a group of devotees of Mahākāl in Ujjain who follow similar customs (Anandagiri's *Śankaradigvijaya,* cited in Deppert, 1977: 102). At the *jatrās* where a hunt or war expedition is celebrated, as for instance during Dasarā at Devaraguḍḍa, the devotees gallop like horses, whipping themselves with horsewhips, as they also do in Andūr near Naldurg, and even at the Somvatī Amāvāsyā festival in Jejurī one may see devotees possessed by the power of the god moving like horses in front of the palanquin. The sacrifice of sheep is done today only to Bāṇāī and outside the temple in Jejurī, because some say that Khaṇḍobā is a Liṅgāyat and is after all Śiva, and thus does not tolerate animal sacrifice.

But this Khaṇḍobā receding and merging into his pure form of Śiva—a development found also in the Sanskrit texts in general and in the Māhātmyas pertaining to Khaṇḍobā, which tend to be selective—had his earlier stages not only when it was usual to sacrifice sheep, but when people used to identify themselves with the sacrificial sheep of the god. We know from Kannada inscriptions that devotion to a cause drove people to commit suicide in order to accelerate their unity with their god. This can also be seen on memorial tablets in Karnataka where the *pādukas* of the god are depicted surrounded by heads of rams and human beings (Settar, 1975: 99 and n. 53). Even in Khaṇḍobā's temple at Jejurī we can see such a tablet under the structure which was used for the hookswinging ceremony: the *pādukas* of the god are encircled by four heads of rams. In several other Khaṇḍobā temples, e.g. in Phalṭaṇ (Sātārā Dt.), we find the same tablets with heads of rams *and* human heads. From the traditions of the famous god Mhaskobā of Vīr in Puṇe District we know that

Śāhū Mahārāj of Sātārā suppressed human self-sacrifice committed because of *bhakti*. This forgotten leaf in the history of Khaṇḍobā, Mailār, Mairāl, etc., is also found in the medieval Telugu work from Warangal referred to above. In this work the suicidal devotees of Mailār are called Vīrabhaṭṭas: we read that the Vīrabhaṭṭas used to pierce themselves with red hot iron bars as hot as the blazing sun, that they walked over pits from which spears protruded, that they used to hook their bodies to an iron hook and swing in midair. In the exertion of a *jatrā* they would cut their trunk and thus lay their life at the feet of the god. They would perform *ārati* in a peculiar way (most probably as the Kañcavīras of Devaraguḍḍa in Karnataka still do it today, having the oil lights of the *ārati* fixed on an iron needle piercing the arm). And the *Kṛḍābhirāmam* concludes on these *vīras* (heroes): Mailāravīrabhaṭṭas are daredevils, embodiments of heroism, they are beyond any act of cowardice.

The spirit of the mountain, sometimes living in an anthill as a snake in the forested region, associated with the sun, took shape in stones, called *svayambhū liṅg*. This is just a rough, round lump of stone, and the worship of Khaṇḍobā in the form of a *śivliṅg*, as amongst the Liṅgāyats, is a further stage. Thus even Bāṇāī and Mhāḷsā are, as in Jejurī, primarily worshipped in the form of similar, though smaller, rough-shaped, roundish stones (sometimes called *piṇḍ* or *piṇḍī*). A silver mask or *mūrti* is added, but often the *mūrti* is preceded by the "*vāhanas*", by votive figurines of cattle, horses, and rams, and by such attributes and weapons as the spear and the flagstaff.

The tribes with their oral literature, the Liṅgāyats and Gosāvīs (the followers of the Nāths and of Kālbhairava), the influence of the tribal chief and eventually the local *daṇḍanāyaka* or ruler, the Brāhmaṇs (mainly) with their selective textual versions and codification of the local tradition in terms of the Purāṇas: these do not destroy the cult, but add new layers of belief, ritual, and myth. Whatever was added, gained prominence or receded into the background, the belief nowadays tends to stay that the destination of Khaṇḍobā is the realization of his true, immutable, and pure form as Śiva. Khaṇḍobā (like Śiva) delegates and shirks many of his former functions. Religious suicide or the hook-swinging ceremony in Jejurī has long been abolished—no doubt by the British—but nobody had any serious objection to the abolition; in fact, this is in accordance with the development of Khaṇḍobā. Today the access to the temple in

Jejurī is being beautified with trees and flowers—which would not be in accordance with the origins of this outlandish god. The function of healing ailments and fractures has been delegated to a minor god outside at the outer wall of the temple precincts. Sacrifices of sheep are now offered to Bāṇāī, outside the temple, and non-vegetarian offerings are shown to Khaṇḍobā at the most from afar. The poplar print of Mhāḷsā and Khaṇḍobā fighting the *daityas* actually shows Mhāḷsā piercing one of the *daityas* with a lance, as pointed out once to me by Madame Biardeau, whereas Khaṇḍobā just wields his sword. Khaṇḍobā perhaps never gained the exalted, undisputed position of Murukaṉ in Tamilnāḍu. He used to be classed amongst the not-so-high gods and his contact with outlandish regions and people, with the magical and so forth did not please some of the Vārkarīs or those with a brāhmaṇical attitude. Yet even the Brāhmaṇs acknowledged with wonder that he combines all groups and that he even counts Brāhmaṇs amongst his ardent followers.

The Mallāri/Khaṇḍobā Myth as Reflected in Folk Art and Ritual

1. INTRODUCTION

THE FOLLOWING study utilizes a variety of sources which are brought together in order to portray, in an integrated way, the nature of a cult on the Deccan (India) which is of considerable importance with respect to its spatial spread and historical antiquity.

The cult is that of Mallāri, popularly called Khaṇḍobā in Maharashtra, mainly Mailār (Mairāḷ) in Karnataka, and Mallaṇṇa in Andhra. Another name is Mārtaṇḍa Bhairava, especially used with reference to the form Śiva took when he fought the demon. For the sake of simplicity I shall generally use the name Khaṇḍobā. The emphasis here is on the reflection of the cult and the myth in folk art though I use other sources like oral literature, observed ritual performance and festivals (*jatrās*), and texts as well. Many published and unpublished manuscripts in Marathi of the Mallāri/ Khaṇḍobā myth were composed from the 17th to the 19th century; I have used some of them here.[1] I have emphasized other aspects of the cult in previous publications (Sontheimer 1976, 1978, 1982, 1983).

2. THE MYTH OF MALLĀRI

The myth is, in short, the battle of Śiva as Mārtaṇḍa Bhairava against the *daitya* Malla or the two *daityas* Maṇi and Malla. As familiar from the Purāṇas, the *daityas* had usurped the three worlds and were ruling over them, in this case from a city built on the mountain Maṇicūl (*MV* 8.14). The extremely brave *daityas* or *rākṣasas* set out to kill cows and Brāhmaṇs (*MV* 8.17) and became enemies of the gods (*MV* 11.60: *pratāpa-sindhu nirjara dhvaṃsī*). Indra, Viṣṇu and the Ṛṣīs requested Śiva to join and lead them. In the gigantic battle which ensued between the gods and the demons and their armies, Maṇi and Malla were killed by Śiva, but at the same time they were released from their blindness or bondage and they became forever associated with Khaṇḍobā.

This reminds us of the myth of the great demon king Bali, who was defeated by the gods led by Indra. Indra was supported by Agni or Viṣṇu (Tripathi 1968: 53). The positive features of the demon Bali also emerge in the Purāṇas. He is actually close to Viṣṇu as Vāmana, but does not or only vaguely and belatedly realize the presence of the god and then willingly fulfils his promise though it seems that he is doomed (Tripathi 1968: 54f., 117, 143 *et passim*). As Shulman remarked, Bali's self-sacrifice is the secret of his salvation (Shulman 1980: 338). Similarly the battle of Malla against Khaṇḍobā seems to be a kind of sacrifice and Khaṇḍobā is pleased by Malla's bravery (*MV* 16.44; 18.181, 232; 34; 40: Maṇi and Malla pleased Śaṅkara with their war; cf. Sontheimer 1983). There is another feature in the Bali-Vāmana legend which reminds us of a practice in the Khaṇḍobā cult. Bali is tied and thrown into a mountain cave or into the underworld as a punishment (Tripathi 1968: 65). In later Purāṇa versions Bali is tied until he is released by Viṣṇu's third step on his head (Tripathi 1968: 233). This is reminiscent of the chain-breaking rituals in Khaṇḍobā's festivals. The heavy iron chains (Marathi *langar*; Sontheimer 1983) were broken—as informants would say—in order to experience or verify the nearness of Khaṇḍobā or because the breaking implies the true existence (*sattva*) of the god. The fetters are said in the texts to be Varuṇa's serpents. Informants also compare the iron chains in the Khaṇḍobā cult with serpents.

They myth of Mallāri, that is, Śiva as the enemy of Malla, is extremely old, though only at a rather late stage was it somewhat loosely attached to the *Brahmāṇḍa-purāṇa* as the *Mallāri Māhātmya* (see note 1). Some elements of the myth may also be seen in the battle of Indra against Vṛtra, the demon who is described as a giant serpent which arrogantly raises its head over a mountain and is in the possession of supernatural magic power (*māyā*). Vṛtra bars the waters enclosed in the mountain, and robs and swallows the celestial rivers, until Indra kills him, whereupon the waters are freed and run roaring like cows towards the sea.[2]

In other myths Indra is also the liberator of the cows after a fight with the demon Vala, who holds them captive in a mountain cave. In the postvedic literature Vṛtra and Vala are considered to be brothers, as are in our case the two brothers Maṇi and Malla.[3]

3. REFLECTIONS ON THE MEANING OF "MAṆI" AND "MALLA"

The association of demons with mountains prior to their defeat by gods is ubiquitous whether we think of the Veda or other (e.g. the old Tamil) literature.[4] The mountains, like the demons, who either live on them or are sometimes homologous with them, are beyond the human habitat and are the embodiment of everything which is outlandish and dangerous. The (popular?) etymology of *malla* may be Tamil *malai*, Kannaḍa *male*, Marathi *māḷ*, etc. = "hill, mountain", and we have the reference by Plinius to Malli, who live in the territory of the mountain Mallus (Majumdar 1960: 341). The connection of the demons with the mountain is well expressed in *MV* 20.49: The five sons of Malla become mountains after their defeat. In another passage it is said that on the mountain Maṇicūl the *daityas* built their city and ruled over the three worlds (*MV* 8.14; 9.57: near the mountain Maṇicūl) in consequence of a boon given by Brahmā. In the *MMVi* (16.26) we hear that Malla created mountains as his weapons against Śiva. In *MV* (34.40) it is said that Maṇi, or rather Maṇi and Malla, had created a mountain, called Maṇicūl, and founded a city called Maṇipūr on it. From there they ruled over the three worlds (*tribhuvana*). The Lord of the city was Mallāsura (*MV* 1.77). The god who defeats the demon associated with the mountain is called Mallaṇṇa in Telugu, Mallayya in Kannada, and Malaikiḻavōṉ in Tamil (the name of Murukaṉ), i.e. "the Lord of the Mountain", as Śiva is called *giriśa*.[5] After his defeat the mountain, or the demon identified with the mountain, becomes the seat of the god, as Kailās is the throne of Śiva. In the *MV* Malla becomes the throne of Mārtaṇḍa Bhairava (20.56).

The demon Malla seems also to be connected with the Mallas, who were Kṣatriya Vrātyas, according to the *Manusmṛti* (10.22), and were outside the brāhmaṇical fold. They are mentioned as early as the *Jaiminīya Brāhmaṇa* (III 199f.; Bollée 1981: 172ff., esp. 178). In this text, in fact, an old relationship is found between Indra and the Mallas. Indra's charioteer Kutsa is chased away by Indra with the words "be a *malla*" or "be Malla", because he was sexually misbehaving with Indra's wife, as the *daityas* Malla and Maṇi misbehaved and carried away the women of the Brāhmaṇs while raiding their hermitage.[6] Previously, when Kutsa had misbehaved with Indra's wife, he became the first to wear an *uṣṇīṣa*. This is a "turban" also worn by Rudra/Śiva and by the outlandish Vrātyas,[7] whose association with Rudra was very close.

In early times the Vrātyas were well known for their wandering habits and predatory activities (Heesterman 1962: 6, 30; Parpola 1973: 55ff.) and their aggressiveness even against Brāhmaṇ householders and Veda scholars (Heesterman 1962: 11). In tune with this, Malāsur (Malla) not only raids the hermitage of Brāhmaṇs but is also compared with a waylayer harassing travellers (*MMRā* 228: *mārgaghna*).

The Mallas were an ancient tribe and a kind of guild of pugilists and wrestlers. The *Harivaṃśa* mentions the wrestlers Cāṇura and Muṣṭika, whom Kṛṣṇa and Baladeva defeated. Kṛṣṇa thereby acquired the name Mallāri: the enemy of Malla (or the Mallas). In this connection it is interesting that Malla and Śiva as Mārtaṇḍa Bhairava/ Khaṇḍerāyā wrestle for nine days and nights according to the *MV* (18.162ff., 180).[8] Moreover, wrestling bouts take place during the *jatrā* on the full-moon day of the month *Pauṣ* (December/January) at Jejuri. The encounter between Kṛṣṇa and Cāṇura and Muṣṭika is depicted in an old relief on one of the light-pillars (*dīpmāḷ*) in front of the temple of Khaṇḍobā at Jejuri. It may also be the fight between Mallāri (Khaṇḍobā) and the demons Maṇi and Malla.

It is well known that many kings in the Deccan, in Rajasthan, and in Nepal had *malla* as their *biruda* in their name, e.g. the Kalacuri (12th century) King Sovideva was called Bhujabalamalla, "the strong wrestler".[9] One may also mention the titles Tribhuvana-malla and Trailokya-malla = "Wrestler of the Three Worlds", which were in frequent use amongst the Hoysaḷas (Derrett 1957: 22 *et passim*) and other dynasties.

Malla and Maṇi, though *rākṣasas*, are nevertheless great kings, according to the *Mallāri Māhātmya* (see e.g. *MM* 9.33; 13.49: he is the *rājā* of the *daityas*). The *MV* says that Malla was the king of the *daityas* (11.26: *daityanāth*); *mallaṉ* in Tamil means not only "wrestler", but also "a great, important personage".[10] Maṇi and Malla are reputed to have destroyed the *mūrtis* of other gods and to have compelled people to worship their own *mūrtis*, according to the *MMVi* 7.27. In Jejuri, the *mūrti* of Malla, who became a devotee of Khaṇḍobā, is impressive and still ardently worshipped. The crown shows Malla's royal background. One may also see in the demon king an allusion to the medieval kings or chiefs in the Deccan and South India who dominated outlying areas and formed a constant threat as invaders or usurpers to older, more established kingdoms. Thus the "hill-chiefs", variously called in Kannaḍa *malapar, malavar,* or *malepar,* were notorious raiders and robbers, but occasionally rose to high positions and even established kingdoms (Saletore 1935: 69 *et passim*; Derrett 1957: 7 *et passim*). The Hoysaḷas, for example, called themselves *maleparoḷ gaṇḍar* = "champions among the hill-kings", and are said to have started as successful brigand chiefs (Derrett 1957: 14ff.). They emerged from the predatory communities of the Beḍars (Marathi Beraḍs) or Rāmośīs (Marathi), who are famous devotees of Khaṇḍobā (Sontheimer 1976: 85 ff.). The attack on settlements of the Brāhmaṇs (*agrahāras*), cattle-lifting, and capturing women was not only their pursuit, but also at times that of officers of kings like *maṇḍaleśvaras* and *daṇḍanāyakas* (Saletore 1935: 60ff.; Sontheimer 1976: 29). Bravery and prowess like that of Malla were the prerequisites for fortune and rise to power. A good example of such a connection between Malla and a minor king who threatened the Hoysaḷas and Kākatīyas was a king and hero called Sarvajña-Khaḍgamalla = "The Omniscient and Strong Man with the Sword". He belonged to the Kāḍava or Pallava race and ruled from Kāñcī in the 12th century (*Tirupati Devasthanam Inscriptions,* vol. I, 10: 17). He is described as the "master of horsemen" and had a sword painted on his banner. Malla, whose possession of sword and horse is emphasized, thus looks like a demonized replica of kings like Sarvajña-Khaḍgamalla. Some of these features of Malla have been transferred onto Khaṇḍobā himself. Thus he is the "Lord of the Sword" and the "Master of Horses" (*MMŚ* 1.94: *hayapatī,* in popular Marathi *haibatī*). But, before Śiva turns into Mārtāṇḍa Bhairava/Khaṇḍobā and becomes a divine warrior king, he is ridiculed by Malla and described as a rather indigent Śaivite mendicant (*MMVi* 11:11: *jogaḍā*). "How can he have an army? He has only a bullock and is clad in a tiger skin", Malla muses (*MMRā* 9.11). "You are poor, go to the Kailās", he advises Śiva and boastfully continues: "I have many elephants. You have only one bull to ride. I have superb celestial clothes, you are clad in a bloody elephant skin. Your body is adorned with serpents. My ornaments are of gold. I am anointed with sandal paste mixed with gold. You throw about the ash of the funeral ground. You have only the powder made from bones" (*MMRā* 9-12).

When Khaṇḍobā kills Malla he—according to most of the versions—doesn't use a sword, but his *triśūl* (e.g. *MV* 18.193ff.). Thus Śiva, the *yogī*, who becomes a warrior king, assimilated the attributes of Malla and is often depicted in folk bronzes with two arms holding a sword and a shield and another two arms holding the typical hour-glass-shaped drum (*ḍamaru*) and a trident (*triśūl*). According to the texts his weapons consist of the hour-glass-shaped drum (*ḍamaru*), the sword (*khaḍga*), a vessel (*pānpātra*), and the trident (see *MV*24.57-63; see note 25).

The Maharashtrian saint Rāmdās (1608-1681) seems to refer to the apparent distinction between Śiva and Khaṇḍobā, who are both modelled on the conception of a warrior king like Malla. Rāmdās sang: "The god is an *avatār* of Śiva. He has settled on the hill-fort (of Jejuri). One [Khaṇḍobā] is seated on a blue horse. The other is on a white bull. One [Śiva] has white ash as his ornament. The other [Khaṇḍobā] has turmeric powder (Marathi *bhaṇḍār*). For Rāmdās they have become one. He does not distinguish between the two" (Rāmdāsī 1928: 32, *abhaṅg* 70).

In summary, we may say that the semantic connotations of Malla which are also associated with the conception of Khaṇḍobā include "mountain, hill", "an outlandish hill demon", "pugilist", "wrestler", "mountain dweller", "hill chief with predatory propensities", and "king".[11]

What about Maṇi? As we have seen, the mountain is occupied by the demon before the victory of the god. In the case of Indra's fight, the demoniac enemy who occupied the mountain was the huge, monstrous serpent Vṛtra. Similarly the termite mound—a homologous representation of the mountain—is the seat of serpents (*nāg*) (see e.g. Sontheimer 1976: 182ff., 204f.). Thus the two demons may be identified not only with the mountain, but also with the serpents living in it. There is no reference to Maṇi and Malla connecting them with serpents in our texts. However, in the Khaṇḍobā temple of Mailārpūr (Prempūr/Pember, near Bidar), we find a stone image of a serpent in the place where one usually expects a *mūrti* of the *daitya* facing the god. The god may here be more properly Maṇi (Maṇimalla may also mean "Maṇi, the Malla"). Maṇi is perhaps still a reflection of Maṇibhadra, or Māṇibhadra, the *yakṣa*, who was the guardian deity of caravans.[12] If this is so, it fits well that Mailārpūr was on an old north-south trade route and was notoriously unsafe because of waylaying robbers (Sontheimer 1976: 151f.).

4. THE PRIMEVAL UNITY (*SĀYUJYATĀ*) OF GOD, DEMON, AND BHAKTA

When Śiva/Khaṇḍobā kills Malla, the demon is freed from his illusion and arrogance and before he dies he turns into a *bhakta* of Śiva/Khaṇḍobā. Śiva grants him a boon and Malla wishes to be absorbed in Śiva's name: Hence the name Mallāri or Mallakṛtānta. Both features are clearly represented in the silver plaques (Marathi *ṭāk*) which show the demons under the feet of the god. This indicates the liberation from illusion and the achievement of union with Śiva (*śivasāyujya pavlā. MV* 20. 98). The two heads of the demons, sometimes three,[13] are shown to support the seat of Śiva. Malla is actually *ahaṃkāra* personified (*MV* 19.11). Śiva/Khaṇḍobā shows mercy and removes the blindness and *avidyā* from the demon, indicating the virtual consubstantiality of Śiva and the demon or any human soul.[14] The demons suddenly turn into followers of Khaṇḍobā, become members of his army or his doorkeepers, like the *rākṣasas* in the famous Tripura myth (Māṇikkavācakar's *Tiruvācakam* 14.4; 15.9;—Yocum 1977: 20ff., 23). Thus, in popular representations we come across not only the heads of the two demons supporting the throne of Khaṇḍobā, but also two warriors preceding Khaṇḍobā and his entourage. The *MMŚ* (2.115) says that Maṇi and Malla seated on horseback became *dvārapālas* of Śiva forever (see Figs. 1, 2, 3, and 4).

The *bhakti* for Śiva and Khaṇḍobā has occasionally taken such severe forms that people seem to have committed religious suicide in order to transpose themselves into the state of nearness or union with Śiva. Thus we find a number of *pādukās* of Khaṇḍobā surrounded by heads of rams, but also by rams *and* human heads (Sontheimer 1982: 272f. and plates 21-3). From Kannaḍa inscriptions we know that such memorial monuments indicate ritual suicide. Incidentally, it is curious that a somewhat similar arrangement occurs in the early prescription for the building of the fire-altar (*agnicayana*), which aims at the restoration of the primeval unity of Prajāpati. Similarly, the devotee, through his self-sacrifice, aims at unity with Śiva, or rather with Khaṇḍobā, who resembles Rudra in many respects. Rudra, identified with Agni, plays a central role in the *agnicayana* ritual as the flaming fire (Parpola 1973: 33). The flame of life violently left Malla and entered the mouth of Mārtaṇḍa Bhairava (*MV* 19.78). Malla, thus sacrificed, merged into Śiva. It may be a coincidence that in Jejuri during festivals the devotees constantly pour oil into the flames on a light pillar which is just by the side of the *pādukās.* The *pādukās* are located in a pavilion which is topped by the pole of the once widely practised hookswinging rite (*MV* 19.65; Rāmdāsī 1928: 32, *abhaṅg* 71).

In the first layers of the fire-altar, in its centre, five skulls must be placed: a human skull in the middle; west, east, south, and north of it skulls respectively of a horse, a bull, a ram, and a he-goat (Heesterman 1967: 30). If we assume that *pādukās* have replaced the human skull as the homologous representation of Prajāpati/Brahmā, and that Śiva in many respects has eventually replaced Prajāpati/Brahmā, we can see the survival of an element of the ancient classical *śrauta* ritual which itself is based on folk cults. However that may be, we find that all the animals mentioned in the *agnicayana* ritual occur in the Khaṇḍobā cult.[15]

Śiva/Khaṇḍobā is no doubt a perpetuation of the ancient Rudra/Paśupati cult and Śiva is repeatedly referred to as Paśupati in the *MV* and *MMŚ*. Paśupati is the Lord of *paśus*, that is, the Lord of animals *and* human beings, or the Lord of souls. Thus the rams as the sacrificial animals may reach a higher state when they are sacrificed. The human being becomes free from his temporal limitations and merges with Śiva, whether by sacrificial suicide—now no longer practised and forgotten—or by sheer devotion and dedicated worship.

5. THE ELEPHANT

Malla also assumes the form of an elephant during his battle with Khaṇḍobā (*MMVi* 16.16; cf.13.24). This reminds us of Śiva killing Gajāsura and dressing himself in an elephant hide. Only if we know this incident of the battle described in the *MM* (Maṇi as *kunjara*: *MM* 13.32; Malla as *gaja*: 16.17) can we realize that the little elephant rider in front of Khaṇḍobā representations on plaques depicts Malla. This also explains the stone elephant which is placed in front, and a little to the side, of Malla's *mūrti* in Jejuri. Like Malla, the elephant faces Khaṇḍobā. But the elephant rider can also be explained as another representation of Khaṇḍobā, who turns the demon in the form of an elephant into one of his *vāhanas*. Śiva as Khaṇḍobā also means that he has assumed royal functions and rides in state on an elephant, similar to Indra. Thus at the marriage of Khaṇḍobā with Mhāḷsā, celebrated annually at Pali in Satara Dt., the god rides on an elephant borrowed for the occasion from the ex-princely state of Aundh. Actually Khaṇḍobā is tied to the waist of the Pāṭīl (headman) of Pali in the form of a metal face mask of the god (Marathi

Fig. 1: A mould for preparing silver plaques which serve as house gods. It shows Khaṇḍobā/Mārtaṇḍa Bhairava with his two wives, Mhāḷsā (right) and Bāṇāī (left). Under the feet of the god are the heads of the demons Maṇi and Malla (height 10 cm).

Fig. 2: A mūrti *of Mailār/Khaṇḍobā in the temple of Manmailar (Karnataka). Under the seat of the god are the heads of three demons (height c. 80 cm).*

***Fig. 3:** Khaṇḍobā with Mhāḷsā. The hoofs of the horse rest on the heads of the demons Maṇi-Malla (height c. 20 cm).*

***Fig. 4:** A folk bronze* mūrti *of Khaṇḍobā which shows Bāṇāī and the two* daityas, *who have turned into warriors of Khaṇḍobā (height 8 cm).*

Fig. 5: *Side view of Fig. 4. Mhāḷsā, the first wife, has turned away her face as if annoyed by the presence of Bāṇāī, the really beloved of Khaṇḍobā. The omnipresent dog and the two* daityas */warriors are at the base.*

mukhavṭā). Stone elephants as votive donations can also be seen on the way up to the temple in Jejuri, mostly placed to the side of *nandīs*.

6. THE BULL AND THE HORSE

Śiva in purāṇic style invariably rides a *nandī*, and he arrives on his *nandī*, according to the *MM*, before he mounts a horse to fight the demon. Most of the texts tell us that the *nandī* turns into the horse (*turaṅga, haya*), though there are indications that the demons Maṇi and Malla owned the horse before Khaṇḍobā.[16] The connection of Malla, the hill demon, with the horse echoes the mythical, demoniac winged horses which dominated the mountains before human beings.[17] It was Indra, according to the *Ṛgveda*, who cut off the wings of the mountains (= horses?) and thus rendered them immobile (*Ṛgveda* 4.19.4; 6.30.3). In many tribal myths of Middle India the creation of the first human beings by the god was endangered by a demon, mostly a horse, or, more rarely, two horses. As a punishment the wings of the horses were cut off and they were reduced to the state of riding and pack animals (Kapp 1977: *passim*). The horse and the bull (bullocks) are conspicuous in the annual *jatrās* at Nimgav-Davdi in Khed Taluka of Pune Dt. Twice a year, on the full-moon days of the month of *Māgh* (January/February) and the month of *Caitra* (March/April), carts decorated with five bunches of peacock feathers are driven up the hill towards the temple at breath-taking speed. The carts (*gāḍā*) have small solid wheels, are drawn by one or two pairs of bullocks, and are preceded by a rider on horse-back (Pl. *c*).

The *MM* (13.61) and the *MMVi* (3.56) say that Maṇi (Maṇikāsura) was allowed to stay with his horse near Mallāri. This may account for bronze *mūrtis* which show a "groom" leading the horse with the god seated on the horse. Such a "groom" may also be a minor but widespread god like the shepherds' god Bīrappa/Birobā (Murty and Sontheimer 1980: 173). The representations of Śiva/Khaṇḍobā and of numerous similar gods with the horse as their *vāhana* are extremely widespread. They occur on silver plaques and as metal *mūrtis* and may be found in temples as well as in house shrines, especially in Maharashtra. Sometimes small plaques are used as charms tied around the neck. The myth of the battle of the god on the horse against the demons is also often depicted in murals on temples and on old glass paintings, for example in the Municipal Museum of Nasik (Fig. 3, Pl. *a* and *b*).

7. KHAṆḌOBĀ AND THE HERO ON THE HORSE

The omnipresent horse in the folk cults and rituals of the Deccan and western India is so pervasive and historically so old that I wonder whether we should not emphasize this phenomenon much more. It is found as early as in the megalithic burials of the 7th century B.C. in the Deccan[18] and is part of an ancient complex which is essentially outside the brahmanical ritual and culture. Asko Parpola (1973: *passim*) has suggested that Rudra, the Vrātyas, and Aiyaṉār are related to the megalithic burials. The horse is connected with the hero-cult prevalent in western India and the Deccan up to Tamilnadu at least from the time of the Caṅkam literature onwards. Thus Maṇi and Malla are repeatedly described as mighty *vīras* (*MV*8.14, 17; 9.52; 11.130; 12.15ff., cf.16.27). Śiva, the *yogī* turned warrior, is also the Lord of the *bāvan vīr,* the 52 *vīras* who include several demoniac mythological heroes, godlings or deified spirits, e.g. Bhairav, Jaypāl, Vīr Vikramājīt, Hanumān, Ismāl Jogī, etc. (Dāte 1942: II, 283). The Rajputs and the Muslims have only added to the lore of the cult of the hero and to the reverence for the horse, the symbol of *kṣatra.*

Incidentally, in Jejuri, the most famous cult centre of Khaṇḍobā, the horses of the god are traditionally kept by a Muslim family. In some places Khaṇḍobā is called Mallu Khān or Ajmat Khān—the latter said to be the name given to Khaṇḍobā in Jejuri by Aurangzeb, who was compelled to flee from Khaṇḍobā's power. Many late medieval stone sculptures are scattered on the side of the stairs leading to the temple of Khaṇḍobā in Jejuri. They show the heads of heroes who died in battle. The stones are derived from the older innumerable hero stones of (Kannada) *vīragaḷas*, (Tamil) *vīrakkals* of the Deccan and western India. On these older, widely varying stones the hero is often shown to have died in a raid defending his cattle and women, just as Khaṇḍobā came to the rescue of cows and the Brāhmaṇs with their womenfolk when Maṇi and Malla attacked them. On the *vīragaḷas* the *apsaras* are shown to carry the hero towards heaven. There he dwells in the company of Śiva. It is noteworthy that the *yogī* with his *tapas* and the warrior in his fury who dies on the battlefield are often equated with each other. Both are able to pierce the orbit of the sun.[19] Thus we find a wealth of traditions which show warriors and even dynasties (e.g. the Hoḷkars of Indore, who have Khaṇḍobā as their family god) emerging from a tribal or pastoral-nomadic or even predatory past and merging into a religious context in which Śaivite gods and cults dominated.

Plate (a): *A glass painting in the Municipal Museum in Nasik depicting Khaṇḍobā's fight against the two demons.*

Plate (b): *The fight against the demons. Khaṇḍobā's* śakti *wields the spear (=*śakti*). A mural painting in the Khaṇḍobā temple at Khanapur/Pember (Prempūr) near Bidar (Maharashtra).*

Plate (c): *The* gāḍā *(Marāthī cart and cart-race) ceremony in the Pūrṇimā (full-moon) festival* (jatrā) *of Khaṇḍobā at Nimgav-Davdi (Khed Taluka, Maharashtra) at the end of the harvest season in the months of Māgh (February/March) and Caitra (March/April) and the beginning of the New Year. The carts are reminiscent of the Daimabad bronze chariot of 1800-1600 B.C. (See Dhavalikar 1979: 361-66, pl. 35/1-2.) This chariot has solid wheels like the chariots in Nimgav-Davdi. The birds on the bronze chariot may be seen represented by the peacock-feather bunches on the chariots in Nimgav-Davdi. If the bulls in the Daimabad bronze chariot also resemble horses (as Dhavalikar 1979: 362 says), we may see this reflected in the fact that the bullocks are preceded by horse riders. The dog in the Daimabad bronze is also a part of the Khaṇḍobā cult. Ritual chariot races in India have been known since the Vedic period, e.g. as reflected in the Rājasūya ceremony. Chariot races often have the function of regenerating the productive forces in the cosmos, of renewing the world and obtaining new food and life for man and cattle (see Heesterman 1957: 128ff., 133ff.). The cart races in Nimgav-Davdi are also said to increase the strength of the bullocks and the fertility of the fields.*

Plate (d): *A huge statue of Malla in the temple court at Jejuri (Pune District) facing the entrance of the temple. A small elephant to the bottom and the crown indicate Malla's royal background. Malla is also sometimes called Maṇi, "the Malla". Mostly they are considered to be two brothers, Maṇi and Malla.*

From very early times the horse plays a great role in the myths and rituals of many tribals, in those of dynasties emerging from a tribal background, and in the culture of the *kṣatriyas*. Horse figurines e.g. are important in the death rituals of the Bhīls. With the ritual called *nukto*, in which brass figurines of a rider on a horse play a great role, the purified spirit can ascend to reach the clan of ancestors and to dwell with Bhagavān in the beyond (Kramrisch 1969: 23ff.). The depiction of horse and rider in the memorial stones of the Bhīls is not only an imitation of prestigious Rajput styles—in fact, in the Rajput memorials the horse is mostly not shown—but also reflects an incident of the death ritual. Generally, the horse is also a symbol of death and fertility. The horse is used by the shaman for his shamanistic flights to the upper and nether worlds in order to retrieve souls from there. But in the case of Śiva the obstinacy of his *bhaktas* has made him dwell on the human earth in the form of Khaṇḍobā/Mallāri. He was first seen by young herdsmen as he descended on horseback on the high mountainous plateau where the old temple is situated at Jejuri (Khare 1958: 90; Sontheimer 1978: 112).

In the tribal context, the clan god on the horse is often interpreted as some form of Bhairava, a god who protects. He is a warrior, a deified hero, or a saint, and in any case a god who eventually merges into many of those major deities riding a horse. All these deities on horseback point towards gods like Mārtaṇḍa Bhairava (the Khaṇḍobā of Maharashtra) or the Aiyaṉār of Tamilnadu, gods who express this motif in a most complex manner. They are mounted on a horse and surrounded by horses.

8. KHAṆḌOBĀ, HIS DOGS, AND THE DOG DEVOTEES

Bhairava, Mārtaṇḍa Bhairava/Khaṇḍobā is accompanied by dogs or a pack of dogs whether he is on a hunt or defeating *rākṣasas*. The dog or pack of dogs is associated with the art, ritual and mythology of the Mallāri/Khaṇḍobā cult from the earliest times. Ekanāth (b. 1533 at Paithan) seems to refer to a golden *mūrti* of Khaṇḍobā seated on a dog. He says that "Khaṇḍerāv" and the dog are "not different" or are "identical" (*abhinna*) on account of their being linked by gold.[20] In the *MMVi* (3.8; cf. 8.71) we read that Khaṇḍobā is surrounded by dogs, seated on a horse and fond of turmeric powder (Marathi *bhaṇḍār*, Sanskrit *haridra*, Marathi *haḷad*). Turmeric powder is—apart from its medical properties—the poor man's substitute for gold. It also represents the substance of the god and, especially during festivals of Khaṇḍobā like the Somvatī Amāvāsyā festival at Jejuri, everything is immersed in it. Even all the other gods are said to throw it on Khaṇḍobā in his praise at the end of the battle (*MMVi* 8.71). Thus *bhaṇḍār* provides the ritual and substantial link between god, men, *daityas*, and animals which reflects a "communitas" (Victor Turner) of all who are present at the festival. The *daitya* also receives a constant offering of *bhaṇḍār*. Even the black temple dogs in Jejuri or ordinary stray dogs receive a generous coating on their foreheads (Fig. 5).

One of the earliest references to the dog of the god is in the *Śatarudrīya* of the *Taittirīya Saṃhitā* (Sontheimer 1983: *passim*). Rudra is in this text a dog, the Lord of the dogs, and the Lord of those keeping dogs. In fact, there exists an oral legend in Karnataka telling us that in a previous *yuga* a group of special devotees went as a pack of hounds for a hunt with Śiva or to help him fight the demon (Sontheimer 1983: *passim*). The *MMŚ* coincides with this: King Mārtaṇḍa is accompanied by 700 dogs (1.84; *MMVi* 8.16: "wild because of anger and accompanied by many dogs"). In our age these dogs have become human beings keeping a vow which involves that on special occasions they behave like dogs, barking and eating from a begging bowl in a dog-like fashion. It is noteworthy that their behaviour, appearance, and outfit very much reflect the style of the ancient Vrātyas, the Mallas, and the Pāśupatas with their peculiar vow.[21] Some of their attire and behaviour can very well be compared with those of the Cynics in Ancient Greece.[22] These devotees, who beg in the name of Khaṇḍobā/Mallāri, are called *vāghyās* in Marathi and *vaggayya* in Kannada. *Vāghyā* is invariably derived from Sanskrit *vyāghra*. It is said that the *vāghyās* were tigers formerly, but that through the *darśan* of Mārtaṇḍa their bodies became human. They were told by Mārtaṇḍa/Bhairava to bark like dogs. This reminds us somewhat of the ancient Pāśupata vow which involved *avitad-bhāṣaṇa*—uttering senseless or contradictory words. Kannaḍa *uggu*, from which *vaggayya* may be derived, similarly means to "utter repeatedly meaningless sounds".

In any case, the Vaggayyas still occasionally act like dogs during *jatrās*, performing a round dance accompanied by drums and chants. In the middle of the circle devotees throw coins on a black woolen blanket and the Vaggayyas pick up the coins with their mouths, entertaining the devotees. The coins in this instance tend to replace the food which devotees offer in the bowls of the Vaggayyas. One is reminded of the famous scene in the *Chāndogya Up.* (1.12) of the dog dance rite performed with the *udgītha* chant in order to procure food. This is in remarkable accordance with the explanation in the *MV* of the origin of the dog in the Mārtaṇḍa Bhairava/Khaṇḍobā cult: the *Sāmaveda*—somewhat impure when compared with the *Ṛgveda* and *Yajurveda* because it is sacred to the ancestors (*Manusmṛti* IV, 119-20) and thus has something to do with death (Monier-Williams 1970: s.v.)—became the dog of Śiva and would forever stay at Śiva's gate (*MV* 34.50).

The dog is often a metaphor for sexuality and sexual licentiousness, a trait which was, as we have seen, also characteristic of Malla. This feature seems to have been lost in the rites of the Vāghyās. However, I noticed devotees of Bīrappa in Andhra ritually drinking milk like dogs, barking and biting each other, and imitating the copulation of dogs (see Murty and Sontheimer 1980: 174ff.).

The mixing of "tiger" and "dog" is chronic in myth, ritual, and art. Rudra/Śiva—as presumably shown on the famous Indus seal—is also in the company of a tiger.[23] He is seated on a tiger skin or clad in a tiger skin (e.g. *dvipicarmanivāsin, Mahābhārata, Droṇaparva* 173, 32a, crit. ed.; e.g. *MMVi* 6.16). Thus Bhairava's *vāhanas* are occasionally the dog *and* the tiger or two animals which are a mixture of both, as e.g. in a painting from Orissa and a glass painting from Tanjore.[24] The Vāghyās, on the other hand, have to carry a pouch made preferably of tiger skin or otherwise of deer (*haraṇ*) skin. In this pouch they keep the sacred *bhaṇḍār*, the turmeric powder, the substance embodying Khaṇḍobā.

9. THE WIVES OF THE GOD

Rudra/Śiva or Bhairava is not normally shown in the texts as accompanied by his wife when he goes out to hunt or to defeat the demons. Accordingly he occurs in a small brass *mūrti* as riding a horse, carrying a lance or a *triśūl* and holding the head of one of the demons, whereas the other head has fallen on the ground (Fig. 6). This is more in accordance with our texts. In the *MV* and *MM* it is not mentioned that Pārvatī or Umā accompanies him, though there are instructions in the *MV* about what kind of *mūrti* should be used for *pūjā*. Here the wife is specifically mentioned.[25] Popular art frequently shows him with Pārvatī, who is identical with Mhāḷsā in the Khaṇḍobā

***Fig. 6:** Mallāri/Khaṇḍobā is shown seated on a horse. On the left he holds the head of one demon. The other head is on the floor. Remarkable are the long lance and the royal parasol. At the back of the* mūrti *is (not visible) the dog (height 7 cm).*

***Fig. 7:** Khaṇḍobā with his two wives—for once peacefully united (height 15 cm).*

cult. In some more "classical" representations she sits in the Umāpati fashion more or less awkwardly on Śiva's left thigh. Both are seated on a horse in this style (Fig. 3). But very often she sits either in front of or behind him. Rarely we may also find popular brass *mūrtis* where both wives are seated peacefully on the horse before Khaṇḍobā (Fig.7).

Khaṇḍobā's second wife is Bāṇāī, who comes from the shepherd community of the Dhangars. Khaṇḍobā and his equivalents in the Deccan and in South India always have a second wife from a community with a tribal background. Thus Murukaṉ's "second" wife comes from the Kuṟava tribe (Zvelebil 1977: 233, 244f.). It is Bāṇāī whom Khaṇḍobā dearly loves and who—coming from the forest—is more erotic, beautiful and earthy. Mhāḷsā, on the other hand, is from the higher community, but of a somewhat jealous nature, even cantankerous, and too domestic. She sits high up on the horse, her nose turned towards the sky, whereas poor Bāṇāī is standing on the ground holding a sheep in her arm and reaching up to hand Khaṇḍobā some fruit or other food. She essentially reflects the fertility and the eroticism of the early Tamil Vaḷḷi in the old Tamil (*akam*) love poetry (Figs. 4 and 5).

In popular pictorials it is Mhāḷsā who kills the demon with the lance, whereas Khaṇḍobā just lifts his sword as if he were about to strike. It is the *śakti* of Khaṇḍobā who seems to bring liberation to the demons. According to our texts (e.g. *MV* 8.90), the lance is often an embodiment of the *devī* (Pl. *a* and *b*).

10. THE HUNTER WITH THE SPEAR

Since Vedic times if not earlier, Rudra/Śiva is the great hunter armed with a spear or a bow and arrows. In an inscription of the year A.D. 1369 from Ainavōlu near Warangal in Sanskrit and Telugu it is said that the god Śiva, in order to protect Arjuna, assumed the form of a hunter (*Śabara*), fought the demon Malla, and killed him, thereby acquiring the name Mallāri or Mailār (Sircar [ed.] 1961: 8-9, 21; Murty and Sontheimer 1980: 168). Mallāri has always been the god of the hunting tribes, like the Niṣādas, Śabaras, or others. The 13th century text *Krīḍābhirāmamu* from Warangal says that Mailār is the god of those "Who are fond of hunting with spears". Even today shepherds bring their ceremonial spears (another embodiment of the god) for the Somvatī Amāvāsyā festival at Jejuri and participate

Fig. 8: A mould for preparing silver plaques. It shows in a typical fashion Khaṇḍobā and his first wife, Mhāḷsā, as riders on the horse. To the right at the bottom one can see Bāṇāī, the second wife. It may also be Malla as bhakta.

in the ceremonial hunt of the god. Many of the Vāghyās or Vaggayyas are recruited from the shepherds and also carry spears. The same spear is also shown in old illustrations as Khaṇḍobā's weapon. A group of Dhangars was actually called Barge Dhangars and was said to go for a hunt with bear spears (*bargā* = staff?). The spear appears prominently in the Murukaṉ cult and in the early texts Murukaṉ is called *vēlaṉ* after his frenzied attendants who carry a spear (Tamil *vēl*) (Sontheimer 1976: 20f.). Murukaṉ, Skanda/Kārttikeya, and Khaṇḍobā can also be mutually connected because of possessing a lance or a spear (Fig. 6).

11. CONCLUDING REMARKS

Thus folk art, rituals, oral myths and legends, besides the written versions in Sanskrit and Marathi, link up the age-old Rudra/Śiva cult with the Khaṇḍobā/Mallāri myth and cult. Taken together, these features are mutually informative and represent an internally cohesive body of evidence which illuminates the record of peoples outside brāhmaṇical circles, peoples whose history is extremely ancient. Because of its vigorous and exuberant expression in visual art, oral literature and festivities, this culture, with its irresistible mixture of temporal joy and potential otherworldly spirituality, has remained an invaluable treasure in the devastating spiritual and cultural emptiness of modern times. Khaṇḍobā/Mallāri combines *bhukti* and *mukti* and is accessible to all, irrespective of caste or religion, including Mlecchas, i.e. Muslims. This the *MV* stresses repeatedly (*MV* 29.30; 5.12: *neṇe varṇa-jāti-kuḷā*).

NOTES

This is a substantially enlarged and revised version of a lecture which was published in J. Deppert (ed.), *India and the West. Proceedings of a Seminar Dedicated to the Memory of Hermann Goetz*, New Delhi, 1983.

I am grateful for the financial support of the German Research Association (Deutsche Forschungsgemeinschaft) in the year 1979. Professor S.G. Tulpule has been helpful in reading with me the texts and mss. mentioned in note 1. Asko Parpola, Willem Bollée, and M.L.K. Murty have made helpful observations. Jim Laine has made editorial comments as regards the English of this paper. I should also mention Mr. Ramdas Atkar and Rajaram Zagade, who have, as usual, assisted me in my field research. I am also grateful to Mr. Richard Werny, who has taken the photographs of Figs. 4, 5, and 6. The photograph of Fig. 3 was taken with the permission of Mrs. M. Happe.

Some of the plaques and metal figurines are in private collections from the Deccan and Western India, mostly Maharashtra. Their exact place of origin is unfortunately unknown.

1. The *Nirṇayasindhu* by Kāmalākarabhaṭṭa of the year 1612 refers to the Campāṣaṣṭhī festival on the 6th of the light half of the month *Mārgaśirṣa* as famous in Maharashtra and cites the *Mallāri Māhātmya* [*MM*] in the *Brahmāṇḍapurāṇa* (Nirṇayasindhu Nirṇayasāgara, Muṃbaī, 1949: 228 (cited by R.C. Dhere 1961:8).—The *Caturvarga-cintāmaṇi* (1260-1271) of Hemādri mentions the *vrata* of Kumāra (Skanda) on Campāṣaṣṭhī, but not Khaṇḍobā/Mallāri (Dhere 1961:8). The *MM* was probably composed after that and before Siddhapāl Kesarī, according to Dhere.
   The texts which have been used are:
   Śrī Mallārimāhātmya [*MM*] by Siddhapāl Kesarī [composed in Marathi in 1585, according to Dhere], Mumbaī [several editions].
   Śrī Mārtaṇḍa Vijaya [*MV*] by Gaṅgādhara (R.C. Dhere [ed.]). Pune 1975 [composed in Marathi 1823].
   Śrī Malhāri Māhātmya by Śrīdharasvāmī Nājharekar [*MMŚ*] (R.C. Dhere [ed.]). Puṇeṃ, 1975. [Śrīdhara lived between 1580 and 1651.]
   Śrī Mallāri Māhātmya by Vināyaka [*MMVi*]. Bombay? 1872 [composed in 1871].
   Khaṇḍerāyācī Ādī [*Kh. Ā.*] by Jagjivan [photocopy of an unpublished ms. from Dhule, 18th century].
   Śrī Mallāri Māhātmya by Rāmdās, "Sadāśiva's servant" [*M.M.Rā*] [photocopy of an unpublished ms. belonging to S.G. Joshi, Puṇeṃ, composed in 1857].
2. Gonda 1978: 55; cf. *Ṛgveda* 5.30.6; 6.17.8, 9.—Indra frees the rivers of Vṛtra: 4.17.1. Rivers and cows are metaphors for food and are often mutually exchangeable, according to Deppert 1977: 121, 199f.—For Indra as the adversary the demon Vṛtra and the subsequent parallels of Prajāpati and Namuci and of Buddha and Māra, see Bollée 1977; 371-81.
3. Gonda 1978: 57. Indra frees the cows locked up in the cave by Vala. *Ṛgveda* 1.174.4; 3.32.16 etc.
4. Deppert 1977: 128. See Zvelebil 1977: 223ff., 234.—The malevolent forces of the hills and the anxieties and terrors in the souls of men were personified as Cūraṉ, whom Murukaṉ overcomes in battle. *Patiṟṟuppattu* 11.5. Cūr is Murukaṉ's enemy who seeks to possess people, especially women. It is a personalized demonic force. *Naṟṟiṇai* 329.7-9; 373.5. See also Clothey 1978: 28, 30. Cūr in his battle against Murukaṉ takes various terrifying forms, such as that of a huge mountain. See Shulman 1979: 27-40, esp. 31. Malla consecrates mountains by *mantras*, using them as weapons in his fight against Mallāri (*MMVi* 16.26).
5. *Tirumurrukāṟṟuppaṭai* 317, 77; Sontheimer 1976: 20; Zvelebil 1977: 235ff.—Zvelebil tends to derive Skanda/Kumāra/Kārttikeya and Murukaṉ from an "Ur-Murukaṉ" (236f.), but I would believe that the Vedic Rudra, Śiva, Murukaṉ, Kārttikeya, etc. are all versions of one god genetically and historically connected with a proto-Indian pre-Vedic god. Note that Rudra is the *youngest* son of the Creator and that *kumāra* is one of the names of Rudra (this has been suggested by Asko Parpola). Rudra is also *inter al.* derived from *rud* which means "lament, cry" (cf. Kannada *uggu* = "repeatedly to utter unmeaning sounds" [sic], Kittel's *Kannaḍa-English Dictionary* [1968; *s.v.*] see below in text).—Moreover, any god

in folk religion, as well as in the Veda, may assume the form of a young god. For Rudra as *giriśa, giriśanta, giritra* see *Taittirīya Saṃhitā* XVI, 2f. *giriśa, Mahābhārata* XIII. 6348 (Cal. ed.).

6. *M.M.* 1.53ff. Malla raids the *āśram* of the Brāhmaṇs while on a hunt: *MV* 1.88ff.
7. For the *vrātyas* in this context see Sontheimer 1981: *passim*; Dandekar 1979: 207ff.; Bollée 1981: 173ff.
8. Cf. 18.66ff.: Though the *daitya* may be a highly accomplished wrestler (*parama catur malla*) he can achieve nothing against Śiva, as the Kolhāṭīs—a caste of acrobats—can perform acrobatic feats of a high order, but how can they measure themselves with Hanumanta!—For Cāṇura and Muṣṭika, the "Mallas", and Kṛṣṇa as Mallāri see Bollée 1981: 183; *Harivaṃśa* 2.121. 119 in the Poona edition of 1936 (cited by Bollée).
9. Sontheimer 1976: 193. One of his successors (Śaṅkama) had the *biruda* Niḥśaṅkamalla—"The wrestler without fear"! His brother was called "Ākavamalla"— "The wrestler who is a challenge" (see *Maharashtra State Gazetteer* 1967: 351f.).—For the dynasties of the Mallas in Nepal, see Bollée 1981: 184. For the Malla dynasty of the ancient kingdom of Mallabhum in West Bengal, see Östor 1980: 24-26, 203-4.—On the Mallas as an ancient people in Buddhist and Jaina works, see Law 1973: chapter 50.
10. Burrow and Emeneau 1961-1968, s.v.; Sontheimer 1976: 189. Sindhi *malu* means not only "wrestler" but also "brave man" (see Turner 1966-1971: 9907; I owe the reference to Asko Parpola).
11. A rich *māla* (= *malla*) is mentioned in the 13th century Marathi *Līḷācaritra* (Kolte 1978: *līḷā* 30). He lived at Warangal and had 500 *mālās* under him. Here *mālā* means "masseur" rather than "wrestler", though the two professions are closely linked; cf. Koḷī = "fisherman", "hunter", and "ferryman". Cf. Bollée 1981: 184 fn. 97, and as regards *niṣāda* = "hunters", "fishermen", "robbers", etc. > "ferrymen", *ibid*: 8. 181.
12. See Sircar 1971: 133ff., 136, and fn. 3, 144ff. Sircar connects Maṇibhadra with Maṇināga, whose *tīrtha* at the ancient city of Rājagṛha is mentioned in the *Mahābhārata*.
13. According to the *Kantapurāṇam, kāṇḍam* 2-4 by Kacciyappar, the demon Cūr, together with his brothers Ciṅkamukaṉ (Sanskrit *Siṃhamukha*) and Tarakaṉ, worshipped Śiva and in this world won control over the universe. See Shulman 1980: 30f. and fn. 49. This may explain the three heads of demons shown in the *mūrtis* and pictorial representations of Mallaṇṇa in Andhra, e.g. at Iloni (Ainavōlu) near Warangal and at other places in the Karimnagar Dt. (see also Fig. 3). The three demons of the Tripura myth were Tārākṣa, Kamalākṣa, and Vidyunmālin; they faced the necessary destruction and death to gain Śiva. See O'Flaherty 1975: 125ff.
14. *MV* 20.98; see also 19.78. On the *ahaṃkār* of the demon, see also Shulman 1980: 317ff., 321f.
15. I was told that the head with horns in the *kīrtimukha* style at the base of the threshold of the temple door is that of "Dakṣa". Besides "pure" animals, like "man", horse, bull, and ram, having a function in the cult, there are great fairs for horses and camels at Malegaon (near Bid) in the month of *Pauṣ* (December/January) and of donkeys during the *Purṇimā* day in *Pauṣ* at Jejuri. Gifts of bullocks, horses, buffaloes or cows to Mārtaṇḍa are recommended in fulfilment

of a promise in exchange for a request for increase in cattle (*MV* 33.43ff.).

16. According to *MMŚ* 1.80; also *Kh. Ā.* 83; *MMVi* 8.25. According to *MV* 34.51ff. Maṇi already had a horse. Śaṅkar ordered the moon to become a horse and, seated on it, he cut off the head of the *daitya*. Ever since the horse as a *vāhana* has been dear to the god. The *MMVi* (13.24) tells us that Maṇi became "horse-faced" (*hayamukha*) after his head was cut off by Mārtaṇḍa and he started neighing. Eventually, the upper half of him became an elephant. According to the *MM* 13.59 the horse, chariot, and elephants derive from the demon (Dhere 1961: 31).
17. See Jettmar 1975: 295; cf. 252: flying horses. On the horses of the Hephtalite peoples of the Pamir area the Chinese have preserved an origin myth: There was a mountain in which a divine horse lived. Mares were driven into the mountain (see Eberhard 1978: 146; I owe the reference to P. Snoy).—Amongst the Dhangars of Maharashtra we find the belief that the horse was hidden in a mountain cave in the form of wind, before Khaṇḍobā fetched it to ride to his beloved Bāṇāī of the Dhangars (Sontheimer 1976: 190).
18. Excavations of megalithic burials conducted by S.B. Deo at Mahurjhari and Naikunth in the Vidarbha region of Maharashtra have yielded horse skeletons with horse bits *in situ* as well as skeletons of dogs (see below). Lances of the length of 2 m. and arrow tips in the bodies of enemies point to a nomadic, warring community dominating over agriculturists. The site excavated is near a present-day Goṇḍ village. The Goṇḍs may sacrifice and eat any animal except the horse (and presumably the dog) (personal communication by S.B. Deo). This explains the continued importance of the horse *and* the dog in cults, especially cults like that of Khaṇḍobā. Lance and bow are still extant in representations of Khaṇḍobā. Brass figurines of Khaṇḍobā with a bow and on horseback, his wife seated behind, also occur. The persistent estimation of the horse is also reflected in its worship amongst tribals like the Goṇḍs and the Bhīls. They may not own horses themselves, but at least their gods are made to ride horses.
19. See Sontheimer 1981. The famous *śloka: dvāv imau puruṣau loke sūryamaṇḍalabhedinau/parivrāḍ yogayuktaśca raṇe cābhimukho hataḥ//* is alluded to in *MV* 16.27.
20. *vānārūḍha Khaṇḍerāvo/suvarṇācā karavilā pahā ho/tethem̱ pāhatām̱ śvāna āṇi devo/suvarṇānvayem̱ abhinna//Ekanāthaḥ Catuḥślokī Bhāgavata* 580, in: Paṇasīkara (ed.) 1968.
21. See Sontheimer 1981 on the Vaggayyas of Devaraguḍḍa in Karnataka. On the Paśūpatas see Lorenzen 1972: especially ch. VI, p. 185, e.g. *avitatkaraṇa* (acting as if devoid of judgment) and *avitadbhāṣaṇa* (uttering senseless or contradictory words). The *Śaṅkaravijaya* refers to the followers of Mallāri at Ujjain "who were endowed with the dress and language of a dog which is the form of the *vāhana* of Mallāri". They pleased Mallāri with their dance and song. They wore as a special mark a necklace of cowries—which is still typical of *vāghyās* and Gorappas. Cf. the *niṣka* of Rudra. The followers of Mallāri based their faith in Mallāri on the authority of the *Śatarudriya* reference to the "dogs and the lord of dogs" (see Veezhinathan [ed.] 1971: ch. 29, p. 117f.).
22. The Cynics were followers of the principles of Diogenes who had received the nickname of *kýon* (dog) because they rejected all conventions, tried to live on

nothing, and advocated shamelessness (*anaideia*) *The Oxford Classical Dictionary* [Oxford, 1949; repr. 1957]). The return to a state of nature and to the life of animals; not external wealth, but the possession of the soul; and freedom from all desires were some of their teachings. They were dressed in a rough coat (cf. the rough woollen coat of the *vrātyas* and Vaggayyas), they had a satchel for keeping the food they received as alms, and a staff. The life of the first human beings and of animals presented an example to them. The similarity with gods was seen in their complete exigency, which led to begging. The humiliation experienced when they begged unsuccessfully for food led to spiritual merit. Corporal and spiritual asceticism and self-mortification were necessary to gain spiritual freedom. Sexual licentiousness in public and opposition to a settled social life and institutions and the attempt to salvage the freedom of the individual were other features of the school of the Cynics. See Helm in Pauly 1925: Kynismus. See Ingalls 1962: 281-98.

23. For another, more plausible interpretation of the "proto-Śiva" seal see Hiltebeitel 1978: 767-97.
24. Bussaberger and Robins 1968: 158.—"Madurai Vīran" in Appasamy 1980: plate 4: "... Below the group is a dog chased by a cheetah...". Rāmdās (1608-1681) speaks of "dogs as big as tigers" in one of his *abhaṅgs* on Khaṇḍobā (Rāmdāsī [ed.] 1928: *abhaṅg* 1170).
25. The instructions in the *MV* (24.57-63) on how *mūrtis* are to be made are worth quoting: "Preferably one should make for worship an image (*pratimā*) of gold, alternatively of silver or copper. Otherwise it can be made of stone or clay. There are two types [of images] for meditation: seated on the horse with Mhāḷsā. In the hand shine sword (*khaḍga*) and drum (*ḍamaru*), two hands are [thus] adorned, with the heads of Maṇi-Malla near the feet (57). The second type is prescribed according to tantra (*tantrokta*). The *mūrti* is adorned with four arms (*caturbhuj*), it shines with Gaṅgā and Mhāḷsā on either side of the god (58), with *triśūl*, *ḍamaru*, and drinking vessel (*pānpātra*), and the sword shining in the right hand. The *mūrtis* should be made beatiful with all ornaments (59). The horse should be nearby. In the front should be set the Nandī as well as a metal dog. Near the feet should be the heads (60). [Or] one should bring clay, consecrating it with prayers, and moisten it with water consecrated by *mantras*, make a square pedestal (*śāḷuṅkā*) and provide a channel (61). The shape of a horse should be made out of clay [at the end of the channel]. On the top one should form two *liṅgs* with highest devotion (62). The Mārtaṇḍa *liṅg* should be big, that of his dear Mhāḷsā one-third in size. On the head of the Mārtaṇḍa-*liṅg* one should place a lump of clay, taking it to represent Gaṅgā (63).

Dasarā at Devaraguḍḍa: Ritual and Play in the Cult of Mailār/Khaṇḍobā

INTRODUCTION

INCIDENTS reminiscent of very ancient cults are still evident in the cult of Khaṇḍobā in Maharashtra, the corresponding cults of Mailār(a) in Karnataka, Mallaṇṇa in Andhra Pradesh, and in particular the Dasarā Festival at Devaraguḍḍa (in Karnataka). In fact, it is difficult to resist the conclusion that we can find striking similarities with the Vedic or even pre-Vedic culture of the Vrātyas, the Mahāvrata festival (which has been connected by J.W. Hauer with the rites of the Vrātyas),[1] the Vrātyas as they appear in the Vrātyastoma, and Rudra as the deity of the Vrātyas (who is also called Ekavrātya).[2] Asko Parpola has even suggested a connection between the ancient Mahāvrata festival and the Dasarā festival.[3] The rituals and the festivals of the Vrātyas were marked by dance, accompanied by singing and musical instruments like harps and drums, a ritual kind of vile speech, chariot races, black magic, etc. They were antithetical to the classical Vedic *śrauta* ritual. All these features of the rites of the Vrātyas persist in present-day folk religion and especially in the Khaṇḍobā/Mailār/Mallaṇṇa cult. In the context of this paper I shall not enter into a detailed comparison of this cult and the festival with the Vrātyas and their parallel culture as reflected in the Vedic texts, but shall only point out some striking parallels as I discuss the festival.

DRAMA AND RITUAL IN THE DASARĀ FESTIVAL

It may seem somewhat far-fetched to present a *jatrā* (Ma.) or *jātrā* (Ka.), a popular pilgrimage and its rituals, as a drama. But this is how I experienced it when I first observed the festival. The notion of a drama corresponds to what has been said about the Vrātyas and their rites above, and the use of the term may be permissible in the wider framework of the concept of "play" or "sacred play". The term "play" is used in its equivalents in many rituals and festive occasions in India. For example, the nomadic Haṭkar Dhangars of Maharashtra describe their annual festival—which takes place between Dasarā and Divālī, just before their eight months' migration—as *kheḷ* (Ma. "game", "dance") and *nāc* (Ma. "dance"). The festival lasts for two days and centres around a dance of the shepherds accompanied by drums and *sanaīs*. The dead ancestors are enlivened and may possess one or the other dancer. And even the *bhūts*, malignant spirits, which have been possessing shepherds and causing illness, may be worked up on this occasion and driven out by the god who protects the shepherd community. We thus witness a veritable battle between the malignant spirit and the god.[4] We experience, so to say, in a ritual micro-cosmic context what is again and again a subject in the great mythological texts: the battle between gods and demons. We should add to this a reference from the *Jaiminīya-Brāhmaṇa,* which has very close affiliations to the Vrātyas; there, in the Mahāvrata ritual, a fight between an Ārya and a Śūdra takes place on the border between sacred and profane space. The Ārya and the Śūdra represent the gods and demons fighting for the sun.[5]

The element of play is ubiquitous in such festivals. Thus the god "plays" when he crosses the border of the village (Ma. *śilaṅgaṇ*, Skt. *sīmollaṅghana*) in a magnificent procession on the festival of Dasarā. Moreover it is said that Śiva, or Khaṇḍobā, spent much of his time playing chess with Pārvatī/Mhāḷsā, and when he lost once, he had to hand over everything to Pārvatī, including his clothes, one by one. Only his begging bowl, his iron chain, and his *triśūl* were left and have since been worshipped by his devotees.[6] Famous is the dance of Śiva, who dances the world out of and into existence. Everything the god does is, in fact, his *līlā*, i.e., the divine activities are visualised as "sports". In Tamilnadu the "plays" or "sports" (Ta. *viḷaiyāṭu, viḷaiyāṭal*) of Śiva[7] are especially associated with Cidambaram. He is also a magician at Tillai (Cidambaram).[8] But we need not digress and may e.g. refer to the *Mallāri-Māhātmya* version in Marathi written in 1857 by a certain Rāmdās, who described Śiva/Khaṇḍobā as *nānā-nāṭaka-līḷā-avatār*—"the embodiment of various roles and *līḷās*".[9] For the sake of the world, for the sake of his obstinate bhaktas, he re-enacts his primordial deeds, e.g. the killing of the demon. This happens on a special, auspicious day, out of ordinary time. It is an attempt to re-enact the mythical age of the *satyayuga.*

On this sacred day the god assumes the role of a king and hunter and his devotees can participate actively in his *līlā*, as we shall see. The ritual is a *dromenon*, something which is *done*. What is presented is a drama: that is, an action which incarnates a mythical, primordial or cosmic event, not as a representation of, but as an identification with it.[10] We should emphasize that what the observer experiences and describes as a drama does not necessarily correspond to the subjective experience of the active participants in the festival, who feel themselves anything but "actors on a stage".

The ritual re-enacts or recollects the mythical event and derives its efficacy from the fact that it is a dramatic performance of mythic incidents. The "script", in the case of the Dasarā festival's dramatic performance, is unwritten and unfixed, because it is based on oral myths and legends. It is remarkable, however, how persistent some of the mythologemes and images are which determine the roles of the participants. They have their origin as far back as e.g. the *Śatarudriya* of the *Taittirīya-Saṃhitā* and the Vedic Rudra. Besides the Śiva of the Purāṇas, the Murukaṉ cult, the Khaṇḍobā cult, the Mallāri myth which is found e.g. in the *Mallāri Māhātmya* (supposed to be part of the Sanskrit *Brahmāṇḍa-Purāṇa*, with several written Marathi versions), and the *Mārtaṇḍa Vijaya* by Gaṅgādhara[11] have added to the mythological and ritual background.

We may also recall that the tenth day, *Vijayādaśamī*, commemorates the day of victory, on which Durgā killed the demon Mahiṣa, Arjuna defeated the Kauravas, and Rāma killed Rāvaṇa and conquered Lanka. War expeditions are supposed to have begun on Dasarā. If a king started an expedition without celebrating *Vijayādaśamī* he would secure no victory for a year in his kingdom, says the 13th century author Hemādri in his *Vratakhaṇḍa*.[12] An important incident of Dasarā in the case of nobles and kings has been the "sporting" or parading of horses, elephants, and soldiers (*nirājana*) and the marching out. The crossing of the village border (*sīmollaṅghana*), the worship of the *devī* Aparājitā (the "Invincible"), and the worship of the Śamī tree (*Mimosa Suma*) are other features of the festival. Hemādri says that the king should take the Viṣṇu steps, first towards the east and then towards the other directions. After making an effigy of his enemy or merely bringing him before his mind, he (the king) should pierce him in the heart with an arrow with a golden shaft.[13] The latter comment also indicates that a feature of the ceremony and similarly of the myth need not be acted out in detail, but may be mentally assumed and be reduced to suggestive actions (similar to the *mudrās* in the dance style of the Bhārata Nāṭyam,

Kathakali, or the more popular Yakṣagaṇa). Thus the mythologemes in the Dasarā festival at Devaraguḍḍa also manifest themselves in the ritual in an abbreviated and coded way, but are not absorbed or obliterated by the ritual at the cost of the *drama*. In this respect the ritual differs from the brahmanical *yajña* of the classical *śrauta* ritual. We may usefully cite some observations by J.C. Heesterman in this context:

> The essential feature of Vedic ritual is the all but obsessive precision in the execution of the standardized liturgical acts and their fitting together into an unbroken concatenation. It is to this exacting precision that all the ritual effort is directed. That is why the word for truth, *satya*, in the ritual context means precision, exactitude....The rigorous precision of the ritual act exhausts its meanings....That is: all possibilities for a richly variegated complex of deeply layered meaning have been willfully reduced in favour of an utterly regulated world of the mind, a sovereign universe, and therefore divorced from the confusing realities of the mundane world and its contingencies. This, it would seem, sets the Vedic *śrauta* ritual apart from rituals as we generally understand them, tied up with the life of the community in a comprehensive, many-stranded web of meanings.[14]

The Dasarā festival at Devaraguḍḍa has, as we shall try to suggest, this comprehensive, many-stranded web of meanings tied up with the life of the community. It may tend to lose its mythological meanings, but is nevertheless still consciously related to its mythological heritage. Most of the devotees would say that it was on that day that the god Mailār prepared for the fight with the demon Mallāsur or Maṇikāsur in a magnificent show of fortitude. And the *jatrā* differs essentially from the classical Vedic ritual in as much as it is determined by *līlā* and *kheḷ* whereas the Vedic ritual is straightforward, complicated, hard work, appropriately called *karma*, and it lacks the spectacular.

THE NINTH DAY IN DEVARAGUḌḌA

Devaraguḍḍa is a small village on a hill between Dharwad/Hubli and Harihar, near Ranebennur, not far from the National Highway No. 4. The date of the festival is the ninth and tenth days of the month of Aśvin (September-October). The nine days of Durgā (*Durgā-navrātra*) have come to an end. Either on the ninth or on the tenth day the "pots" (*ghaṭa*) in which the goddess (or the god) was worshipped for nine nights are thrown into the river. Many pilgrims (including Liṅgāyats) visit Devaraguḍḍa during these days, especially villagers, shepherds, members of the middle class from nearby towns in Karnataka, but also vagrant devotees permanently serving deities like the goddess Yeḷamma and the god Vīrabhadra. Devotees of Vīrabhadra may pose in a kind of *imitatio dei* at the access to the temple. Prominent are the Vaggayyas, who are special devotees of Mailār and to whom we shall directly return.

On the ninth day, the day before Dasarā, the god leaves the temple on the hill to go to a small temple situated in a Banyan grove about two miles away. Here Mailār is also called Kariāladamarayya—"Lord of the Black Banyan Tree". According to some traditions it was on that day that Śiva as the killer of the demon Malla—who infested the neighbourhood—became Mallāri, the "enemy of Malla". Other names of Mallāri are Bhairava or Mārtaṇḍa Bhairava. There is also the tradition that Mallāri used to go hunting with a pack of hounds. When he was enshrined on the hill the dogs became men and served as his followers under the name of Vaggayyas.

THE VAGGAYYAS: THEIR PERFORMANCE AND OUTFIT

The Marathi equivalent of the term is *vāghyā*, popularly derived from *vāgh* = "tiger", or *vāghī* = "a bag made of tiger's skin" (Molesw.), which the Vāghyās, the special devotees of Khaṇḍobā, use. *Vāghyā* ("dog") may also be derived from Ka. *uggu* = "to utter repeatedly unmeaning sounds"; Ka. ogga is a follower of the god Mailār.[15] One may also plausibly derive "Vaggayya" from Ka. baggu = "barking, crying out" and Ka. *baggu* = "tiger".[16] Whatever the correct derivation may be, two aspects of the ancient Rudra/Śiva as *paśupati* ("the Lord of the animals or souls") blend: the dog is the *vāhana* of Bhairava, and we have noted Rudra's association with the dog in the *Śatarudriya.*[17] Moreover the *Atharvaveda* associates dogs not only with Yama,[18] but with Rudra: "To Rudra's howl-making, unhymned-swallowing(?) dogs I have paid this homage".[19] On the other hand we have the relationship of Rudra/Śiva with the tiger. Śiva is seated on a tiger's skin or is clad in a tiger's skin, and Rudra is, like the tiger, the lord of the forest (*āraṇyānāṃ patiḥ*).[20] In fact, Śiva becomes identified with the tiger, as e.g. the Vāghobā cult in Maharashtra shows.[21] Thus the performance of the Vaggayyas may be an imitation of dogs *or* tigers.[22] In any case the Vaggayyas carry a bag (*bhaṇḍāracīlu*) which is made of tiger's skin and in which they keep *bhaṇḍāra* (turmeric powder).

These Vaggayyas act and bark like dogs when pilgrims arrive at the grove. They have placed their wooden or brass begging bowls on the ground before the temple within the grove and the pilgrims fill them with bananas, milk, curds, ghee, sugar, millet-bread and rice. Formerly the Vaggayyas would act it out much more. They would run to their bowls, would howl, bark and quarrel amongst themselves, and would lie flat on the ground to eat like dogs. This behaviour may seem to disappear and may perhaps be less and less considered "respectable", but it can still be seen in Devaraguḍḍa, and is still common in other places. At other *jatrās* of Mailār and on the special request of devotees, the Vaggayyas perform a round-dance accompanied by drums and chants. In the middle of the circle devotees throw coins on a black woollen blanket and the Vaggayyas pick up the coins with their mouths, entertaining the devotees, If food is offered into the bowls, they will fight like dogs, trying to tear away food from each other's mouths. One is reminded of the famous scene of the dog dance in the *Chāndogya-Upaniṣad* (1.12), performed with the *udgītha* chant of the *Sāmaveda* in order to procure food. This again is in remarkable accordance with the explanation in the *Mārtaṇḍa Vijaya* (34.50) of the origin of the dog in the Mārtaṇḍa Bhairava/Khaṇḍobā cult: the *Sāmaveda*—somewhat impure when compared with the other Vedas, because it relates to the *pitṛs*, according to the *Manusmṛti* (4.124), and has thus, we may add, something to do with death—became the dog of Śiva. It would forever stay at Śiva's gate.

Even a Brāhmaṇ may become a Vaggayya, but as the old Dharwar Gazetteer of 1884 says, such Brāhmaṇs dress like Vaggayyas, but do not bark in public and when the term of their vow is over they doff the Vaggayya's dress and go home. We should remember here that when Śaṅkara came to Ujjain he met, according to the *Śaṅkaravijaya* of Anantānandagiri, a special group of Brāhmaṇs who were followers of Mallāri. They pleased Mallāri with their dance and song. They wore as a special mark a necklace of cowries which is still typical of most of the different groups of Vaggayyas and Gorappas and may be compared with the *niṣka* of Rudra. The followers of Mallāri at Ujjain based their faith on the authority of the *Śatarudriya* reference to the "dogs and the Lord of the dogs".[23] The Pāśūpatas also continued the tradition of the Vrātyas. They were much given to dance and song and *avitadbhāṣaṇa* (= "uttering senseless or contradictory words") was an important incident in the *pāśupata* vow.[24] Ingalls has compared them with the Cynics of ancient Greece,[25] but we can also compare them with the Vaggayyas. The term "cynic", after all, is derived from "*kýon*", which means "dog"..

The real, life-long Vaggayyas mainly come from the Kuruba community. The Kurubas are traditionally shepherds (Uṇṇikaṅkaṇ-Kurubas) and husbandmen with a pastoral background (Hattikaṅkaṇ-Kurubas).[26] In Devaraguḍḍa there are sixty families of Hattikaṅkaṇ-Kurubas who traditionally dedicate one or more children in each family as Vaggayyas to serve Mailār. They have a special right to serve the god of Devaraguḍḍa as "dogs",[27] which means begging in his name and praising him. Through the Kuruba-Vaggayyas in Devaraguḍḍa as well as in other places, Śiva/Mailār maintains his traditional link with tribals or outlandish people, a link which is mentioned as early as in the *Śatarudriya* of the *Taittirīya-Saṃhitā.* Śiva/Mailār thus combines all: from the Brāhmaṇ to the lowest.[28] Mailār and all the equivalent gods in the Deccan have, moreover, a second wife, or lover, from a tribal people. In the Kurnool District (Andhra Pradesh) there is e.g. a rather "raudric" Narasiṃha in a primarily pre-Vaiṣṇava context. He is a hunter with a bow who turns into an animal robbing sheep. His first wife is Lakṣmī, whereas his beloved second wife is Saddalakkama, who comes from the Motāḍikāpus, a subcaste of the Kāpus.

Thus there are two types of Vaggayyas (also called Gorappas): namely, those who beg in the name of Mailār for their whole life on account of a vow of their parents, and those who have taken the vow to serve the god for a certain period. All Vaggayyas have a peculiar long, black, woollen overcoat. On the back of the overcoat the sun and the moon are stitched in colourful designs. The borders are beset with colourful zig-zag patterns. The sun and the moon in the Khaṇḍobā cult indicate that the god is stronger than the sun and the moon.[29] Similarly the Vrātyas wore two ornaments, one of gold and one of silver, which represented the sun and the moon.[30] The sun and the moon along with a dog are also sometimes engraved on the brass begging bowls (Ka. *doṇi,* Ma. *koṭambā*) of the Vaggayyas. They also carry a *triśūla* or a *śūla* (spear), often a cowrie-necklace (though not those Vaggayyas belonging to the sixty Kuruba families attached to the cult of Mailār at Devaraguḍḍa), and a *ḍamaru* (the hour-glass shaped drum) or a *ghaṇṭā* (hand bell), besides the begging-bowl. A scarf is worn around their colourful turbans. They may also tie tiger- and bearskins around their waist. A slightly different group of Gorappas-Gokayyas not only wears a long, black, woollen overcoat, but also a bearskin cap of tremendous size.[31] They also beg in the name of Mailār or Mallaṇṇa. The Vaggayyas or Gorappas remind one of Rudra and the ecstatic, outlandish people associated with him. Rudra is dressed in black in the *Aitareya-Brāhmaṇa* (v. 14) and the Vrātyas, very much associated with Rudra, wore a turban, were dressed in black, woollen garments, had a white and black ramskin over their shoulders, a *pratoda* (goad or whip?), which later is said to have become the *triśūla* or *śūla,* a *niṣka* (a necklace like Rudra's), and an "unstrung" bow (*jyāhroḍa*).[32]

The Vaggayyas of Devaraguḍḍa and the slightly varying groups from other places make long begging expeditions (which have not been studied so far) within Karnataka, Maharashtra, and Andhra Pradesh. They visit e.g. Karvar on the west coast, where they are known as "Mailār's dogs" (*Mailāra kunni*). The Vaggayyas attached to the five major centres (as understood in Devaraguḍḍa) of the Mailār/Khaṇḍobā cult (Devaraguḍḍa; Mailār, near Devaraguḍḍa; Maṅgsūli, near Athṇī, Dt. Belgaum; Mailārpūr [Pember or Prempūr] near Bīdar, and Jejurī, Pune Dt.) disavow the use of black magic. But some Vaggayyas, possibly from other places, are known to practice black magic, with which they try to intimidate people and extract money. With these somewhat predatory habits one may compare the opinion of Heesterman on the Vrātyas. He says about their wandering and aggressive habits: "It may be that they claimed presents and hospitable accommodation under the threat of violence, either real or magical."[33]

THE KUDURAPPAS: THE HORSES OF THE GOD

A vow (Ka. *harike*) which can be taken by members of *all* communities consists of acting as a horse of the god during the festival. In fact, the distinction between horse and rider is vague. Like horses, the devotees gallop forward and backward, beating themselves mercilessly with whips. They loudly shout the name of Mallāri. Devotees feed them bananas etc. straight into their mouth, keeping the eatables on the open hand as one would feed horses. These devotees are called Kudurappas ("who serve a horse" or "who control a horse") and the *jatrā* is thus also called "the festival of the horse" (Ka. *kudure-habba*). To act as the horse of the god is a very widespread vow in the Mailār/Khaṇḍobā cult. The god enters the person in the shape of wind; it is called a "playing wind" in Marathi (*kheḷtem vārem*). But "wind" is also popularly associated with, or contaminated by, *vāru,* which means a "war-horse, a steed, a charger". Skt. *vāyu* means "wind" as well as "horse". It will no longer come as a surprise that Vāyu is, along with Rudra, mentioned as the god *par excellence* of the Vrātyas.[34]

It is the god who possesses the person and uses the whip. And we may cite the comment of a Maharashtrian shepherd on the phenomenon:

After the god has come into the body he beats with the whip. Why does he beat with the whip? If the afflatus (*vāreṃ*) of the god is fierce, then the god whips. Because of the whipping the afflatus subsides, the god becomes peaceful.

In one whose body the god truly enters, it will not show [on the body] after the beating. He whose body the god does not enter fears the beating. If he beats himself, it will show and because of his fear the afflatus disappears. If it is the true afflatus [of the god], then it does not disappear and the beating of the whip does not affect him.[35]

The horse is one of the main *vāhanas* in the cult of Mailār/ Khaṇḍobā, and, according to some versions, it was acquired from the demon. Śiva originally came on his *nandī* and then mounted a horse to fight the demon Malla. We can see that between humans, animals and even the god there exists consubstantiality. The *Mārtaṇḍa Vijaya* e.g. says that the *nandī is* Śiva (17.82). The dog is worshipped on festivals as Khaṇḍobā and the usually black dog may be thoroughly covered with yellow *bhaṇḍār*. The dog *is* also the god, and men act like dogs. God—man—horse are similarly consubstantial.[36]

THE NINTH DAY (CONTINUED): THE EXPEDITION OF THE GOD AND THE PROPHECY

To return to the ritual of the ninth day: the god goes for a hunting expedition to the grove. Or is it the preparation of a war expedition to kill enemies or rather the demon (*rakṣasa*)? We cannot say which is the dominant view, because, in a cult in which oral traditions abound and have not been put down in a single authoritative and univocal scripture, the answers are conflicting. Moreover, not much difference is made traditionally between a hunt and a war-like expedition of a king in mythology. In many places it is maintained, however, that the demons (Maṇi and Malla, Maṇikāsura and Mallāsura) were killed on Campāṣaṣṭhī day, in the month of Mārgaśīrṣa (Nov./Dec.). The *Mārtaṇḍa Vijaya* says that on this day the *liṅg* appeared in Prempūra, near Bīdar (31.5.).

That the god is also the king appears from the fact that he is treated with pomp (Ka. *vijṛmbhaṇe*) as if he were a king. Besides, he has a minister (*pradhān*) or *heggaḍe* (Ka. "headman of a village"), whose temple is to the north of the main temple. The minister is at the same time supposed to be Viṣṇu. The god's bow (Ka. *bil*) and that of his first wife, Māllava, are also carried to the grove. With this bow the god is said to have killed the demon. The god's bow is about fifteen feet high, that of his wife being somewhat smaller. Both bows are generally kept in the main temple, where there can also be seen a number of wooden horses presented to the god on account of vows. There is another huge, unstrung bow which is permanently kept to the south of the main temple in a niche. The lower part of this bow rests on the head of the demon. Another feature of the expedition of the god to the grove is that many devotees accompany him with torches topped by a piece of cloth soaked in oil. This is also in fulfillment of a vow. Thus one may see dozens of lighted torches, which adds to the impression of the god being a hunter "on a wild hunt", especially the more the day merges into the twilight of the evening. At this time the bows are carried to a free space in the middle between Devaraguḍḍa and the grove. A large crowd of spectators, including the Vaggayyas, has gathered there.

Everybody now waits for the eldest Kuruba, who belongs to one of the sixty families and has been unanimously selected on account of his special devotion as a life-long *kāraṇikadavaru*: that is, a "person in charge of the ritual". For eleven days he has been fasting, having no food nor water, and sitting in the main temple on the hill. On this day he has been sitting quietly in the grove. He is now led at high speed by two Vaggayyas from the grove to the space where the two bows are erected. He climbs the god's bow as high as possible so that he can stand on the shoulders of the men holding the bow, or he may even climb higher up without their support. Then he shouts "*sad*", which is supposed to mean, "No sound! Silence!", but which may also mean—we may conjecture—that now the divine word (Ka. *sad* = *śabda*) can be heard. Even the blowing of wind or rainfall is said to stop at this moment. He then looks in all four directions and is in contact with the god, or rather, possessed by him (Ka./Skt. *avirbhūta*), though he says that he personally does not know what is happening to him. Then the god makes three utterances through him which, according to the old Dharwar Gazetteer, may be very cryptic, e.g. "thunderbolt strikes earth", "cat quarrels with dog", "head cut off", which foretell, respectively, for the new year a famine, war, or change of rulers.[38] On one of my visits the prophecy was that the *rabi* and *kharif* crops (the first and the second harvest) will be equally good. This prophecy was also published in Kannada dailies.

It is tempting to compare the *kāraṇikadavaru*, the leader of the Vaggayyas, with his great, ancient predecessor, the Ekavrātya. The eldest Kuruba, after having fasted for eleven (cp. the eleven *rudras*) days, becomes a seer. When he climbs the bow he is in communion with the cosmic powers. He becomes, at least for some moments, Mailār/Rudra as the Vrātya becomes Ekavrātya and is one with *mahādeva* and *īśāna* (i.e. Rudra), according to the famous *Atharva-Veda* chapter (XV.1). In this text even the bow is mentioned as a seemingly indispensable implement (XV.1.6): "He became the Ekavrātya; he took to himself a bow; that was Indra's bow."[39]

THE TENTH DAY: DASARĀ

The next day, on the actual Dasarā day, the god has returned to the hill. He is still in the palanquin, which is kept on a roofed pedestal (Ka. *maṇṭapa*) overlooking an open square to the north-western side of the main temple. A *hukka* is kept to the side of his palanquin. He is supposed to smoke *gāñjī* (hemp) like Śiva. The begging bowls are kept near the open square and there is a continuous stream of devotees going to the palanquin and into the various temples to have *darśan;* none of the devotees forgets to make some offering of eatables into the bowls of the Vaggayyas. To the northern side of the main temple are exhibited two tremendously large-sized pairs of sandals. They are the leather sandals which the god and the goddess used to protect their feet while they were hunting in the wilderness.[40] They are also worshipped because they have power to bestow not only all kinds of merit, but even *mokṣa.* This may be compared with the foot of the *devī* who tramples on Mahiṣāsura or the hoofs of the horse of Mailār/Khaṇḍobā, which in some brass *mūrtis* are placed on the heads of the two demons Maṇi and Malla, or, in our case, the bow which rests on the head of Malla. Malla, in fact, achieved eternal *sāyujyatā* (communion) with Mailār/Mallāri; this is indicated by the name *Mallāri.*[41]

During the whole morning vows are fulfilled by devotees who act like horses and keep on dancing on the open square, whipping themselves. The eldest Kuruba sits on the southern side of the main temple, facing the southern door of the temple.

At three p.m. the atmosphere at the open square gets tense. A large crowd of spectators has gathered and sits around the square on walls, balconies, and roof-tops. On the northwestern side, in front of the palanquin, some dignitaries, e.g. a district judge, are seated. Once I saw a Brāhmaṇ, who had been invited, seated on a chair under a parasol. He was considered as (another) manifestation of the god. In front of these guests a large, black, woollen blanket is spread and on it are a number of well-polished wooden tentpeg-like instruments, wooden hammers, some pointed iron bars (about one and a half inches in diameter), a thick rope about five meters long, swords, some coconuts and numerous small coins offered by the spectators.

THE *PAVĀḌĀ*: THE BRAVE AND MAGNIFICENT PERFORMANCE OF A VOW[42]

Eventually a particular spot is selected in the open square and one of the Kañcavīras,[43] who may be Kurubas or members of a former untouchable caste, sits down and pierces the calf of his leg by driving one of the pointed pegs through it with the help of a wooden hammer. The rope is smoothed with bananas, then it is passed through the hole in the leg and subsequently two twigs of the *babbuḷi*, the thorny *Acacia arabica*, are pulled through the hole simultaneously in opposite directions. One or two other Kañcavīras may follow. Besides, pointed iron bars may be pushed through the calf of the leg with a jerk. Another method of such self-torture is a kind of *āratī* ("waving of lights before a deity"). A thick needle branching into five needles which are covered with cotton cloth, soaked in oil, and lighted is thrust through the forearm near the wrist and is waved in the usual *āratī* way in the direction of the god. The wounds, from which hardly any blood oozes, are covered with turmeric powder. All these feats of courage and devotion are dedicated to the god with the swinging of swords and the yelling of "*Yeḷkoṭi Mallāri Mārtaṇḍa*", which refers to the seven crores of hosts of Mallāri Mārtaṇḍa.

The finale of the *pavāḍā* and the whole Dasarā festival is reached with the breaking of chains. Again the number eleven plays a role: eleven chains are broken by eleven members of eleven families selected from the sixty Kuruba families. The heavy chains are fixed to a thick stone pillar which is fashioned at the top into a *triśūl*. The pillar stands on the opposite side of the open square seen from the *maṇṭapa* where the god watches from his palanquin. One Vaggayya after the other tries his luck, and mostly they succeed in breaking the chain after one or several strong pulls. Nowadays the breaking is done by hand, but formerly the chain is said to have been fastened around the neck. This method is also mentioned in the *Mārtaṇḍa Vijaya* (33.54ff.). At the end a Vaggayya of a certain family breaks the chain, having a special right to do so. This marks the end of the festival. The god is carried in his palanquin into the temple accompanied by female Vaggayyas, who are called Gorammas or Varammas. They wave fly-whisks to ensure a fresh breeze for their god.

THE KAÑCAVĪRAS

Who are these Kañcavīras and what does their performance imply? These self-mortifications of devotees of the Mailār cult have a very old tradition, as we know from the *Krīḍābhirāmamu* written at the time of the Kākatīya dynasty, who ruled from Warangal.[44] The author of this work not only praises Mailār as a great hunter and leader of those who find happiness in hunting with spears (v. 145), but also refers to the Vīrabhaṭṭas of Mailāra, who are "daredevils, embodiments of heroism, and are beyond any act of cowardice". He also tells of their piercing themselves with red-hot iron bars, of hook-swinging, of their impaling themselves on spears, and of their peculiar way of performing *ārati* (vv. 141-2). Such feats of bravery, even leading to ritual suicide, seem to have been frequent in the cult of Mailār and Khaṇḍobā.[45]

Mailār/Khaṇḍobā was very much a god of the tribal, hunting and martial communities and, as we have seen, was treated very much as a king by these groups. "For the hero the king is god", says the *Mārtaṇḍa Vijaya* (18.27). The two latter terms seem to be interchangeable. Occasionally the soldiers would commit suicide on the death of their general.[46] Sometimes the heroes would make a vow to commit suicide if they won in a battle.[47] Death would grant the hero *sālokya* with Śiva, if not *sāyujyatā*. Courage as shown by the Kañcavīras of Devaraguḍḍa makes them fit for the grace of Mailār.

Thus it is also said that Śiva was pleased with the bravery of the *daityas* Maṇi and Malla. Malla was also a great hero (*vīra*) and achieved *sāyujyatā* on death in battle.[48] In fact, on the mythological plane we can see the battle of Mailār/Khaṇḍobā as a kind of sacrifice in which Malla is the sacrificial victim. This is reflected in the ritual of the Kañcavīras. The Kañcavīras, by their self-sacrifice, achieve the nearness of god not only for themselves, but also for the spectators.

Not only the "horses", but also the Kañcavīras avoid feeling pain by calling out Mallāri's name. And by the application of turmeric powder, which is the very substance of Mailār and has cooling and healing properties, the wounds heal in no time. After all, Rudra/Śiva/Khaṇḍobā is also a physician and the "Lord of herbs".[49]

One may ask whether this is not just devotion bordering on blackmail. The *Mārtaṇḍa Vijaya* speaks of the obstinacy of the bhaktas, which Mārtaṇḍa Bhairava meets.[50] In other words, these *vīras* through their fury and exertion arrive at a stage where sacred energy is produced, resulting in the presence of God.[51] The hero is similar to the ascetic practicing *tapas* and producing extreme heat and *siddhis.* Thus the shepherd "shamans" in the Mhaskobā cult in Mahārashtra "playing" with a sword and achieving possession by the god are called *siddhas* as well as *vīras.*[52] Through *tapas* the ascetic becomes clairvoyant and may incorporate the gods. This power is not a monopoly of the mystics and magicians; it is also obtained in the "excitement" of initiatory military combat. A saint, a shaman, a *yogī* or a "hero" may feel the supernatural warmth to such a degree that, *upon his appointed plane of being,* he surpasses the profane human condition and becomes an embodiment of the sacred.[53]

No wonder the hero is considered equivalent to the *yogī* in the famous Sanskrit *śloka*

> *dvāv imau puruṣau loke sūryamaṇḍalabhedinau/*
> *parivrad yogayuktaśca raṇe cābhimukho hataḥ//*
>
> (*Mahābhārata,* Cal. edn. 5.1031. See crit. apparatus in crit. edn. on 5.33.32; *Pañcatantra* 1.345).

In the *Yājñavalkya-Smṛti* 1.374 the hero and the *yogī* are also grouped together; those who are killed in face-to-face combat go to heaven like the *yogīs.*

The fury of the Kañcavīras and their contact with the wilderness, with unbound and dangerous nature, their "play with death", and the nearness to their deity, who still resembles Rudra and is called Mārtaṇḍa Bhairava, are as yet not completely domesticated and hedged by ritual. Their performances, though to some extent stylized and ritualized, differ from the brahmanical ritual, especially in the sense of the classical *śrauta* ritual. The Kañcavīras still resemble the Vrātyas and the odd assemblage of people beyond ordered society (mentioned in the *Śatarudriya*) who have special relations with Rudra. This lends them a power which, though they may rank low in the social and ritual hierarchy, they can transfer and convey to the spectators who take part in the ritual drama.

THE BREAKING OF CHAINS

In many of the festivals of Mailār/Khaṇḍobā, chains (Ka. *sarapaḷi*, Ma. *langar*) are broken not only as a great spectacle, but also in fulfilment of a vow given in return for a request for prosperity in domestic affairs and agriculture. Generally, *saṃsāra* or *prapañca* (Ma.) will be happy if the chain breaks, and the contrary if it does not break. The chain can only be broken on those special days which are charged with the presence of the god, and the breaking of the chain indicates the real, true presence and existence of the god (Ka. *devara astitva*). But breaking also depends on the purity of behaviour of the one who attempts to break the chain. If he has not kept promises and obligations towards his god, the chain will not break. The god will not consider him a true *bhakta* and will not support him in the new year in the ordinary *saṃsāra*. In Devaraguḍḍa as in so many other places the Vaggayyas and Kañcavīras are professionally close to the god. They invoke the god with their feats and the spectators enjoy the spectacle and at the same time feel reinforced and relieved by the close association with their god, mediated by people who by their very outlandishness and devotion are closer to the god. The chain breaking releases the spectators a little, reassured for the vagaries of the usual *saṃsāra*.

THE INTERPRETATION OF RITUAL INCIDENTS BY THE BHAKTI POETS

The informants may not be very articulate about it, but saints have used phenomena like god's dogs, the chains, etc., as "metaphors" for a more philosophical interpretation, in a way similar to that in which the *paśupati-paśu-pāśa* concept was bound to receive a philosophical interpretation.

Thus the Tamilian Māṇikkavācakar in his *Tiruvācakam* repeatedly refers to himself as the dog-like self.[54] He considers Śiva the great bestower of release who destroys his births and deeds. He uses martial metaphors for Śiva's action against *malam* (filth, dirt) and *pācam* (rope, bondage). Like Mailār/Khaṇḍobā, Śiva rides on a victorious war horse, cutting the bonds.[55] It is through death that Malla achieves *mukti.*

For the *bhakti* poet the ritual and ritual implements in the Khaṇḍobā cult become metaphors for the "inner religion". For example, with Tukārām, the begging bowl becomes the heart, the handbells strike the unstruck sound, the bag is inexhaustibly full of *bhaṇḍār,* which is "knowledge" (*jñān*), the *bhakta* becoming Him is filled with the "wind" of the god and becomes possessed with love for the god. Just as a mad dog barks, god has made his dog-devotee bark.[56]

The Brāhmaṇ is at the most an onlooker, as we have seen, and generally does not actively participate in popular *jatrās,*[57] and Cakradhara, for example, the 13th-century "founder" of the Mahānubhāv sect in Maharashtra, taught his followers not to visit *jatrās.*[58] But not all the saints turned against participation in *jatrās* and their popular rituals and entertainments. The Maharashtrian saint Rāmdās (1608-81) e.g. gives a vivid description of a *jatrā* of Khaṇḍobā which reflects the fervent exuberance of the festivals in this cult. Rāmdās, "the active saint", knew that one had to be involved in *jatrās* and popular cults to understand and enlist the support of the folk. In this he differed from the puritan Vīraśaiva saints and Jain munis of Karnataka who ridiculed the Mailār cult.[59] Yet Rāmdās advised the participants to exert their sense of discrimination (*viveka*) amidst the dazzling chaos of a *jatrā.* In one of his songs on Khaṇḍobā he gave "The Description of the Pilgrimage Festival of Jejurī":[60]

I saw God Khaṇḍerāv / All the pilgrims gathered/How can I tell of the manifold splendour / Crowds of people, the mass of horsemen/Throngs of pilgrims, bands of musical instruments//1//

Huge drums, kettle-drums, cymbals, tabors / The *burugas* [and] the tabors merging into a tumultuous noise / The horns and the cymbals join the symphony//2//

Elephants trumpet, camels grunt / Horses neigh, bullocks bellow loudly / The name [of God]//3//

One would not know who is where / in the *yātrā* / One gets lost in surprise //4//

In front there is a dense crowd, behind there is a dense crowd / On both sides are the shops huddled together / Up in the sky are clusters of parasols //5//

Standards bearing the sign of the Bull, all kinds of flags / The huge banner poles / Parasols and fly-whisks, ornamented standards//6//

I saw the God diffusing with fragrance / Shining with glory / I saw those holy grounds, soft and pure//7//

All kinds of flowers, garlands of flowers / All kinds of jewels, garlands of jewels / The Three[61] are the very substance of beauty//8//

Fierce and horrid [are] Vetāḷ and Khaṅkāḷ / [Being] the watchmen on both sides [of the gate] / Both are seated on a horse [and] watch motionless //9//

Who has counted the dancing girls owning the glory of the art [of dancing], who came / Glittering and started dancing under the various festive canopies//10//

The glories [of the God] are sung with the accompaniment of tambourines / There was stick-fighting of different kinds / When a group was formed / The competition started//11//

If one went to the bazaar there was wonder / what to buy and not to buy / There is no limit to the blessed glory of the God//12//

On one side there was the silent heath / Where the simple and innocent should go / One should go to the God['s temple] at a quiet time //13//

In the night the time was quiet / In many a place music sounded / One felt as if Kokilas were singing//14//

Rāmdās says: with the strength of discrimination / One should be in the midst of all and yet remain aloof / That is the highest happiness//15//

In *jatrās* of supralocal importance, the antagonistic competitions between villages tend to be replaced by ritualized mock contests without the usual prize money, as e.g. in the stick-fighting to which Rāmdās refers.[62] These mock stick-fights are still practised by many groups in the annual full-moon *jatrā* for Khaṇḍobā at Pali, District Satara, Maharashtra, in the month of Pauṣ (December/ January). As the song by Rāmdās shows, all these performances (including those of animals) become acts of praise, devotion and dedication to Khaṇḍobā, and, we may add, follow a fixed pattern of rules, which is not necessarily hierarchical, but assigns honorary privileges (Ma. *mān*) to perform rituals to definite groups of devotees or individual devotees (*mānkarī*). This assures some order amidst the chaos of the *jatrā*. Rāmdās also shows the effects of worshipping Khaṇḍobā:[63]

Victory to Khaṇḍerāyā, who has Mhāḷsā and Bāṇāī, the two beautiful wives //1//

The stubborn hero, the warrior-king / The eternal hero of the battlefield, to whom turmeric powder is dear//2//

He directly shows his feats to the folk / Worshipping him the bhaktas become strong/ Bhaktas [who act like] dogs and tigers break the chain / Vile people are instantly put to rest//3//

CONCLUDING REMARKS

The breaking of the chains by the Kañcavīras represents a ritual which may offer some immediate relief and joy through the vision or the felt presence of the divine unfathomable *līḷā*. This the enlivened spectators take home into the world of *saṃsāra* till the drama is re-enacted the next year. Some of them may even consider the broken chain an image of being freed from bonds and the tearing of evil, of transcending the human condition and of achieving freedom and deliverance. Of this their traditional literature is full.[64] It would be in any case facile to generalize by drawing categorically the borderline between the practical object of the ritual (children, increase of wealth, cattle, etc.) and the unconscious merger into a more transcendental aim which brings freedom from desires or at least relativizes the importance and worries of *saṃsāra*. The festival with its various rituals, some of which can be performed individually or by families and some of which are performed by the Vaggayyas and Kañcavīras for the sake of all, integrates the segments of the individual and communal lives of the participants, both morally and spiritually, and re-establishes the channels between man and God.[65] It provides a regeneration of life-forces, enabling the participants to continue living with a renewed sense of purpose[66]—which, possibly, should also be the result of watching a good drama.

The "play with death" is common in Dhangar and Kuruba *jatrās* and has entered from there into popular *jatrās* of gods worshipped by all communities, as in the case of the Mhaskobā cult of Vīr in Maharashtra.[67] The Dhangar *devṛṣī* ("shaman") would belabour his stomach with a (rather blunt) sword, or dance holding the sword tip pressed against his mouth, tongue and teeth, as in the Mhaskobā *jatrā* at Vīr. Or, in the *kheḷ* of the Dhangars, the dancing *devṛṣī* would lean with his bent body on a stick or sword the grip of which is placed on the floor. This reminds us of the Vīrabhaṭṭas of Mailār impaling themselves on spears.[68]

These rites and the Dasarā festival at Devaraguḍḍa show that the gruesome self-sacrifices of earlier times resulting in death[69] have been brought under control by a performance which tends to be ritualized and stylized by more or less symbolic actions. This reminds us of the development in the Vedic *śrauta* ritual: there is a long, great fight described in the *Jaiminīya Brāhmaṇa* between Mṛtyu (Death), who is very much associated with the Vrātyas, and Prajāpati.[70] Ultimately, as J.C. Heesterman observes:

> Prajāpati overcomes his rival through the discovery of the symbolical and numerical equivalences (*saṃpad, saṃkhyānam*). This meant that Prajāpati, by means of the numerical equivalences brought the ritual "weapons" of Death under the same denominator with his own "Weapons".... Thus Prajāpati's victory over Death expresses the break-through of the classical ritual.... The most important point in the Prajāpati-Death contest, however, is that Prajāpati's victory means the elimination of Death as a participant in the ritual; or, rather, by means of the symbolical eqivalences his power can be ritually made subservient. By the same token the rival is excluded from the ritual. In the same way as Death, he can be dealt with ritually, without his active participation....[71]

The "archaic rites" which were the weapons of Death were contests like chariot races, dancing, singing, drumming, lute-playing, and copulation. In one or the other form, these rites recur, as we have stated, in the cult of Mailār/Khaṇḍobā, and though they may be stylized or ritualized to some extent, they were never absorbed to such an extent as to become abstract or lose their draṃatic effect.[72] The dance of Śiva is similar: it may result in death, but it may also result in life, if it is well-ordered and controlled. In this sense Śiva becomes Kālāntaka, the "Destroyer of Death".[73] The ambivalence and danger of the god, if ill-controlled, is well expressed by an incident told by a Dhangar shepherd:

> A Dhangar *siddha* "playing with the sword" danced and became possessed by the god Birobā [the great pastoral god of the Deccan]. A rival of the *siddha* had evil intentions in his mind. He made the drummers suddenly change the rhythm. The [indispensable] drum (*dhoḷ*) and the *siddha* fell on the floor. His vital breath (*prāṇ*) left him....

It is the well-ordered rhythm of the drum which holds Death under control, or pleases the god, and turns the powers of the god into beneficial ones.

ACKNOWLEDGEMENTS

To the German Research Association (DFG), for financing field research in Maharashtra, Karnataka, and Andhra Pradesh in 1977 and 1979.

Dr. Asko Parpola, for comments on an earlier draft and valuable references in a letter dated 12 February 1982.

Dr. S.G. Tulpule, for help in translating the *Mārtaṇḍa Vijaya.*

Dr. P.K. Aithal, Dr. G. Bandini and Dr. Anne Feldhaus, for helpful comments.

Mr. Ramdas Atkar and Mr. Rajaram Zagade, for help in field work.

Dr. S. Settar, for help on various occasions in Karnataka.

NOTES

1. Hauer 1927: 246ff. Heesterman (1962: 10) accepts this.
2. See Dandekar 1979: 209f. *Atharva-Veda* XV. 1.4. For a description of the Vrātyas, see Parpola 1975: 34ff.
3. Parpola 1982. See also Hauer 1927: 251 and the important article Goṇḍa 1943.
4. Sontheimer 1976: 141-3. The verb *khel* or rather *khelaunu* (Nepali) is used in spirit exorcism in Nepal as well. It literally means "to make play", "to fascinate", i.e. to force the *vīr* or *masān* etc. to obey the *dhāmi*, a kind of shamanistic healer, fortune-teller, and ritual specialist for life cycle ceremonies. Höfer and Shrestha 1973: 54.
5. Hauer 1927: 259. *Kaṭha-Saṃhitā* 34.5; 39.3-6. *Pañcaviṃśa-Brāhmaṇa* 5.5.14-17. Cited in Parpola 1979. Caland 1970: paragraph 165.
6. Told by M.K. Tambe and R.E. Waghmode (in Marathi). For purāṇic parallels see Meyer 1937: volume II, 145ff.
7. Zvelebil 1974: 108.
8. For Śiva's "sporting" at Cidambaram see Māṇikkavācakar's *Tiruvācakam* 21.7. For the perception of Śiva as a magician playing at Tillai, see *Tiruvācakam* 31.7. Similarly the pastoral deity Birobā in Maharashtra is often called *gāruḍi* (Ma. snake-charmer, juggler, conjurer, Molesw., s.v.). See now also Yocum 1982: 154ff., dealing with the *Tiruviḷaiyāṭal Purāṇam*, the *sthalapurāṇa* of Madurai describing the "holy sports" or "plays" of Śiva at Madurai, and (p. 157 ff.) with the concept of *līlā* in general. For the epithets of Śiva, i.e. "conjurer" (*māyaṉ*), "trickster" (*eṭṭaṉ*), and "magician", see ibid., p. 148.
9. *Mallāri Māhātmya* (4.2) by Rāmdās, "disciple of Sadāśiva". Cp. also 6.1: *līlā-vigrahī-ādipuruṣa.*
10. See Huizinga 1958: 21.
11. *Gaṅgādhara kavi-viracita Śrīmārtaṇḍa Vijaya,* edited by Rāmacandra Cintāmaṇ Ḍhere (Puṇe: Varadā Buks, 1975).
12. See Kane 1974: 191.

13. Ibid.
14. Heesterman 1981: 54. Heesterman is commenting on the performance of *śrauta* sacrifice (and its filming) amongst the Nambudiri Brāhmaṇs in Kerala.
15. Kittel 1968: volume I, 220, 313.
16. *DED* 4256. Kittel 1968: volume III, 1126.
17. *Taittirīya Saṃhitā* 4.5.4 (*Kṛṣṇa-Yajurveda-Saṃhitā*).
18. Macdonell 1974: 151 and 173.
19. *Atharva-Veda* XI.2.2; 30. Dandekar 1979: 235. Macdonell 1974: 76; the reference there has to be corrected. Rudra is also accompanied by jackals. *AV* XI.2.2. Cf. *Vājasaneyi-Saṃhitā* 16.28.
20. *Aitareya-Brāhmaṇa* VIII.6, cited in Sprockhoff 1981: 40.
21. Kosambi 1962:89. Sontheimer 1976:53, fn. 46. Cp. Höfer and Shrestha 1973 on the Bāgh Bhairab, i.e. Tiger Bhairav [Bhairava], impersonated by the *dhāmi's* assistant.
22. Cf. the *puruṣavyāghrāḥ* mentioned in *Śatapatha-Brāhmaṇa* XIII.2.4.2.4 and *Jaiminīya-Brāhmaṇa* II.423. Sprockhoff 1981: 35. The origin of the Vāghyās (or Vāghes) is described in the *Mārtaṇḍa Vijaya* (29.12-14): The Vāghyās were tigers formerly. When they devoured all the sheep of Ajāmel the Dhangar [Shepherd], Mārtaṇḍa became furious and sent the dogs.... These dogs caught the tigers and brought them to their lord. When the tigers had *darśan* of Mārtaṇḍa, they became human beings. Mārtaṇḍa ordered the "tigers": "Bark like dogs [and stay] near me". Note the "confusion" between man, dog, and tiger, and compare Rāmdās' *pada* 1167, below (fn. 63).
23. Veezhinathan 1976: chapter 29, p. 117f.
24. Lorenzen 1972: 185.
25. Ingalls 1962: 281-98.
26. Sontheimer 1976: 105ff.
27. In the area of Karwar (South Karnataka) the Vaggayyas are known as Mailāra Kunni, "dogs of Mailār".
28. See e.g. *Mārtaṇḍa Vijaya*: *bhaktas* can be Mlecchas, i.e. Muslims (24.30-31), and Caṇḍālas (24.40). The god is accessible to all *varṇas* through *dhyān*, says the author of the same work (21.52). Women devotees can present betel to the god in Devaraguḍḍa, something which is done only to regular husbands otherwise. The Kañcavīras (on whom see below) are often former Untouchables.
29. See e.g. *Kavi Śrīdhara Nājharekara kṛta Malhāri Māhātmya*, edited by R.C. Dhere (Puṇe, 1975), 1.98. For the significance of the sun and the moon in the Khaṇḍobā cult and in the context of the Somavatī-Amāvāsyā festival, see Stanley 1977.
30. Hauer 1927: 129. *Baudhāyana-Śrautasūtra* XVIII.24: *AV* XV.
31. Their forehead is besmeared with ash and they also carry a *ḍimkī* (an hour-glass-shaped drum). See Misra *et al.* 1971: 17f.
32. Hauer 1927: 124; Dandekar 1979: 207ff.; Heesterman 1962: 13; Eliade 1977a: 112. That the garments are made from wool is mentioned in *Lāṭyāyana-Śrautasūtra* VIII.6.20 (Hauer 1927: 110).
33. Heesterman 1962: 6f., 11, 29f.
34. Caland 1970: No. 146. According to the *Jaiminīya-Upaniṣad-Brāhmaṇa*, the *ekavrātya* is Vāyu. *JUB* 3.4.5.2.1-4 (Sharma 1966).
35. Sakharam Babu Lakade. Cf. the Keśin hymn in the *Ṛgveda* (10.136.4-5), where

it is said that the muni flies through the air. He is the horse of the wind, the friend of Vāyu, driven by the gods. See Eliade 1977a:111. Cp. Höfer and Shrestha 1973: 52f. The spirits of the dead are called *bāyu* (*vāyu*) and the term is used as a synonym for *pret* (ghost of a dead person). In *śrāddha* ceremonies ten kinds of *vāyu* (winds) play a role. Höfer and Shrestha 1973, citing Shastri 1963: 58-69. The forty-nine *bāyu* are mentioned in the *mantras* in the texts of the *bāyu* and may thus be connected with the forty-nine *maruts*, the storm gods (Höfer and Shrestha 1973: 53). In a narrower sense the word *bāyu* applies only to those ghosts which inflict misfortune upon the living. Cp., on a different level of sophistication, the *vāyu-abhibūta* which occurs amongst the ritual prescriptions of Pāśupatas: one should practise, *inter alia*, *spandana* (shaking one's limbs as if afflicted by "wind-disease"). Lorenzen 1972: 185. The "folk ritual" also involves the shaking and tossing about of the medium possessed by the *bāyu*. Höfer and Shrestha 1973: 53. The wind humour is the cause of a great number of disorders, according to Hindu medical works. Filliozat 1964: 61-79, 196-228 (cited in Lorenzen 1972).

36. Thus Revanta, son of Sūrya, and the patron deity of horses, is sometimes viewed as a horse. *Garuḍa Purāṇa* 201.6 etc. See Moeller 1966: 174.
37. Cf. also *Mārtaṇḍa Vijaya* 35.60: the god is worshipped like a king and Jejurī (ibid., 35.63) is his capital (*rājadhānī*).
38. *Gazetteer of the Bombay Presidency*, Dharwar 1884: 721. Cf. Thurston 1975: volume IV, 154.
39. Whitney's translation (1905).
40. In the *Paripāṭal* XXI, Murukan is the god of the hunters in the mountains who carries a lance, rides on an elephant and wears leather sandals. In the *Paḻaṉittalapurāṇam* XX.51, protection from impurity for the feet of the god is given as the reason for the sandals (information from Kamil V. Zvelebil). But see the curious parallel in e.g. *Kātyāyana-Śrautasūtra* XV.6.23-24: The freshly anointed king is not allowed to go on the pantomimic war expedition without leather sandals (of boar skin), because he should no longer touch the earth with his bare feet. Deppert 1977: 142—In Madduleti, near Betamcherla in the Kurnool Dt. (Andhra Pradesh), the similar and hardly Vaiṣṇavized god Narasiṃha goes on a hunting expedition which is not to be seen by anyone. Sandals are kept, and, on the return of the god after a week's hunt, the sandals are said to be worn out and to have thorns sticking to them. The heavy sandals of the nomadic Dhangar shepherds are notorious. Thus the sandals (*upānaḥ*) also form part of the outfit of the wandering Vrātyas. See Hauer 1927: 96 (*Lāṭyāyana-Śrautasūtra* VIII.6.23-24) and 110 (*Baudhāyana-Śrautasūtra*, chapter 25).
41. *Mārtaṇḍa Vijaya* 20.56: the dead body becomes the throne of Mārtaṇḍa; 20.98: Malla achieves *sāyujya*.
42. Kittel 1968: s.v. In Marathi it is a panegyric ballad about a hero or great personage.
43. See Khare 1958: 97.
44. *Krīḍābhirāmamu* 1972.
45. See references in Sontheimer 1982: 272f. (figures 21-23). Dhere (1961: 18) cites the *Samayaparīkṣā* (a Jain work), which euhemeristically considers Mailār to be a deified hero (*vīra*).

46. E.g. the suicide of the general of king Vīra Ballāḷa, Kuvara Lakṣmaṇa, and his wife along with soldiers, recorded on a pillar in Halebid. Thakur 1963: 61f. See Settar 1982: 196f.
47. Sontheimer 1982: 271f.
48. See e.g. *Mārtaṇḍa Vijaya* 16.44. On Malla as a hero, see Sontheimer 1984.
49. *Taittirīya-Saṃhitā* IV. 5.2.1. For Rudra as a physician see Macdonell 1974: 76.
50. *Mārtaṇḍa Vijaya*, chapter 19, describes the obstinacy of Malla as a *bhakta* of Mārtaṇḍa, receiving ultimately a boon from the god.
51. Eliade 1977b: 91f., 146ff.
52. Sontheimer 1976: 196.
53. Eliade 1977b: 150. One may compare the Kañcavīras with the story in the *Kirāta Parvan* in which Arjuna makes a self-sacrifice to Śiva. On Arjuna as the "warrior yogin" see Biardeau 1972: 195-96, 160-66.
54. *Tiruvācakam*, e.g. 8.7: He makes my dog-like self his own.
55. *Tiruvācakam*, e.g. 8.3, cf. 8.21. Siva, disguised as an Arabian horse-dealer, saves Māṇikkavācakar from the persecution of the king. The role of Śiva as a horse-dealer is played by a Muslim on the Avani-Mula-Day. See Frenz and Nagarajan, translators 1977: ixff.
56. *Tukārām-Gāthā* 1972: number 4429.
57. Cp. Heesterman 1964: 21f.
58. *Līḷācaritra*, *Uttarārdha* 585 (Kolte, editor 1978).
59. See Cidānandamūrti 1966: 41-62. I owe the reference to S. Settar and was helped in the translation of the article by Rajaram R. Hegde, Pune, Department of Archaeology, Deccan College.
60. Rāmdāsī, editor 1928: *pada* 1171.
61. That is, Khaṇḍobā; his first wife, Mhāḷsā; and his second wife, Bāṇāī.
62. Cp. Beals 1964: 99-113 and Heesterman 1967: 27.
63. Rāmdāsī, editor 1928: *pada* 1167.
64. See e.g. *Bhāgavatapurāṇa* III.25.20 on *pāśa*, which binds man to the world but is a door to *mokṣa* if directed towards the saints (*sādhus*). Gail 1969: 88.
65. Long 1972: 37. Cf. also V. Turner 1977: 198-215.
66. Long 1972: ibid.
67. Sontheimer 1976: 143, 218.
68. For ritual suicide of low caste warriors see also Elmore 1925: 111: "The Madigas returned to Katama Razu. . . and when he saw that they returned without fighting any battle or winning any victories, he was angry and would not speak to them. . . . They threw their weapons into the air and baring their breasts were slain by the falling swords and spears. For this act they were immediately admitted into the heaven of heroes." Cp. also Hassan 1920: 240ff., on the caste variously called "Goundala", "Gouda", "Idiga", and "Kalal". The caste worships Mallaṇṇa by a hook-swinging festival. "Sometimes two or more devotees are suspended simultaneously from the beam and, with swords and shields in their hands, make a pretence of fighting with one another" (245f.).
69. Settar and Sontheimer 1982: 196f., 212ff. *et passim*.
70. *Jaiminīya Brāhmaṇa* 2. 69-70. See Heesterman 1994: 12f. The *JB* passage is cited and discussed by Asko Parpola in a study to be published in the *Wiener Zeitschrift für die Kunde Sudasiens* ("The Epic Bard and the Early History of Indian Religions").

71. Heesterman 1964: 12f and 1962: 20.
72. For ritual chariot races and obscene ritual imitation of dogs see Sontheimer 1984. One may compare the Muraḷīs in the Khaṇḍobā cult, the Gorammas, and the second, more erotic and more beloved "wife" of the god (Bāṇāī in the case of Khaṇḍobā, Vaḷḷi of Murukaṉ, and Kurubattyavva of Mailār) with the *puṃścalī* (harlot) of the Vrātyas. Mailār is said to visit his "wife" outside the village on the ninth day of the light half of the month of Aśvin.
73. O'Flaherty 1981: 138.

Rudra and Khaṇḍobā: Continuity in Folk Religion

If we compare Rudra, as a folk god, with Khaṇḍobā, one of the most famous folk gods of Maharashtra, we discover a surprising degree of correspondence between these deities and their cults. By "folk god" we mean a god who is directly accessible to his followers, exists on earth "here and now", and is not preponderantly located in a distant Purāṇic heaven. Consequently we leave aside for the moment in our comparison the Śiva of the *Mahābhārata*[1] and the *Purāṇas*. It seems preferable to see in the presentation of Rudra/Śiva in these texts reflections on what was basically a folk god. For this reason, we also ignore for the moment the texts relating to the ritual and philosophy of various Śaivite "sects", e.g. the Pāśupatas.[2] We would like to suggest that the expressions of beliefs about Rudra varied according to the different levels of the social groups which were involved in the worship and, moreover, may have been caused not only by a social, but also by an ecological or spatial separation. Thus it seems difficult to assume that there was one unilinear evolution of a monolithic conception from Rudra to his "successor" Śiva, and we must rather think of mutual adjustment, incorporation and subordination of different conceptions and attitudes of different social groups. One may enlist the well-known concept of "universalization and parochialization" to describe this interaction.[3] Other concepts which could be used to describe the interaction are "inclusivism"[4] and "reflexivity",[5] but we can only draw attention to them here and shall not examine their applicability in detail.

In our opinion it seems improbable that the Śiva of the Sanskrit texts is the exclusive successor of Rudra, from whom Khaṇḍobā eventually emerged as a "parochialized" cult or perhaps even as an "aberrant" version of a Purāṇic Śiva. One may with much more justification say, as we shall try to show, that there was also always the folk god called "Rudra" in the Vedic texts (among other names, e.g. Śarva, Bhava, Paśupati), who lived on in cults like that of Khaṇḍobā or the related Mailāra (Karnataka) and Mallaṇṇa (Andhra). These cults existed parallel to the Rudra/Śiva of the *Purāṇas* and of the Śaivite "sects", which had their own peculiar mythology, ritual and philosophy. The Khaṇḍobā cult was linked to the scriptural "great tradition", as we see in the *Mallāri Māhātmya,*[6] but this link was late and superficial and failed to fully "universalize" the folk god Rudra-Khaṇḍobā and his cult. This link is not even fully acknowledged in the standard *Purāṇas:* the *Mallāri Māhātmya* is said to belong to the *Brahmāṇḍa Purāṇa,* but the text is not included in the Veṅkaṭeśvara edition of the same *Purāṇa.* Today the content of the *Māhātmya* is still hardly known to the majority of the devotees. Where it is known, the struggle of Khaṇḍobā against the *daityas* as an "*avatār* of Śaṅkar for the sake of his *bhaktas*" is emphasized, but not the myth told in the *Māhātmya.* According to the *Māhātmya* the god descended to defend Brāhmaṇs, their *āśram,* and their *yajña* from the depredations of Maṇi and Malla, the *daityas.*[7]

When and where the myth of the *Māhātmya* was known, it tended to be only partially accepted and was made to function within the framework of folk religion. This happened apparently also with an earlier attempt to identify Khaṇḍobā with the Brāhmaṇical-purāṇic Skanda.[8] In short, we may say that folk tradition, oral literature and folk rituals still prevail in the Khaṇḍobā cult.

Especially in the texts of the later Vedic period (the period of the *Atharvaveda,* the *Brāhmaṇas* and the *Śrautasūtras*) we find Rudra reflected as a god who had to be integrated into the *śrauta* sacrificial system, but it seems obvious that he belonged primarily to the Vrātyas, rather than to the brāhmaṇical sacrificial priest. The picture of Rudra as portrayed by Vedic texts shows a god on the whole unaffected by later interpretations. That is, we get evidence of a god who has not yet been dynamically interpreted by Purāṇic authors, "sectarians", classical poets and philosophers.

Thus the faithful transmission of the Vedic texts has preserved for us the picture of a folk deity who was worshipped under various names by Āryans other than those responsible for composing the *Ṛgveda.* In fact, Asko Parpola suggests that Rudra was a god especially connected with the pre-Ṛgvedic Āryans who mixed with the culture and population of the late Harappan period. He has actually identified them as the *dāsas* or *dasyus,* which originally just meant "man" and not yet "slave".[9] According to Parpola the rituals of the pre-Ṛgvedic Āryans with their admixture of the religion of the late Harappan period were antithetically opposed to the Vedic *soma* sacrifice and the classical *śrauta* ritual.[10]

Parpola's thesis offers good reasons not to assume one unilinear historical development from a single Rudra to Śiva, but suggests a more complex development of several distinct parallel traditions. We also particularly agree with his thesis as it makes it unnecessary to postulate Rudra as an "outsider" in the sense that he was (primarily) a non-Āryan deity who was "reluctantly brought into the Vedic-Āryan fold."[11]

The comparison between Rudra and the folk deity Khaṇḍobā involves reading the Vedic texts on Rudra in the context of field research in Maharashtra, and also in Andhra and Karnataka, and then the study of the cult as reflected in regional literatures. The reaction of the authors of *Māhātmyas* (e.g. the *Mallāri Māhātmya*) and of "sectarian" texts written sometimes in Sanskrit but chiefly in Kannada, Telugu, and Marathi—though providing a new layer or a different way of looking at the god—are important, as they show which aspects of the folk cult were emphasized, de-emphasized, added, rejected, ignored, or interpreted anew.

Indologists have tended to overstress one aspect in their interpretations of Rudra. For example, Arbman regarded him primarily as a god of death.[12] But if we consider e.g. Rudra's dogs primarily as "messengers of death" connected with inauspiciousness, impurity, blood, and hell, we take the position, and remain in the sphere, of a Brāhmaṇ *śrauta* ritual expert, or of the student of the Veda whose study (*adhyāya*) may be disturbed at the sight or sound of a dog (*Āpastamba Dharmasūtra* I.10.17 *inter al.*). For the hunter or the itinerant merchant and other followers of Rudra, as mentioned in the *Śatarudrīya* (see below), the dog has no such terrifying implications and has vital importance in their life. The hunter needs the dog for hunting, the shepherd for protecting his camp or flock, the itinerant merchant to protect the caravan, and so on. The faithful and brave dogs (often imitated by the *bhaktas* of Rudra and Khaṇḍobā, see below) are even given memorials and are depicted as devoted to the god, as, for example, in two memorials dedicated to two dogs at Phaltan on the way to Shingnapur (Satara district). Folktales told by Dhangar shepherds emphasize the faithfulness of dogs. Khaṇḍobā's dogs are nowhere associated with Bhairava and his brahminicide, rather they are said to have come with Bāṇāī, the second wife of Khaṇḍobā and a shepherdess. It was R.N. Dandekar, following R.G. Bhandarkar, who clearly pointed out Rudra's malevolent as well as benevolent features.[13] The ambivalence of gods like Rudra is a frequent and essential component in the cult of any Indian folk deity, and this has been virtually ignored in Indological studies of the past.[14]

There is another curious feature which emerges if one compares Rudra with Khaṇḍobā: folk rituals in general and the rituals in the Mailār/Mallaṇṇa/Khaṇḍobā cult in particular resemble in many ways the folk elements of the Vedic *śrauta* rituals, or rather the rituals which were "assimilated away"—to use the expression of Jan Heesterman—in the classical Vedic *śrauta* rituals.[15] If one observes the *jatrās* of Mailār, Mallaṇṇa, or Khaṇḍobā, and if one reads, for example, the descriptions by Rāmdās of the *jatrā* at Jejuri,[16] one discovers many archaic folk rituals which are mentioned in, but are eliminated from, the classical Vedic *śrauta* ritual. Heesterman has shown that the classical *śrauta* ritual "eliminated" or "assimilated away" the "preclassical" rituals based on communal celebrations, agonistic dualism, music, dance, ritual abuse and ritual copulation. It purified and individualized the "preclassical" rituals by breaking the dualistic pattern and cyclical exchange, making the *yajamāna* the centre of the ritual. The sacrifice became independent from ritual rivalry and the complementary pattern of purity and impurity. The classical *śrauta* ritual eventually became the domain of absolute purity. The *mahāvrata*, which was originally a cyclical festival and has been compared with the Dasarā festival, became a normalized *soma* ceremony, but it still preserved archaic rites, such as different kinds of contests, e.g. chariot races, dancing, singing, drumming, and ritual copulation. These rituals were the weapons of Mṛtyu, who was close to Rudra, and who, according to the *Jaiminīya Brāhmaṇa* (*JB* 2.69-70, fought a ritual battle with Prajāpati which ended in the victory of Prajāpati and the breakthrough of the classical Vedic ritual. All the incidents of the "preclassical" Vedic ritual occur, however, in the Khaṇḍobā cult and are not completely eliminated, however stylized they may have become.

We cannot compare here all the features common to Rudra and Khaṇḍobā and a few examples must suffice to illustrate the point. One of the most important texts is the *Śatarudrīya* of the *Taittirīya Saṃhitā*. There are small differences in the text of the *Śatarudrīya* of the *Vājasaneyi Saṃhitā*. Of course, references from other Vedic texts like the *Vrātyakāṇḍam* of the *Atharvaveda* (Book XV) are important. The *Śatarudrīya* is sometimes considered a description of the ubiquity, and thus the philosophical universality, of Rudra. But, as one sees in the folk-religious context, in addition to an emphasis on Rudra's ubiquity, the text gives a concrete and unmistakable impression of Rudra through the description of his specific, personal characteristics. These characteristics reappear in slightly different terms in the Khaṇḍobā of folk belief.

SPATIAL SEPARATENESS OF THE FOLLOWERS OF RUDRA

Rudra is the Lord of the mountain. He wanders in the mountains. He is called *giriśanta, giritra, giriśa* (*TS* IV.5.1). In the *Maitrāyaṇī Saṃhitā* (I.10.20) the mountain is specifically mentioned as the abode of Rudra. Rudra, the hunter, lives among the mountains with his wife Rudrāṇī. She plays a more a vital role than the wives of the other Vedic gods.[17] Khaṇḍobā is a mountain deity, who is called Mallayya in Andhra or Mallappa in Karnataka. Etymologically the term is derived from Tamil *malai*, Kannada *male*, etc. Mallayya also refers to the famous deity of Śrīśailam in Andhra, who at the folk level has many similarities with Khaṇḍobā. Mallayya/Mallikārjuna is especially associated with the tribe of the Ceñcūs. Pilgrims from Maharashtra in the 12th century already called him Sirigiri (Śrīgiri) Mallayya.[18]

The close association of Khaṇḍobā with his wife while they kill the demon or go for a hunt is familiar in folk art and ritual. From the *ṚV* we already gather that the goddess Vāc stretches the bow for Rudra (*ṚV* 10.125.6). Rudra's "sister" Ambikā (considered in this context to be the autumn season) joins him on his kill (*TB* I.6.10; *MS* 1.10.20; cf. e.g. *Mahābhārata* 3.40.17; 40.55 [critical edition]). Near Jejuri, in the villages of Sakurdi and Murti Modhve, we find two similar, very old reliefs (presumably 13th c.) of a hunter with a Bhairava halo. He is accompanied by his wife, who wears a *mukuṭa* like that of a queen. Both have bows and hunt a wild boar and deer. They are accompanied by dogs and demon-like hosts. Today the god is called Vandev and the goddess Yogeśvarī. Apparently the god was worshipped as a hunter around Jejuri. The Somvatī Amāvāsyā festival in Jejuri still has vestiges of a hunting excursion of Khaṇḍobā. Khaṇḍobā is accompanied by his wife Mhāḷsā and *inter alia* by a host of "hunters" represented by the Dhangars with their ceremonial spears. Formerly, it is said, wild animals were actually hunted and a drop of blood was put on the *pālkhī* of the god and goddess. On this day many people worship their ancestors. It is as if the living and the dead (the *vīras* or *bhūtas*) were equally alive and united on this day. But it is made clear in the *Mārtaṇḍa Vijaya* that Jejuri is not a place for *śrāddha*, but the capital of king Mārtaṇḍa (*MV* 35.62-3). Rudra, like Khaṇḍobā, is the lord of the *gaṇas* (*TS* IV.5.4e) and the lord of the *bhūtas* (*TS* IV.5.11: *bhūtānām adhipati*).

Rudra is not only connected with the world of demons, but also, according to the *Hiraṇyakeśigṛhyasūtra* (1.5.16.10), associated with serpents: he sits in a place infested by serpents—that is, we may presume, in a termite mound. The termite mound can be seen as spatially separated from the settled habitation and is, so to say, a miniature mountain in the forested area. G.H. Khare mentions[19] that Khaṇḍobā/Mailār cannot be exclusively a mountain deity because some important cult centres are not on a hill or a mountain, e.g. Adimailār in the Bellary district, where Mailār is called Maṇ-Mailār, the "Mailār made out of clay". But here Mailār manifested himself in a termite mound in which he was said to have lived with frightful serpents. In Prempur/Khanapur (near Bidar) the *mūrti* of the demon Maṇi is in the form of a huge serpent.[20]

In the Vedic *agnicayana* ritual "the head of the sacrifice" as the essence of the universe plays a big role. Originally in the preclassical ritual the "head of the sacrifice" must have been a great object of contention between rivalling parties.[21] Without going here into the intricacies of the Vedic ritual we may say that an "anthill" and the "sacrificial head" are seen as identical. At one stage Agni or the sun is worshipped in an "anthill" and he is considered to be hidden in the "anthill" as the sun discerning the world at daybreak (*TS* IV.1.2.h.k.).[22] Rudra is "identified" with or "substituted" for by Agni in the ritual context of the *śrauta* sacrifice. Now Khaṇḍobā in Adimailar (Karnataka) is considered to have been hidden in the termite mound from which he emerged as Mārtaṇḍa Bhairava, the sun. The termite mound, which in the Vedic ritual stands symbolically for the head of the sacrifice, is in popular legends also the seat of the god and of gold, turmeric, and wealth in general. The association of Mārtaṇḍa Bhairava or Khaṇḍobā with gold or rather *bhaṇḍār*, turmeric powder, is well known. The sun spending the night in the termite mound or in the underworld and emerging at daybreak is also reflected in the

Mārtaṇḍa Vijaya (28.2ff.), in the explanation of the origin of the turmeric powder: the night changes into turmeric. In an oral legend from Andhra we hear that the termite mound was the seat of the sheep (= wealth) and of Mārtaṇḍa Bhairava in the form of a dog.[23]

THE SOCIAL SEPARATENESS OF SOME FOLLOWERS OF RUDRA AND KHAṆḌOBĀ

The *Śat.* already mentions the "outlandish" communities which are also involved in the worship of Khaṇḍobā. Thus we have all types of robber groups and thieves (*TS* IV.5.3: *taskarānām, stāyūnām, paricarāyāraṇ-yānām...patiḥ; paricarāyāraṇyānām patiḥ* means "chief of those who roam about in the woodlands"). But Rudra is not only the lord of thieves and robbers, the lord of the trees and of the forest, but also the lord of the fields: *kṣetrānām pati* (*TS* IV.5.2g). He is primarily the lord of the forest people and vagrants, but he also belongs to the agriculturists. He could be invoked to protect them and is their guardian. One can compare the robber groups with the Rāmośīs or Beḍars/Beraḍs, who were the traditional robbers and waylayers and have special rights in the Khaṇḍobā cult. On the one hand he is the lord of the robbers and on the other hand he is the *kṣetrapāl par excellence.* The Rāmośīs were notorious robbers of the harvest and they waylaid merchants, but at the same time they could be made watchmen of the fields etc. Close to Rudra are also the *niṣādas* (*TS* IV.5.40), who were hunters, fishermen, robbers, etc., and the *puñjiṣṭas* (ibid.), who were fishermen or fowlers etc. As the leader of these tribes Rudra is called *sthapati,* which is also the title of a *niṣāda* chief.[24] These tribes may be compared with the Malhār Koḷīs and Mahādev Koḷīs, who were the tradi-tional Maharashtrian hunters and fishermen, leaning towards predatory activities. The goddess Bāṇāī at Jejuri is served by *pūjāriṇīs* of the Mahādev Koḷīs. We might add that in many places in Maharashtra the Koḷīs and the Gavḷīs were the first to serve a Mahādev cult before it became a holy *kṣetra* of Śiva: Mahādeva is one of Rudra's names in the Veda (*AV* XV.5.6; *MS* II.9.1).

In the *Śat.* Rudra is addressed as the best of traders, the trader *par excellence* (*TS* IV.5.2k: *vāṇija*). Khaṇḍobā/Mailār is very much also a god of the Banajigas, a traditional Liṅgāyat merchant caste. The cult of Mallaṇṇa at Odela in Karimnagar district was, for example, founded by a Banajiga. Khaṇḍobā's wife is Mhāḷsā, who is supposed to be a Liṅgāyat *vāṇī* (merchant) by caste. An important trade centre between the northern and southern Deccan associated with Khaṇḍobā is Malegaon in Usmanabad district. There is also a well-attended *jatrā* in the month of *Mārgaśīrṣa* which is called *ghoḍyācī jatrā*, because there is a considerable trade in horses, cattle, and camels. In a folk song he is called the "Merchant of Jejuri" (*Jejuricā vāṇī*) who loads pack-oxen (?) with sacks of turmeric powder, rice, coconuts, arecanuts, and oranges, takes them to Jejuri and unloads them in the courtyard of Bāṇāī's house.[25]

Rudra's special weapons as a lord of the hunters is the bow. Bow and arrows are actually more natural to him than the *vajra*. Sometimes the *vajra* is said to part into three arrows, thus when Indra hurled his thunderbolt against Vṛtra it divided into three arrows (*TS* VI.1.4, 4-5). Whether the *vajra* and the *tisṛdhanva*[26] are precursors of the *triśūla*, ancestors (also called *vīra*) are depicted with three arrows, a bow and a sword on the memorial plaques (*ṭāk*) used in the ancestor worship of the Khaṇḍobā cult. These vīras look like an *imitatio dei* of Rudra/Khaṇḍobā.

In the *Śat.* Rudra is asked to loosen the string of his bow (*TS* IV.5.1.1 and o.). The bow (*jyāhnoḍa*) is also the weapon of the *vrātyas* and of the Ekavrātya, the primordial chief of the *vrātyas* mentioned in the *Vrātyakāṇḍam* of the *Atharvaveda*. The unstrung bow of Mailār plays an important role in the Dasarā festival of Devaragudda. The height of this bow is about 8 meters and it is climbed by the eldest Vaġgayya of the Kuruba caste at the peak of the festival. His communion with Mailār at this moment very much reminds us of the activities of the Ekavrātya, or rather, the *sthāpati* of the *vrātyas*, who becomes the Ekavrātya by performing certain cosmogonic rituals. He is thereby identified with Mahādeva, Rudra, Īśāna, etc. In *AV* XV.1 the bow is mentioned in the connection as a seemingly indispensable implement: "He became the Ekavrātya; he took to himself a bow, that was Indra's bow."[27] Rudra is often identified with Vāyu, the wind.[28] According to the *JUB* the Ekavrātya is Vāyu (3.IV.5.2. 1-4). Now, when the eldest Kuruba climbs the bow in Devaragudda, thus communicating with Mailār, wind and rain are supposed to come to a halt and, in fact, the wind is said to be located in the god personified by the Kuruba.

The wind is often identified with the horse.[29] *Vāyu* may mean "wind" as well as "horse". To act as the horse of the god by galloping and whipping oneself is a common ritual in the Khaṇḍobā cult. The god enters the devotee in the form of wind which is called *kheḷteṃ vārem̐* in Marathi. But *vārem̐* is also popularly associated or confused with *vāru*, which means "war-horse, steed, a charger". The *jatrās* of Mailār are therefore also called *kudureya habba*—"the festival of the horse" and the devotees performing the vow are *kudurappas*. Vāyu, along with Rudra, is mentioned as the special god of the *vrātyas*.[30] We must therefore examine the *vrātyas* more closely at this stage.

They are described as constantly wandering bands and, as Heesterman writes: "It may be that they claimed presents and hospitable accommodation under the threat of violence, either real or magical."[31] The dress and equipment of the leader of the *vrātyas*, the *sthapati* or *gṛhapati*, resemble that of Rudra: he has long hair (*AV* XV.2) and wears an *uṣṇīṣa*. He has a dark garment like Rudra (*AB* V.14), which is of black wool. He has an upper garment of black and white goat- or ramskins and a *pratoda* (goad or whip?); he wears a jewel or amulet (*maṇi*); he wears neck ornaments—two, according to the *AV* (XV.2)—and the *BŚS* says (18.24) they are of silver and gold (cf. below, the sun and moon stitched onto the gowns of the Vaggayyas); he also wears a *niṣka* like Rudra's and carries an unstrung bow (*jyāhroḍa*). The other *vrātyas* were equipped like their leader, wearing woollen, black clothes with band fringes or ribbons, as well as a pair of girdles (*dāmani*) and sandals (*upānahau*), and black and white ramskins over their shoulder. They were accompanied by the *puṃścalī*, which is usually translated as "harlot" or "dancing girl", and a bard (*māgadha*).

If we compare the habits and the outfit of the *vrātyas* with those of the Vaggayyas of Mailār and the Vāghyās of Khaṇḍobā we find some striking similarities. All Vaggayyas or Goravas, as they are also called, have peculiar long, black, woollen gowns. On the back the sun and the moon are stitched in colourful designs. The borders of the gown are beset with colourful zig-zag patterns. The sun and the moon, along with a dog, are also sometimes engraved on the brass begging bowls of the Vaggayyas. They also carry a *triśūla* or a *śūla* (spear), or a staff, a cowrie necklace, a *ḍamaru* or a *ghaṇṭā*. They may also tie ramskins around their waists. Members of a slightly different group, called Gokayyas or Gorappas, wear not only long black woollen overcoats, but also black bearskin caps of tremendous size. The Vaggayyas go out on begging excursions; sometimes they try to intimidate people in order to extract money from them. Some of them are known to practise black magic. It is perhaps not too far-fetched to see in the *puṃścalī* the ancestress of the *muraḷī*,[32] the woman "married" to Khaṇḍobā. The Muraḷī is accompanied by a Vāghyā, who is the bard of Khaṇḍobā.

The specialty of the Vaggayyas and to a lesser degree of the Vāghyās is their performance of dog imitation rites. The dog plays an important role in the Mailār/Khaṇḍobā cult. The Vāghyās accompanied the god in a former age as dogs on his hunt. But the term *vāghyā* may also be derived from Sanskrit *vyāghra,* and the mixing of "tiger" and "dog" is chronic in myth, ritual and folk art.[33]

One of the earliest references to Rudra and the dogs is in the *Śat.*: here the "dog leaders", "dogs", and the "lords of dogs" are mentioned (IV.5.4 q and r). Once the Ekavrātya is addressed as "dog" in the *HGS* (2.7,2).[34] In the *Śatapatha Brāhmaṇa* (XII.2.IV.2.4) we find a reference to the *puruṣavyāghrāḥ.* Thus we discern a relationship between Rudra, the dogs, and the tiger. Rudra is seated on or clad in a tiger skin (*cf. Śat.* IV.5 k). Like the tiger he is the Lord of the forests (*AB* VIII.6: *araṇyānāṃ patiḥ*); this we may compare with the Vāghobā cult of Maharashtra. Vāghobā ("Father Tiger") is not the Śiva of the *Purāṇas,* but a stage preceding him. Note that the Vaggayyas and the Vāghyās carry a pouch with *bhaṇḍār* which should be preferably of tiger or deer skin.

Ṛudra as Paśupati is also perpetuated in the Khaṇḍobā cult. *Paśu* means primarily cattle in the *Ṛgveda,* but generally also animals that live in the air, in the forest and in the village (*ṚV* X.90.8). Yet Rudra is not *a priori* an animal protector like the later saints, e.g. Buddha or Cakradhara. He is after all the hunter who lives in the forest and wears the tiger skin, that is, he has killed the wild animals and assimilated their power, which we may see reflected in the drop of blood of the hunted animal which is applied to the palanquin of the hunting god (see above). His unpredictability and ambivalence are also experienced by man—who is one of the five sacrificial *paśus* in the *agnicayana*—and his cattle. Whenever there is an outbreak of disease among men or cattle a sacrifice is offered to Rudra (*AV* XI.2.26). Thus, if worshipped, he can bring blessings to his worshippers and generally looks after the welfare of men and animals (*ṚV* 1.43.6). He sees to it that the inhabitants of the village are well-fed and free from disease (*ṚV* 1.114.1). Though he brings death he also is a great physician (*ṚV,* e.g. II.33.4).

Khaṇḍobā is the perpetuation of Paśupati on the folk religious level. Man, tiger, dog, horse, cattle, elephant, bull, and ram: all are united in the cult, for the distinction in mythology and ritual is not a sharp one between man and animal. Rāmdās expresses this in the description of the *jatrā* at Jejuri.[35]

Elephants trumpet, camels grunt
Horses neigh, bullocks bellow loudly
the name (of God) //3//

Khaṇḍobā's unpredictability is preserved in folk mythology. Like Rudra, who occasionally slaughters cattle (*PB* VI.9.7-8), Khaṇḍobā slaughters the herd of sheep of Bāṇāī, the shepherdess, and only when she follows him, recognizing his magic powers, does he restore the animals to life by throwing a pinch of *bhaṇḍār* over the heap of killed sheep. The healing powers of the great physician are contained in the *bhaṇḍār*. The slaughter of Bāṇāī's herd is not an isolated story. In a medieval Sanskrit work called *Vīracaritra* Mairāla is said to destroy a herd of sheep and goats.[36] According to an oral legend in Andhra Pradesh, Narasiṃha on the folk level, a god clearly reminiscent of Khaṇḍobā, robs the sheep of the Vempalas until they are persuaded to worship and offer sacrifices to him.[37]

The martial aspect of Rudra, his association with the heroes, is also prominent in the Vedic texts. Rudra is the brave warrior (*TS* IV.5.6m: *śūra*. *TS* IV.5.10: *tavas*). He is also called *mahāvīra* in the context of the Vedic *pravargya* ritual. Rudra is connected with the *vrātīnas*, a group similar to the *vrātyas*. They are warriors who are not *kṣatriyas*, but *yaudhas*. Rudra is the leader of various kinds of troops, according to the *Śat.*, and he is associated with horses and the masters of horses, the *aśvapati* (*TS* IV.5.3r), which immediately reminds us of Khaṇḍobā as the *hayapati* (or Marathi *haybati*) and of the *śiledārs* of Maharashtra, the cavaliers who were more often than not followers of Khaṇḍobā.

Even though the bow was the most prominent weapon of Rudra, he was also a swordsman (*niṣaṅgin*: *TS* IV.5.7d)—a feature which was emphasized in the Khaṇḍobā cult.[38] Rudra, like the folk deity Khaṇḍobā, was the Lord of heroes in a context which was not yet primarily determined by the later ethical concept of defending cows, women and Brāhmaṇs. Cattle-lifting and the sheer virtue of prowess (*vīrya, tejas, mahas, tviṣi*, etc.) were admired and the hero was admired as hero, without regard to moral considerations. On the death of a hero his surviving powers were worshipped, similarly as the hero stones of the Caṅkam literature were worshipped for no ethical reason, but for fertility and gaining strength. Whereas later *vīragaḷas* implied that the heroes had reached Śiva's Purāṇic heaven, Khaṇḍobā remained the earthbound lord of the *bāvan bīr*, the Lord of the fifty-two *vīras*, who include all possible martial ghosts and godlings. We do not gain the impression that Rudra as the Lord of the *bhūtas* is a god living in heaven; on the contrary, he is earthbound and omnipresent. Closely attached to Khaṇḍobā and his regional variants—Mallaṇṇa and Mailār—were the living heroes, the Vīrabhaṭṭas and Vīramuṣṭis, mentioned in the 13th century *Krīḍābhirāmamu*, the Kañcavīras in the cult of Mailār, and the *vīras* in the Khaṇḍobā cult, of whom we have records from the time of king Śāhū of Satara (18th century). The *vīras* survive in the Mhaskobā cult of Mahārashtra.[39] From Andhra we have a description of how two or more devotees of Mallaṇṇa of the Goundala toddy tapper caste are tied to the crossbeam of the hookswinging pole, and, with swords and shields in their hand, make a pretence of fighting with one another.[40] All these heroes practiced and still practice ritual self-mortifications, e.g. in Devaragudda, and, in earlier times, even ritual self-sacrifice. Thus we have numerous late medieval memorials of stone heads (Marathi *muṇḍkī*) in Jejuri and other places, evidence of heroes who sacrificed their life either in battle or by ritual suicide. Often these heroes were from low or untouchable castes who in this way had a chance to rise either spiritually or socially. Other memorials show the *pādukās* of Khaṇḍobā surrounded by heads of rams or heads of human beings, the *vīras*, aspiring to some kind of *sāyujyatā* ("union with God").

REACTIONS TO "RUDRA"/MAILĀRA IN JAIN AND VĪRAŚAIVA LITERATURE

The "sectarian" reflections on Rudra/Mailāra, the folk deity, can be illustrated with references from Jain and Liṅgāyat literature in Kannada. It is interesting to observe that his status as a deity, let alone as Śiva, was not recognized, and that he remained a demon in the eyes of his opponents.

Barring two possible exceptions, Mailāra appears earlier in inscriptions and regional literature than Khaṇḍobā.[41] Kannada inscriptions dated as early as A.D. 922 tell us that women were called Mala; inscriptions from A.D. 1032 refer to men as Maila. *Maila* can mean peacock and Mailāra may be linked with Murukaṉ, whom we must ignore here, though the early Caṅkam literature reflects a basic affinity among Murukaṉ, Khaṇḍobā, and Rudra. Mailāra is probably derived from *maila* and *arasa*, that is, "King Maila".[42] The earliest reference to Mailāra in literature is found in the Jain work *Dharmāmṛta* of Nāyasena (A.D. 1112), who mentions the Goravas of Mailāra beating themselves in excitement (*Dharmāmṛta* 3.206). In the *Samayaparikṣe* of the Jain author Brahmaśiva (c. 1150-1160) we find an interesting piece of information: a person worshipping Mailāra is unworthy to be called a Jain, he is *kāla* (= "sinful"? IV.125). Mailāra belongs to the *kṣudradevatās* like Keṭa, Kata, Marige, and Masaṇige, who cannot give boons (9.128). In 9.105 we read: ...in the name of deities like...Baḷari, Bhairava, Mailāra, Masaṇi, Marabbe, etc., many people sacrificed their life, but without purpose. 2.71: A person of Jain faith who had fought and died with obstinate valour on the battlefield later on became known as Mailāra. Brahmaśiva also seems to suggest that the worship of Mailāra was recently initiated by a certain Manevagadde Chaṭṭappa. The title and name of this person occur also in inscriptions (e.g. shortly before Brahmāśiva's time) and refer to a Mahāsamanta. On the whole, Mailāra was worshipped by simple folk, heroes, officers, and kings of minor dynasties. He was, however, the *kulasvāmī* of the Kākatīyas.[43]

The tradition that Mailāra was a Jain was carried on by Vīraśaiva authors and he is at times called Mallideva or Mallinātha. Apparently some common Jain folk must have worshipped him under that name. Mallinātha is also mentioned in connection with a Bhairava temple in the *Līḷācaritra* of Cakradhara. Mallikārjuna of Śrīśailam is also called Mallinātha in an inscription from Karnataka and in the *Līḷācaritra.*[44] Thus it is likely that the first inscription (A.D. 1246) in Jejuri on a Jain *mūrti* of the *yakṣa* of the *tīrthaṅkara* Mallinātha may refer to a Jain worshipping Mailār/Khaṇḍobā under the name Mallinātha.[45] The *mūrti* is actually dedicated by the Jain devotee to Kapardi, the *yakṣa* of the *tīrthaṅkara.* Kapardi as a name of Rudra already appears in the *Śat.* (*TS* IV.5.9c).

According to Vīraśaiva literature the offering of hair and fingers was a widespread practice and was usual in the Mailāra cult. The imitation of dogs by the devotees of Mailāra is frequently mentioned and also that they wore cowrie shells. Very common in the Vīraśaiva texts is the reference to an episode according to which the Vīraśaiva saint Śaṃkaradāsimayya established in a dispute that he was the true Rudra and not Mailāra. A detailed account is found in the *Śaṃkaradāsimayyapurāṇa* by Mallikārjuna. A few excerpts from the description of the dispute between the Goravas[46] and Vaggayyas/Voggas with Śaṃkaradāsimayya may be relevant in our context.[47]

Dāsimayya is holding a discourse on the experience of truth before the Śivaśaraṇas at the Mailāra temple in Pimbera town, probably Pember/Prempur near Bidar. A devotee of Mailāra, Maiḷādevī, comes and brings offerings for him. She offers the rest, the *prasād*, to Dāsimayya, but he refuses it because a devotee of Śiva does not take *prasād* given to another, especially a petty deity. She asks whether Mailāra is not himself Śiva and Dāsimayya replies that he is not Śiva, but a *graha* (an evil spirit). Then they call the Goravas, who come along with the *voggas* (from Sanskrit *vyāghra*—tiger, or Kannaḍā *oggu*—to shout unintelligibly). They had applied *kuṃkuṃ* and *gandha* to their bodies; had a necklace of cowries, fly-whisks of peacock feathers, and umbrellas; wore a woollen gown; had *liṅgas* tied to their waists; had shaven heads; and wore woollen caps.

The Gorava leader is enraged that their god should be an evil spirit and argues that Mailāra is none other than Śiva himself. He narrates the following story:

While a demon, called Malla, was torturing the people in the form of a wild animal, Śiva came in the form of a hunter with his *paśupata* weapon to kill him. The four Vedas followed him in the form of four dogs and Gaṅgā in the form of Maiḷādevī.[48] After slaying the demon and wearing the garlands made of his intestines, necklaces of his teeth, and robes of his skin and drinking his blood, Śiva comes to a camp of shepherds. The leader of that camp bows down to Śiva, the hunter, and requests him to protect their sheep from a wolf. Śiva kills the wolf and marries the leader's daughter.[49]

Dāsimayya replies: Śiva indeed killed the demon Mallāsura. But Śiva/ Mallahara is not Mailāra. Mailāra is an evil spirit. He was a warrior. He came to a Jain monastery and asked to be instructed in asceticism. He was instructed in asceticism and also given a jasmine flower (as a test?) with a magical spell to attract women. One day Mallideva saw a shepherd woman (note the similarity with the folk story of the hunting excursion of Khaṇḍobā which ends with the marriage to Bāṇāī, the shepherdess), called Māḷi. He forgot all his ascetic observances and with the help of the jasmine flower made Māḷi elope with him. But her husband raised a loud cry and some hunters came and killed both with their arrows. They became evil spirits known by the names Māḷi and Malla.

The Goravas are naturally enraged about this story and challenge Dāsimayya to make their god work for him. Dāsimayya calls Mailāra, who comes out of the temple and willingly agrees to follow Dāsimayya and carry his umbrella. The Goravas surrender to Dāsimayya and ask him to pardon them for talking nonsense, but he should know that after all the followers of Mailāra are used to barking. They request the release of Mailāra and Mailāra reluctantly returns to Pemberi. From that day they have called him Koḍeya Mailāra, "the Mailāra with the Umbrella".

Here we can see the vehement sectarian Vīraśaiva reaction to a folk deity. The folk deity was relegated to his original position as a demon or evil spirit, at the most an orderly of a saint. He was not even given the position of a Vīrabhadra, who is worshipped amongst Liṅgāyats. Yet in practice we find Liṅgāyats serving as temple priests of Mailāra in Devaragudda. The Jains had a tendency to recognize him as a guardian of their *tīrthaṅkara.* Nevertheless Mailāra remained a god close to peasants, tribes of fishermen and hunters, pastoral groups, merchants, robbers, heroes—dead or alive—and minor dynasties of ambitious kings; his special devotees were the Goravas and Vaggayyas. Even Brāhmaṇs could be found amongst his followers, observing the *vrata* of becoming a Vaggayya, if not for life, at least temporarily.[50]

Perhaps from the 14th century onwards we find the rise of folk deities. This coincides with the prophecy of Cakradhara in the *Līḷācaritra*: the great temples of Viṣṇu and Śiva will decay and gods like Mairāḷ-Mailār, that is, *kṣetrapālas,* rise.[51] At least one Maharashtrian saint had little respect for the worshippers of Mallāri who go to him with their *divṭyās* (Marathi, = torches) to have *darśan.* He ranked "Malhāri" amongst the *bhūtas.*[52] But there were subtle variations in the reactions of the Mahārashtrian saints and they cannot be dealt with here.[53] Malhāri gained "respectability" by means of a victory over an *asura* and the full literary elaboration of this feat in the *Māhātmya,* which effectively linked the god to the great tradition. The god had to transcend his own asuric form.

MALLA, THE ROBBER KING

We suggest that Khaṇḍobā/Khaṇḍerāyā/Mārtaṇḍa Bhairava as the *avatār* of Śiva is to a great extent modelled on the example of Malla, the *asura* or *daitya.* Malla resembles more the original Rudra than the Purāṇic Śiva. The myth of Mallāri = "Śiva, as the enemy of Malla" is very old and has its precursor in Kṛṣṇa Mallāri defeating the two wrestlers or *mallas* Cāṇura and Muṣṭika.[54] The "destroyer of Mallayeśa" is also mentioned in one of the Ajanta inscriptions.[55] In a 14th century inscription at the Malleśvara/Mailāra temple in Ainavolu near Warangal it is said in Sanskrit and Telugu that Śiva in the form of a hunter (Śabara) saved Arjuna by killing the demon Malla, thus acquiring the name Mallāri, which in course of time became Mailāra.

The goddess Māḷacī accompanied her consort as a huntress.[56] The myth is told *in extenso* in Sanskrit and Marathi, without reference to Arjuna and the *Mahābhārata*, in the *Mallāri Māhātmya*, of which many Marathi manuscripts by different authors with small but important variants and additions exist. There are also Kannada and Telugu versions of the *Mallāri Māhātmya*. In addition there are such works as the *Mārtaṇḍa Vijaya* (1823), the *Khaṇḍerāyācī Ādi*, and the *Jayādri Māhātmya* in Marathi.

Malla may be derived from Tamil *malai*, Kannada *male*, Marathi *māḷ* = "hill" or "mountain". This is probably a folk-etymological derivation, but both the demons Maṇi and Malla are often connected with mountains in the texts. For instance, the five sons of Malla become mountains after the defeat (*MV* 20.49). From the *MMVi* (16.26) we learn that Malla consecrated mountains as weapons against Śiva. The *daitya* Maṇi created a mountain and on it the two *daityas* built their city Maṇipūr, from where they ruled over the three worlds (*MV* 8.14). The lord of the city was Mallāsura (*MV* 1.77).

The god who defeats the demon associated with the mountain is called Mallaṇṇa in Telugu, and Malaikiḻavoṉ in Tamil; the latter is a name of Murukaṉ, i.e. the "Lord of the Mountain". The god had to defeat Cūr, the personification of the evil powers on the mountains. The mountain or the evil, dangerous spirits identified with it become the seat of the god, the way that Kailās is the throne of Śiva. In the *MV* (20.56) Malla becomes the throne of Śiva as Mārtaṇḍa Bhairava.

Malla may also be traced to Vedic *marya*, which means a "young, strong man" and also a "stallion". The *maryas* are a people or a sodality. The *maruts* are said to be Rudra's sons (*ṚV* 1.61V.12; VI.66.11) or Rudra's *maryas* (*ṚV* 1.64.2; II.33.6).[57] Old Indian *marya* has changed into *malla*.[58] The *mallas* were *vrātyas*, or, according to the *Manusmṛti* (10.22), Kṣatriya Vrātyas. They were also a guild of wrestlers or pugilists. Wrestling bouts still take place during the *jatrā* on the full-moon day of Pauṣ at Jejuri. The chief wrestler in the villages of Karnataka often comes from the Kuruba shepherd caste, which is closely connected with Mailār/Mallaṇṇa. In Devaragudda a sculpture of two wrestlers can be seen on the otherwise sparingly decorated temple wall. According to the *MV* (18.162ff., 180) Malla and Śiva wrestle for nine days and nights. "But though the *daitya* may be a highly accomplished wrestler (*parama catur malla*) he can achieve nothing against Śiva; similarly the Kolhāṭīs can perform acrobatic feats of a high order, but how can they measure themselves with Hanumanta?" (*MV* 18.166ff.). It may be the encounter of Cāṇura and Muṣṭika which is depicted in an old relief on one of the *dīpmāḷs* in front of the temple of Jejuri, but it could also be the fight between Mallāri (Khaṇḍobā) and the demons Maṇi and Malla. We may add that Tamil *mallaṉ* means not only "wrestler", but also "a great, important personage"; Sindhi *malu* means "wrestler" as well as "brave man".

It is well known that many dynasties in Rajasthan, Nepal, and the Deccan were called Malla or had *malla* as a *biruda* to their name. Especially at the time when the Mallāri/Mallaṇṇa/Mailāra cult arose in the Deccan, we find *malla* as a frequent epithet of kings, e.g. Bhujabalamalla as the epithet of the Kalacuri King Sovideva (12th century).[59] Trailokyamalla appears as an epithet of rulers, and sometimes this seems a tall claim if we see that they were subordinates of the Cālukyas of Kalyāṇa in the 11th century.[60] One may also think of the *malepar, malevar,* or *malapar,* who were notorious hill-chiefs, robbers, and raiders. The Hoysaḷas, for instance, called themselves *maleparol gaṇḍar*—"champions among the hill-chiefs". Another frequent title in Kannada inscriptions is *giridurga-malla* = "the Malla of the hill-forts". The parallel in folk religion is found in the name of Mallaṇṇa/Mallikārjuna in Andhra, who is called Parvatāla Mallu = "the Malla of the Mountain" in oral legends. He is also called Tribhuvanamalla and is said to rule over the seven hills.[61] The Hoysaḷas themselves emerged as successful brigand hill-chiefs and a number of rising dynasties seeking power had a predatory background amongst people like the Beḍars or Rāmośīs, who are famous devotees of Khaṇḍobā. Not only hill-chiefs, but at times officers of established kings, like *maṇḍaleśvaras* and *daṇḍanāyakas*, raided settlements of Brāhmaṇs (*agrahāras*), lifted cattle, and abducted women.[62] In comparison with the established king, the robber chief and hero had everything to gain and nothing to lose except his life. A good example of such a parallel between Malla the demon and a minor king who threatened the Hoysaḷas was a king and hero called Sarvajña-Khaḍgamalla = "the omniscient, strong man with the sword".[63] He belonged to the Kāḍava or Pallava race and ruled from Kanci in the 12th century. He is described as "the master of horsemen" and had a sword painted on his banner. Malla's and Maṇi's possession of a horse and a sword is emphasized in the texts.

The robber king, the daring potential usurper of the realm, by whom the established king in the centre was constantly threatened, corresponds on the mythological plane to the demon king who tries to usurp the centre of the world and to rule over the three worlds, like Malla in the *Mallāri-Māhātmya* and the *rākṣasas* in the famous Tripura myth. While hunting in the forest Malla raids the *āśram* of the Ṛṣis (which one may compare with the *agrahāras* of Brāhmaṇs), destroys their *yajña*, takes their cows, and misbehaves with their women. He is also compared with a waylayer harassing travellers (*MMRā* 2.28: *mārgaghna*). Maṇi and Malla are frequently described as great heroes: *pratāpa śūra, pratāpa sindhū, parama vīryavān*, etc. (*MV* 8.14, 17; 9.152; 11.126, 130; 12.15ff., *cf.* 16.27 etc.). Malla, the *daitya*, is called *mahāvīra* (*MM* 10.2). His followers, the *vīras*, even worship Malla, the great hunter, the chieftain and predatory king. "For the hero the king is god", says the *MV* (16.30).

In the *MM* and other texts Śiva becomes an *avatār*, assumes the form of Mārtaṇḍa Bhairava/Khaṇḍerāyā and kills the two *daityas*. For the sake of the *bhaktas* he remains on earth. He rules on the mountain fort of Jejuri, his capital, and is worshipped like a king (*MV* 35.60). The god had to become a king. The Yogī (or *jogaḍā*, as Malla calls him contemptuously: *MMVi* 11.11) becomes a divine warrior. We read in the *MMRā* that Malla wonders: "How can he have an army? He has only a bullock and is clad in a tigerskin." "You are poor, go to Kailās," he advises Śiva and boastfully continues:

> I have many elephants. You have only one bull to ride. I have celestial clothes, you are clad in a bloody elephant hide. Your body is adorned with serpents. My ornaments are of gold. I am anointed with sandal paste mixed with gold. You throw about the ashes of the funeral ground. You have powder made from the ashes of bones. (*MMRā* 9-11)

Śiva assimilates many of the attributes and paraphernalia of the demon king, e.g. the sword and the shield, and his gold, which in our times has become *khobareṃ* (coconut kernels) mixed with *bhaṇḍār*. He also takes over his elephant and *rathas*. According to some the *nandī* becomes the horse, but there are suggestions that the horse, along with the *rathas* and the elephants, can be traced back to the demon. Rāmdās, an astute observer of the Khaṇḍobā cult, notices the apparent original separateness of the two conceptions of the god when he says: "The god is an *avatār* of Śiva. He has settled on the hill-fort (of Jejuri). One (Khaṇḍerāyā) is seated on a blue horse. The other (Śiva) is on a white bull. One (Śiva) has white ash as his ornament. The other (Khaṇḍerāyā) has turmeric powder (*bhaṇḍār*).

For Rāmdās they have become one. He does not distinguish between the two."[64] Rāmdās is an objective observer of the Khaṇḍobā cult. He accepts the powers of Khaṇḍobā, the folk deity, and attributes the defeat of the *turuks* to these powers.[65] He has no difficulty in seeing in Khaṇḍobā a manifestation of Rāma, the upholder of Rāmarājya.[66] His personal belief he keeps to himself as a mental reservation: "One should be in the midst of it all and yet be aloof from it," he concludes his beautiful description of the wondrous *jatrā* of Khaṇḍobā. He does not interpret Khaṇḍobā metaphorically in terms of the "inner religion."[67]

THE COMMON BOND AMONG KHAṆḌOBĀ, THE DEMONS, AND THE BHAKTAS

The resolution of the conflict between god and demon has philosophical overtones. It is sophisticated, but texts like the *Mallāri Māhātmya* and the *Mārtaṇḍa Vijaya* often express what is yet vaguely felt on the folk level. For instance, the breaking of chains at the festivals of Khaṇḍobā means the fulfilling of a vow (*navas*), but it also means the breaking of worldly fetters (*bhav-baṃdhana*), as the *MV* says (34.54-5). A Vāghyā informant considers the chain an attribute or emblem (*śikhā*) of the demons. In other words, if the chain, which is also considered to be a serpent, is broken in the ritual (*canpar thoḍṇeṃ*) it is a sign that the demon or the *bhakta* is freed and obtains nearness to god. A Dhangar informant said that the breaking shows the existence and power (*sattva*) or nearness of the god. The texts repeatedly stress that Khaṇḍerāyā grants *bhukti* as well as *mukti* (e.g. *MMVi* 10.90).

The fate of Maṇi and Malla resembles the fate of the demon king Bali as described by D.D. Shulman in his *Tamil Temple Myths.*[68] Actually the *bhaktas* can associate themselves with the fate of the demons. Before the demons die, their *ahaṃkār* is dispelled; they are released from their blindness or bondage; they achieve *sāyujyatā*, that is to say, the flame of life enters Khaṇḍobā (*MV* 19.78), or *sannidhi*, that is, they become his *dvārapālas* or *bhaktas.* The battle against them is conceived as a sacrifice (*raṇa-yajña* or *raṇa-utsava*) instituted by Mārtaṇḍa Bhairava.

Khaṇḍobā is pleased at the bravery of the *daityas* (*MV* 16.44 etc.). The *daityas* had to be sacrificed to obtain their salvation or *mukti.* Their sacrifice—like the violent self-sacrifice of the *vīras*—is a necessary precondition for their salvation. Thus they achieve their primordial unity with Śiva and the god sheds his asuric form. Accordingly, "Yeḷkoṭi", the famous cry in the cult of Khaṇḍobā, remembering the victory of Khaṇḍobā, has an ambivalent meaning: *yeḷkoṭi* are the "seven crores" of enemies whom the god defeats, but they are also the "seven crores" of *bhaktas*. Rāmdās expresses this succinctly:[69]

sāt koṭi daitya mārile/
yeḷkoṭi bhakta bolile//

He killed the seven crores of *daityas*
They are known as seven crores of *bhaktas*.

THE TREND TOWARDS "PURITY" AND "RESPECTABILITY"

The direction which the evolution of the cult took was towards purity, away from the violent realm of death, from the life of a hunter and the predatory habits of the *daitya*. The *daitya* becomes *nirmala*.[70] But before he dies and achieves *sāyujyatā* or becomes a *bhakta*—his name being absorbed into Śiva's name—Śiva grants him another boon: the god is to fulfill the wishes of those devotees who [still] practise *ugra bhakti:* that is, animal sacrifice (*paśuvadha*), the rite of hook-swinging (*gaḷ ṭocṇeṃ*), or piercing one's leg (*tīra jaghanīṃ ṭocūni ghetī*) (*MV* 35.53). But this kind of *bhakti* is given a low rank in the ninefold modes of *bhakti* according to the *MV* (35.46). It is called *rākṣasī bhakti.* Another way of *bhakti* is to invoke the wind, that is, Khaṇḍobā, and to diagnose the afflictions in the victim, taking him on the way of *bhakti* (*MV* 35.55; *Jejuri Māhātmya,* ch. 20, p. 73). This is probably a reference to the *devruṣi,* who summons the god and treats afflictions. But this was branded as *piśācī bhakti* (*MV* 35.47). In this context even Rāmdās and other *bhakti* saints ranked Khaṇḍobā amongst the lower gods Vetāḷ, Kaṅkāl, Mhaisobā, Brahmā, Māyarāṇī, etc.[71] On the other hand, it is suggested that *sāttvikī bhakti* consists of feeding a Brāhmaṇ who has to be imagined to be a form of Mārtaṇḍa (*MV* 35.61 and *Jejuri Māhātmya,* ibid.).

There are more instances of the trend of purity and abstention from violence. I am not sure whether Khaṇḍobā can still effectively be invoked in black magic like Rudra (see e.g. *ṚV* II.33.11, 14) to harm others, though, it is said, it can still be done in the case of Mhasobā. The usual answer would be in the negative: "because he is Śaṅkar".

The sacrifice of animals is still performed on a large scale during the festivals of Khaṇḍobā, but already the texts tell us that this happens on the special request of the demon (*MV* 33.5-7). It is said by informants that the sheep are offered for the nourishment of the demon as a special concession of Khaṇḍobā. In Jejuri, Dhangars now exhibit the non-vegetarian *nived* (*naivedya*), lifting it up in the direction of the god or carrying it to Bāṇāī, the shepherd-goddess. That does not mean that in remote places they may not still offer it directly to their *kulasvāmi* Khaṇḍobā. An oral legend suggests that Rāmdās contributed towards the abolition of animal sacrifices to Khaṇḍobā:

> When he came to Jejuri on his pilgrimage from Pandharpur to Alandi he enquired who lived in the fort. He was told that it was Mallāri. When he saw the blood of many sacrificial sheep flowing near the Nandī at the foot of the hill he moved on and rested in the Lavathaḷeśvar temple on the outskirts of Jejuri. Khaṇḍobā heard about the arrival of Rāmdās and wondered why Rāmdās did not come to have *darśan*. He took the form of King Śivājī seated on a blue horse and appeared before the saint. Rāmdās realised that the rider was Khaṇḍobā, went to the temple to have *darśan*, and established a Māruti shrine at the entrance gate of the temple court.

Today the general answer is that animals are not sacrificed to Khaṇḍobā "because Khaṇḍobā is Śaṅkar." As the demonic Rudra, who was fond of blood sacrifices and to whom one should sacrifice cattle (*PB* 1.8.3; *TB* I.11.5. 8-9), was transformed into the classical Purāṇic Śiva, who does not accept blood sacrifices in the "standard" *śivaliṅg* temples, Khaṇḍobā is slowly being transformed into the vegetarian deity Śiva/Śaṅkar.

Similarly the world of heroes, of the *vīras*, who used to practise self-mortification and even offered their head to fulfil a vow for the sake of their king, chief, or god, tends to belong to the past. Naturally the royal elements of the Khaṇḍobā cult are on the wane. Today even the name Khaṇḍerāyā seems to be more common in the traditional oral and written texts than in modern parlance, in which the god is simply called Khaṇḍobā. Hunting is a thing of the past, and only occasionally may we see, for example, a group of Māṅgs, Rāmośīs and Marāṭhās go to the temple of Khaṇḍobā (in Pali) in order to get the blessings of the "Lord of the dogs" for themselves and their dogs before they leave for their hunt. They remind us of the "hunters" and "dog-leaders" in the *Śat.* (*TS* IV.5.4q). Khaṇḍobā's powers as a *kulsvāmi*, of granting fertility to fields, cattle, and marriages, remain, however, unabated, as his festivals show. The festivals are still tumultuous, though they may have lost the grandeur which Rāmdās describes. Khaṇḍobā is still the Lord of the ancestors and of the living. As rituals die hard, one may during field work unexpectedly discover many old vestiges going as far back as the time of the Vedic Rudra.

But the direction of the evolution was the same in the Khaṇḍobā cult as in the classical Vedic *śrauta* ritual, which shed its folk elements of agonistic dualism and competition and its connection with Mṛtyu and became the domain of absolute purity. Moreover, modern and urban sensibilities run counter to "primitive" institutions like rites of animal imitation, or of the *muraḷīs*. But somewhere the trend towards ritual purity had to stop, because, just as Rudra was the god of Caṇḍālas and Brāhmaṇs alike, so Khaṇḍobā is the god of all: *neṇe varṇa-jāti-kuḷā* (*MV* 5.12). Even Mlecchas, i.e. Muslims, can be his *bhaktas* (*MV* 24.30).

CONCLUSION

Our comparison between Rudra and Khaṇḍobā—incomplete as it is for want of space—suggests an amazing persistence of folk religion. Though there are regionally varying aspects of the deity (like Mallaṇṇa in Andhra and Mailāra in Karnataka) and adaptations to historical factors, there was basically little change but rather variations of the same theme. Folk religion thus emerges as one of the stable constituents of Hinduism or Indian religion. Notwithstanding its relation and interaction with other constituents of Hinduism, it has to be taken in its own right and not as an adjunct to the so-called "great tradition". Taken seriously, folk religion can throw much light on other religious traditions and their texts and *vice versa*.

We have thus traced "reactions" of some of the religious traditions to this folk cult. The zealous reaction of the orthodox Jains did not prevent their admission of folk deities as *yakṣas* of their *tīrthaṅkaras*. The vehement antipathy of the Vīraśaivas to the Vrātya-like followers (the Vaggayyas and Goravas) amounted to their acceptance of the cult in practice. The *Māhātmya* of the Brāhmaṇical authors endeavoured to make the cult respectable and pure, to distinguish between the demonic and the divine, and to identify it with the Śiva/Śaṅkar of the Purāṇic heaven. Though we have largely ignored the interesting reaction of Vaiṣṇavism and the Vaiṣṇava *bhakti* saints of Maharashtra to the cult of Khaṇḍobā, we have noted the reaction of the ascetic Brāhmaṇ saint Rāmdās, who recognized the cult as legitimate and even praised it, while condemning other aspects, especially blood-sacrifice.

NOTES

This paper is partially based on new material gathered during a stay in Maharashtra from August 1984 to April 1985. I am grateful to the DFG (German Research Association) for financial support. Dr. S.G. Tulpule has helped me in elucidating Old Marathi texts and Prof. András Höfer has read and commented on an earlier version. Dr. James Laine has made comments as regards the English style. To all of them I am most grateful.

1. A recent study is Jacques Scheuer, *Śiva dans le Mahābhārata* (Paris: Presses Universitaires de France, 1982).
2. Bhairava, who plays an important role in the cult of Kāpālikas, Kālāmukhas, Nāthas, and Śaivite Gosāvīs, is not, for all his capacity to absorb local folk cults, basically and initially a folk deity, but a version of Rudra primarily sponsored by Śaivite ascetic "sects". Though Khaṇḍobā appears as Mārtaṇḍa Bhairava when he kills the demons Maṇi and Malla, it would be rash to declare Khaṇḍobā in all his aspects identical with the Bhairava of the *Purāṇas* or of the Śaivite "sects".
3. McKim Marriott, "Little Communities in an Indigenous Civilization", in *Village India*, ed. McKim Marriott (Chicago, 1955), pp. 171-222.
4. See Gerhard Oberhammer, ed. *Inklusivismus. Eine indische Denkform* (Wien, 1983). Hacker's thesis (pp. 11-28), which seems to be confined to the religious-spiritual sphere, has been cautiously extended by A. Wezler to "psychologische, soziale und ähnliche Gegebenheiten" (pp. 61-91, at p. 89).
5. A.K. Rāmanujan, "Where Mirrors are Windows: Towards an Anthology of Reflections" (unpublished ms). Ramanujan applies his concept of "reflexivity" to the "dynamic interrelations" between texts and families of texts which form a "simultaneous order" and suggests its applicability to other aspects, e.g. to ritual, philosophy, eating, and sociolinguistic patterns.
6. See notes as regards the *Mallāri Māhātmya* in Sontheimer 1984:155.
7. One of my best informants, Sakhārām Bābū Lakaḍe, who belongs to the Dhangars, the large shepherd community of Maharashtra, and who is an extremely knowledgeable devotee of Khaṇḍobā, never mentioned the *Mallāri Māhātmya*. Nor did he know of the Campāṣaṣṭhī festival, which is celebrated on the 6th day of the light half of the month of Mārgaśīrṣa (November-December) according to the written texts, e.g. the *Mārtaṇḍa Vijaya* (31.5). Śiva became an *avatār* in the form of a *liṅg* at Prempur (near Bidar) on this day. A special *vrata* (vow) in this festival is to feed daily ten Brāhmaṇs from the first day of the month to the 6th. Campāṣaṣṭhī is sacred to Skanda, and there seems to have been an effort afoot to link Khaṇḍobā to the classical Skanda, but this link has remained very tenuous, unlike the connection between Murukaṉ and Skanda. Cf. Fred W. Clothey, *The Many Faces of Murukaṉ* (The Hague, 1978), p. 123.
8. Scholars, especially in Maharashtra, have for long been divided in their opinion as to whether 'Khaṇḍobā' is derived from 'Skanda'. The desire to

discover a unilinear *paramparā* of a particular deity tracing his or her ancestry in the *Purāṇas* often becomes foiled, because one can usually argue one way or the other. All "Śaivite" deities have similar or overlapping features or, we may say, a structural affinity. Thus certain features of Khaṇḍobā can be compared with similar ones of Skanda. However, such features may also be shared by Rudra, the folk deity. If we take Rudra, Murukaṉ, and Khaṇḍobā *inter alios* first of all as folk deities and then proceed to inquire when, where, and how these deities were linked or identified with their versions in the *Purāṇas*, many questions are resolved. The problem is ably discussed by G.H. Khare, *Mahārāṣṭrācim cār daivatem* (Puṇe, 1968), pp. 146ff., who criticizes Rājvāḍe's etymology; see also Rā. Ciṃ. Ḍhere, *Khaṃḍobā* (Puṇe, 1962), pp. 25ff.; Rā. Śaṃ. Nagarakar, "Skanda. Devatāvijñānātīl ek camatkār", in *Jñāneśvar traimāsik*, varṣa 10, aṃk 4 (October 1978), pp. 45-61, at pp. 57ff.

9. Asko Parpola, "The Pre-Vedic Background of the Śrauta Rituals", in *Agni: The Vedic Ritual of the Fire Altar*, ed. Frits Staal (Berkeley, 1983), vol 2, pp. 41ff.
10. See also the discussion in Asko Parpola, *Arguments for an Aryan Origin of the South Indian Megaliths* (Madras, 1973), p. 34.
11. Doris M. Srinivasan has recently argued for the "insider" theory and shown *inter alia* that primary Vedic Āryan traits may belong to Rudra from the outset. She shows the importance of Rudra in the framework of the sacrificial *śrauta* system, the affinities between Rudra and Agni and the importance of Rudra as *uccheṣaṇabhāga*. See "Vedic Rudra-Śiva", JAOS 103 (1983), 543-56.
12. E. Arbman, *Rudra: Unterschungen zum altindischen Glauben und Kultus* (Uppsala, 1922), ch. 7. For a discussion of previous interpretations of Rudra see R.N. Dandekar, "Rudra in the Veda", *JUPHS* 1 (1953), 94-148 (cited as reprinted in *Vedic Mythological Tracts* [Delhi, 1975], pp. 199-277).
13. Ibid., p. 203. R.N. Dandekar, "Vaiṣṇavism and Śaivism", in *Ramkrishna Gopal Bhandarkar as an Indologist*, ed. R.N. Dandekar (Poona, 1976), p. 58. Recently the "bi-polar and ambivalent" nature of Rudra was discussed by J. Bruce Long in "Rudra as an Embodiment of Divine Ambivalence in the Śatarudrīya Stotram", in *Experiencing Śiva: Encounters with a Hindu Deity*, ed. Fred W. Clothey and J. Bruce Long (Delhi, 1983), pp. 103-28.
14. Khaṇḍobā, like Rudra, protects his followers and punishes, possibly with death, his enemies and the detractors of his followers. He may send his black dogs, which are just another manifestation of the god. An incident told by a follower of Khaṇḍobā who is a *devruṣī* (Sanskrit *devarṣī*), the "shaman" of Khaṇḍobā, summarily illustrates the ambivalent nature of the god:

> Dhoṇḍibā, a Vañjārī [a caste of traditional itinerant merchants carrying grain or salt] from Pimparvadi, used to vilify the Vāruvālās. Then the people of the village said: "Viśvanāth [the *devruṣī*] is capable of solving this problem." On a Sunday he came to me. He wanted to test the existence (*sattva*) of the god. The Lord possessed me. While I was possessed [the Lord] said: "On the sixth day you [Dhoṇḍibā] will receive a blow." On this very day, in the evening a black puppy appeared. It bit him and ran away. He wanted to kill the dog, but could not catch it. Then the people of Pimparvadi asked me: "Sir, why did this happen?" I asked them: "What did the dog look like?" They said: "It was a black puppy." Then I told [Dhoṇḍibā]: "Perform the ritual of *jāgraṇ*." Now he did not have money to arrange for a *jāgraṇ*. He went to his father-in-law, but could not

get money. Then he went to Jalna and he was admitted [to a hospital]. On the sixth day he died. Then the people realized that one should not abuse [Khaṇḍobā's] *bhaktas*.

The *devruṣī* who told this incident is also a Vāghyā (for whom see below): Śrī Viśvanāth Jijobhāū Vāghe, Partud, Dt. Usmanabad. The Vāruvālās are followers of Khaṇḍobā who, like the Kudurappas of Karnataka, enact horse imitations. They trot like horses and beat themselves with a whip (Marathi *vāsarī*). The horse is the favourite *vāhana* of Khaṇḍobā. Sunday, the day on which the *devruṣī* gets possessed by Khaṇḍobā, is the special day of god. The "sixth' day brings to mind Campāṣaṣṭhī; see note 7. *Jāgraṇ* is a night-long vigil in honour of the god for which Vāghyās and Muraḷīs have to be invited; see below.

15. Heesterman, "Brahmin, Ritual and Renouncer", *WZKSO* 8 (1964), pp. 2ff., at p. 17.
16. Anantadās Rāmdāsī, ed., *Śrīsamarthāṃcā Gāthā* (Puṇe, 1928), *pada* 1171. See Sontheimer 1981: 1ff., at pp. 60ff.
17. Dandekar, "Rudra in the Veda", p. 114. In *TB* 1.6.10, Ambikā is Rudra's sister.
18. Śaṃ Go. Tuḷapuḷe, *Marathi Vāṅgmayācā Itihās, khaṃḍa pahilā* (Pune, 1984), pp. 41ff.
19. *Op. cit.*, p. 152.
20. Sontheimer 1984: 159.
21. J. Heesterman, "The Case of the Severed Head", *WZKSOA*, 11 (1967), 22-43.
22. Heesterman, pp. 37, 39.
23. G.R. Varma, *Mailāra Deva* (Tadepalligudem: Varman Publications, 1973), p. 38.
24. *MS* II.2.4. Wilhelm Rau, *Staat und Gesellschaft im alten Indien* (Wiesbaden, 1957), p. 16. Cf. *TS* IV.52.i; *sthāpalaye.*
25. Vā. Su. Ahire (collector of the song) in Sarojini Bābar, ed. *Ek hotā Rājā* (Bombay: Mahārāṣṭra Rājya Lokasāhitya, Puṣpa 10ve, 1964), pp. 50ff.
26. A bow with three arrows. See *MS* IV.5.9 and *BŚS* 16.22; 18.24. Cf. Parpola, "Arguments", pp. 41ff.
27. W.D. Whitney's translation in *Atharvaveda Saṃhitā* (Cambridge, Mass., 1905).
28. Caland, *Jaiminīya Brāhmaṇa in Auswahl*, No. 146.
29. Sontheimer 1981:9.
30. Ibid.
31. *IIJ*, 6 (1962-1963), pp. 6ff., at p. 11.
32. *muraḷī* = "the flute of Kṛṣṇa". I suspect that the term is folk-etymologically derived (like so many terms in the Khaṇḍobā cult) by metathesis from Kannada *maruḷī* = a mad woman" (Kittel, *Kannaḍā-English Dictionary*, s.v.), i.e. a god-intoxicated woman. This gains some plausibility from information given by a *pūjārī* (Śrī Gopāl Tātobā Pūjārī) of Mangsuli (Belgaum district), who described *muraḷīs* as women dedicated because of "*bhakti* and custom". He compared them to Mahādēviyakka, the famous "mad" Lingayat woman saint and devotee of Mallikārjuna, who wandered wild and god-intoxicated in the wilderness till ultimately she found Mallikārjuna and lost herself. She became his "husband", as the *muraḷīs* were wedded to Khaṇḍobā in a more ritualized context. On Mahādevīyakka see A.K. Rāmanujan, *Speaking of Śiva* (Harmondsworth: Penguin, 1973), pp. 111ff. The term *maruḷa* appears in one Kannada *abhaṅg* attributed to Jñāneśvar (*akkā nī keḷe mātu/katoḍalana dasega*

maruḷādene). A little brother or sister tells his or her sister (*akkā*) that he or she has become mad (*maruḷādene*) after Viththala. See the discussion in Caṃdraśekhar Kapāḷe, *Sāhityasaṃved*, (Gulbarga, 1985), pp. 1-21.

33. Sontheimer 1984: 163ff.
34. I owe this reference to Harry Falk from his forthcoming work *Das Würfelspiel in Veda*.
35. *Śrīsamarthāṃcā Gāthā, pada* 1172.
36. H. Jacobi, "Über das Vīracaritam", in Bernhard Kölver, ed., *Hermann Jacobi. Kleine Schriften*, Teil I (Wiesbaden, 1970), p. 378 (*Vīracaritra*, ch. XXI). See also ch. VIII, 57 (p. 400): *Mairāla iva mṛṇmayaḥ* and cf. above *Maṇ-mailāra*—"the Mailār [made of clay]". R.C. Ḍhere, op. cit., p. 144.
37. Sontheimer 1985: 47.
38. *niṣaṅga* may also mean "quiver".
39. See Sontheimer 1976: 196. In Jejuri one Vir family still survives.
40. Syed Siraj ul Hasan, *The Castes and Tribes*...(Bombay, 1920), p. 240.
41. There are the well-known references to Khaṇḍaka, the patron *yakṣa* of Pratiṣṭhāna according to the *Mahāmayūri Mantra*, which dates possibly from the 4th century A.D., according to D.D. Kosambi, *Myth and Reality* (Bombay, 1962), p. 121. For the Ajanta cave inscription see below.
42. These and the following remarks on Jain and Vīraśaiva Kannada literature are mainly based on M. Cidanandamurty, "Kannada Kāvya, śasananagaḷalli Mailāra mattu Māḷaci", *Prabuddha Karnāṭaka*, 48/3 (1966), 41-62. I am grateful to Dr. Rajaram R. Hegde for help in translation.
43. Sontheimer 1985: 148.
44. Ānaṃda Nā. Kuṃbhār in *Mahārāṣṭra-Sāhitya-Patrikā*, aṃk 227 (1983), 34-74, at p. 34. *Līḷācaritra*, ed. S.G. Tulpule (Nāgpur-Puṇeṃ, 1967), *Uttarārdha*, *līḷā* 384, p. 74.
45. Cf. Khare, op. cit., p. 89ff. Cf. p. 151.
46. The "Goravas" were Śaivite ascetics, according to medieval Kannada inscriptions. Perhaps the Śaivite non-brāhmaṇical "Guravs" who are priests in Khaṇḍobā temples are their successors.
47. Ed. V.B. Halbhavi, chapter 13. The excerpts are from M. Cidanandamurty's essay cited above. See also Khare, op. cit., pp. 134ff.
48. One may compare this with a description of Dattātreya in the *Līḷācaritra*, Kolte's edition, *Uttarārdha*, *līḷā* 146. *Cf. Kañcippurāṇam*, (Nākaliṅkamutaḷiyār, ed.) (Madras, 1910), *Tiruvekampappāṭalam* 78: when Śiva changes into the form of a hunter, the four Vedas turn into his dogs (Tamil *nali*). I owe this reference to Eveline Meyer.
49. There are some improbabilities regarding the two wives of the god. Normally the identifications are: the first wife is Maiḷādevī = Mhāḷsā = Pārvatī = Yogeśvari. The second wife is the shepherdess = Bāṇāī = Gaṅgā.
50. Sontheimer 1981: 7.
51. Kolte's edition, *Līḷācaritra, Uttarardha*, *līḷā* 436.
52. See the *abhaṅg*, wrongly attributed to Jñāneśvar, in J.T. Molesworth, *A Marāṭhī-English Dictionary* (Poona, 1975; reprinted), p. xxvi.
53. See G.D. Sontheimer, "Bhakti and the Khaṇḍobā Cult", paper read at the Third Conference on Early Devotional Literature in New Indo-Aryan Languages,

Leiden, December 1985 (to be published). (Editors' note: See "Bhakti in the Khaṇḍobā Cult" in the present volume.)

54. Sontheimer 1984: 157.
55. B.C. Chabra, "The Incised Inscriptions", in *Ajanta,* ed. G. Yazdani, vol. 4 (London: Oxford University Press, 1955), pp. 121-4, p. 124, line 5: *Mallayeśa-karttānta.* In line 12 *Khaṇḍe[śva]ra* (= Khaṇḍobā?) is mentioned. On paleographic grounds the inscription has been recently assigned to the late seventh or early eighth century. See Geri Hockfield Malandra, "The Date of the Ajanta Cave 27 Inscriptions", *WZKS* 26 (1982), pp. 37-46.
56. M.L.K. Murty and G.D. Sontheimer 1980: 164.
57. R.N. Dandekar, op. cit., p. 102.
58. W.B. Bollée, "The Indo-European Sodalities in Ancient India", in *ZDMG* 131 (1981), 172-91, at p. 181.
59. See *Maharashtra State Gazetteer, History, Pt. 1. Ancient Period* (Bombay, 1967), pp. 351ff.
60. B.R. Gopal, *Minor Dynasties of South India: Karnataka* (Madras, 1982), pp. 123ff.
61. According to an oral version of the Mallaṇṇa myth recorded near Karimnagar, Andhra Pradesh.
62. Sontheimer 1976: 29.
63. Sontheimer 1984: 158.
64. *Śrīsamarthāṃcā Gāthā, abhaṅg* 70.
65. *Śrīsamarthāṃcā Gāthā, pada* 1170.
66. Lakṣmaṇ Rāmacandra Pāṃgārkar, *Śrīsamartha-grantha-bhāṃḍār,* 2nd ed. (Bombay, 1978), p. 633, no. 8: [translation]...Rāmdās says he (Khaṇḍerāv) is Rāmrāv, Rām is verily Khaṇḍerāv.
67. *Śrīsamarthāṃcā Gāthā, pada* 1172. For a translation of the *pada* see Sontheimer 1981: 17ff.
68. (Princeton: Princeton University Press, 1980), pp. 14., 134, 316ff.
69. *Śrīsamarthāṃcā Gāthā, pada* 1170.
70. By the touch of Śiva's feet (*MM* 16.57).
71. *Dāsbodh* 3.2.27-32.

Between Ghost and God: A Folk Deity of the Deccan

A. INTRODUCTION: SPREAD AND ANTIQUITY

One of the most famous folk gods of Andhra Pradesh is Mallanna, often identified with Mallikārjuna of Śrīśailam in the Kurnool district.[1] Śrīśailam, in the Nallamala Hills of the Eastern Ghats, was nearly inaccessible until recently. The ancient cult of Mallikārjuna also attracted pilgrims from Maharashtra from at least the twelfth century onwards. They called the god Sirigiri Mallaya, a name still used in Karnataka, Andhra, and Maharashtra.[2] Many religious currents have met in the cult of Mallikārjuna, especially those of Śaivite "sects", beginning from the Pāśupatas and Kāpālikas to the Liṅgāyats, and it also has its epic and purāṇic contacts.[3] As is so often the case with famous cults, forest tribals (Ceñcūs) and/or pastoralists (Gollas) are said to have been the discoverers of Mallikārjuna. The immediate access to worshippers of all castes and religious affiliations is characteristic not only of Mallanna/Mallikārjuna but also of the god Mailāra of Karnataka and Khaṇḍobā alias Mallāri/Malhāri/Mairāḷ of Maharashtra. Scholars usually compare these three deities, whose interregional identity is confirmed by itinerant devotees and medieval literature. The identification is explicit in border areas of the three adjoining states, e.g. in Pember/Prempur (Khanapur), near Bidar, at the border of Maharashtra and Karnataka. Here Mallanna is also known as Mailāra as well as Khaṇḍobā. Such is also the case at Warangal in the Telengana area of Andhra Pradesh, where Katta Mallanna is called Khaṇḍērāyā. A folk song from Malegaon, further north of Pember, in the Nanded district of Maharashtra, identifies Khaṇḍobā with Mallanna:

On the stony heath of Malegaon
surrounded by four bastions

there Malhāri resides
the god Mallanna...[4]

We are dealing here primarily with the folk deity Mallanna/ Mailāra/Khaṇḍobā (MMKh) rather than with the sectarian or the purāṇic Śiva. Folk religion has its own identity and may not necessarily subordinate itself to the values of the Brāhmaṇ. Moreover, other hierarchical models may exist beside that of the Brāhmaṇ, as Richard Burghart has argued.[5] According to him, there are the Brāhmaṇ, the ascetic, and the king, each claiming highest rank and godhood within his respective hierarchy. The hierarchies do not face each other as rigid structures, but interact. Elements of each hierarchy are incorporated into the other hierarchical model. The highest ranking person of the other hierarchy was assigned an honourable, but subordinated rank within the enlarged model. Similarly I would like to suggest that the cult of MMKh, though borrowing values from the other traditions, is expressive of an autonomous current, that is, folk religion, which interacts with other currents, but is not necessarily subordinated to them. Ecology certainly also plays a role. MMKh are mainly worshipped in dry or (now diminished) forested areas of the Deccan. The devotees belong to a wide range of groups which are known by different names in the three states, but follow the same traditional occupations. Prominent among them are the traditional agricultural, trading, pastoral nomadic, hunting, and predatory castes. Many of these castes had martial proclivities in the past. Devotees include Untouchable castes as well as Brāhmaṇs. In Maharashtra it is mainly Deśastha Brāhmaṇs who worship Khaṇḍobā as their family deity. This link with the Brāhmaṇs might tempt us to label MMKh as the usual Bhairava, who is connected with Brāhmaṇicide and the destruction of the yajña (as in the case of Dakṣa's sacrifice). But the link to the Brāhmaṇical ritual-social order of the world, as formulated in terms of the *cāturvarṇya* system, is generally not emphasized. No doubt this is also a theme, but it is introduced by Brāhmaṇical sources, like the Sanskrit *Mallāri Māhātmya*, which I briefly deal with at the end of this essay. Considering the transgression of the sacred, social order, we come to learn that MMKh transgress more orders than that of the Brāhmaṇs, e.g. that of the Liṅgāyats and the Muslims. In short, the mythological, ritual, historical, social, and ecological context of the cult does not permit us to emphasize *a priori* the importance of the *varṇa* hierarchy, the Brāhmaṇical value of ritual purity, or the Brāhmaṇ's spiritual superiority (in Dumont's terms) over worldly power (*kṣatram*). Often MMKh resemble a bandit, or a rising, pre-imperial king rather than a pacified *kṣetrapāla* and protector of the *cāturvarṇya* system, of Brāhmaṇs and cows. MMKh convert and accumulate their devotees from many groups by means of aggression, robbery, love marriage or marriage by capture (apparently in the inverted *pratiloma* order), feats of prowess, tricks, and miracles. They create their order of society not primarily by seeking sanction in the Brāhmaṇical order and becoming a *kṣetrapāla* or a "demon devotee". Hierarchy is determined by bhakti (which does not necessarily correspond to the "classical" modes of bhakti) and tapas. From the point of view of sects and the Brāhmaṇ's point of view the deity may be considered to be just a bhūta, or an inferior godling, that is, a *kṣudradevatā* or *kṣetrapāla*. But for the actual worshippers he is *central to their life and beliefs*, irrespective of what others choose to call him.

Folk religion seems to be singularly conservative and there are striking continuities between MMKh and their antecedent Rudra. Rudra was primarily a god of certain groups mentioned, e.g., in the *Śatarudrīya* of the *Taittirīya Saṃhitā*. Their culture was outside, though interconnected with, that of the Vedic sacrificial priests who subordinated Rudra as Agni in the agnicayana ritual. For the latter he may have been a "demonic" intruder connected with impurity and death, which had to be eliminated. Vedic passages reflect a god who is earthbound, "demonic", with magic powers, potentially ubiquitous in nature, yet very much bearing personal characteristics. These would usually suggest iconic worship, but, if we take texts like the *Śatarudrīya* literally, we must conclude that Rudra's followers viewed him as the "charismatic" living leader of their respective groups. He is the mediator between the divine, unmanifest, untamed elements of *nature*, which he incorporates and controls, and his followers, who worship him. But the borders are fluid and all three partake of each other. The follower imitates his leader; the leader, in turn, imitates Rudra in dress and ritual. Here we find the early roots of bhakti, the verbal root of which is *bhaj* = "to participate". Rudra is called *sthapati* (*TS* 4.5.2.i), which may refer to a chieftain or to the leader of the Vrātyas;[6] *mantrī* (*TS* 4.5.2.k)—the lord of the "spells"; *senānī* (*TS* 4.5.2.a)—the leader of the army; *vāṇij* (*TS* 4.5.2.k.)—the merchant; and *daivya bhiṣaj* (*TS* 4.5.f)—the divine doctor. Rudra is connected with robbers and thieves, heroes, and warriors, lords of horses, and dog keepers. Horses, dogs, and cattle are his animals, and he often manifests himself in these animals. He is a hunter with bow and arrow and is associated with forests and mountains. He is the lord of the fields, that is, a *kṣetrapati* (*TS* 4.5.2.g.) rather than a mere "protector" (*kṣetrāpala*). All these features survive and are reflected in the MMKh cult. For example, Mallanna is said to be "indistinguishable among bandits" (Tel. *dongallō dorakaḍu*) in Golla traditions[7] and Khaṇḍobā is reputed to be "close to thieves"[8] and is associated with ex-predatory communities like the Rāmośīs (Beraḍs). Most noteworthy are the special followers of Rudra, the Vrātyas, whose dress and rituals closely resemble those of the special devotees of MMKh, the Voggus of Andhra, the Vāghyās of Maharashtra, and in particular the Vaggayyas of Karnataka. That the Vaggayyas actually envisage an *imitatio dei* is demonstrated in the Mailāra temple of Aduru in the Dharwar district. Here the typical long woolen black gown of a Vaggayya is displayed on the wall inside the shrine and it is said to be the gown of Mailāra. The imitation of the human leader who incorporated the divine and himself became Rudra, e.g. the Ekavrātya in his cosmogonic ritual (*AV* XV), seems to have been a common feature before manifestations of the divine in *mūrtis* became popular (but cp. *TS* 4.5.6.c: "to him of the amulet"). We need not view the later sects worshipping Śiva or Bhairava with their peculiar rituals of *imitatio dei* as the antecedents of the Voggus etc., but would rather suggest direct continuity between the ancient Vrātyas and the present day Voggus etc. Parallels of such impersonations of the deity also include the devotee of the early Murukaṉ, the *vēlān* dancing in a frenzy until he became Vēlān, that is, Murukaṉ himself.[9] Similarly the *devṛṣī* ("shaman") in the Khaṇḍobā cult is possessed by the god in the form of the wind and virtually becomes Khaṇḍobā. The Svāmi at Mailar (Hadagalli Taluka, Ballari District) impersonates Mailāra in the form of a king. In the traditions of the Gollas Mallanna/ Mallikārjuna may turn up as a Jaṅgama, a Liṅgāyat renouncer, a "walking *liṅga*", as it were, to test his bhaktas. And in the cult of Khaṇḍobā the god may turn into a Vāghyā for the same purpose.

B. MANIFESTATIONS OF THE FOLK DEITY

THE LIVING GOD ON EARTH, GOD AS KING AND OTHER APPEARANCES

For the devotee MMKh is a living, powerful god (e.g. Ma. *jāgṛt*) who exists "here and now" on earth and is not confined to a purāṇic heaven. He is worshipped in a temple primarily in the form of a *svayaṃbhū liṅga* (Ma. *piṇḍa*), which has to be distinguished from the *liṅga* installed in the usual Śiva temple where the *liṅga* has to be enlivened by Brāhmaṇs in the ceremony of *prāṇapratiṣṭhā*. Accordingly the temple priests of Mallanna are not Brāhmaṇs, but Gollas (at Warangal, Yerru Gollas) or Liṅgāyats, and, in the case of Khaṇḍobā, Guravs rather than Brāhmaṇs. In addition to the *liṅga* there are usually brass *mūrtis* of the gods. In the case of Mallanna the *mūrtis* are four feet high (e.g. in Komarelli, Jangaon Tk., Warangal Dt.; in Warangal, Katha Mallanna; and Ailōni/Iloni/Inoli, near Warangal) and made of clay (see plates e and f). Mailāra's *mūrti* at Mailar is also made from the clay of a termite mound. It is from this mound, filled with dreadful serpents, that the god is said to have appeared for the first time. Possession, firewalking, hook-swinging, and animal sacrifices are still practised and point to a folk deity *par excellence*. It is only in recent times that such customs have receded, except in outlying areas. MMKh are worshipped by different groups as their leader, reflecting their respective occupations. But they are especially worshipped like a royal god, or like a god as a king, and as such the god of dynasties and would-be dynasties of kings. For instance Mallanna was the *kulasvāmī* of the Kākatīyas (thirteenth century), Mailāra of a chief of Bhujanganagar (fourteenth century), Khaṇḍobā/Khaṇḍerāyā was the family deity of the Holkars and the Gaikwads (eighteenth century), and so on. It was especially in Karnataka and Maharashtra that the royal and martial aspects of the cult flourished. The temples of Khaṇḍobā often resemble fortresses, as e.g. in Jejuri (Pune District), which is said to be his capital (Ma. *rājdhānī*; see plate g). The brass *mūrtis*, often donated by kings, resemble kings. They reflect the historical period of the Vijayanagara empire and, in the case of Khaṇḍobā, they resemble, when dressed, a Maratha Sardār. The face of Mallanna is usually adorned by a Muslim beard. Representations on silver plaques used as house gods or as amulets and brass *mūrtis* show him seated on a horse accompanied by his wife or *śakti*. His weapons show the martial and sacrificial background of the cult: trident (*triśūl*) and hourglass-shaped drum (*ḍamaru*), sword (*khaḍga*) and shield (Ma. *dhāl*), or a bowl (Skt. *pātra*, Ma. *paral*).

MMKh are also treated like a king and act like a king. At Jejuri Khaṇḍobā is carried in a palanquin for a hunting expedition on Somvatī Amāvāsyā, that is, on a no moon day falling on a Monday. The procession moves from the Gaḍkoṭ (Hill-Fort) to the river, where the god takes a bath with his devotees after his hunt. The ritual is reminiscent of the *aśvamedha*: Khaṇḍobā's horse is led by a Muslim

***Plate (e)**: Images of Mallanna, Golla Kētamma (left), and Balaji Māḍaladevi at Kommarelli, Jangaon Taluk, Warangal District, Andhra Pradesh. Contemporary lithograph.*

Plate (*f*): *Images of Mallanna and his wives in the temple of Ailōni, near Warangal. Contemporary lithograph.*

Plate (g): *The Khaṇḍobā temple on the Gaḍkoṭ ("Hill Fort") at Jejuri. The temple in the so-called Peśvā style was recently renovated in the Tamil style.*

far ahead of the palanquin. The devotees (e.g. the Dhangar shepherds acting as hunters with spears) eagerly try to touch the hooves or the head of the horse and walk with it. The "hunt" concludes with a common bath of the god and all the participants. At the end of the Vedic sacrifice the king takes a final bath (*avabhṛtha*). His followers join him and become free of sin.[10] In the old (nineteenth century) songs of the Vāghyās (bards of the god), the hunt to the river Karhā is mentioned, as well as Khaṇḍobā's circling the earth on a horse.[11] In the *VS* (23, 17-19) the sacrificial horse is identified with Agni, Vāyu, and Sūrya. According to the *Śatapatha-Brāhmaṇa* (13, 2; 7, 13-15) the mantra says that the victim will conquer the same realms as these deities. Agni, Vāyu, and Sūrya are forms of Rudra, the war god. Khaṇḍobā is similarly identified with fire, such as the indispensable torches (Ma. *divṭī*, Ka. *divaṭī*), or the flame that is worshiped on a platter. He is the sun as Mārtaṇḍa Bhairava, and in the form of turmeric powder (Ma. *bhaṇḍār*, Ka. *baṇḍāra*. Tel. *baṇḍāru*). MMKh's special day is Sunday. But he is also the wind (Ma. *vāreṃ*) who possesses devotees and makes them act like horses. Horse and dog are associated with Rudra as well as with MMKh. Dogs (preferably black) are worshipped throughout the cult of MMKh. The elementary, undomesticated manifestation of the divine in the form of a wild dog, not yet tamed, is still experienced by the Kois, who belong to the Gonds. They revere wild dogs even if they kill cattle.[12] A similar concession is made to Rudra, whose connection with the dog is close, as for instance in a passage from the *BŚS* (14.23; *TB* 2.4.1.6): If a dog passes between the *garhapatya* and *āhavanīya* fires, impurity is removed by making a cow walk over it, and the sacrificer hands over his cattle to Rudra (who is Agni). Unlike those made over to Rudra (*TS* 2.1.7), cows are, of course, not sacrificed to MMKh, although sheep used to be sacrificed to them and were slaughtered by Khaṇḍobā, according to oral traditions, such as when he destroyed the herd of sheep of Bāṇāī, his second wife. Mallanna's army consists of seven dogs, a number which may easily increase: King Mārtaṇḍa has 700 dogs, and sometimes they amount to seven crores (*yeḷkoṭi*, Tel., Ka., but the term is also very much used in the Khaṇḍobā cult). The horse or the dog may appear in the dream of the devotee and summon him to Jejuri. For those who are not worshippers of MMKh the dog may spell death and disaster. Khaṇḍobā may take the form of a dog and punish those who insult his bhaktas. But the god also grants freedom from the state of a wild animal, and the present day Vāghyās, the special devotees of Khaṇḍobā, are examples of this: they were actually tigers, but gained their human form, or rather turned into the faithful dogs of the god, by having a vision of the god.[13] The dog and also the humans impersonating it are epitomes of faithfulness and protection. The dog is useful to the hunter and the shepherd; hunting and protecting are characteristic activities of the king. Thus there are famous examples of Maratha kings and Sardārs which show much loyalty and affection between masters and their faithful dogs. In this light it may not sound so ridiculous that King Śāhū (1707-49) would dress and treat the dog that had saved him from a tiger as a Sardār,[14] or that Malhārrāo Holkaṛ would not dine with the Peśvā unless his dog was admitted to the dining hall. He would rather eat with his dog outside on the verandah.[15] We should add that Śāhū as well as Holkar were devotees of Khaṇḍobā. The same reverence for dogs prevails in the Mallanna cult. When Mallanna and his brother Bayanna sleep during the night, the dogs keep watch (Tel. *kāvali*) for wolves, jackals, and tigers. When Mallanna distributes the milk of sheep, he makes twelve leaf cups: seven for the seven dogs, one for the goddess Pōśammā, one for Agni, one for Nāgasarpam, one for Bayanna, and one for himself. There may be a thirteenth cup for the wind god. It goes floating in the air and Mallanna tells Bayanna that the wind god is carrying away his cup.[16]

THE LIFE-INCREASING GOD

MMKh accept promises and fulfil wishes (Ma. *navas*, Ka. *harike*, Tel. *mokkubaḍi* = vow). Such wishes may be earthbound, like victory in battle, children, rain, a good harvest, cattle, recovery from illness, and good marriages. Especially fertility and marriage are important incidents. The marriage has to be sanctioned by the god, and the couple have to present themselves to their *kulasvāmi*. In Warangal at the Katta Mallanna temple Yerra Gollas enact a ritual on an elaborate design on the floor on which the marriage of Kētamma, the first wife of Mallanna, is performed. Newlyweds still wearing their marriage clothes (coloured yellow with turmeric) come to the Katta Mallanna temple and perform the marriage of Mallanna with Kētamma as a fulfilment of their vow. After the marriage ritual Golla and Kuruva women dance on the design and some get possessed. In Pali (Satara District) Khaṇḍobā's marriage with Mhāḷsā, his first wife, from the Liṅgāyat Vāṇī (merchant) community, is performed annually. Dense clouds of turmeric powder envelop the marriage procession. Turmeric powder is reputed not only to heal but also to cause fertility in marriages. It is also identified with the life-giving sun (= Sūrya [masc.]), who, in oral traditions, impregnates women. The custom of girls being "married" to MMKh is especially emphasized (and nowadays disapproved of) in the cult of Khaṇḍobā, where they are called Muraḷīs. Along with the Vāghyās, the bards of Khaṇḍobā, the Muraḷīs perform dances at *jāgraṇs,* which are vigils in honour of Khaṇḍobā arranged by patron devotees of the god. These parties of devotees who sing and dance in honour of Khaṇḍobā may remind us of the *puṃścalī* ("harlot"), the Vrātya, and the *māgadha* or *sūta* (bard), who jointly wandered and must have performed and begged in the name of their god, Rudra.[17]

The Desire for Nearness to or Unity with the God

Not only is earthly life enriched and increased in the constant company of the god in thought or in ritual, but death promises nearness to or even unity with the god. This even led to ritual suicide by heroes (*vīras*), as in the case of the Vīramuṣṭis mentioned in the *Krīḍābhirāmamu,* the Kañcavīras of Mailāra, and the Vīras of the Khaṇḍobā cult.[18] Unity or nearness may thus be rather violently achieved by special devotees (in the past), or comes with the normal death of those devotees who worship MMKh as their *kulasvāmi.* Numerous stone *mūrtis* and new as well as weathering inscriptions on steps, now more and more replaced by new steps and thus forgotten forever, commemorate heroes and/or ancestors in Jejuri. Similar to the ancestor cults of tribals like that of the Dhangars of Maharashtra or the Gonds, the ancestors are close to and eventually merge imperceptibly with the clan deity in worship. But MMKh are not just deities of a single clan or caste or group, but are lords of many clans and castes, as if of a confederacy. MMKh are the leaders of hosts, dead and alive, like Rudra. In accordance with the notion that the god is living here and now, it is not the distant Kailās on which the departed soul rests. A certain concession seems to be made to this folk god on earth in a Marathi *āratī* appended to the Sanskrit *Mallāri Māhātmya* when it is said:

> The mountain of the fortress of Jejuri is in the form of a *liṅg.*
> In the world of mortals this is the peak of another Kailās.

Jejuri is Kailās, an old Vāghyā song confirms.[19] The same claim is made in Kommarelli in the case of Mallanna. Similarly the mountain of Shingnapur (Satara District) is said to be the seat of Śambhu or Mahādeva, who is rarely called *Śiva* except in a Sanskritic text or context; and Śrīśailam (Kurnool District) is the seat of Mallikārjuna. Mallikārjuna also serves as a kind of Śiva on earth, other than the distant purāṇic Śiva, perhaps reflecting the notion preeminent amongst tribals that gods live on the surrounding mountains. Ancestors in the Khaṇḍobā cult, and Khaṇḍobā himself, are also worshipped in the form of metal plaques which depict heroes (Ma. *vīras*; see plates h-i). The worship of these plaques on Somvatī Amāvāsyā on the Karhā river at Jejuri is accompanied by songs and dances performed by the Muraḷīs and Vāghyās. A common meal is shared by ancestors and living descendants. The ancestors appear and possess their descendants. What happens to ascendants after three generations nobody knows. They certainly do not become *viśve devāḥ* according to the classical *śrāddha* ritual, which, anyway, the *MV* maintains is not performed at Jejuri. Perhaps the lesser known Brāhmaṇical "folk" *antyeṣṭi* rituals as dealt with by the 16th century Nārāyaṇabhaṭṭa explain the folk belief: here the deceased is transformed into Rudra by the ritual.[20]

Criteria for Ranking of Bhaktas

A blend of *tapas* and *bhakti* determines rank in the cult of MMKh, although there is no written explicit formulation for it. Translated into the notion of god as King, it is bravery (*śaurya*) and loyalty (*bhakti*). This reflects the historical relationship between king and loyal followers, e.g. in the Vijayanagara empire.[21] Feats of bravery are reflected (historically) in the self-mortifications of the various kinds of heroes (*vīras*) in the MMKh cult. The ritual of hook-swinging may have been performed mainly to pay off vows in order to get life-increasing wishes fulfilled, like fortune or children (a wish which after all may ultimately express a desire for "immortality"), but the essential aim of *bhakti* is nearness or unity with god. A Vāghyā song typically expresses these aspirations:

Give me the banner of success, O King Mālurāyā Mārtaṇḍa// But don't give me the sense of pride, [lest] people will laugh at you // This is all I beg from you // Your eternal, famous banner signals protection and death // 1 //

Plate (h): *Metal mould used by goldsmiths for preparing plaques. Such plaques are used in house shrines in the cult of Khaṇḍobā, and also in the cult of Mallanna. They depict ancestors as warriors* (vīras) *and are used in ancestor worship (actual size* $2\frac{1}{2}$ *x 2 inches).*

Plate (i): *A mould depicting Khaṇḍobā and his wife. At the bottom the usual dog is shown.*

Don't give me so many riches, I request you // I don't want the distinction between man and man. How is it that you make one serve with a flywhisk and grant another a huge vessel of success // 2 //

Just give me kith and kin, for having a family, for making my clan grow // Don't send me away and make me wander, my life remains with you // Your eternal, famous banner of success flutters // 3 //

Keep, O keep your shadow over Śivaji Vāghyā // With the mercy of love, let me and my companion Rāmcandra sit beneath it. People will resort to your feet, O Lord, with the new sword in your hand // 4 //[22]

The most faithful *bhakta* does not wish anything except the company, nearness, or unity of or with the god. The god himself is (Ma.) *bhūkela* = "hungry for true *bhaktas*" (*MV* 5.12), or (Tel.) *bhaktavatsala* = "gracious to his *bhaktas*". Thus according to a legend it was a member of the "untouchable" Māṅg (Mātaṅga) caste who sacrificed his life for the foundation of the fortress in Jejuri. This is interpreted as an act of *bhakti* because by his sacrifice he wanted to persuade Śiva to stay forever on earth, that is in Jejuri (which Śiva did). The Māṅg became the guardian god of the temple, having his shrine near the main gate of the outer temple wall. His name is Yeśvant Rāo and he became a *havildār* (officer of a fort). Today he is famous for healing bone fractures when vows are made to him. Thus it appears that the divine doctor, Rudra, alias Khaṇḍobā, has delegated some of the medicinal powers to Yeśvant Rāo and thus moved to a greater degree of purity, because traditionally doctors are ritually impure.[23] Similarly the existence and practice of values of faithfulness and bravery may elevate the devotee or hero while transferring something of his own lowliness to his god or lord. Yeśvant Rāo's legend reminds us of the Velugoṭi family to which the chiefs of Venkatagaon belonged. They first came into prominence during the reign of the Kākatīya king Gaṇapati, who ruled at Warangal from A.D. 1198 to 1263. The founder of the Rēcerla clan, of which the Velugoṭi family is an offshoot, was a farmer at the village Anumangallu, called Cevvi Reḍḍi.[24] The *Vēlugōṭivarivaṃśāvaḷi* contains variants of the story of Cevvi Reḍḍi.

According to one version, Cevvi Reḍḍi discovered by chance a treasure trove, to take possession of which he had to sacrifice his faithful Untouchable servant Rēca. The servant willingly offered himself as the victim. In pursuance of a promise Cevvi Reḍḍi changed the name of his *gotra* to Rēcerla in commemoration of his faithful servant who had cheerfully faced death for his benefit.

According to another version, Cevvi Reḍḍi, while returning home from his field after dark, encountered a *vetāla*, a demon. Cevvi Reḍḍi bravely defended himself with a club; the demon, pleased with his bravery, conferred upon him certain favours and vanished. From then on Cevvi Reḍḍi became popular as Bēṭāla Reḍḍi, whom King Gaṇapati invited to his court and granted favors, including the government of a district. Finally he established a kingdom at Rēcerla.

The *Mallāri Māhātmya* explains the name of Mallāri in a similar way: Mārtaṇḍa Bhairava is pleased by the bravery of the defeated demon hero (*vīra*) Malla (*M.Mah.* 16.41), and on the request of Malla his name becomes part of Mārtaṇḍa's name. Mārtaṇḍa is now called Mallāri = "the enemy of Malla" (*M.Māh.* 17.36).

Devotion and *tapas* are also the elements in another prototype of a *bhakta* in the Khaṇḍobā cult. Local traditions in Jejuri tell of a *bhakta* who every day climbed up the path to the old Khaṇḍobā temple on the distant, high plateau (Karhe Pathar). He certainly did not go there for material wealth, but to be near his god. When the *bhakta* grew too old to make the arduous ascent, the god descended from the high, distant hill to the hill just above the town of Jejuri. On account of his devotion and self-sacrifice the devotee and his descendants were given the first rank amongst the *mānkaris* (Ma.), that is, those *bhaktas* entitled to ritual privileges in temple rituals. Thus the flagstaffs of the descendants of the devotee still have precedence over those of other *bhaktas* in processions.

C. THE FOLLOWERS OF MAILĀRA, MALLANNA, AND KHAṆḌOBĀ ACCORDING TO RITUAL, ORAL LITERATURE, AND HISTORY

The Vaggayyas and the Festival at Devaragudda and Mailar

Especially noteworthy are two great festivals which are celebrated in the cult of Mailāra: the Dasarā festival at Devaragudda (at Ranebennur near Harihar, Dharwad District) and the festival at Mailar (Hadagalli Taluka, Bellari District) in the month of Māgha (February/March). The latter lasts for eleven days, beginning with Rathasaptamī day and ending two days after the full-moon day. On both occasions the struggle is against the demons Maṇi and Malla. Some say in Devaragudda that Malla was killed in Devaragudda and Maṇi at

***Plate (j):** A Vaggayya or Gorappa from Karnatak in his black woollen overcoat that is beset with a zigzag pattern and has the typical fringe at the bottom. The indispensable begging bowl, from which he eats like a dog at rituals, is not visible.*

Plate (k): *A Vaggayya from southern Andhra/Karnataka with a bearskin cap and a necklace of cowrie shells.*

Mailar, but in Mailar we are told that it was here that both Maṇikāsura and Mallāsura were killed in battle. A mock battle against the demon is enacted in Mailar. The special followers of Mailāra, the Vaggayyas (see plates j and k), who closely resemble the ancient Vrātyas, the followers of Rudra, play a prominent role in the ritual. They are also called Gorappas or Goravvas and are mentioned in medieval Kannada inscriptions. Although most of the Vaggayyas are from the Kuruba shepherd community, there are also members of other communities, from the low Taḷvāra (sword) caste up to (allegedly) the Brāhmaṇs. But, whereas the Kurubas are Vaggayyas for their whole life, most of the members of other communities observe the rites of a Vaggayya/Gorappa only on special occasions. Among the Taḷvāras, the eldest son should become a Gorappa after his father dies. He does not regularly wear the typical attire of a Gorappa. He is supposed to wear it on every full-moon day, on Sundays, and during the (Ka.) *jātrās*. On these days he goes begging.

On the first day of the battle ritual a black flag is hoisted as a sign that war is declared against the demons. Milk is boiled and is allowed to spill over as a good omen forecasting the victory of Mailāra. Again the Vedic Rudra comes to mind: it is milk which is boiled in the *pravargya* ritual in a vessel called *gharma*. The vessel is also called *mahāvīra* and Rudra is identified with it.[25] The next day group fighting is enacted which involves throwing sweets at each other. This is said to be a sign that war has begun. Whereas Maṇikāsura is defeated easily (it is not shown how), Mallāsura accepts defeat only on the eleventh day. Early in the morning, before sunrise, thousands of devotees, many of them temporary or lifelong Gorappas dressed in their long, black woollen gowns, converge on a hillock outside Mailar. They are the army of Mailāra. The whole army of devotees, said to (mythically) consist of seven crores (Ka. *yeḷkoṭi*), moves towards the hill in complete silence. Many devotees carry brass torches which evoke the impression of a nocturnal wild hunt of Rudra. The god is represented by the Svāmi of the Devasthān (temple), who rides a white stallion and is accompanied by a bearer of a royal parasol. Besides there are *mūrtis* of Mailāra and his wife mounted on a wooden structure covered by cloth. When the top of the hill is reached the masks and the huge leather sandals of the god and his wife are quickly carried around a platform seven times, accompanied by thick throngs of devotees who loudly scream "Yeḷkoṭi Mallāri Mārtaṇḍa".[26] *Yeḷkoṭ* may also refer to the seven crores of enemies defeated by Mailāra, but throughout the tradition of MMKh it is also suggested that enemies may become devotees of the god. Finally, the god has defeated and slain the demon: a cloth which has so far concealed the huge wooden mask of the demon is pulled away from under the feet of the deities. The day closes with the *karṇikotsava* (festival of prophecy). This ritual is more or less the same at Devaragudda. It takes place there during the Dasarā time and is performed on the ninth day.[27] In Mailar an old Kuruba who has fasted for eleven days (in Devaragudda on the ninth day) climbs a bow (Ka. *billa*) which is eighteen feet high. After climbing the bow to the top he is possessed by the god in the form of wind. He then utters prophecies for the coming year. He does not participate in the activities of the other Vaggayyas, but (as observed in Devaragudda) quietly sits under a banyan tree in a grove until his appointed moment has come. At his side the huge bow is placed against the tree (see plate 1). The Vaggayya's attire and the rite he performs remind us of the Ekavrātya, as described in *AV* XV, who becomes Rudra and is described as having a red back and a black belly (*AV* XV.1.7). The shoulders and back of the Vaggayya who becomes Mailāra are covered by a red cloth with the zigzag border characteristic of the dress of the Vaggayyas and imitative of a rugged fur; in front the black woollen gown is visible.

Another important ritual in Mailar and Devaragudda is the *pavāḍā*, a "heroic, magical feat".[28] In Mailar it is celebrated after the slaying of the demon, in Devaragudda on Dasarā day. It is performed by the so-called Kañcavīras, recruited especially from Kuruba Vaggayyas, and (in Devaragudda) also by Māḍigas. Their heroic feats reflect an aggressive loyalty towards their god. They wield weapons like iron prongs, swords or tridents, and pierce their calves with painted iron rods, or with an instrument resembling a pointed tent peg made of the wood of a palm tree. The most important incident of the ritual is carried out by a young, unmarried Vaggayya, preferably twelve years old. He is the first who has to perform the ritual of piercing the leg in front of the god. He then simultaneously passes two thorny twigs of the *babbuli* tree through the wound. After that he passes a long rope through the wound. One might wonder whether the rope in this act of bravery does not indicate the tie with which an initiate symbolically binds himself to the god. The whole ritual also has (self-) sacrificial undercurrents. Thus, it is said that once upon a time the god demanded human sacrifice. Some exquisitely carved medieval

Plate (l): *The oldest Kuruba, who climbs an eighteen-foot-high bow (on the right) during the Dasarā festival and in the process becomes "Mailāra". Devaragudda, Dharwad District, Karnataka.*

stone heads, apparently from *mūrtis,* are deposited behind the temple in Mailar where the *pavāḍā* is performed. They are said to be the heads of *vīras* who died in self-sacrifice. The term Kañcavīra (so far the etymology is unclear) is locally said to be a corrupt form of *pañcavīras,* that is, "five heroes" who voluntarily cut off their heads in front of the god. Curiously this story resembles the tradition of Mhaskobā in Maharashtra where the god demanded as a proof of faith the five immature children of the founder of the cult. The god obligingly allowed lambs to be the victims instead, and the children were left unscathed. Dhangar shepherds of Maharashtra still offer a "row" (Ma. *dāvaṇ* < Skt. *dāmanī*) of five sheep to Khaṇḍobā. There are persistent and pervasive suggestions that in the past young rams and humans could be alternate sacrificial victims.[29] The Kurubas are said to have gained their importance in Mailar because Mailāra slew the demon in the form of a Kuruba. A reflection of this may still be the substitute sacrifice of a lamb by Kurubas on the day of the battle. It is taken to the hill where the demon manifests itself in the form of a wooden mask, actually somewhere to the side of the hill.[30] Again we have the suggestion that the enemy of the god, the demon, becomes the follower (alive, or dead in the form of a *bhūta*), or, we may say, the demon becomes a devotee. While considering the sacrificial connotations in the ritual connected with Mailāra we may start wondering whether the "sacrifice" of the Kuruba youth which takes place at the end of the battle does not faintly echo an incident in the *aśvamedha* sacrifice. Both festivals, at Mailar and Devaragudda, have close connections with horse rituals and they resound with the cracks of the whips of Gorappas. They enact the galloping of horses and are possessed by the wind of the god. The Gorappas, who are also called Kudureyappas, are said to be the cavalry of the god, and the festivals are also called (Ka.) *kudureya habba* (the festival of the horse). It does not, therefore, seem too farfetched to refer to the Vedic *Vādhūlasūtra,* which says that at the end of the *aśvamedha* the immature, weeping son of a *sūta* (bard) is to slaughter the horse, whose head falls off in the process. They youth is to lose his own head if he does not know how to properly cut up the horse, as the latter has to be restored thereafter. Falk suggests that the youth has been selected by a game of dice in which the loser is called "dog". In younger texts the youth, as the dog, is no longer the scapegoat, but an actual dog is killed.[31] No actual *aśvamedha,* of course, or anything resembling it is practised in Mailar or Devaragudda, but we should keep in mind the importance of the horse in the Dasarā ritual, which may have had its antecedent in the classical *aśvamedha* sacrifice. Horses in the Dasarā ritual were especially conspicuous at the spatially and historically close capital of the Vijayanagara empire.[32] Moreover, the young Kañcavīra who is the "dog" of Mailāra and who sacrifices himself to his god, the "Lord of the Horses" (Skt. *hayapati*, or *aśvapati*), tying himself to the god by passing a rope through his leg, strengthens the impression that the ritual has contacts with the Vedic Rudra. In the *Vādhūlasūtra* the young *sūta* is taught a song with which earth, ether, and wind are requested to heal the injuries of the horse, and heaven and the *nakṣatras* are involved to restore the form of the horse.[33] In the cult of MMKh it is a pinch of turmeric powder, the very substance of the sun, which heals the wounds of the victims with immediate effect.

The Expelled Son of the Kāpus/Reḍḍis

The Kāpus or Reḍḍis are the most important agriculturist caste of Andhra, equivalent to the Marathas of Maharashtra and the Gāvḍās of Karnataka. In the traditions of Komarelli and Ailōni, Mallanna is said to have been born miraculously as the seventh and youngest son of Ādireḍḍi and Nīlamma, king and queen of Kollapuri Paṭṇam.[34] According to the myths told in these traditions, when these two treat Parameśvara with miserliness and forgetfulness, the god appears in the form of a Jaṅgama and turns the tide of their fortune. Their kingdom becomes ridden with drought and famine, and the cattle perish. Kollapuri Paṭṇam becomes a ghost city. Ādireḍḍi and Nīlamma leave Kollapuri with their six sons. They live in the wilderness, or rather on the outskirts of Kalyāṇapuri Paṭṇam. They are not allowed by the "*liṅga*-wears", i.e. the Liṅgāyats, to enter the city. They live by selling firewood, work as laborers, and collect food in the forest for twelve years. During this period they pray to Śiva to rescue them from their plight. It is then that Śiva the *bhaktavatsala* turns up in the disguise of a Jaṅgama, promising them a son who will be of great strength, illustrious, and named Mallanna. Mallanna is born (Tel. *māyāmānuṣa vigrahaḍu*) and eventually restores his family to power and rules Kollapuri Paṭṇam. But the brothers, or rather the six sisters-in-law, turn against him, and when the property is divided (land, cattle, and houses) Mallanna receives as his share uncultivable land, that is, hilly and forested areas, and bullocks not capable of drawing the plough. Mallanna clears the forest for cultivation by felling trees, digging up termite mounds (Tel. *puṭṭa*) and burning the undergrowth. While digging the termite mound, he hits upon a golden nose ring. Once upon a time Pārvatī was presented a young sheep by Śiva which multiplied until there were one crore of sheep. Pārvatī kept her nose ring as a lock on the sheep. Satisfied with the *bhakti* of Mallanna, Pārvatī directs him to tend them for seven years and to take care to kindle the fire near the termite mound perpetually. In accordance with the command of Pārvatī, Mallanna makes a perpetual fire in a bowl-shaped brazier (Tel. *kumpaṭi*). He milks the sheep every day, boils the milk in the *kumpaṭi*, and worships the termite mound by pouring the boiled milk into it.

In the different versions of the story told by the Gollas, who are the traditional pastoralists of Andhra, certain motifs remain constant: the youngest brother who has to be satisfied with the wilderness as his share and is driven out, like Rudra, the youngest son of Brahmā, or the *kaniṣṭha* of the Vrātyas, who becomes *nirvasita* and has to seek his fortune to establish himself. In the case of the Vrātya, cows had to be gained on an expedition as the basis for establishing his own household.[35] Throughout the oral traditions of Mallanna we hear about the adventurous efforts of Mallanna to win recognition and supremacy over his adversaries, like the *kaniṣṭha* Vrātya, "who wants to come to the top".[36]

Another recurring feature of the oral tradition is the association of fire with the termite mound from which Mailāra/Mārtaṇḍa Bhairava (the "sun") also emerged in Mailar. When the fire—indispensable to boil the sheep milk, which is ambrosia (Tel. *amrutamu*)—near the mound is extinguished, Mallanna has to steal Agni from a Rākṣasa who holds captive the Brāhmaṇ girl Ratnāṅgi. Slaying the demon he gains both the fire and the girl. There is no mention in this version to this effect, but we may surmise that the Rākṣasa is a Brahmarākṣasa.[37] His skull (Tel. *netti, pucca, kapālamu*) serves as the bowl for gruel (Tel. *ambali toṭṭi*). The fire seems to be closely connected with the termite mound and the origin of Mārtaṇḍa Bhairava. In another legend Mallanna finds sheep and Bhairava in the form of a dog in the mound.[38] Oral traditions call him Bayanna, and identify him as Mallanna's brother, who is found in the mound. He is a naked (cf. Nagna-Bhairava), rather stern character, particularly bent on protecting the purity of the sheep flock.[39] He is one-legged and may be compared with Ekapad Bhairava or *aja eka-pāda*, who, besides being one of the Māruts in the *Ṛgveda* and *AV*, is also identifiable with Rudra and Indra.

THE MARRIAGES OF MAILĀRA, MALLANNA AND KHAṆḌOBĀ

Mallanna, although miraculously born as the son of Ādireḍḍi and Nīlamma, exists or moves outside of or between castes, and that is the seed and precondition of his eventual power and rise to a king of all. Much to the displeasure of his brothers and sisters-in-law he does not marry a girl from their caste. He marries Ratnāṅgi, a Brāhmaṇ girl; he also marries Pagiḍikāḷḷi Padmākṣi after miraculously performing several tests. Ultimately he has five wives, like Khaṇḍobā. But it is mostly two wives who are prominent in the cult of MMKh. One is closely connected with the Liṅgāyats. She is said to be a Vāṇī (Ma. grain merchant) and is variously called (in Tel.) Bhramarāṃba Mēdala, Māḍala, Mādaci, or (in Ka.) Māḷaci, Māḷavva, Gaṅgi Mālavva, or (in Ma.) Mhāḷsā. Thus Mallanna also takes the form of a merchant, and is often mentioned in connection with itinerant merchants like the Perikes or the Gōne Kāpus (Tel. *gōne*: jute bag).[40] In Malegaon, the Khaṇḍobā center in the Nanded district, Khaṇḍobā is said to have manifested himself in a jute bag of a merchant caravan.[41] The god coming along with merchants in the form of a stone lodged in the hoof of a pack ox is a frequent motif in the oral traditions of the Dhangar shepherds. In this way Khaṇḍobā comes to marry Mhāḷsā, the daughter of Timma Śeṭ, a Liṅgāyat Vāṇī, at Pali in the Satara district. According to the Golla traditions at Kommarelli Mallanna comes riding on a horse to the Balijas in Sindhu Paṭṇam in the form of an itinerant bangle seller named Gājula Mali Seṭṭi. The Balijas have amassed their riches by cheating the traders and others who pass through their town. By his powers Mallanna outtricks the traders, acquires all their wealth, and marries Balije Māḍalamma, showing her his greatness (*mahimā*). She fails to recognize it in him when he turns into a leper. Thus again he moves out in search of a true, devoted wife and finds her in Golla Kētamma. She is the daughter of rich Gollas who own a big herd of sheep. They are courteous, truthful, and generous.[42]

The god marrying a tribal woman is common all over the Deccan and goes back to the Caṅkam literature, where it is the tribal Vaḷḷi who is the beloved of Murukaṉ.[43] The "marriage" with the tribal woman often has elements of transgression and is an occasion to display the miraculous feats of the god. In the case of Bāṇāī, he herds nine lakhs of sheep all alone and even slaughters all of them, only to restore them to life with a pinch of turmeric powder.[44] Invariably the oral traditions about two wives, one coming from the merchant community (identified with Pārvatī on the Sanskritic level), and the other coming from the "forest' (often identified with the classical Gaṅgā), oscillate between the two poles of, on the one hand, a love relationship (as between the early Murukan̲ and Vaḷḷi) and, on the other hand, *bhakti* and/or renunciation. In the old songs of the Vāghyās, Khaṇḍobā is often blamed by Mhāḷsā for his infatuation towards the dirty Bāṇāī. The songs of the Vāghyās regarding Khaṇḍobā's wives are often ambiguous; they may be understood as erotic, but the listener may also interpret them in terms of *bhakti*. Khaṇḍobā, who may turn up as a Pathān on horseback, actually has five wives in Jejuri: Mhāḷsā, the Liṅgāyat; Bāṇāī, the Dhangar shepherdess; Phulāī Māḷin, from the gardener caste; Rambhāī Śimpin, the tailor woman; and Candāī Bhāgvāni, the Muslim woman. By his marriages he transgresses the normal social order, yet this transgression fuses together heterogeneous groups with different social and ecological backgrounds. Notions of ritual purity and impurity tend to be obliterated in his cult. No wonder the cantankerous "first" wife, Mhāḷsā, coming from the vegetarian Liṅgāyat caste, complains about Bāṇāī, who has polluted the house, is uncouth and stinks, and should actually stay in the wilderness (Ma. *rān*) where she came from.[45] Yet Mhāḷsā catches fish and Bānū (Bāṇāī) watches the fun (Ma. *tamāśā*). "Where is the Liṅgāyat in this?" Not only that, but

> Bānū and Mhāḷsā are of different castes
> For the god Mallāri they eat from the same plate
> The Bāṇāī of the Dhangars, the Mhāḷsā of the Vāṇīs
> How can she swallow (even) a morsel?[46]

In Devaragudda the episodes of the hunt and the love adventure of the god with Kurubattyavva, the shepherd girl, are enacted by the devotees after Dasarā. The god is taken to the river on horseback and is accompanied by one group equipped with whatever weapons there are in the temple. There are by agreement two parties. One is Mailāra's and the other is his father-in-law's. During the mock hunt—some people pretending to be tigers and others chasing them—Mailāra is understood to make love with the Kuruba girl. The news leaks out and reaches his first wife, Gaṅgi Mālavva. Thus, by the time the first party returns from the mock hunt, the Gorappas and Gorammas who are already in the temple do not allow them to enter. The party in the temple enacts the anger of Mailāra's first wife by evicting Mailāra as well as the hunters. After Mailāra's party confesses the mistake they are allowed inside.

THE ENCOUNTER WITH OTHER RELIGIONS

The recognition of MMKh as Mallikārjuna, Sadāśiva, Tribhuvana and so on, although claimed by his followers, was not undisputed by certain other groups. Some Jains seem to have accepted Khaṇḍobā as their *tīrthaṅkara* Mallinātha, perhaps confusing him with Mallinātha = the "Lord of Malla" (*M. Māh.* 19.3), according to the earliest inscriptional reference in Jejuri.[47] They also called the Mallikārjuna of Śrīśailam Mallinātha.[48] Maṇi, the demon, is mentioned in the context of earlier Jain *basadis* superseded by MMKh cults. The temple at Mailar is thus said to have been a Jain establishment. Actually it may have been Maṇibhadra, the tutelary deity of caravans, popular among Jains, who was worshiped amongst Jains, e.g. in Prempur near Bidar in Karnataka. The present-day temple is situated on a traditional trade route leading from the Godavari Valley via Malegaon to Bidar. A Jain *mūrti* of a person in *dhyāna* posture shows the Jain affiliation. The *mūrti* is now relegated to a small shrine at the border of the *kṣetra.* The Brāhmaṇical *Mallāri Māhātmya,* which is connected with Prempur, expressly refers to the place as "the capital of the enemy of Maṇi" (18.9: Maṇidvisa) and not to Malla, or "Maṇi *and* Malla". In front of the temple a huge stone *nāga* (serpent) faces Khaṇḍobā in the temple and takes the position of the defeated demon who has turned into a *bhakta.* If it is true that Maṇibhadra and Maṇināga are identical this would further suggest a connection with the Jains. Maṇi, who is a great hero (*vīra*) in the *Mallāri Māhātmya,* may be one of the fifty-two *vīras* (*bāvan vīr*) mentioned in Jain sources.[49] The Jain author Brahmaśiva (c. 1150-60) of Karnataka classed Mailāra amongst the *kṣudradevatās* and claimed that he was a Jain warrior who died with obstinate valour in battle.

Reputed Vīraśaiva saints like Śaṅkaradāsimayya tried to prove that Mailāra was none other than a *demon* and that it was Śiva and not Mailāra who slew Malla.[50] Yet Liṅgāyats, especially the common folk, accepted MMKh and are often temple priests (as in Devaragudda). Or else they established temples, such as one in Odela (Karimnagar District) which was founded by a Balajiga.

Cakradhara, the "founder" of the Mahānbhāva sect, predicted in the thirteenth century that the Viṣṇu and Śiva temples would decay and *kṣetrapālas* like Mairāḷa would become established in the

Kaliyuga.[51] This prediction can actually be said to have been confirmed by historical facts if we think of the fall of the Yādava empire and the eventual decay of its ("Hemādpanti") temples. In the fourteenth century the *Krīḍābhirāmamu* praises the village deity Mailāra as the "great hunter", "ocean of kindness", "who makes an impossible task possible (such as catching an invisible deer)", and commends him "to the praise of noble people".[52] It may have been about the same time that the *Mallāri Māhātmya* established an "etymological" identification of Mailāra/Mallāri and Mairāḷa with Śambhu and Viṣṇu.[53]

Some Maharashtrian *bhakti* saints also tended to classify Khaṇḍobā as a *kṣetrapāla* or *kṣudradevatā* or simply as a *bhūta*. Saint Rāmdās, in one place in his works, ranked him amongst the village deities or ghosts and in other places identified him with Rāma. He also called him Mallu Khān.[54]

According to the Golla *kathā* of Hyderabad the confrontation between Mallanna and the Balijas (i.e. Liṅgāyats), the brothers of Māḍalamma, ends by Mallanna turning them into dogs and causing them to be reborn as Voggus. They behave like dogs (in rituals), get possessed by Mallanna and make predictions.[55] Mallanna or Khaṇḍobā is also called Rautrāy at Devara Hippargi near Bijapur. The temple clearly has Muslim antecedents. Rautrāy fights a Liṅgāyat Rākṣasa called Dariyappa who lives in a *maṭha*. Instead of the usual Nandī in front of the temple, at Devara Hippargi we find the horse as *vāhana*.

MMKh's relationship, as we have indicated, also extends to the Muslims. Thus a Golla *kathā* tells us how Mallanna acquires turmeric powder (Tel. *pasupu baṇḍāru*), which he needs for his marriage with Bhramarāṃbā.[56] He has to fetch it from Mecca (*sic*), where he goes in the guise (*avatāra*) of a fakir. The inhabitants of Mecca are Śiva *bhaktas*. They wear a waist band (Tel. *mola dāram*), and never drink liquor or eat meat (Tel. *māḍhu māṃsamu*). But he spoils their customs and traditions (Tel. *ācāra vyavahārālu*). Mallanna spends twelve years in Mecca as a servant. He makes the well go dry. The inhabitants of Mecca ask him if he knows any means of restoring the water to the well. He tells them that if they slaughter a black cow (Tel. *kaṛri āvu*) and eat it, the water in the well will be restored. He makes them cook *kanduru* (Tel. for a biryani-like dish) with the meat of the black cow and causes them to smoke *gāñjā*. He then asks them to look into the well and they see water. They develop great faith in Mallanna.

When after twelve years the well is again filled with water, *baṇḍāru* (which may also mean *gold* and is the substitute for gold in the rituals of the MMKh cult) erupts near the well. The inhabitants of Mecca get engrossed by the sight of water and gold and, infatuated, they fall into a deep slumber (apparently caused by Mallanna). When they wake up, Mallanna has disappeared with the *baṇḍāru*. They launch a hunt for Mallanna, whom they call Malkhān. They almost catch up with him. At that moment Mallanna jumps into the Gaṅgā (a general name of a river), from which an outstretched arm emerges. The Turakas (Turks) wonder whose hand it could be and chop it off. Gaṅgā thus saves Mallanna with the hand. In return for this help Mallanna promises Gaṅgā that she will be known as Bipatma (Bibi + Padma) and worshipped every year. She will be taken in a procession on an elephant on the day of the *urus* of Pīrla Panduga.

Although the particular place of the celebration of Gangā could not be ascertained and this tradition seems to be confusing, the general background becomes clear if we think of the historical symbiosis in the Deccan between Liṅgāyats and Muslims on the level of folk religion and in the realm of mysticism. Sufis and Liṅgāyats could identify to some extent on the level of mysticism. Rituals in which a *jaṅgama* turns up in a procession dressed as a Pīr are known from Bidar.[57] Mallanna and Khaṇḍobā were worshipped by Liṅgāyats *and* Muslims. In a Marathi inscription dated Śaka 1625 and Faslī 1113 (1703) the Śiva of the Liṅgāyats is identified with Mallukhān: *Śrī guruli(ṅ)ga ja(ṅ)gama vibhūtarudrakṣa-bhuśena sadās(ś)ī(i)va s(ś)aṅkara s(ś)ambhu Mahādeva Mā(a)hārudra: Maluṣ(kh)ān.*[58] It is, however, Khaṇḍobā who is very often called Mallu Khān or Ajmat Khān and his affiliation with the Muslims is visible in the style of his temples (as in Jejuri or in Andur, Osmanabad District). He appears as a Paṭhān on horseback, one of his wives is Muslim, and the keeper of the god's horses and his *kotvāl* is a Muslim in Jejuri. In the *Mārtaṇḍa Vijaya* (24.30-1) Muslims are expressly said to be his *bhaktas.* A typical instance of this mutual appreciation is a special order issued by the Sultan of Bijapur, Ibrahim II, in 1614, in which he assured the right of pilgrims to perform rituals to Khaṇḍerāo or Mallāri at Naldurg and the reinstatement of the annual *jātrā.*[59] It is only when attacked that Khaṇḍobā reacts violently. Thus the *Mārtaṇḍa Vijaya* (36.43) also mentions that Mārtaṇḍa Bhairava annihilated the Mlecchas, i.e. Muslims. At Prempur, near the capital of the Bidar Sultanate, the *daityas* Maṇi and Malla are said to have been Muslim kings. And in the *Jayādri Māhātmya,* which pertains to Jejuri, the *daityas* are said to have been born in the "Yavanakula".[60] According to the local legend and songs of the Vāghyās, 900,000 hornets were sent by Khaṇḍobā through a hole in the wall of the fortress at Jejuri to drive away the army of Aurangzeb. The same story involving hornets is told by Gollas about Śrīśailam:[61] in this account, Chatrapati Śivājī, while fighting Aurangzeb, enters the forest of Śrīśailam. Feeling very thirsty, he approaches Pārvatī and requests her to give him a bowl of milk (Tel. *pāla cambu*). Before Śivājī can empty the bowl Pārvatī manifests herself in innumerable lives (Tel. *janmālu*), or rather *bhramaras* (Tel. *tummeda*: hornets), attacks Aurangzeb, and uproots his army. When Śivājī sees the slain enemies, he addresses her: "From now on your name is not Pārvatī, you are Bhramarāṃbā". To this day one can hear the sound of hornets (Tel. *tummedala jhuṃkāramu*) in the wall behind Bhramarāṃbā.

On the whole we may draw the conclusion that, like the ancient Rudra, MMKh seemed to be acceptable to the common folk irrespective of caste and creed. The *Mārtaṇḍa Vijaya* (5.12; 24.30 and 33) summarizes this in its own way: "Hungry" for devotees, Mārtaṇḍa Bhairava does not known of *jāti, varṇa,* or *kula* (eminent family). Caṇḍālas and Mlecchas are welcome as *bhaktas.*

The Position of the Brāhmaṇs and the *Mallārī Māhātmya*

Seen from the viewpoint of folk religion, the position of the Brāhmaṇs in the cult of MMKh was not and is still not dominant. Nor was it *a priori* established according to orthodox-śāstric principles. Yet many Brāhmaṇs claimed MMKh as their *kulasvāmī.* The Brāhmaṇs' principles and ideals tended to be incorporated and subordinated to folk religion. Sanganna, the son of Brāhmaṇs of the Visvāmitra *gotra,* is born at the same time as Mallanna, according to the traditions of the Gollas. He becomes Mallanna's companion, is equal to him, and is also called his disciple.[62] On the purāṇic level Viṣṇu is identified with the brother-in-law of Khaṇḍobā, who is on the folk level his minister (Heggaḍī Pradhān), the brother of Mhāḷsā and a Lingāyat (Śaivite) Vāṇī. Śrī Venkaṭeśvara of Tirupati in Andhra is also a brother-in-law of Mallanna. Mallanna, while testing the *bhakti* of his wife Balija Māḍalamma, keeps her in a fort on a mountain. He goes away and returns as a leper. She curses him, and wishes that he would die. Her duty is to fetch water to cure him, but Mallanna makes all the water disappear. Māḍalamma plans to go to Tirupati, to her brother Veṅkaṭeśvara (popularly known as Veṅkanna), to fetch water. Before she goes to him, Mallanna arrives at Tirupati and warns Veṅkaṭeśvara not to give her any water. Not to displease his sister, and rather scared of Mallanna, Veṅkaṭeśvara leaves Tirupati to avoid her. This episode shows that Mallanna was still superior to Veṅkaṭeśvara.[63]

In Devaragudda the minister is actually represented as Viṣṇu with sword, mace, conch, and "book", but he is assigned a place outside the temple precincts. The *Mārtaṇḍa Vijaya* knows a story which shows that the Brāhmaṇs not only were worshippers of Khaṇḍobā, but had to respect and accept certain basic incidents of the cults lest they be confronted with evil consequences:

> A mischievous Brāhmaṇ mocks at a Vāghyā and the chain he (then) carries around his neck: "How can your Mallāri possibly break the worldly fetters (Ma. *bhavabandhana*)? If you bind it to your neck, and, calling his name, break it with one jerk, then I shall rest assured". To the dismay of the Brāhmaṇ the Vāghyā breaks the chain with a single jerk, calling upon Malhāri, "the liberator from worldly fetters" (Ma. *bhavamocaka*). The Brāhmaṇ turns into a dog and bites people so that they take to their heels. His wife makes a vow to Mārtaṇḍa to perform a *yātrā* without footwear so that her husband may get freed from his affliction. His *ahaṃkār* vanishes and he becomes Malhāri's *bhakta* (*MV* 34.54-70).

Versions of the myth of Mallāri probably precede the Sanskrit *Mallāri Māhātmya*. According to an inscription at the temple of Ailōni dated 1369, it is Arjuna, with the help of Śiva, who kills the demon Malla. Śiva is from then onwards called Mallikārjuna.[64] The *Mallāri Māhātmya*, considered to belong to the *Kṣetrakaṇḍa* of the *Brahmāṇḍapurāṇa*, purports to point out the authoritative, purāṇic grounds and to establish the Brāhmaṇical credentials of the cult of Mailāra and Khaṇḍobā. The work is a masterpiece not only because of its beautiful narrative style, but also for its skillful attempt at transforming a rather "rustic", "demonic", "impure", and "violent" cult. Śiva becomes an *avatāra* on the request of the seven Ṛṣis, or Brāhmaṇs (*dharmaputras*), as Indra and Viṣṇu are unable to defeat the demons, who have become invincible on account of their *tapas*, which has elicited a boon from Brahmā. As Mārtaṇḍa Bhairava, Śiva fights the demons Maṇi and Malla, who have raided the *aśrama* of the Ṛṣis, overthrown the *yajña* (and even urinated into the sacrificial fire), killed cows, and molested the women of the Brāhmaṇs. Thus everything that is sacred to the Brāhmaṇical order is at stake, but the demons are defeated in a tremendous battle, a *raṇa-yajña,* or battle-sacrifice. After the defeat of the valorous demon kings, their *ahaṃkār* disappears and on their death they attain the god (*sannidhi* or *sāyujyatā*; another term used in the *M.Māh.* is *vilaya*: 17.42). We have attempted to show elsewhere that Maṇi and Malla, the demon kings, are an epitome of the rising king, the "robber king", and of communities not exactly belonging to the Brāhmaṇical fold or paying respect to its orthodox-śāstric implications like *yajña, varṇa,* etc.[65] The Brāhmaṇical attitude to the "outlandish", impure manifestations, as exemplified by the Purāṇas and, in this particular case, in the *Mallāri Māhātmya,* was to incorporate or ignore some aspects of these cults and demonize others. Maṇi and Malla were said to belong to the Prahlāda *kula.*[66] That they made their followers worship their *mūrtis* is noted as especially aggravating and objectionable.[67] We may sense here perhaps an attitude which was opposed to the old notion that a king could be a god who stands at the top of his own spiritual, ritual, and social hierarchical model without overriding Brāhmaṇical control. According to the *Mallāri Māhātmya,* the folk deity was split into the pure, purāṇic Śiva and the demon, who is impure until he is defeated and becomes the demon devotee and a *dvārapāla.* He is now subordinated to a Śiva who protects the *yajña* and *dharma* of the Brāhmaṇical order. As Shulman has observed of the bandit king or pre-empire king: "His world is the ancient sacrificial universe, which allows destruction its place—before the splitting of Brahmin and kingship in the interests of maintaining the Brahmin's ideal, uncon-taminating sacrifice".[68] Historically, many Deśastha Brāhmaṇs were worshippers of Khaṇḍobā and seem to have been warriors rather than "ideal Brāhmaṇs". For instance, a Maratha general of the artillery, Panse, whose fort was called Malhārgaḍ, donated a huge sword to Khaṇḍobā in the eighteenth century.[69] The sword was given a mythical ancestry which was traced back to Aśvatthāman and his avenging sword.[70]

The splitting of the folk deity into the demon and Śiva is also reflected, in our view, in the battle ritual at Mailar. At the end of the battle, the head of the demon, which is not to be seen before this moment, appears at the feet of the god, as if the god has shed his own asuric form.

The status of the folk deity is also slowly eroded by the texts. The *Mallāri Māhātmya* (18.14) still mentions amongst the offerings of the gods to Mallāri/Mairāḷa incense, lights, betel, and animals (*paśu*).

The Marathi version by Siddhapāl Kesarī is also explicit and stresses that plates filled with meat etc. are offerings to the god Mairāḷa (18.19). In the *Mallāri Māhātmya* the dying demon Malla requests that Śiva should fulfill the wishes of those *bhaktas* who worship him by *chedapātādi*, by "causing themselves to be cut etc". This may refer to the hook-swinging rite, which nowadays continues only in a mild form, or the self-mortification of the *vīras* (17.37). The Marathi translation of the *Mallāri Māhātmya* by Siddhapāl Kesarī, however, renders these customs disparagingly as *ugra* (violent, demonic) *bhakti*. The *Mārtaṇḍa Vijaya* (by Gaṅgādhara, of 1821) goes even a step further and styles animal sacrifices and self-torture as (demonic) *rākṣasī bhakti* (35.53).

In accordance with this evaluation of the modes of *bhakti*, worship was further restructured in the texts. For instance, possession (so essential in folk religion) by the god in the form of the wind has the still lower demonic appellation of *piśācī bhakti*. But *sāttvikī bhakti*, "true *bhakti*", is the feeding of a Brāhmaṇ in the form of Mārtaṇḍa (*MV* 35.47, 55; 35.48, 61).

It was on a Sunday, on the sixth of the month of Mārgaśīrṣa (Campāṣaṣṭhī), that Mārtaṇḍa and his wife (*śakti*) Mārtaṇḍa Bhairavī manifested themselves at Prempur as *svayaṃbhū liṅgas* made of clay under a wishing tree, together with Maṇi, who rides a horse (*M.Māh.* 18.3f.). He manifested himself on the request and for the protection (*rakṣārtham*) of the *dharmaputras* (*M.Māh.*18.5f.). In the "city of Prempur" the god was made accessible to all *varṇas* and *jātis* through *dhyāna* (meditation) (*M.Māh.* 18.9); and he fulfills wishes: cattle, sons, horses, women, and a kingdom without enemies, full of horses and elephants, for kings (18.28f.); and, for Brāhmaṇs, recognition by the king and victory in disputes against those who speak wrongly or pervertedly (18.30).

We must voice some caution as to the results and influence of the *Mallāri Māhātmya*. Its full contents are only vaguely known by circles beyond the Brāhmaṇs. Most of the devotees apprehend that Śiva has become an *avatār* to kill the demon, "for the sake of the *bhaktas*", *not* specifically for Brāhmaṇs and their values. Numerous depictions show Khaṇḍobā with his wife Mhāḷsā killing the demons, but nowhere is it shown who the particular *bhaktas* were whom he rescued. The songs of the Vāghyās rarely refer to the story of the seven Ṛṣis or *dharmaputras*—but this, admittedly, may not have been the function of the songs.

D. CONCLUSION

Mallanna could shelter under the umbrella of the ancient cult of Mallikārjuna of Śrīśailam and thus obtain his legitimization as Śiva. Mallikārjuna, however, had and still has a cult which involves worship by people from various quarters, including tribals, who have free access to the temple. It is not a monopoly of purāṇic mythology or of Brāhmaṇical worship. Mailāra and Khaṇḍobā gained their Brāhmaṇical credentials through the *Mallāri Māhātmya* (and other texts like the *Jayādri Māhātmya* and *Mārtaṇḍa Vijaya*), in which Śiva becomes an *avatāra* to defend the orthodox-śāstric Brāhmaṇical order. It is, however, doubtful how far the *Māhātmya* has become an authoritative scripture for groups of devotees beyond the immediate addressees. Māhātmyas are not compulsory law which sanction the traditions of a particular cult once and for all and for all devotees. The acceptance of the tradition "codified" by Māhātmyas depends on the degree other groups of devotees are aware of its contents and are persuaded by it. This awareness may spread nowadays more easily and quickly with the increasing literacy and proliferation of printed temple pamphlets (which, however, mostly do *not* or only marginally refer to the Brāhmaṇical features of the *Māhātmya*). Even if devotees know of the existence of the *Māhātmya*, and may or may not know of its contents, acceptance may just amount to lip-service. The focus is still on the folk-religious character of the cult, which derives its innate values from its direct accessibility to a god who lives "here and now" and not in some distant purāṇic heaven. His worship is based on forms of *bhakti* and *tapas* which do not necessarily correspond to the codifications of the ninefold *bhakti* in "classical" *bhakti* texts. *Bhakti* and *tapas* can take violent forms and reflect the attitudes of the hero and ascetic. MMKh are folk gods, but they are more than local village deities (*grāmadevatās*) or caste gods, who are normally said to be typical examples of folk religion and only to cater to practical, material wishes of the devotee. The closeness and company of the god, or god as king, in this life or an afterlife is one of the ardent wishes of the devotee. In the Khaṇḍobā cult it is voiced by the desire expressed in the songs of the Vāghyās: let us go to Jejuri.[71] The wishes of the devotee are often expressed in simple words, not in classical terminology: I do not want anything. Just remember me and let me be near you. There is no reason to give me anything.

An unwritten principle of the cult is that the god tests the *sattva*, genuine-ness, of his devotee. The *bhakta* has to recognize the god in his disguise, something which is possible only if one sheds one's *ahaṃkār.* Thus the demon bragging about his riches and mocking at the obscure ascetic on his Nandī is nearly doomed. It is his bravery that saves him in his death. Bāṇāī suffers the loss of her sheep until she recognizes the god in the old leper.

The position of the god also resembles that of the nascent or robber king, or even the king at the imperial center, like Kṛṣṇadevarāyā of Vijayanagara. The robber king has no (or not yet an) axe to grind as regards *varṇa* and impurities. His followers are recruited from all groups without reference to caste and creed. The king at the centre may have to pay attention to *varṇa* and *śāstric dharma,* but how far is a matter to be examined in each case. Notwithstanding the *dharmic-śāstric* order, he will have to take an "ecumenical" or "secular" attitude towards other castes and religions, e.g. the Muslims. MMKh tend to have the same neutral attitude towards the hierarchy of caste and religion.

The openness to all communities and the earthboundness which is an essential ingredient of folk cults, but results in impurity, exposed the cult to moral censure from various quarters and other religious currents. That Khaṇḍobā as an *avatāra* of Śiva remains on earth is anathema to the Purāṇas. Mostly Śiva is represented on earth by Bhairava, Vīrabhadra, or some other partial manifestation who fulfils mundane, impure functions. Most of the devotees would emphasize that Khaṇḍobā is a full *avatāra* of Śiva/Śaṅkara and not the usual Bhairava. Śiva as Khaṇḍobā on earth also takes over many attributes and characteristics of the defeated demon, like royal insignia, weapons, and animals, e.g. the horse.

A cult of a god on earth who admits access to all communities and allows violent rituals to be performed in his name, besides animal sacrifices (now offered to Bāṇāī or the demon), Muraḷīs (*devadāsis*), and so on, always evoked a mixed reaction in old Marathi literature. The quick metamorphosis from an ascetic beggar who rides an old bull and carries an ant-eaten club (*khaṭvāṅga*) to an illustrious king with rich clothes and a horse with a saddle studded with jewels is "a touchy point not to be disclosed". This is the view of the poet Nirañjanamādhava (d. 1790) in a humorous praise song (*stotra*) dedicated to Khaṇḍobā.[72] Because Khaṇḍobā is reputed to be rather fierce and impetuous in his reaction to those who fail in observing their family duties towards him, and to cause the trouble and affliction characteristic of ghosts, he must be a ghost (*bhūt*). This is the argument of a Christian missionary apparently supported by a Kokaṇastha Brāhmaṇ in a discussion with a Deśastha Brāhmaṇ. The discussion took place around 1855.[73]

At the end of the nineteenth century a Maharashtrian Brāhmaṇ on a pilgrimage through India reached Jejuri and remarked with some disdain:

> There the Pūjārīs are Guravs and many of the Śūdra caste etc. come for *darśan.* Therefore Ragunātha could see that ritual purity and impurity were very little respected. After he had performed the *yātrā* according to family *dharma* he went to Moreśvar (Morgaon) to have *darśan* of Gaṇpati.[74]

Marathi proverbs and expressions emanating from sources outside the cult reflect that the cult could not be ignored, and yet tend to discredit it. The dramatic performance of rituals, the participation in the play (*kheḷ*) of the god, is an important ingredient of folk religion, and very much so in the cult of MMKh. The Marathi term *kheḷkhaṇḍobā* actually refers to the wind of the god possessing the devotee and tossing him around, but it is taken to mean "utter demolition", "devastation", or "destruction". Essentially, the MMKh cult remained then a cult that preserved the identity of Rudra between, on the one hand, the classical-purāṇic Śiva, who is worshipped in a Brāhmaṇical temple in the form of a *liṅga,* and, on the other hand, the Śaivite sects such as Kāpālikas and Kālāmukhas, who became extinct, and their successors the Nāthas and Liṅgāyats—though, admittedly, the cult incorporated and shared features of these two other important currents of Hinduism. In fact, we may say that the cult is a mirror of all currents of Hinduism, but it is *folk religion* that is emphasized.[75]

NOTES

1. This paper includes material which was collected during a stay in Maharashtra from August 1984 to April 1985. I am grateful to the German Research Association for financial support. Dr. M.L.K. Murty, Deccan College, Pune, has helped me in my field research in Andhra Pradesh and in transcribing and translating oral texts. I received the same help from Dr. Rajaram R. Hegde, Deccan College, Pune, in Karnataka. To both I am most grateful. Data taperecorded and observed in the field are not specifically documented here. The reader is referred to a previous article of mine (see n. 47) where further references will be found.
2. S.G. Tulpule, *Marāṭhī Vāṅgmayācā Itihās, khaṃḍa pahilā* (Pune, 1984), 41ff.
3. N. Ramesan, *Temples and Legends of Andhra Pradesh* (Bombay, 1962), 12.

4. Tārā Parāñjpe, "sīmā pradeśātīl bhāvagamgā: sāngīte", *Paṃcadhārā* 14 (1981), 22.
5. Richard Burghart, "Hierarchical models of the Hindu social system", *Man* (N.S.) 13 (1978), 519-36.
6. *Pañcaviṃśa Brāhmaṇa* 24.18,2; *BŚS* 28.24; Harry Falk, *Bruderschaft und Würfelspiel* (Freiburg, 1986), 18.
7. *Golla Kathā I* (Hyderabad). Told by Voggu Mallesh, Ray Mallesh et al.
8. According to a story told by a Dhangar shepherd, N.K. Mane; the story is at least 137 years old, as it is referred to in the *Jñānoday*, a missionary journal. See G.N. Morje (ed.), *Jñānoday-Lekhan-Sār-Sūcī* (Bombay, 1986), 459: What was told by the Dhangar with humour and visible relish proves the depravity of the cult from the point of view of the *Jñānoday*.
9. A.K. Ramanujan, *Hyms for the Drowning* (Princeton, 1981), 115.
10. P.V. Kane, *History of Dharmaśāstra*, vol. II, pt. II (Poona, 1941), 1236.
11. Śrī Sadguru Bhāūmahārāja yāṃcyā saṃgrahāṃtūl *Śrī Khaṃḍobācīṃ padeṃ* (publ. by V.D. Gokhale, Pune, 1951), *pada* 22 (*Somvatīpada*), *pada* 19.
12. Syed Siraj ul Hassan, *The Castes and Tribes of H.E.H. The Nizam's Dominions* (Bombay, 1921), 231.
13. Rā. Rā. Bāpurāv Khaṃḍerāv Khāḍe, *Śrīkṣetra Jejurī-mahātmya* (Pune, 1924), 51. This story is a *verbatim* translation of a passage in the (unpublished) Skt. *Jayādri-Māhātmya*.
14. *Maharashtra State Gazetteers, Satara District* (rev. edn., Bombay, 1963), 140, fn. 1.
15. Mukund Wamanrao Burway, *Life of Subhedar Malhar Rao Holkar* (Indore, 1930), 183.
16. *Golla Kathā I* (Hyderabad).
17. J.W. Hauer, *Der Vrātya* (Stuttgart, 1927), 149.
18. G.D. Sontheimer, "Dasarā at Devaraguḍḍa. Ritual and Play in the Cult of Mailāra/Khaṇḍobā", *South Asian Digest of Regional Writing*, 10 (1984), 1-20. (Editors' note: See also this volume.)
19. *Khaṇḍobācīṃ padeṃ, pada* 24.
20. I owe this reference to Klaus W. Müller, who is working on the *antyeṣṭipaddhati* of Nārāyaṇabhaṭṭa for his Ph.D.
21. Günther D. Sontheimer, "Folk Deities in the Vijayanagara Empire: Narasiṃha and Mallanna/Mailar", in A.L. Dallapiccola (ed.), *Vijayanagara—City and Empire* (Wiesbaden, 1985), 144ff., 158. See Upendra Thakur, *The History of Suicide in India* (Delhi, 1963), 61f. for the devotion between master and servant in the case of Kuvara Lakṣmaṇa, a general of the Hoysaḷa King Vīra Ballāḷa II (1173-1220) who committed suicide along with his wife and some of his soldiers. The relationship between lord and master, as in the case of MMKh and devotee, is indicated in the inscription: "Between servant and king there was no difference: the glory and the marks of royalty were equal in both". Kuvara Lakṣmaṇa and his wife became united with Garuḍa and Lakṣmi, respectively, suggesting that the Hoysala king was Viṣṇu. This fits well with the notion that for the "hero the king is god".
22. *Śrī Khaṇḍobācīṃ padeṃ*, 2.
23. Joachim Deppert, *Rudras Geburt. Systematische Unterschungen zum Inzest in der Mythologie der Brāhmaṇas* (Wiesbaden, 1977), 96f.
24. K. Venkata Ramanayya, *Vēlūgoṭivarivaṃśāvaḷi* (University of Madras, Madras, 1939), 2.

25. J. W. Hauer, *Der Vrātya*, 129f. I could not see the ritual myself, but was told about it by Shri Guru Jayachandra Wodeyar Swamy, who also provided other information about the cult of Mailāra.
26. Sontheimer, "Dasarā ...",12 and n. 40.
27. Sontheimer, "Dasarā ...", *passim*.
28. Sontheimer, "Dasarā ...", 13ff.
29. Young boys often are the first to discover Khaṇḍobā or Mhaskobā or similar gods. Young boys are priests in some temples in Anantapur District. For the representation of heads of rams and humans alternating under the *pādukās* of Khaṇḍobā, see S. Settar and G.D. Sontheimer (eds.), *Memorial Stones* (Dharwad, N. Delhi, 1982), 272f. (figures 21-3).
30. I am not sure whether the lamb is actually killed nowadays.
31. Falk, *Bruderschaft*, 160ff., 162.
32. Sontheimer, "Folk Deities...", 150f.
33. Falk, *Bruderschaft*, 161.
34. Dharmapuri Venkatayya Pantulu, *Ailōni Mallanna Kathā*. (A Compilation from the *Golla Kathā*) (Warangal, 1964), 1ff. (cited as *Golla Kathā II*); G.R. Varma, *Mailāra Dēva* (Varman Publications, Tadepalligude, 1973), 38.
35. *Golla Kathā I* and *II*; Falk, *Bruderschaft*..., 52; Deppert, *Rudra*, 94ff., 108.
36. Falk, *Bruderschaft*..., *ibidem*. *Jaiminīya Brāhmaṇa* 2.227: *agrakāma*.
37. *Golla Kathā I*. According to this oral version it was just a *rākṣasa*, but the narrators are sometimes confused about the sex. It is also a *rākṣasa* according to the traditions at Komaravelli: Varma, *Mailāra Dēva*, 38. According to *Golla Kathā II*, however, it is a Brahmarākṣasī.
38. Varma, *Mailāra Dēva*, 30ff.
39. *Golla Kathā I*.
40. Varma, *Mailāra Dēva*, 30ff.
41. Sontheimer, *Birobā, Mhaskobā und Khaṇḍobā. Ursprung, Geschichte and Umwelt von pastoralen Gottheiten in Mahārāṣṭra* (Wiesbaden, 1976), 151; *Census of India 1961*, vol. X, pt. VIII-B, *Fairs and Festivals of Maharashtra* (Bombay, 1969), 190f.
42. *Golla Kathā II*, 19ff.
43. The name of the village Kommarelli or Kommaravelli in Jangav Taluk, Warangal District, has been associated with Kumāra (Murukaṉ, Skanda) and his wife Vaḷḷi. The three heads in front of the *mūrti* in the temple of Mallanna may be the three demons, Cūr, Ciṅkamukan, and Tarakan, whom Murukaṉ killed (*Kantapurāṇam, kāṇḍam* 2-4 by Kacciyappa Civācāriyar. See Kamil Veith Zvelebil, *Tamil Literature* [Wiesbaden 1974], 185ff.).
44. Sontheimer, *Birobā*, 63ff.
45. *Khaṇḍobācaṃ padeṃ, pad* 14.
46. Tārā Paranjpe, "...sāngīte", 22.
47. G.D. Sontheimer, "Rudra and Khaṇḍobā: Continuity in Folk Religion", in Milton Israel and N.K. Wagle (eds.), *Religion and Society in Maharashtra*, University of Toronto, Centre for South Asian Studies (Toronto, 1987), 1ff., at 13ff. (Editors' note: See also this volume.)
48. Sontheimer, "Rudra", ibid.
49. Vasudeva S. Agrawala, *Ancient Indian Folk Cults* (Varanasi, 1970), Appendix, Nos. 2 and 4.
50. Sontheimer, "Rudra", 14f.
51. V.B. Kolte (ed.), *Līḷācaritra, Uttarārdha, līḷā* 436 (Mumbaī, 1978).

52. Vinukonda Vallabhārayadu, *Krīḍābhirāmamu*, v. 145 (Secundarabad: Andhra Pradesh Book Distributors, 1972).
53. *M. Māh.* 18.11-13: The syllable *ma* means Śambhu, the syllable *a* Viṣṇu; if these two [gods] are on earth, the word *mela* (*ma + a + ila*) comes into existence. He is an enemy (*ārati*) to this *mela*. On account of this word analysis Mallāri's name has become Mailāra. The syllables *ra* and *la*, it is said, are homophones: from this Mairāla comes into existence.

    In 18.10 we are told that the *mūrtis* of "Śambhu and Mārtaṇḍa Bhairavī are made of clay" (*mahīmayī*), but the traditions that Mailāra/Mallanna emerged from a termite mound are omitted.
54. Sontheimer, "Rudra", 19ff.
55. *Golla Kathā I.*
56. *Golla Kathā I.*
57. H. K. Sherwani, *The Bahmanis of the Deccan* (Hyderabad, 1953), 195; Richard Maxwell Eaton, *Sufis of Bijapur 1300-1700* (Princeton University Press, Princeton, 1978), 250.
58. G.H. Khare, *Mahārāṣṭrācīṃ cār daivateṃ* (Pune, 1958), 150; *Epigraphia Indo-Moslemica 1921-1922*, 20.
59. Eaton, *Sufis*, 99.
60. Khāḍe, *Jejurīmāhātmya*, 70.
61. *Golla Kathā I.*
62. *Golla Kathā II.*
63. According to traditions recorded from Gollas in Sultanabad (Karimnagar District).
64. D.C. Sircar (ed.), *Annual Report on Indian Epigraphy for 1957-58* (Delhi: Government of India Press, 1961), 8-9, 21; M.L.K. Murty and Günther D. Sontheimer, "Pre-historic Background to Pastoralism in the Southern Deccan in the Light of Oral Traditions and Cults of Some Pastoral Communities", *Anthropos* 75 (1980), 163-84, 168.
65. Sontheimer, "Rudra", 16ff.
66. *M.Māh.* 14.14; *M.Māh.* (by Cintāmaṇi, in Ma., A.D. 1821) 1.23.
67. *M.Māh.* (by Cintāmaṇi) 1.97: they called themselves *īśvara*. Cp. *M.Māh.* 7.27 (by Vināyaka, in Ma., A.D. 1872): they uprooted *svayaṃbhū liṅgas*, destroyed the *mūrtis* of other gods, [and] caused their own *mūrtis* to be worshiped.
68. David Dean Shulman, *The King and the Clown in South Indian Myth and Poetry* (Princeton, 1985), 344.
69. Keśav Raṅganāth Pānse, *Pānse gharāṇyācā itihās* (Puṇeṃ, 1929), 130.
70. Khāḍe, *Jejurīmāhātmya*, 72: Aśvatthāman promises to offer the heads of the five Pāṇḍavas to Duryodhana. After praising the gatekeeper at the camp of the Pāṇḍavas, that is Śiva/Tripurahara, he receives a sword from Śiva to kill the Pāṇḍavas. He enters the camp and beheads five youths who resemble the Pāṇḍavas (according to *MV* 35.23, Aśvatthāman mistakes them for the five Pāṇḍavas), offers the heads at the feet of Duryodhana and returns the sword to Śiva. This curious version again reminds us of the *pañca vīras*, and the *dāvaṇ* of the Dhangars, see *supra*.
71. *Khaṇḍobācīṃ padeṃ*, *pada* 21: *calā jāūṃ pāhūṃ jejurī*....Whether a particular act of devotion, like bringing water from the river in *kāvaṭis* (a water vessel and the ritual) and bathing the god, has practical (*bhukti*) or transcendental (*mukti*)

results depends on whether it is practised *sakāma* or *niṣkāma*, according to *MV* 22.34ff. See also John M. Stanley, "Niṣkāma and Sakāma Bhakti: Pandharpur and Jejuri", in Milton Israel and N.K. Wagle (eds.), *Religion*, 52-67.

72. L.R. Pāṃgārkar (ed.), *Nirañjanamādhavāṃcā kavitāsaṃgraha*, pt. 1 (Poona, 1919), 64ff., 66. See also Rāmdās, in Sontheimer, "Rudra", 19.

73. R.C. Dhere, *Khaṃḍobā* (Puṇeṃ, 1961), 117-19. Referring to Mare Micel, *Khaṃḍobācī goṣṭ* (Mumbai, 1855).

74. Gaṇeś Sadāsiv Śāstrī Lele, *Tīrthayātrā Prabaṃdha* (Pune, 2nd edn., 1964), 134.

75. Cp. G.D. Sontheimer, "Hinduism: The Five Components and Their Interaction", in G.D. Sontheimer and H. Kulke (eds.), *Hinduism Reconsidered* (New Delhi: Manohar, 1989), 197-212.

The Myth of the God and His Two Wives:
Two Pastoral Versions from Maharashtra

1 INTRODUCTION

1.1 THE SPREAD OF THE MYTH IN INDIA

THE MYTH of the god and his marriages with two wives is found in many parts of India. The pattern is mostly the same: The first wife comes from an upper stratum (or heaven) and the second wife from a lower stratum of society (or the underworld). The second wife usually belongs to a forest tribe or migrant community and, in any case, comes from a spatially separated area, such as a forest or a pastoral region. In this paper I want to present two versions of this myth from the oral literature of a nomadic shepherd group, the Hāṭkar Dhangars of Maharashtra. But before I refer to their oral literature and discuss the two versions, I shall mention some of the regional parallels of the myth. The myth is connected in the South with the cult of Murukaṉ and Aiyaṉār. It occurs in the poetry of old Tamil literature (see e.g. Zvelebil 1977: 227-46), in the *Kantapurāṇam* of medieval Tamil literature (Zvelebil 1974: 185ff.), and in the folk literature of Andhra Pradesh and Karnataka (see e.g. Sontheimer 1985; 1989a) and Maharashtra (see e.g. Sontheimer 1976: 61ff.). It is also known in Pushkar, Rajasthan, in a brahmanical sacrificial context (see Malik 1993; Shulman 1980: 274f.). In Pushkar the second wife of Brahmā, Gāyatrī, comes from the Ābhīra tribe, whereas the first wife is Sāvitrī. Though there are three wives in the Hindi oral epic *Lorikī* of Uttar Pradesh and Bihar, Mañjarī and Candā play prominent roles and we should probably include the epic in our list (Pandey 1982).

In Bihari folk literature, we again meet with the myth. Here Mahādev, as a trader, leaves and forgets his home, marries a second time and returns after 12 years (Sarkar 1974: 96). Again, in medieval Bengali literature, Śiva is said to mix freely with low caste and tribal people and Gaṅgā appears as a woman of the Koch tribe (Sarkar

1974: 75-7; 166). Whereas in the Sanskrit Purāṇas the marriage of Śiva with Pārvatī is emphasized rather than that with Gaṅgā, folk sources insist that there are two marriages, whatever problems the second marriage may create or however contemptuously people of the upper social groups may think of the second liaison. Another solution on the Sanskrit level for avoiding this question seems to be that it is Pārvatī who appears in the disguise of a tribal woman or that Pārvatī becomes a *yoginī* or a *kāminī* respectively, according to the mood of Śiva (O'Flaherty 1973: 7). It would be tempting to analyse the myth by comparing the regional versions and reflections of the myth in Sanskrit literature with our case. But we shall limit the discussion to the two texts from the oral literature of the Hāṭkar Dhangars.

1.2 The Hāṭkar Dhangars and their Nomadic Way of Life

The Dhangars of Maharashtra are a large community of heterogeneous groups which basically live on nomadic or semi-nomadic pastoralism, though many of them also follow agricultural and other occupations (Sontheimer 1975: *passim*; 1976: 139-70). This essay deals with the Hāṭkar Dhangars, who are mostly nomadic shepherds. During the monsoon they live in their monsoon encampments in the eastern parts of the Pune, Ahmednagar and Satara districts of Maharashtra. These camps (*vāḍās*) are situated on their own pasture lands. Some of them have built houses which have replaced tents and mud-and-stone huts. But rainfall is scanty and with the end of the monsoon the Dhangars are forced to migrate because of withering pastures. Some "camps" (*vāḍās*) migrate to the Western Ghats, others to the coastal (Konkan) area. In both areas there are better opportunities for grazing sheep. Besides they can pen their sheep in the rice fields of the farmers in exchange for rice or cash. With the beginning of the monsoon they return to their home area, which was dominated by a pastoral economy until regular agriculture spread and encroached on the region during this century and especially in recent years.

2 THE ORAL LITERATURE OF THE HĀṬKAR DHANGARS

The oral literature of the Hāṭkar Dhangars consists of myths about their gods, goddesses and exemplary heroes and devotees. The myths are sung in a kind of folk *ovī* or rather free rhythmic composition, e.g.

bhāy-yā-sū-ra va-nā-lā (ta)
bhāy-yā-sū-ra va-nā-lā

The first half of the *caraṇa* may be combined by a syllable like *va* or *ta* which is generally non-semantic. The whole narration as sung in consecutive *caraṇas* is called an *Ovī* (written here with a capital 'O' when the whole composition is meant) by the Dhangars, perhaps because they consider the whole composition to be a "series of *caraṇas* wreathed together". The word *ovī* is derived from the verb *ovaṇeṃ* = "to wreath" (Tulpule 1979: 451). It may also be that the Dhangars know the religious import of the word *ovī* in Maharashtrian *bhakti* poetry and thus use the same word for their composition, which has a great religious significance for them. Thus any *Ovī* invariably starts with *sum-ba-rāna mān-ḍi-lā* / and may continue with *sum-ba-rā-na de-vā-cā* //

The remembrance is set //
The remembrance of God //

The *caraṇa* is sung by two main singers and repeated by two back singers. The Dhangars would call the two main singers *mhore* [= *mohoreṃ*, in archaic (S) M] *mhaṇāre* = "who sing ahead or in front" and the latter *māge mhaṇāre* = "who sing behind". One of the main singers is the actual leader whereas the second main singer keeps up with him as much as possible. Like him the two back singers are also informal apprentices, in the sense that there is no formal compulsion to learn an *Ovī*. From childhood *Ovīs* are heard and learnt and any Dhangar male who believes that he is able to sing may join in the performance of an *Ovī*. In fact, an *Ovī* is easy to sing because any story with a religious content can be spontaneously turned into an *Ovī* by a talented singer. The contents and the message of the *Ovī* are thus absorbed in a casual, playful manner at a very young age. In some *Ovīs*, as in the one which has been translated and discussed here, the second line of a *caraṇa* may change and thus speed up the narration, e.g.

vā-ḷū-ta-lā kha-ḍā-kā /
pā-ya-man-dī śi-ra-lā //255//

But rarely do the two main singers immediately continue with a new *caraṇa*, mostly they just repeat it. Then the back singers repeat the *caraṇa*. After this the main singers may again rejoin with the same *caraṇa*, which will again be sung by the back singers. This may draw out the *Ovī* enormously. But, as there is no hurry, the *Ovī* can be spread over several nights, e.g. during Navrātri, the "Nine Nights" before the Dasarā festival in the month of Āśvin (October/November). Thus there is no need to finish the *Ovī* in one session. Moreover, as the whole contents of the *Ovī* are well known, only a section of the narration may be sung on any occasion.

The *Ovī* of the Hāṭkar Dhangars, as in the present case, is normally sung without the accompaniment of musical instruments. However, during the *khel*, the annual festival for ancestors and gods, the Hāṭkar Dhangars use big drums (*dhol*) for the dance. Other instruments are played by Hoḷārs, that is, members of a caste of musicians, during the *khel*. (Sontheimer 1988: 108-30; 1976: 137, 140, 142f.).

Sometimes a Hāṭkar Dhangar who serves one of the temples of Birobā of other family caste gods of the Dhangars may visit the monsoon camp, and during his stay he may initiate an *Ovī* (*ovī lāvṇeṃ* = "to commence an *Ovī*") as the main singer. It is mostly in these cases that the main singer will introduce spoken passages. The second main singer may respond to such passages in prose. This is sometimes described as *saṃpādani*, a term which, according to Molesworth, means "the dressing up (...of any legend-exposition) with rhetorical embellishment". The Dhangars would normally describe the prose parts of the *Ovī* simply with the phrase *ovī toṇḍaṇe sudhārūn karāycī* = "improving the *Ovī* by making it intelligible".

Prose or spoken passages are also frequent in the *Ovīs* of the Dhangars in the districts of Kolhapur, Satara and Sangli. Unlike the Hāṭkar Dhangars, they are mostly settled, though young men may practise semi-nomadic pastoralism. The *Ovī* is elaborately accompanied by dance and by musical instruments, namely, one or more drums (*dhol*), cymbals (*jhāñj*), and flutes (*pavā*). These Dhangars' performance is more spectacular than that of the Hāṭkars, who preferably sing their *ovīs* sitting. A typical sight amongst nomadic as well as settled Dhangars is that the singers close one ear with their hand while singing. Only Dhangar men sing *Ovīs*. Women sing the usual rural *ovīs* while grinding millet on the grinding-stone—wherever it still exists. They also specialize in cradle songs (*pālṇā*).

The Dhangars are also good story tellers, who vividly narrate the contents of *Ovīs* and folk tales to children and friends. Dhangar women also tell stories. Such narratives are simply called *goṣṭi*, that is, "stories". Unlike the *Ovīs* these stories contain many details and often abound with humour. The style of narration depends upon the narrator. The story translated here (LS) is essentially a version of the myth sung in the *Ovī*, but the drastic description and the idiolect of the narrator lend it a character of its own when compared with the *Ovī* version.

3 THE *OVĪ* OF KHAṆḌOBĀ, BĀNUBAI AND MHĀḶSĀ

The *Ovī* which has been translated here was sung by nomadic Hāṭkar Dhangars during the night at a monsoon camp on 7 November 1979. The leading singer was Sakhārām Bābū Lakaḍe, an extraordinarily well-informed Dhangar. The *Ovī* has the merit that it was sung in one stretch without much repetition and was thus completed within one night. An added advantage is that the *Ovī* is a nearly comprehensive statement of the relationship of the Hāṭkar Dhangars to their major god Khaṇḍobā through Bāṇāī/Bānubāī, who is said to belong to the Dhangars. Bānubāī is the second wife of Khaṇḍobā, but the myth also tells of the origin of the relationship with his first wife. A major centre of the Khaṇḍobā cult is Jejuri (Pune District). The myth of Khaṇḍobā and Bāṇāī is known in many cult places of Khaṇḍobā in Maharashtra and is sung in *padas* by Vāghyās and Muraḷīs, the special male and female devotees of Khaṇḍobā. Their songs are primarily meant for listeners from other, mostly settled, communities and not for the Hāṭkar Dhangars. One of the main themes in them is the relationship between the two wives, but not the events which lead to the marriage of Bānubāī with Khaṇḍobā. The myth has also been the subject of a very popular Marathi theatre play (*Khaṇḍobāce lagin*) produced by the Indian National Theater (Bombay), but this version is a modern—and no doubt successful—adaptation and de-emphasizes the religious and ritual meaning which the myth also has for the Hāṭkar Dhangars. Seen from this point of view the present version has a certain authenticity and preserves the essentials of the myth according to the notions of the Hāṭkar Dhangars.

3.1 The Language of the Text and Comments on the Translation

A linguistic analysis of the text is not the aim of this paper. The language, moreover, does not provide major difficulties beyond those which have been described previously (Sontheimer 1975b:83-110). To be noted is that the inherent */a/* of (S)M is mostly pronounced while singing, as in song-poetry generally. For example: *mā-nā-man-dī bo-la-to* //78// [(S)M: *bolto*].

I have transcribed the inherent /*a*/ only in passages or terms in 3.3.

The translation adopts a middle course between the order of words in the *Ovī* and the intelligibility of the *contents*, which is the main object of this paper. For this purpose punctuation was used only where absolutely necessary. To save space a consecutive, linear system of writing has been used instead of columns. The counting follows the system in Marathi *pothīs* numbering with //1// again after each 100 *caraṇas*. The reason again is mainly to save space. As has already been stated, each half of a *caraṇa* is repeated. In the cases where the second half is just a repetition, the translation is not repeated and the end of the *caraṇa* is marked with two vertical strokes (//). If the second line differs, this has been indicated by a single vertical stroke (/) after the first line.

3.2 Translation of the Ovī

//The remembrance [of God] is set //1// in the name of God [we sing his *Ovī*] //2// Yāmū and Khyāmū, the two brothers //3// Their means of living was enormous //4// Sheep, goats //5// A herd of horses //6// But there was no son //7// Yāmū said to Khyāmū: //8// "Look after our cattle wealth //9// I am off to somebody". //10// Away he went//11// The Mirdā of the *vāḍā* //12// For the sake of a son //13// Away he went //14// For the sake of a son //15// He went to the first forest //16// To the frightful forest //17// Demonesses were pounding [bones into] flour //18// Tigers and other wild-cats were lying about//19// She-bears were performing Phugaḍī dances //20// Thieves and robbers were shouting //21// Different kinds of snakes were writhing //22// Yāmū went on //23// He went on //24// Came into the [second] frightful forest //25// There was a temple //26// He said to himself: //27// "The god has to be served". //28// He took some branches of a tree //29// Swept the shrine //30// Had his bath and worshipped //31// Poured water over the god //32// Put flowers on the god //33// Many days passed //34// The god was in difficulty //35// After twelve years //36// The god said to Yāmū: //37// "What is it that you want?" //38// Yāmū said to the god: //39// "I have a lot of cattle //40// But no son. Give me a son". //41// The god said: //42// 'Sap from the ocean plant pour over me". //43// Yāmū went away //44//With a pot in this hand. //45// To the shore of the ocean //46// Who was in difficulty now?

//47// The lord, who creates and maintains //48// "I must give him a child". //49// In Indra's court //50// He said at that time: //51// "Drop one leaf / promise it to me. //52// Twelve years' service //53// He has done for me". //54// In Indra's court //55// The maid-servant of the god //56// The god let fall down, //57// The Raṃbhā of the god //58// A net of flowers //59// She became //60// On the shore of the ocean. //61// Yāmū took off his clothes //62// Entered the water //63// Splashed and struggled //64// Yāmū said to himself: //65// "If I take this thing, //66// If I place it on the god, how much light it will spread". //67// Yāmū went on swimming / Water waves //68// The net drifted ahead //69// Yāmū swam after it //70// Half into the ocean //71// The net would not come near //72// He was overpowered by fatigue //73// He could not swim further //74// The net was too far //75// "To reach the net //76// Is beyond me". //77//. He said to himself: //78// "I am born to die. //79// Let people say, he drowned. //80// Nobody is near me". //81// In his mind [was] the thought: //82// "Life is gone anyway". //83// He went on swimming. //84// The god was in a fix //85// He was puzzled: //86// "He wants to die". //87// He [Yāmū] reached the flower net //88// Brought it back //89// To the shore of the ocean //90// He performed the full ritual //91// He filled the spouted vessel with water //92// Came back //93// Returned to his temple //94// Poured water on his god //95// Worshipped //96// When the flower net unfolded //97// A girl was born. //98// The flower net //99// On the head of the god //100//

He placed. //1// Yāmū said to the god: //2// Why did you give a girl? //3// Was it in your fate //4// That it was to be a girl?" //5// He took her under his armpit //6// Held the girl to his stomach//7// By the same way //8// He wandered back //9// Returned. //10// Demonesses were pounding [bones] into flour //11// Ghosts were whistling //12// Thieves were shouting //13// Serpents were writhing //14// Female bears were dancing Phugaḍī dances //15// Yāmū went on //16//To his *vāḍā* //17// Near the *vāḍā* he thought: //18// "Twelve years have passed //19// My beard is as long as a winnowing basket //20// My hair as long as an arm //21// They will recognize me". //22// There was a dense thicket //23//In the middle of the thicket //24// He swept the floor //25// And camped //26// The girl started crying //27// There was no milk to drink //28// "How to feed her?"//29// He felt sad //30// The sound of crying //31// Reached the sheep //32// Hemū's [flock of] sheep //33// Grazing in the forest //34// There was a young ewe //35// She sniffed it out //36// A child was crying //37// She left the sheep //38// Came near the thicket //39// She sniffed //40// Came near //41// Yāmū was frightened: //42// "Some wild animal has come //43// It will carry away the child". //44// The sheep in the thicket //45// Yāmū recognized it //46// Said to himself: //47// "A virgin ewe //48// The miraculous deed of the god //49// Could it have milk?" //50//Then the milk broke forth //51// A stream of milk came //52// The girl started drinking //53// The crying stopped //54// He became happy //55// At sunset //56// The ewe would not return to the camp //57// He pondered //58// Went off //59// Took her under his armpit //60// Held her to his stomach //61// Yāmū went in front //62// The ewe followed him //63// The ewe was bleating //64// Near the *vāḍā* //65// Where did the [other] sheep go? //66// The shepherds drove out the sheep //67// Near the *vāḍā* //68// The sheep scattered //69// Yāmū went to the *vāḍā* //70// At that time the shepherds drove out the sheep //71// Yāmū went to the *vāḍā* //72// To the border of the *vāḍā* //73// He carried the girl in his arms //74// At midnight //75// What wonder happened? //76// The miracle of the god //77// The little child //78// A sky-high house //79// At that time //80// A three-storeyed house she built //81// At dawn //82// All the Gāvḍās got up //83// "What is this," they said //84// They started throwing stones //85// "What is this high thing?" //86// At the mirrors of the three-storeyed house //87// At the glass panes //88// At that time Yāmū said: //89// "Don't throw stones". //90// At that time //91// During the first rule of god/In the beginning of the Kaliyuga //92// People did not know houses [then] //93// People lived in tents //94// People lived in caves //95// The three-storeyed house //96// A resplendent Mahāl //97// O my little Woman! //98// Yāmū spoke //99// To the Gāvḍās of the *vāḍā*//200//

The Gāvḍās started asking: //1// "Who are you, to whom do you belong?" //2// Twelve years had passed //3// A beard as long as a winnowing fan //4// Hair as long as an arm //5// They would not recognize Yāmū //6// And questioned him //7// "I am Khyāmū's brother //8// The Mirdā of the *vāḍā* //9// My name is Yāmū".

//10// Joy filled the *vāḍā* //11// [And filled] all the Gāvḍās. //12// "From where is the child?"//13// "A gift of god". //14// The people in the *vāḍā* //15// Were happy //16// "Twelve years he was away. //17// After twelve years he came //18// Yāmū, our Mirdā.//19// A girl //20// God has given //21// Let us decide the name according to the horoscope". //22// They went to the Brāhmaṇ. //23// He looked up the horoscope.//24/ "Bānubāī she is named //25// The Mirdīn of the Twelve *Vāḍās* //26// She will become". //27// Thus said the Brāhmaṇ//28// They were happy //29// Came back //30// [Celebrated] the "fifth day after childbirth" //31// And [on the twelfth day] the "name-giving day" //32// Named her Bānu //33// The small child / became tall //34// Began to grow up //35// Twelve years passed //36// She employed the Gāvḍās //37// In different directions //38// She sent the *vāḍās* //39// They grazed the sheep //40// Where there fell rain //41// There would be grass //42// They grazed the sheep //43// [She was] the Lady of the Twelve *Vāḍās*. //44// The herd of the shepherds //45// When the *vāḍā* was at a certain place //46// He killed //47// At that time he grazed [?] //48// The god Khaṇḍobā //49// Decorated the Nandī //50// Covered him with the bodycloth //51// Put the ornaments on the horns //52// Fixed the little bells //53// Sat on the Nandī //54// Went off //55// To the terrific forest //56// Started wandering //57// To the river Tārāḷī //58// In the middle of the river //59// The Nandī stopped //60// A stone in the river sand/ Got stuck in his hoof //61// The Nandī stopped //62// He remembered //63// In the town of Pal //64// Tuḷsīrām, the Grocer //65// His daughter Mhāḷsā //66// He went into her dream //67// Started saying //68// To Mhāḷsābāī: //69// "In the river Tārāḷī //70// The Nandī got stuck //71// The *ārati* should be waved". //72// The woman filled the *ārati* plate //73// A silken wick / With a camphor flame //74// At midnight / She went out //75// To the river Tārāḷī / To the middle of the river //76// Waved [the *ārati* platter] around the Nandī //77// The stone in his hoof / Fell into the *ārati* platter //78// In the town of Pal //79// To the courtyard studded with mirrors //80// The Tuḷsī plant in front of the door //81// She went home //82// The stone on the *ārati* platter //83// She worshipped in the Tuḷsī shrine //84// She served "him" //85// To the town of Pal //86// At that time the god went //87// Said to Mhāḷsā: //88// "I shall make you my wife / Become my wife". //89// Mhāḷsā said to the god: //90// "I shall be your wife,

//91// But you have to win me". //92// "What is it, tell me?" //93// "Out of the leaves of the tamarind tree / Stitch a leaf-plate //94// With an unfired earthen pot / Bring water //95// A game of dice / You play with me //96// Five umpires should be called". //97// Thus the game was arranged //98// The game of dice //99// The first throw [of dice] was cast //300//

The first throw / Mhāḷsā lost //1// Mhāḷsā said: //2// "The first throw is invalid". //3// Thus, at that time //4// Her luck was reversed //5// When she threw //6// This time the god lost //7// He was to take the pot / Was to go to the water //8// He took the pot / Went to the water //9// To the river Dūdhanī / In the middle of the river //10// Washed and rinsed his mouth //11// Immersed the pot //12// The pot dissolved //13// He became angry / Filled with anger //14// He returned //15// Went to the tamarind tree //16// To the trunk of the tree //17// Began to make leaf-plates //18// But they could not be made //19// He started making leaf-cups//20//But they could not be made //21// He became angry //22// He remembered //23// That a bride should be brought //24// He went away //25// In search of [another] bride //26// He went to a stable //27// To a horse stable //28// Searched the stable //29// But he could not find a horse //30// He went to a second and a third stable //31// But he would not find a horse //32// He went to a sixth and a seventh stable //33// But he could not find a horse //34// It struck him / He remembered //35// In the mountain cave [there is] a horse //36// At the opening of the cave //37// There was a rock like a dish //38// How to remove the rock? //39// The miracle of the god //40// The hand in the [magic] pouch / A handful of *bhaṇḍār* //41// He threw / He flung //42// The rock toppled over //43// He tied his turban //44// Around his waist //45// He went into the cave //46// Silken ropes //47// He tied to the horse //48// He brought water //49// Washed the horse and it looked spick and span //50// He examined the horse //51// On its back a *śāḷuṅkhā*//52// At its tail a *pucavarā* //53// At its navel a diamond //54// On its forehead sandalpaste //55// The horse attracted his attention //56// A horse with five auspicious marks //57// He put on the felt and saddle //58// Secured it with the red girth //59// Tied ornaments on the mane //60// Put on the pronged bridlebits //61// Put on the stirrups to support the feet //62// Sat on the horse //63// The neck with the whip //64//

With the whip he hit it //65// Went into the sky //66// Hegāḍe Pardhān accompanied him //67// "He is gone off and away //68// On the way to the forest". //69// As he went ahead //70// Mhāḷsābāī //71// saw the god //72// "The god is on his way //73// How to make him come back?" //74// The form of a woman //75// Who carried kindling [she took] //76// Came across his path//77// The god passed her //78// Went ahead //79// The form of a Mahār woman //80// With [a load of] cow dung on her head //81// She took and came across his path //82// The god passed her //83// Went ahead //84// The form of a Māḷī woman //85// With a flower basket on her head //86// She took and came across his path //87// The god passed her //88// Mhāḷsā said: //89// "He does not recognize me".//90// The form of Mhāḷsā //91// She took and came across his path //92// The god passed her //93// He was filled with anger //94// She held the bridle: //95// "God , where are your off to?" //96// "I am in search of a bride //97// I shall bring a bride". //98// That much he said //99// Mhāḷsā said: //400//

"If something happens to you //1// How shall I know? //2// Give me a sign". //3// "If the ring on your toe / pinches you //4// If the pearls on your neck / Fall down //5// If the red dot on your forehead / turns black //6// Then something is happening to me/ Something is about to happen //7// This will be my sign". //8// The god went on //9// To the frightful forest //10// The god became thirsty //11// Thus Hegaḍyā Pardhān //12// In search of water //13// Took a pot //14// Nowhere was there water //15// Came to the god: //16// "Nowhere is there water". //17// "My throat is dry //18// If you bring water //19// My life will go on //20// Go and search for water". //21// Hegaḍe Pardhān //22// Went in search of water //23// Nowhere was there water //24// There was a thick grove //25// In the middle of the grove //26// A huge cobra //27// Was entangled in the thicket //28// Entangled it had died //29// It hung upside down //30// In the hollow of a rock the saliva //31// Saliva dripped //32// Poison flowed //33// It was filled to the brim //34// Hegaḍe Pardhān //35// Went to look for water //36// Saw the hollow in the rock //37// Plunged the pot into it //38// Came back //39// The god had fallen asleep //40// "How to wake him up?" //41// Put it beside his pillow //42// Mhāḷsābāī //43// The ring on her toe / Pinched her toe //44// The pearls on her neck //45// Fell down from her neck //46// She looked into the mirror //47// At the red mark on her forehead //48// Mhāḷsā thought //49// "The god has died". //50// Mhāḷsā took //51// The form of a kite //52// Flapped her wings //53// Rose into the sky //54// Flapped wildly //55// The pot toppled over //56// From his sleep //57// The god awoke at that time //58// He was filled with anger //59// He shot an arrow //60// Brought her down to the earth //61// Her head was flung away //62// Mhāḷsābāī //63// [In] the form of the crab //64// For water she dug //65// A heap of earth she scratched out //66// He was filled with anger //67// He did not drink the water. //68// He went on //69// "Hegaḍe Pardhān, //70// Go and search for water". //71// Hegaḍe Pardhān went //72// There was a Dhangar //73// Grazing sheep and goats //74// Hegaḍe Pardhān //75// Asked the Dhangar: //76// "Where is there water?" //77// The Dhangar was mad //78// He ignored him //79// Would not tell [where there is] water //80// He went back / To the god //81// Hegaḍe Pardhān //82// Said to the god //83// A black Dhangar, thin like a stick //84// I asked him for water //85// And he would not tell [where there is] water //86// He attacked [me] //87// He was mad". //88// [Hegaḍe Pardhān] collected dry cow dung //89// Heated the branding rod //90// Branded the Dhangar //91// Branded [him] on the forehead //92// Then the Dhangar said: //93// "O god, I will tell you [where there is] water //94// Towards the sun //95// At Candanpur is Bānubāī's *vāḍā* //96// There you will get water". //97// Hegaḍe Pardhān //98// Took a pot //99// Went off //500//

To Bānubāī's *vāḍā* //1// "Please give us water //2// The god is thirsty //3// The god's throat is dry //4// He is very thirsty". //5// Hastily she got up//6// Bānubāī got up //7// Her own pot //8// She cleaned and //9// Filled with water //10// "Hegaḍe Pardhān //11// Go to the god //12// Give him water". //13// Hegaḍe Pardhān //14// Took the pot //15// Went to the god //16// The god drank the water //17// Became peaceful //18// The god looked at the pot //19// On the pot //20// Bānubāī's name //21// The god said: //22// "Hegaḍyā Pardhān, //23// Go back home //24// Alone I will go ahead".//25// Khaṇḍū, the god //26// At that time changed his form //27// An old, infirm man

//28// A decrepit, sick horse //29// A sore as long as an arm on the back [of the horse] //30// He walked on pulling the horse behind him //31// To Bānubāī's *vāḍā* //32// Ghule and Mogare, the dogs, were chained up//33// The dogs got loose //34// Fell onto the god / Onto the old man //35// The old man fell / On the thorny fence //36// Bānubāī saw it //37// The Gāvḍinīs of the *vāḍā* //38// Began to shout curses //39// The dogs kept onto the old man //40// Bit the old man //41// She [Bānubāī] shouted curses //42// "Where are you from, old man," //43// Bānubāī asked //44// "I came in search of work //45// I want to serve //46// I want to stay here/ And serve". //47// It was evening time //48// The Gāvḍās gathered //49// "What work can you do?" //50// "Whatever you say, I shall do". //51// "We will tell you what [to do] //52// Sweep the whole *vāḍā* //53// On one heap throw [the droppings of the sheep] //54// That is your work". //55// When dawn broke //56// At nine o'clock //57// The sheep started moving out //58// The old man just sat / In the shadow of the fence //59// In the afternoon //60// The Gāvḍinīs looked //61// "How is the old man's work". //62// He would not work //63// Did not sweep the *vāḍā* //64// In the afternoon //65// The miracle of the god //66// In the [magic] pouch the hand / A handful of *bhaṇḍār* //67// He flung //68// [The dirt of] the *vāḍā* collected //69// Flew on the heap //70// The Gāvḍinīs saw it //71// "Just now he had not yet swept the *vāḍā* //72// How quickly he has swept it". //73// Bānubāī, the Mirdīn //74// "The fellow is good," //75// Bānubāī said //76// At sunset //77// All the Gāvḍās gathered //78// "What work will there be tomorrow?" //79// Bānubāī said //80// At sunset //81// All the Gāvḍās gathered //82// "What work will there be tomorrow?" //83// "The sheep he should drive". //84// "I shall go with the sheep //85// Alone I shall go //86// I don't want you". //87// The sheep he drove //88// Nine lakhs of ewes / Nine lakhs of lambs //89// Not counting the barren ewes //90// A hot day //91// There was no grass for the sheep //92// He took the sheep //93// The miracle of the god / The miracle of Bhagavān //94// The hand in the magic pouch / A handful of *bhaṇḍār* //95// He flung //96// Here and there //97// Grass had sprouted //98// The sheep were fed //99// At evening time //600//

The Gāvḍās said: //1// The old man is a great trickster //2// The lambs which they had pushed away //3// The mothers have accepted now //4// "What work will there be tomorrow? //5// He has to be told to do some other work //6// For the lambs an enclosure //7// How will he bring the thorny bushes [for it] //8// We want to watch". //9// The god left //10// A blunt axe in his hand //11// He took it and went //12// He hacked at the thorny bushes //13// But they could not be cut //14// The miracle of the god / The miracle of Bhagavān //15// The hand into the pouch / A handful of *bhaṇḍār* //16// He assembled the host of spirits //17// All the bushes they cut //18// Threw them amongst the lambs //19// All the lambs/they killed //20// They got entangled in the thorny bushes //21// At sunset //22// The ewes came to the *vāḍā* //23// Calling for their lambs //24// "Why has he done so/ What has happened ?" //25// They told Bānubāī: //26// "He has killed all the lambs". //27// She was grieving //28// Bānubāī //29// "What kind of service does he do? //30// My lambs have to be brought back to life". //31// The miracle of the god / The miracle of Bhagavān //32// The hand in the [magical pouch] / A handful of *bhaṇḍār* //33// He flung //34// The lambs came back to life //35// Suckled at the teats //36// Six months passed //37// "What work tomorrow," //38// They asked Bānubāī //39// "You wash the sheep". //40// Said Bānubāī. //41// During the morning time //42// Nine or ten o'clock //43// The sheep had left //44// The Gāvḍās told the old man: //45// "The sheep should go for bathing". //46// To Bānubāī they said: //47// "You follow us //48// And bring an offering //49// To the washing place". //50// The sheep went //51// The Gāvḍās washed the sheep //52// The miracle of the god / The miracle of Bhagavān //53// In the magical pouch the hand / A handful of *bhaṇḍār* //54// He flung //55// The sheep he killed //56// Of the flesh a heap //57// Of the skin a heap //58// Of the heads a heap [he made] //59// The river turned red //60// As a red stream flowed [into it] //61// Bānubāī came //62// With an offering. //63// Nine lakhs of lambs / Nine lakhs of ewes //64// Not counting the barren ones //65// That many sheep he killed //66// Bānubāī said: //67// "What has happened?" //68// She threw herself on the floor //69// Rolling over and over //70// She cried loudly: //71// "What has happened? //72// Who has done this ? //73// My wealth he destroyed. / My livestock he killed". //74// She cried loudly //75// The old man went //76// To Bānubāī //77// Said to Bānubāī: //78// "Listen to me for a moment //79// I shall bring your sheep to life //80// What will you give me?" //81// "What do you want to take ? //82// Whatever you ask for / I shall give". //83// "Promise me" //84// "Promised". //85// "With the turmeric pouch around my neck / The *koṭamā* in my hand //86// I came to your *vāḍā* / For *you* I have come. //87// I shall make you my wife //88// Do not say 'no' //89// I shall bring your sheep to life". //90// "I agree to it. //91// I shall marry you //92// Bring my sheep to life". //93// The miracle of the god //94// The hand in the magical pouch / A handful of *bhaṇḍār* //95// "Seven Crores, Seven Crores," he roared //96// Threw the turmeric powder / Flung the turmeric powder //97// All of them [were] as before / The sheep //98// The stream of blood disappeared //99// She was weeping/ Started laughing //700//

Bānubāī laughed //1// To her *vāḍā* / She went //2// In the early morning //3// She got up to grind grain //4// The god then got up //5// The god took his former shape //6// The black and brown horse //7// He made it as before //8// He became the former *avatār* //9// He took hold of Bānubāī /Placed her on the horse //10// And rode away //11// In the early morning //12// Bānubāī said: //13// "Don't take me away like this, O God //14// What about us? //15// What will they say about me? //16// She ran away //17// With an old man. //18// The Mirdīn of the Twelve *Vāḍās* //19// Let her go to the place she belongs to //20// Let us arrange for a marriage / Let us marry here //21// Let us marry and go". //22// At evening time //23// The marriage was ready //24// "What is the marriage band?" //25// "At evening time //26// The ewes will come to their lambs [bleating] //27// That is our marriage band". //28// "What are the grains of rice?" //29// "The droppings of the sheep". //30// At evening time //31// The marriage was arranged //32// The droppings of the sheep as grains of rice //33// The god distributed them [among the Gāvḍās] //34// The ewes came to the lambs //35// The marriage of the god took place //36// In Bānubāī's *vāḍā* //37// In those times //38// They started weeping //39// All the Gāvḍās //40// "Our chief is going //41// What shall we do? //42// The sheep are in our possession //43// How shall we meet again?" //44// "I tell you, listen //45// With a bag of turmeric powder around your neck //46// In your hand the *koṭamā* //47// On your shoulder the *laṅgar* //48// You should take //49// On Somavati Āmuśā //50// Every six months //51// To our Darbār //52// You will come //53// You will offer *bhaṇḍār* and *khobāra* //54// And meet us //55// From generation to generation". //56// He gave them a common name //57// "The Dhangar *samāj* //58// Of Bānubāī's *got*". //59// The two went away //60// When they had gone half way //61// Daityas confronted them //62// A big battle took place //63// The god killed them //64// He brought the Daityas //65// He brought us //66// The Daityas said: //67// "Give us something to remember //68// Give us a *mān* //69// Our name will be remembered". //70// "You will eat [meat] //71// I am a Liṅgāyat grocer //72// The people of Bānubāī's *got* //73// Will break the chain //74// They will make me famous //75// They will give pure offerings / Will break coconuts [for me] //76// At the back they will offer sheep //77// The offering for you / The offering of sheep". //78// From there they went and came //79// To the nine lakhs of steps //80// To Kaḍi Paṭār //81// Mhāḷsābāī saw him coming with Bānubāī //82// Towards the Kaḍi Paṭār //83// Mhāḷsābāī saw //84// Anger filled her //85// She came running //86// And came across them half way //87// She took two stones //88// "With these two stones / I shall break your head," //89// Mhāḷsā said to Bānubāī //90// "You cannot come up //91// You should stay in the fort of Jejuri //92// In the lower half of the fort". //93// There is now //94// Bānubāī's temple //95// Near the goats and sheep //96// In the fort of Jejuri. //97// He gave a *mān* //98// On the six months' Āmuśā //99// On Somavati Āmuśā //800//

The *jatrā* gathers //1// From the olden days //2// It will go on //3// Bānubāī's *got* //4// The Dhangar *samāj* //5// A Liṅgāyat Vāṇī //6// The god is a Vāṇī //7// For the Dhangars how is it? //8// They are of Bānubāī's *got* //9// Therefore, very much so //10// Because of his attachment to Bānubāī //11// The god is a Dhangar, too //12// First he was of the Vāṇīs //13// At his neck a bag of turmeric powder / In his hand a *koṭamā* //14// The god went mad //15// On account of Bānubāī //16// He is a mad man, my Mhalārī //17// They shout "Yeḷkoṭ" now //18// A mad man, Mhalārī //19// From then onwards //20// The marriage takes place at the *vāḍā* //21// Ever since they have dedicated Vāghyās and Muraḷīs //22// Before it was not so //23// Having brought Bānubāī //24// Ever since they have arranged *jāgraṇ* //25// They sacrifice sheep //26// What happened then / Now still goes on //27// Finished is our / god's *kittā* //28//

3.3 Notes

1: *Sumbarāna māṇḍala.* (S)M: *maṇḍilā,* literally, "the memory or remembrance [of God] is set." This is the usual beginning of an *Ovī* of the Dhangars in Maharashtra. Cp. Skt. *smaraṇa* and Kabīr's *sumirān* "mental prayer" (Vaudeville 1974: 140).—Cp. Pandey 1982: 9, where the story is begun with a "prayer" (*sumiran*) to Rām and Durgā.

12: Mirdā, (S)M: Mirdhā, is an old word for the overseer of a village (Molesworth), here of a *vāḍā,* which means in the context of Dhangar life "a more or less fixed or temporary settlement of herdsmen", "a herdsman's camp on migration", or "a sheep-fold".

19: *vāgā vagrā* = (S)M *vāgh* and Skt. *vyāghrā.* Such double words indicate variety. Cp. 22; *sapāsarpā,* (S)M *sāp* and Skt. *sarpa.*

20: There are various forms of Phugadi (pl. *phugaḍyā*) dances which are normally performed by girls or young women, e.g. during the Hoḷī festival. Two or four girls hold each other's hands crosswise, lean back and dance in a circle (Devdhar 1906; 219ff.).

31: The term used is *aṅgūl aśtyāna,* cp. (S)M *aṅghoḷ anuṣṭhān* = "ablution and worship of a certain deity" (cp. Molesworth *aṅghoḷ* and *anuṣṭhān*).

40: *jingānī* means literally "livelihood" or "means of support", but in the pastoral context of the Dhangars it also assumes the meaning of "cattle-wealth", "cattle", cp. 4 and 9.

43: *samindrasākoca,* cp. (S)M *samudraśok:* a creeping plant, *Convolvulus argenteus,* used medically (see Molesworth and *Gazetteer of Bombay State, Botany, Pt. I,* 1953: 28). This plant grows outside villages in the Deccan and the Konkan and *not* "on the shore of the ocean" (46). But Yāmū will find something else more important on the shore of the ocean, namely Bāṇāī (97ff.).

112: Jhuṭiṅg or Jhoṭiṅg is the spirit of a dead person wandering as a goblin, sometimes the spirit of a deceased Muslim. But in some places the spirit has been laid to rest and given a cult and has become a respectable deity, as near Mhasvaḍ (Satara District).

181: *tina tāḷa māḍī.* Literally "an upper-storey of a house with three storeys". The singer mixes up *tīn tāḷ* which could refer to "the three storeys of the world" with *māḍī* = "upper storey", but what he wants to convey is clear: a tremendously high house with three storeys.

183: Gāvḍā is an old, disappearing name for the Dhangar pastoralists. Note that the narrator switches over more and more to the term Dhangar. The name comes from the Ka. Gauḍā—a member of a caste of cultivators and cattle-breeders. (See further Sontheimer 1976; 159 *et passim*).

222: *nāvarasa tijī bagāicī* = (S)M *nāvrās ticī baghāycī.* See 224.

224: *nāvarasī bagtyāta* = (S)M *nāvraśī baghtāt.* He looked up the *nakṣatra* name or the name of the child according to the horoscope (See further Sontheimer 1976a: 144).

226: *bārā vāḍyā mīrdi* = (S)M *bārā vāḍyāncī mirdhīn.* The title describes Bāṇāī/Bānubāī as the head of the twelve endogamous groups of pastoralists living in one of twelve different settlements, camps or villages. *Vāḍī* or *vāḍā* may also appear as *haṭṭi/hāṭa, pāḍī/pāḍā,* meaning "pen" or "fold" or "pastoral village" (Cp. *DED* 3199 and 3309). The term also occurs in the oral myths of pastoralists in Karnataka and Andhra. For instance, we hear in the myth of Mallanna, a pastoralist deity, prevalent in Andhra and of a settlement inhabited by twelve Paṭṭi Kāpūs, who are farmers with a pastoralist background. Nowadays this term is elusive and to my knowledge is found in Maharashtra only in the oral traditions of the Dhangars. See Sontheimer 1976: 124-6. However, in the Hindi epic *Lorikī,* which is situated in the pastoral context of the Ahīr herdsmen of Uttar Pradesh, the "twelve hamlets" (*bārah pālī*) of Gauṛagaḍh are mentioned (Pandey 1982: 34)

231: *pāca divsā pācavī* = (S)M *pācavyā divsā[lā] pācavī. Pācavī* is the fifth day after parturition, on which the goddess is worshipped.

232: *bārasa* = The ceremony of naming a child on the twelfth day after its birth.

246-59: The story falters here a little. The singer probably wanted to make a premature reference to the deeds of the god Khaṇḍobā, who will later on watch and kill the sheep of Bānubāī, before he proceeded to tell of Khaṇḍobā's encounter with his first wife, Mhāḷsā. The text runs as follows:

vāḍā yākā yā jāgyālā //46//

mārāyālā yā pāḍalī //47//
cāranī tavhā māṇḍalī // 48//
dyāvayācā [?] khaṇḍubāna //49//
mendī [nandī?] tyāna sajīvala //50//

262ff.: The story differs from the usual tradition, which makes Mhāḷsā the daughter of Timmaśeṭ, a rich Liṅgāyat merchant from Nevasa near Paithan. Cp. Dhere 1961: 50-2.

280: *kāsūbandī*, better = *kācabandī* = inlaid with glass, mirrors (Bābar 1973: 57).

289: The present version of the encounter seems to be confined to the Dhangars. *sogai mi bī karnāra... mājī sogai vhavāva. Sogai* means "close marital relationship". See *sagai* (Molesworth) and *sogayā* (Bābar 1973: 360).

294: It is an impossible task, because the leaves of the tamarind tree are too small.

336: *bhoiryā* = (S)M *bhuyār* = "a subterraneous cavity", especially in a hilly region (Molesworth). Cp. Sontheimer 1984: 162.

352: *saluṅkā* = (S)M *sāḷuṅkhā*. The stone in the center of which the *liṅgam* of Śiva is placed.

353: *pucavarā*, perhaps Skt. *puccha* + *camara* = a flywhisk serving as a kind of decoration for the tail of a horse.

357: *pañcakhalānya* = (S)M *pañcakalyāṇī*. The five auspicious marks are: the four legs white up to the knees and a blaze on the forehead (Molesworth).

367: Hegāḍe Pardhān = Ka. Hegaḍe and (S)M Pradhān is a double word, both meaning "minister". Sometimes, as in Jejuri (Pune District) and in Devaragudda, near Ranebennur in Karnataka, he is identified with Viṣṇu. "Hegaḍyā" (523) is a more intimate and slightly condescending form of "Hegaḍe". See also Dhere 1961: 55-7, on the background of Hegaḍe Pradhān.

389-92: The instant "cure" seems to be based on the method which Dhangars employ to cure sheep by branding them at the spot where the source of illness is suspected.

338: Gāvḍīn and Mirdīn (561) are the feminine forms of Gāvḍā and Mirdā [(S)M Mirdhā].

602: *cāravḍā*: *cār* m. pl. = "light habits, mischievous or idle tricks, pranks, frolics" (Molesworth).

674: *daulata* = wealth: *jinagānī* = livestock.

686: *koṭamā* = (S)M *koṭambā* is a small, rectangular or square wooden begging bowl used by the Vāghyās, the special devotees of Khaṇḍobā.

696: "Seven Crores" = *yeḷkoṭ(i)* (Ka.) is the famous epithet of Khaṇḍobā and refers to the seven crores of hosts constituting Khaṇḍobā's army in his fight against the demon Malla (hence Khaṇḍobā is called Mallāri) or to the seven crores of hosts serving Malla in his fight against Khaṇḍobā, but who become his devotees (cp. Sontheimer 1987: 20).

748: *laṅgara* is the heavy chain carried by the Vāghyās and other devotees which is ritually broken (774) during the festivals for Khaṇḍobā and Mailāra (see Sontheimer 1981: 16; 1984: 156).

750ff: Somạvati Āmuśā = (S)M Somvatī Amāvāsyā. The new moon day which falls on a Monday and is celebrated with a great *jatrā* (801-2), a folk pilgrimage festival.

754: *khobāra* = (S)M *khobareṃ*. Pieces of coconut kernel which are usually mixed with *bhaṇḍār,* turmeric powder.

758: *samāja* is a modern version of the older term *jāti,* which tends to become deprecated (cp. 805).

769: *māna* is a privilege which entitles devotees to perform certain rituals in the cult of the deity.

773: *gota* = relatives, kinfolk, caste, community.

781: Kaḍi Paṭār or (S)M Kaḍe Paṭhār is the name of the plateau or the mountaintop at Jejuri (District Pune). It is the original place from which the god later moved down to a lower hill, on which the more recent temple complex, called Gaḍkoṭ ("Fort"), is situated.

817: Mhalārī is a variant of Malhārī, Mallāri, i.e. Khaṇḍobā.

825: *jāgraṇ* is a festival in honour of Khaṇḍobā celebrated after a marriage and visit to the family deity Khaṇḍobā. Vāghyās and Muraḷīs, the male and female devotees, dance and sing the deeds of Khaṇḍobā before a temporary shrine consisting of a wooden board over which four stalks of sugar cane are tied together at the upper end. The particular ceremony is called *ghaṭa sthāpana* as two copper pots, representing Śiva and Śakti, are placed on a heap of wheat. The pots are crowned with coconuts. Flower garlands are hung over the pots.

828: *kittā,* better (S)M *kissā.* In the speech of the singer /s/ is often replaced by /t/, e.g. *phaksa* instead of (S)M *phakta.* Between vowels /s/ tends to become /t/, e.g. the deity

Mhasobā is in some places called Mhatobā. (Sontheimer 1976:176) *Kissā* means "a story, an account, history, or *bakhar*" (Dāte).

4 LIṂBĀ'S STORY

The story was told in August 1966 by Liṃbā Bāḷku Torve, a nomadic Hāṭkar Dhangar, then aged about 50-60 years. He died during the migration of his *vāḍā* (see *Ovī* 12 and note) to the Konkan in 1977. He was a respected *devruṣi*, that is, a medium of several Dhangar gods. The events which led to his becoming a *devruṣi* have been told elsewhere (Sontheimer 1976: 141ff.). The present story is a version of the myth of Khaṇḍobā and Bāṇāī. The Dhangars have simply called it Liṃbā's story (*Liṃbācī goṣṭ*) and I have retained this as its title (LS). The story was told during the night at a monsoon camp of the Hāṭkar Dhangars. It was occasionally interrupted by peals of laughter from the listening Dhangars, adults as well as children. The narrator asked for somebody to follow his story with an occasional "*huṃ*". This mode of expressing one's attention to a story is, of course, found wherever stories are told. The person who made the sound *huṃkār* is called "the one who makes *huṃ*" (*huṃkār deṇārā*). In this case it was Mādhav Mhanvar, a leader of the *vāḍā* on account of his many abilities and dignified behaviour.

A second recording was made one year later (SR). It did not yield any major variations. We have, however, referred to some of them which supplement the meaning of the text.

4.1 THE LANGUAGE OF THE TEXT AND COMMENT ON THE TRANSLATION

As in the case of the *Ovī* the text provides no special linguistic peculiarities beyond those stated in a previous article (Sontheimer 1975b: 89ff.). The characteristic intonation of the narrator, sometimes in a kind of a singsong, and his low voice, as well as "archaic" terms, require some practice for outsiders to understand him. When the narrator wanted to stress a point he raised his voice and his pronunciation approached (S)M.—The translation tries to make a compromise between the original diction of the story and readability.

4.2 Translation of Limbā's Story

At that time, what happened, Mahāraj? Khaṇḍubā [and] Mhāḷsā, what did they do? Mhāḷsā [and] Khaṇḍobā were sitting side by side—somewhere. At that time they used to sit like this somewhere every day. Hegaḍi Pardhān, his brother-in-law,[1] said: "...your mother,[2] one has to do something to make them bear a grudge against each other". What did the Pardhān do? He came running to Bhoḷā.[3] Bhoḷā said: "Goodness me, Pardhān, why have you come?" "How shall I tell you, my God: the god has asked for the game of dice".[4] "Is it so?" he said, "Yes, so it is", he said. "Ah, what kind of game of dice," he thought, "he has come to instigate some quarrel. Why should he take along the game of dice?" So what did he do? He said: "Alright, now that you have come, pick up these two dice and take them along". What did he do? He picked up the two dice and took them along. He came to the god. "Heh, God, heh, my God". "What are you saying ?" "See, I have brought something to entertain you!" "What is it?" "The game of dice. You just sit there idly and keep quiet. If you play this, it will entertain you". He said: "Good that you brought it. Ah, it's good". To himself he said: "...your mother, he has brought a quarrel into the house. What sort of game has he brought? Well, now that he has brought it, it's alright". Now, Mahāraj, what happened? He threw the game before the god. The god picked it up. What happened now? The god had his bath and performed the rituals and he was to play the game. The god went to play, sat down for the game. For the first throw he called *five.* The throw was *two-and-a-half.* He called *ten*, it was *five.* Now he called *fifteen*, and it was *ten.* Again he called *twenty*, it turned up *fifteen.* Again he called *twenty-five.* It turned up *twenty.* Now the god's turn was over and it was Mhāḷsā's turn. What did Mhāḷsā do? She had her bath and made her toilette, drew a circle,[5] put on her yellow sari, entered the circle of the game of dice with her right foot first, and sat down to play. For the first throw she called *one-and-a-quarter.* It was *two-and-a-half.* Then she called *two-and-a-half.* The throw was *five.* Then she called *five.* The throw was *ten.* Then she called *ten.* It was *fifteen.* Then she called *fifteen.* The throw was *twenty.* Then she called *twenty.* The throw was *twenty-five.* Her turn was over. "Now, oh God," she said, "What shall we do? We should count the throws which we have played so far". "Ah, what is there to count? Someone must have made more points—is there any use of this now?" "Fie, fie", she said, "don't lose your temper and cheat. What is true, will become true. One has to count who has more points. That has to be checked". He said, "...your mother! Check it, do what you want to do". "If I have won more points, you will have to put off whatever you wear. If you have won more points than me, then I shall bring and offer you water in an unfired pot". "I see", he said. "Yes", she said, "how much did you call?" "...your mother, I called *five*". "Then how much did it turn up?" "*Two-and-a-half*, I think". "What did you call then?" "I called *ten*". And how much did it turn up?" "It turned up *five*". "Then how much did you call?" "I called *fifteen*". "How much did it turn up?" "It turned up *ten*". "Then how much did you call?" "I called *twenty*. It turned up *fifteen*. I called *twenty-five* and it turned up *twenty*. Finished is our count". She said: "Well, your count is over, now watch my count". "Well, count. What is your count?" "I called *one-and-a-quarter*. It turned up *two-and-a-half*. Oh God, take off what you have on your head". "It's my turban," he said. "Take it off". He took it off. "Oh God, I said *two-and-a-half*. It turned up *five*. Take off what you have on your body". He said: "It's my coat".[6] "Take it off". He took it off. "What did I call now? I called *five*. It turned up *ten*. Oh God, take off what is around your waist". He said: "It's my waist-cord".[7] "Take it off. How much did I call then? I called *fifteen*. It turned up *twenty*. Oh God, what are you wearing on your finger?" "It's a golden ring". 'Take it off and put it down". The god put it down. "Then I said *twenty*. It turned up *twenty-five*. Oh God, what do you have on your left ankle?" "It's my anklet". He took off his anklet and put it down. Then she said: "Oh God, who has more points?" "You, certainly," he said. "I have more points, oh God, and you have taken off everything, but take off the leather bag on your shoulder too and put it down.'' "Fie, fie," he said, "I won't take off my leather bag ". "Why, oh God," she said, "take it off and put it down". "Fie, fie," he said "do what you want, but I won't put it down. That bag, small like the length of my finger, I need to fill my belly". "With this bag, small like the length of a finger, you will make Vāghyās and Muraḷīs perform the whole night, they will perform *jāgraṇ*.[8] In your name they will sing songs the whole night. There will be *jāgraṇs* [with the help of it]. "The god did not take off and put down his leather bag. He took his flagstaff and begging-bag[9] and went away sulking—where?—to his court. The god went to sleep in his court. When he fell asleep he saw Bāṇāī in his dream. What did he tell the Pardhān? "Ah, ah, Pardhān! Quick! Call the carpenter. A human being has entered this sandalwood pillar". "Ah, oh God, have you become mad or what? How could a human being have entered the sandalwood pillar? Your belly must have swollen up with urine, you must have slept on your back and had a bad dream. How could a human being have possibly entered the pillar?" "How do I know? . . . your mother. But I must have dreamt that someone entered it". "Ah , did you go to piss?" "Of course, I went. I must have gone. To the capacity of a whole ditch [I pissed], and enough, as it were, for a horse to drink". "Is that true or false?" "Ah, truly it was filled". "Well, whatever you have done, is done". What happened now, Mahārāj, while the god was thus sulking, he said: "Pardhān, call the people of this town. After calling them we shall go hunting. Let's go, let's go hunting". Then what did he do? He loaded the cannons and guns. He called the people of the town: "Come, the god is going to go hunting." There was an army of 12,000 men. He was on his way. He left the fort of Jejuri.[10] And the army came down. While he was on his way [he noticed that] he had forgotten the betel leaves. So he told Hegaḍi Pardhān: "Ah, Pardhān, go and get the betel leaves for us". He went back to fetch the betel leaves. Mahār women carrying kindling met him. As they came carrying kindling Mhāḷsā saw them from above [the fort]. "Ah," she said, "the god is on his way sulking. Meet the god, women, take loads of kindling and take five empty pots. Make the god return". The Mahār women said: "Ah, woman, let the god sulk and let Bāṇāī come with her arms loaded with bangles,[11] what do we lose thereby?" "Well and good," she said, "women, don't go. I shall attack you with the smoke of red chillies, I shall burn your huts and I shall blast you with the smoke of chillies". Now, there was an old Mahār woman who said: "If Mhāḷsā has made such a great god sulk how will she have any regard for *you*? Let's go and meet him". So what happened? Some carried baskets of cow dung on their heads, some of them carried bundles of kindling, some of them carried empty pots on their heads and they met the god. The god came from the other side. Hegaḍi Pardhān saw them. "Ah, my God, there is a bad omen for us". "What is it?" "Oh dear, empty pots, loads of kindling and baskets of cow dung are coming. It's a very bad omen for us". "Ah, go and bring what I have told you to bring. We will use the empty pots for drinking water, the cow dung we will use for building a fire, and the kindling we can use for starting a fire. If they give them to us, take them". What did he do? He flung the powerful *bhaṇḍār*[12] and the pots were filled with honey. The cow dung became cakes. The kindling became sugar cane. And the Pardhān went up to them and asked: "Good women, will you give us your loads?" "Of course, we will give them to you, dear fellow". When they threw the loads down from their heads, they became sugar cane. The Mahār women changed their minds and said: "Dear fellow, you won't have that, ah, from place to place, on this and that place where sugar cane is made into sugar, we have collected piece for piece. We are taking them to our children and who would give them to you?" As it happened they changed their minds. Now he went to the cow dung cakes. "Well, my good women, will you give me these baskets?" "Ah, my dear fellow, if you want to take them, we will give them to you". Then when the women put down their loads and looked at them closely they all turned out to be baked cakes. "My dear fellow," they said, "what is there you could possibly take? Going from door to door, waiting in the doorway, taking one offering here and one offering there, in this way we have collected them and are taking them to our children. Why should we then give them to you?" Now "Bābā" went to the empty pots. "Ah, my good women, will you give me your pots?" "Yes, of course, Bābā, we want to give them to you," they said. Now when they put the pots down, they found them filled with honey. "Ah, Bābā, our pots are filled with honey. Ripping open crevices, pulling away stones, bushes and trees, looking for honey here and there, we have collected a little from here, a little from there and we are taking it for our children to eat. So, why should we give it to you?" So it happened. They also changed their minds. But what happened then? He said: "Give me at least one pot according to your promise". Then he got one pot. He went to the cakes and said: "Give me at least five cakes". He got five cakes. He went to the sugar cane, took five canes and went to the god.

"Come, my God, do you want to be beaten with a stick?" "What do you say?" "Do you want to be beaten with a stick? Don't you hear what I say? Do you want to eat a piece of sugar cane?" "Did you speak of a piece of sugar cane? Yes, I want it," he said, "bring it". He took it. Then, Bābā, what happened? He put the pot in the middle of the square and performed a *jāgraṇ*. He tied four stalks of sugar cane over the square, hung a string of cakes underneath. The whole night he performed *jāgraṇ*. Thus the *jāgraṇ* was performed. Then afterwards what happened? The god went hunting. Started hunting. The first time he shouted. His shouting made the forest tremble. The second time he shouted. Trees and bushes were shaken. The third time he shouted. Cliffs and rocks loosened. The fourth time he shouted. He chased herds of animals. The fifth time he shouted [SR: he rounded up the herds of game: sambhar, spotted deer and wild boar] and began to hunt. The sixth time he shouted. He made heaps of the hunted animals. He piled the meat on a wooden scaffold. The god started hunting. Then the army of twelve thousand became thirsty. They became very thirsty. Nowhere was there water and the army of 12,000 went back to the fort of Jejuri. What did the god do? He sat on a black rock and said to the Pardhān: "Ah, I have my life in my mouth. I am thirsty, there is no water at all". The Pardhān looked all over the rock, looked for a well, for a river. There was no water anywhere. When he climbed a big hill, it happened that a cobra had died there. Its saliva flowed thick as a finger into a stream and filled a ditch. ". . . mother," he said, "there is water". He went quickly. He promptly immersed the pot. "How can I drink before the god has drunk?" Thus he carried it to the god. Now it was poison which he had brought. Mhāḷsā knew it by intuition. "Oh my, the god will die. If he drinks the poison darkness will befall the world". So, what did Mhāḷsā do? She called the children of the eagle Garuḍ. "Ah," she said, "quickly, children of the bird. Quickly, with the strength of your neck, with the strength of your feet, with the force of your wings, tip over the pot. Tip over the pot and spill the poison." The children of the eagle Garuḍ flew off. As fast as they had flown off, as quickly they tipped over the pot with the strength of their feet, with the strength of their wings, and with the force of their neck. When they had tipped over the pot the Pardhān fitted an arrow to his bow string and said: ". . . your mother, I have brought water to quench the thirst of the god. . . . Your mother, the birds have tipped it over". The birds flew off and sat on a Kamaḷ tree.[13] When they had sat on the Kamaḷ tree what did he do there? As he was about to shoot an arrow from his bow he saw the cobra. "Oh my goodness," he said, ". . . your mother, a great calamity has happened. If these Garuḍ eagles had not spilled the poison, the god would have drunk it and died". So what did he do? He called the children of Garuḍ. He patted their backs. He let them fly away. Now from where could he bring water? So what did he do, Dādā?[14] There was a huge Banyan tree. He climbed the Banyan tree, climbed it and had a look. The smoke of sheep dung, of a seven months' pile of sheep dung which someone had set on fire, was rising from somewhere. ". . . mother, where that smoke is coming from there must be water". The god was sitting dejected. The Pardhān came running and said: "Water, oh God, where smoke is coming from there must be water. I will go and bring water". "Very well," he said. When he went there, Āḷsī Kuṇḍī and Dubḷī Dhuṇḍī as usual were at the corner of their hut and saw him. They said to each other: "Oh dear woman, good gracious, what is coming this way? Ah, it is probably a White Vulture.[15] When the figure came near, they saw it was a man. They said: "If he comes, this corpse, he comes. What can he take from us? If he takes something, he will take Bāṇāī's property. What can he take from us poor women?" Thus the Bābā came near. When he came near, Bāṇāī saw him. She saw [that he had] a pot [inlaid] with seven jewels. She set down the pot [inlaid] with the seven jewels and gave him a pot [inlaid] with nine jewels and filled it [with water]. When she had filled the pot the Pardhān took it. Now, he would not drink until the god had drunk some water. Now, Bābā, he went to the god. The god was sitting on the black rock. When he [the Pardhān] was as far away as from here to the wall, the god started laughing. When the god started laughing, he said: "Oh God, you are laughing happily and I ran so much I nearly died. Take the water and drink some". "Now my thirst is gone, I am not thirsty at all". Ah, what kind of a god are you?" Then the god said: "Gone is my thirst". At this the Pardhān said: "Oh God, I ran so much I nearly died of exhaustion, and you say 'my thirst is gone'." "Let it be," he said, "now my thirst is gone alright. Drink water yourself. And from where did you bring the water? We will go there". "Oh God, what can one say good about there? There are many women there. They throw their breasts over their shoulders and the lambs and kids suckle from behind". "But will they leave us alive? If you say anything they will beat us". "Oh no, no, I will not say anything. If you tell me, I will not say anything. As you say, I shall behave". "Will you behave like that?" "Yes," he said, "I shall behave like that". Then they both left. When they came nearer and nearer Āḷsī Kuṇḍī and Dubḷī Dhuṇḍī [were] at the corner of their hut. "Ah Kuṇḍī", Dhuṇḍī said, "yesterday it was only one who came. Today there are two! Who are they?" "No, Dhuṇḍī, they are White Vultures". "They must be headed for the sheep pen. Both of them are coming". "Ah, no, they look like human beings". "If they come, they come. What is there for them to take? Whatever they take, it is Bāṇāī's they take." Thus it happened and they came nearer and nearer. 350 Saṅgar[16] women and 350 Dhangar women were ready for them. They threw their breasts over their shoulders. The lambs and kids suckled from behind. And further behind some armed themselves with pestles, some with sticks, some with cudgels, some with grinding-stones, some with mullers. Thus they were ready. When they were thus ready, Bāṇāī said: "Beat them and knead them into a dough". So far so good! Now, when they came nearer and nearer the seven-and-a-half-hundred [*sic*] were ready for them. The god came nearer and nearer. The god was as near as from here to the wall. "Heh," the god said, "do you have husbands and so on or not?" "Ah, at last your corpse has gone for cremation! What reason do you have to mention our husbands and so on?" Then they started beating him; some of them beat him with mullers, some with grinding-stones, some with cudgels. Rather bruised the god slipped away and sat on a heap of sheep dung. Hastily he stuffed sheep droppings into his mouth. Then Bāṇāī came. "Heh, you women," she said, "this fool of fools devours sheep droppings, so why do you beat him?" Thus it happened, Bābā, and they went to their homes. The god, however, remained where he was. The Pardhān came running to the fort of Jejuri, and the god remained where he was. He remained there. At evening time the god went onto the [*vāḍā*]. Just when he went there the sheep and goats gathered at evening time. Thus he came there. "Heh," he said, "Is there somebody who will take me as a servant?" [The story teller now involves the listening Dhangars in the story and questions them as to what they would do in such a situation.] What would you, for instance, say? "I am in a pinched situation. Stay, however, old man, stay with me." Now, suppose you have let him stay, in the morning your wife makes enough millet bread for two, and he alone polishes off your millet bread and still is not satisfied. And now your wife says in the evening, "Oh my, he has polished off our meal, and still his belly is not filled. No, Bābā, we don't want him." [And when the old man returns from work in the evening you would say:] "Heh, Bābā, you have come, old man, we don't want you. We were quite happy without you". [This is what you would say.] Well, now the old man left his work. What did [the Dhangars] think? "Let him work with Bāṇāī". So they made him work with Bāṇāī. Thereupon the god started eating a quarter of a *khaṇḍī*[17] of food and drank a huge pot of buttermilk. He stuffed himself with food. He ate with both hands. He noisily slurped curds and milk. He drove [the sheep] this way when the Dhangars drove them that way. The god's sheep came back full and satisfied, whereas those of the others came back tottery and feeble. "Ah, the old man grazes the sheep well. The old man has grazed the sheep," [the Dhangars said]. What did Bāṇāī say to the old man? "Heh, old man, why are you just sitting there? Why don't you feed neem tree leaves[18] to the 900,000 lambs!" The old man went, took a Babhūḷ tree and threw the whole tree into the enclosure where the 900,000 [lambs] were. The lambs died. Now, in the evening time, after he had killed the lambs, Bāṇāī came to see [what he had done], and she [saw] that all the lambs had been killed. "Oh, oh, who did this? Who has destroyed everything? All the lambs are lying dead. Come and see the lambs". Thus all the Gangāvḍās[19] came to see whether the servant had really killed the lambs. Therefore he flung his powerful *bhaṇḍār* on the dead lambs which they had come to see. And the lambs which they had come to see were—*gucūgucūgucūgucū*[20]—eating leaves. "Oh dear, what a fraud you are. The lambs are eating leaves, are puffed up, and you say, 'the lambs are dead'? Why do you tell a lie?" Thus it happened, Bābā, that they made Bāṇāī tell a lie. Now, further on, what happened? She said: "Go and wash the sheep". As he left, the old man said: "Bāṇāī, come soon and bring millet bread. Bring one-and-a-quarter *khaṇḍīs* of food and a huge pot of buttermilk". Bāṇāī prepared millet bread and stirred 25 maunds of boiled millet porridge. She took a huge pot filled with buttermilk and went away. And he struck each sheep one by one [on the rock].[21] On this side there was a flood of blood, on that side there were the sheep. Bāṇāī, who came there, started tearing her curly hair. "Oh my, oh my, oh my, you corpse, what have you done? Ah, you have killed all the sheep. A flood of blood is flowing. You have piled up the sheep and goats. And did you wash the sheep [as I told you]?" "Ah, wait, Bāṇāī. Let me eat a little first. I am hungry". "Ah, your bier has gone [to the funeral]. What do you want to eat for? You have ruined all my wealth". "Alright, alright, go ahead, go ahead!" He flung the powerful *bhaṇḍār*. The sheep started moving and would not listen to Bāṇāī. While Bāṇāī was walking the thorns of the Sarāṭā shrub[22] stuck in her foot. As soon as she had pulled out the thorns from one foot they would stick in the other foot. Thus she became tired. The sheep were left free and strayed into the millet fields of a Kuṇbī.[23] Bāṇāī lagged behind. What did he do? He emptied the pot of curds onto his plate and swallowed it, eating with both hands. He wiped his moustache. Swallowing the food with two hands he stuffed himself. He drank water. And then he followed the sheep. The millet crop was surrounded by sheep. When he went on, he came across a harrow.[24] He used the harrow as a pillow and slept. He had a specially[25] deep sleep and the sheep concentrated on eating the millet. Now, the Kuṇbī came to watch over his field, and the millet crop was completely eaten up. "Ah, they have scorched the field like the summer heat. Ah, my millet crop has been devoured. Come and let's see about my compensation". Thus five or so people went and when they came there to the ruined crop, [the god] flung the powerful *bhaṇḍār* and the entire millet crop stood there, nicely even in height and stretching to all four corners of the field. ". . . your mother," they said, "you liar. What did you do? Ah, the millet crop is of even height and everything is the same. It is standing and you said that it was eaten up. Give us at least some *hurḍā*."[26] They went to all four corners of the field. He did not dare to break off an ear of millet. He went to three corners of the field and at the fourth corner he yelled loudly. [Since then], see, the millet crop stands well in three corners, but in the fourth corner, it is not good.[27] At that time he did not break off the ears [and that's why it still fails today]. What else happened? At evening time he went and called the Gangāvḍās. "Heh, Gangāvḍās, come here". "What is it, old man?" Marry me to Bāṇāī. And throw these sheep droppings as rice on us two. Open the lamb enclosure. When the lambs start bleating 'baa, baa,' then throw the rice grains on us!" "Just like this," they asked. "Just like this," he said. What happened next, Bābā? It was settled. In the evening the nine lakhs of sheep returned from grazing. They opened the lamb enclosure. And then the *sāmadhuma*[28] [was uttered and] they threw the rice [consisting of] sheep droppings. And when their marriage had taken place, what did he do without delay? He took Bāṇāī on his horse. He flung the powerful *bhaṇḍār*, took Bāṇāī on his horse and went off to the fort of Jejuri. Bāṇāī looked back. "Oh, my God. All the Gangāvḍās have started quarrelling. The whole world [of the Dhangars] has begun to grieve because of me". "Throw," she said, "the powerful *bhaṇḍār* and end their quarrels". He threw the powerful *bhaṇḍār* and ended their quarrels.

As the two lived happily ever after, so you also live.

4.3 Notes on the Text and Translation

(1) For Hegaḍi Pardhān see *ovī* 367 and note. The narrator uses the title "Headman-Minister" as if it were a name in direct speech.

(2) This is a curse which refers to sexual intercourse with the mother, but in the narrator's speech it has lost its original meaning and may as well as be translated as "damn".

(3) Bhoḷā = Śiva or Mahādev(a).

(4) *soṅkṭyā* = "the play of draughts" (Molesw.). It is played with two

or three dice. The exact procedure and rules which the narrator has in mind could not be established and are not found in Devdhar 1905: 180ff.

(5) This half sentence should have followed after "she put on her yellow sari".

(6) *koṭ* = English *coat.*

(7) *karguṭā* = (S)M *kargoṭā* is a silver cord worn around the loins (Molesw).

(8) For the meaning of *jāgraṇa* see *ovī* 812, note.

(9) A *bhaṇḍārī* is a leather bag preferably made from tiger skin, but normally made of deer skin. It contains turmeric powder (*bhaṇḍār*) and is carried by the Vāghyās.

(10) In the SR of the story the narrator adds: *āsā kuṭha, Bāṇāīcyā sodīla* [(S)M: *śoḍhāylā*] *nighlā* [*nighālā*] "Where? He went to search for Bāṇāī".

(11) Wearing green bangles is a sign of imminent marriage.

(12) *kurkurpācā* is an adjective form used by the Hāṭkar Dhangars to describe the power of the divine *bhaṇḍār*. Perhaps it is derived from Skt. *kṛpā* > M. *krupā.*

(13) This "tree" seems to be an invention of the narrator.

(14) Expressions like "Dādā", "Bābā", and "Mahāraj" may be directed to the person pronouncing *huṃ,* but they also simply serve as expletives.

(15) *leṇḍghār* is the White Scavenger Vulture or Pharaoh's Chicken (*Neophron percnopterus* [*Linnaeus*]). It is a dirty-white kite-like vulture with black wing quills and a naked yellow head and bill. A useful scavenger, it stalks about on the ground near the nomadic herdsmen's encampments (Ali 1979: 22).

(16) 350 is a conventional number amongst the Dhangars for counting a group of people, animals, etc. Saṇgar = (S)M Saṅgar (or Khuṭekar) is a member of a caste which specializes in weaving woollen blankets.

(17) I *khaṇḍī* = 200 *maṇ* (Engl. maunds). 1 *maṇ* = 40 *śer* (Engl. seer). 20 *śer* = approximately 20 kg.

(18) *Liṃbābiṃbāce* [an echo-word] *ḍhāḷe. Liṃbā* = (S)M *niṃba* = the Nimb or Neem tree (Molesw.), *Azadirachta Indica. Bābhaḷ* or *bābhuḷ* = *Acacia Arabica.*

(19) Gangāvḍās: For the Gāvḍās see above, *ovī* 183 and note. *Gan* is derived from Skt. *gaṇa.* The term could be translated "the host of Gāvḍās", but it is used as just another designation for "Gāvḍās".

(20) I could not resist leaving untranslated this onomatopoetic description of the sheep feeding on the leaves of the tree.

(21) "... on the rock". This is adopted on the basis of the SR *khaḍkāv* = (S)M *khaḍkāvar*. That Khaṇḍobā struck the sheep *on the rock* occurs in all the versions of the Hāṭkar Dhangars if only implicitly.

(22) *Reullia longifolia* (Molesw.).

(23) Kuṇbī: a member of the agricultural caste which nowadays would rather be more respectfully called Marāṭhās, a denomination used by the narrator in SR.

(24) *kuḷav*—an implement for levelling and smoothing ploughed ground. It is drawn by bullocks.

(25) *peśal nijlā*—Engl. *special*. This is one of the few occurrences where the listener who generally says only *huṃ* suggests the phrase, which the narrator adopts. It also occurs in the following phrase: *miṇḍhyānī peśal jondhāḷī khallā*, which I have translated as: "The sheep con-centrated ...".

(26) Mostly ears of millet (*jovāri* or *bājrī*) which are roasted in the field and constitute a typical rural delicacy on the plateau of Maharashtra.

(27) Because of scarce rainfall, thieves, and, of course, the sheep of the Dhangars, which may invade the fields of the farmers.

(28) *sāmadhuma*—(S)M *sāvadhāna*: The uttering of the words *sumuhūrtta sāvadhāna* at the moment of the completion of the *sumuhūrtta* or auspicious period, and the removing, upon that utterance, of the *antaḥpaṭa* between the bride and the bridegroom. The word is used in marriage ceremonies (Molesw.).

5 NOTES ON THE CONTEXTUAL MEANING OF THE MYTH

5.1 THE PLACE OF THE MYTH IN THE FRAMEWORK OF DIFFERENT TRADITIONS

The focus here is on the meaning of the myth in the context of the living traditions of the Dhangars, and more specifically of the Hāṭkar Dhangars. That is, I would like—not only because of lack of space, but also as a matter of methodology—to investigate what the myth may mean for those people who actually live by it. The next step, which is not pursued here, would be to interpret the myth from the point of view of the traditions of other people who share it. Such people live in the same region or adjacent regions of Maharashtra, but are influenced by other contexts, "milieus" (Hardy 1988: 156 *et passim*), or "literary situations" (L. Lutze, personal communi-cation), and emphasize other traditions. A third step would be then to interpret the myth taking into account its various versions in different parts of India. Though there are striking structural similarities amongst these versions we shall also not discuss them here. To include them in our discussion *a priori* would mean to ignore the implications the myth may have for the Hāṭkar Dhangars. Their two versions are taken here, so to say, as the epicentre of the all-India myth for the purposes of this paper.

The Hāṭkar Dhangars are guided by the myth, and most of it, though the events took place in the Satyayuga (738: in those times), is in con-sonance with their social and religious life. Some of the meaning is expressed in terms of etiological "asides", e.g. the failing crop in one of the fields in LS, but much of it is subconsciously implied in the myth. Thus one has to resort to other sources to explain the myth, if the investigator wants to avoid asking direct questions. Such questions may provoke "theological" reflections by Dhangar informants which they think might suit the outsider, but may also take the informant into another story which, though not answering the question, may be a valuable source eventually. Further sources can be other oral texts, but also the observation of the shepherds' life, especially their rituals, beliefs, and social customs.

Though the Hāṭkar Dhangars lived, and still live to some extent, in spatial separation, they were never cut off from the outside world but interacted symbiotically with other religious, local or subregional traditions. All these traditions have mutually reacted or reflected on each other in multiple ways (following Ramanujan, unpubl. ms.; Sontheimer 1989) and none of them has remained isolated. Thus the very core of our versions of the myth, namely Khaṇḍobā "wooing" Bāṇāī, has probably been introduced into Dhangar mythology from outside. Conversely Khaṇḍobā's involvement in the life of the Dhangars has also imparted, as it were, the quality of a Dhangar (812) to this multidimensional deity. Thus we shall use the other traditions—as far as possible here—as heuristic tools towards analysing the Dhangar versions. These immediate local, or subregional traditions and the culture of the Hāṭkar Dhangars could be called the components of their versions of the myth. The other components interact with their culture, though their influence may be marginal or subordinated. I have listed five components which are relevant here:

(A) The culture of the Hāṭkar Dhangars as the epicentre of the myth. Their oral literature, social customs, beliefs and rituals (= their "culture") reflect pastoralism and "tribal" life, rather than a caste ideology dominated by hierarchical considerations.

(B) Folk religion centering on the folk deity Khaṇḍobā who is god as king on earth. There is a close similarity between Khaṇḍobā and Rudra, the folk deity as reflected in the Vedic texts (Sontheimer 1987). As *kulsvāmi* he is traditionally the Lord of many groups, for instance, merchants, Marāṭhās, robbers, thieves, pastoralists, artisans, Muslims, farmers, fishermen and Brāhmaṇs. His particular devotees are Vāghyās and Muraḷīs, bards and female dancers who have been dedicated to the god by their parents in fulfilment of a vow. They perform *jāgraṇ* and sing of the deeds of the god, and describe his prowess, as well as, often ambivalently, his erotic involvement with Bāṇāī They concentrate on singing about the quarrels between his wives, but also suggest their equality as wives of the god, e.g. when both of them eat from the same plate [Sontheimer: forthcoming (a)]. The Khaṇḍobā cult has attracted most of the variants of the myth of the god and the two wives, because the bards, the Vāghyās, have different social backgrounds and often perform for different clienteles.

(C) Śaivite groups ("sects") like the Nāths, Śaivite Gosāvīs, Liṅgāyats. Śaivite Gosāvīs would say, e.g. that the god won Bānubāī from the king of the underworld, Śeṣnārāyaṇ (Sontheimer 1976: 62).

(D) Brāhmaṇs who are Śaivites and provide the link between the cult and the Purāṇic tradition. They are the authors of the Sanskrit *Mallārimāhātmya* and of many Marathi renderings of the same texts, as well as the *Mārtaṇḍavijaya* and the *Jayādrimāhātmya*. In the *MM*, the most important text, Bāṇāī is not mentioned as such. It is said that Gaṅgā went angrily to the earth (*MM* 20.23,1), and the notorious quarrel between Mhāḷsā (= Pārvatī) and Bāṇāī (= Gaṅgā) is cut short by suggesting that they are one (*MM* 20.24). The *MM* emphasizes the cosmic dimension of Mārtaṇḍa Bhairava or Śiva. The brahmanical texts de-emphasize the worldly involvement of Khaṇḍobā and thus the story of Bāṇāī does not play a role.

Both versions have some resemblance with the descriptions of the forest and the *aśrama* of the "Seven *ṛṣis*" in the *MM*, but also with incidents told e.g. in the Duḥṣanta story of the *Mbh* (1.63-67). In the

MM (1.8 ff.) the *āśrama* of the "Seven *ṛṣīs*" and their families is described: animals like antelopes and tigers, ichneumons and serpents, peacefully coexist (1.10), and the *āśrama* abounds with "fruits of all seasons", besides banana trees and sugar cane (1.11). This idyllic and harmonious retreat, a place of asceticism and Vedic learning which seems to exist out of time, is desecrated by the king of the demons, Mallāsura (1.12-21). Usually the forest in classical texts is terrifying, but ambivalent. In the *Ovī* the forest is also frightful (17ff.), yet there is a comic touch, if we think of female bears performing the *phugaḍī* dance, which is popular amongst Maharashtrian women (20). The several forests which Khyāmu (*Ovī* 16 ff.) and Khaṇḍobā (LS) have to cross in order to reach "the centre out there" (to borrow Victor Turner's well-known phrase) are a frequent theme in the oral literature of the Dhangars, but are also reflected in the *Mbh* (1.63-7, crit. ed.). Duḥṣanta has to cross several forests during his hunt, causes a virtual slaughter amongst the animals of the forest (cp. LS), and finally reaches the *āśrama* of *ṛṣi* Kaṇva. During his march he is accompanied by his army, the people of the town, the ministers (*āmatya*), and his "chaplain" (*purohita*). Like Khaṇḍobā [LS] he leaves them behind one by one and when he reaches Kaṇva's hermitage within the *āśrama* he enters it *alone* (*Mbh* 165.1, cp. Shee 1986: 307). Here he meets Śakuntalā instead of Kaṇva. Again Śakuntalā, who was abandoned by Menakā (of Indra's heaven) in the forest, may be compared with Raṃbhā/Bāṇāī (one of Indra's daughters), who was abandoned in the forest (on which see below, 5.2.1).

(E) Vaiṣṇava Saints of Maharashtra—e.g. Eknāth, Śekh Muhaṃmad, Rāmdās, and Tukārām—and bhakti literature. Most Vaiṣṇava sources reflect folk religion and the Khaṇḍobā cult in terms of the "inner religion" and of the Vaiṣṇava Viṭhobā cult of Paṇḍharpūr. So far they do not seem to have made an impact on the culture of the Ḥāṭkar Dhangars nor do they take notice of the myth. Only Śekh Muhaṃmad disparagingly refers to the "mad" Khaṇḍobā, who searches for Bāṇāī because of his sexual passion (*Yogasaṃgrāma* 14.110; Dhere 1981: 130). His diatribe against Khaṇḍobā is reflected in the erotic relationship of Khaṇḍobā and Bāṇāī as expressed in the songs of the Vāghyās. As Śekh Muhaṃmad lived from 1560 to 1650, we can say that the myth of Bāṇāī, the Dhangar woman, and Khaṇḍobā was known at that time.

The diagram in Figure 9 illustrates what has been said above. The dotted lines indicate the pervasiveness of the myth and suggest the flexible interactions between the traditions:

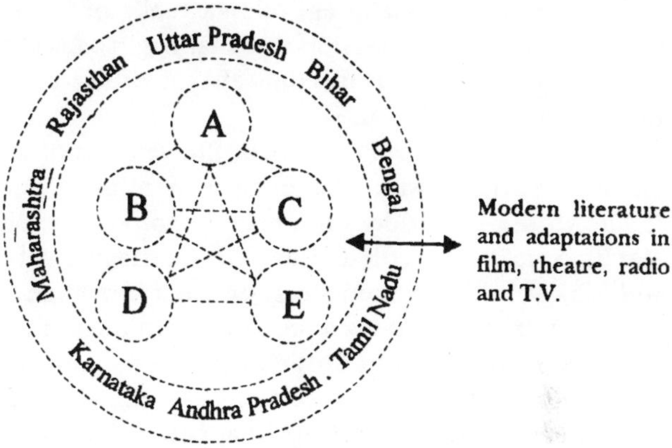

Fig. 9: The Myth of the God and his Two Wives in the Framework of Different Traditions

5.2 Some Incidents of the Myth in the Light of the Culture of the Hāṭkar Dhangars

5.2.1 The Slaughter of the Sheep and Bāṇāī's "Conversion"

The two versions of the myth in a way convey the "creed" of the Hāṭkar Dhangars with respect to Khaṇḍobā and his two wives. The main singer of the *Ovī* calls it a *kissā* ("account") of their god (828 and note). The myth answers the question of how the Dhangars became devotees of Khaṇḍobā through his marriage to Bāṇāī. What is for other groups often a subject of amusement, namely the erotic relationship between Khaṇḍobā and the shepherdess Bāṇāī, is only subtly suggested by the main singer, who refers to Khaṇḍobā rather endearingly as "mad". From the point of view of the other groups worshipping Khaṇḍobā, the marriage can hardly be described as one, except perhaps as a marriage by elopement. Bāṇāī, however, insists on the marriage (717ff.). The main singer shares a sense of propriety which other, settled castes observe in marital relations. The version of LS is more common among the Hāṭkar Dhangars: It is the god or divine king who asks Bāṇāī to marry him and thus forms a marriage alliance. The god searching for a *bhakta* is a common motif in Dhangar mythology. He undergoes *tapas* in the form of exertion and self-degradation. His escape to the heap of sheep dung (LS) is not only a humorous incident, but the climax of apparent self-debasement. It reminds us of the ancient custom of warriors who take refuge on a termite mound and eat grass to indicate their surrender (König 1984: 166). But his act was only one of the tricks of the divine trickster, and the episode is actually the turning point after which the gradual conversion of Bāṇāī begins. According to some other versions, however, it is only after twelve years of service that Khaṇḍobā marries Bāṇāī.

Bāṇāī occupies a central role in the versions of the Dhangars. Mhāḷsā's marriage with Khaṇḍobā is mentioned only in passing (290f.) in the *Ovī*. It does not play the important role it does for Marāṭhās and other settled castes. The marriage ritual of Khaṇḍobā and Mhāḷsā, which is annually re-enacted in a huge festival at Pal (Satara District), is not even mentioned. In the *Ovī* (265f.) Mhāḷsā becomes the daughter of Tuḷsīrām, a merchant of Pal. This differs from the generally accepted version that Mhāḷsā is the daughter of Timmaśeṭ, a rich Liṅgāyat merchant from Nevasa near Paithan (Aurangabad District). It would be wrong just to conclude that the singer is uninformed.

Bāṇāī's birth is usually not mentioned in the *Ovīs* and stories of the Hāṭkar Dhangars. Like Vaḷḷi, the beloved of Murukaṉ in the Caṅkam literature, she is not related to any celestial being. She is just there, is tremendously rich, owns nine lakhs of sheep and goats, "not counting the barren ones", and is the leader of twelve cattle camps (*bārāhaṭṭi*), each inhabited by a different clan (226 and note). Her divinity is rooted in tellurian fertility and prosperity based on cattle wealth. She is the source of the life-giving gift of water to Khaṇḍobā, the god on earth. She also provides him with food and is shown in brass *mūrtis* holding a lamb in her arms and offering food to Khaṇḍobā. Khaṇḍobā is seated on a horse together with Mhāḷsā (Sontheimer 1984: 168). Thus in the LS Bāṇāī's miraculous celestial origin is not mentioned (in 1966), whereas the *Ovī* connects Bāṇāī with Indra, making her an *avatār* of Rambhā, a celestial nymph in Indra's heaven. I was told this episode in 1980, after about fourteen years of contact with Hāṭkar Dhangars. It seems remarkable that earlier the singer never thought it important to relate the incident regarding Bāṇāī's birth. Perhaps in the meantime he had come to know about the episode and wanted to include it in his comprehensive *kissā* of Khaṇḍobā. But again we see the prominence of Bāṇāī, who is credited with a heavenly origin, whereas we are not informed about Mhāḷsā's celestial background. Bāṇāī's birth is elaborated upon much more in versions told by the Vāghyās. According to them Bāṇāī is one of the seven daughters of Indra, and is found by a Dhangar in a golden box in the forest, where she was hidden in a termite mound or in a ditch. The episode in Indra's heaven is here an object of elaborate narration. The version of the *Ovī* is delightfully "original". One has to go through the forest to find the goods of life or physical immortality in the form of children. From "out there" Yāmū brings a living treasure, a girl who turns out to be a source of inspiration and of cattle wealth for the Dhangars. Yāmū is only for a split second taken aback that it should be a girl that he gains and not a boy, perhaps because in the social setup of the Hāṭkar Dhangars girls are as welcome as boys. In any case, Bāṇāī knows how to look after sheep, how to graze them and increase their number. Soon she becomes the Mirdhīn of the twelve *vāḍās*. Thus the celestial credentials of Bāṇāī are established in the *Ovī*.

In the metal plaques (*ṭāk*) which are worshipped by the Dhangars, Bāṇāī is invariably depicted with sheep and with Khaṇḍobā. Both sit on a horse. The Dhangars are obsessed with sheep. They are the basis of their material life and they are connected to them by a firm bond caused by a close symbiosis. The child Bāṇāī is fed milk by a virgin ewe (127ff.). There are detailed myths of the divine origin of sheep which are discovered in a termite mound, the seat of wealth. The details of the life in Bāṇāī's *vāḍā* are minute descriptions of the Hāṭkar Dhangars' life: Thus there are the neem and the *bābhūḷ* trees, the leaves of which serve as fodder (LS), there are the dry, thorny branches of the *bābhūḷ* tree, which are used for the lamb enclosures (607ff.). Then there is the ever present worry about finding sufficient pasture, a problem which Bāṇāī and Khaṇḍobā handle so expertly and miraculously. The daily task of sweeping can be a nuisance (553ff.). But the heaps of sheep dung are bought by farmers and are an additional source of income. The "marriage band" consists of the ewes and nanny goats which return in the evening from the pasture and meet their lambs and kids, which had to stay back in the *vāḍā* the whole day (725ff., cp. LS). The noise which results from this meeting can be deafening. The dogs which are mentioned are indispensable for protecting the *vāḍā*, e.g. against robbers, wild dogs, and wolves (506ff., cp. LS). What we miss in both the versions are references to the wolves (*lāṇḍgā, Canis pallipes,* Molesw.), who raid the sheep pen in the night and sometimes in broad daylight even today. The Hāṭkar Dhangars, however, believe that if "wolves trespass on a flock of sheep" (*lāṇḍgyānī bakrī vālaṇḍne*), the flock will increase. A similar belief is reported of the Kois in Andhra Pradesh, a subdivision of the Gonds. They are said to revere wild dogs even if they kill cattle

(Hassan 1921: 231). Why then this reticence in our versions of the myth?

Perhaps we should consider another trespasser in this context, namely Khaṇḍobā. He resembles Rudra, the folk god, as we have tried to show elsewhere (Sontheimer 1987: 1ff.). As Khaṇḍobā appears in the form of a dog, Rudra can appear as a dog, and his sons are compared with wolves (*ŚŚS* 4.20,1; Falk 1986: 18f.). Khaṇḍobā intrudes into the centre of the world, which is the *vāḍā* in the minds of the Dhangars. In the SR of LS we hear that he crosses the forests, but they are, significantly, counted backwards till he approaches the *vāḍā*:

The god thus crossed the first forest, then the ninth, the sixth, the fifth...
The god crossed the forest...

Ultimately he reaches the *vāḍā*, but first he is wrongly believed to be a White Scavenger Vulture. This is again a realistic description: such vultures—though they have become rare today—move around Dhangar camps and feed on dung and carcasses. It is perhaps a coincidence that the ambivalent Rudra, who brings death as well as life, is also associated with carrion birds (Dandekar 1979: 235; *AV* XI.2.2: *TA* IV.29; cp. *AV* IV.28; XI.2.11). Incantations against them are accompanied by the formula *rudrāya svāhā* (Dandekar 1979: *ibidem*). In the past at least, if not still today, unexpected and unknown outsiders, whether human or animal, meant a potential threat to the prosperity and life of the Hāṭkar Dhangars. Thus Death threatens, whether indicated by the White Scavenger Vultures or by the appearance of the god after a murderous hunt in the form of an old man with a decrepit, sick horse. Though this is humorously narrated in LS we probably do not go astray if we read such a meaning into the myth in the Hāṭkar Dhangar context of life.

However, the myth is also a myth of conversion. The listener is not to mistake the outward signs of danger and death. The miraculous deeds and acts of violence and death do not hide from the listener the fact that the god is searching for a devotee (Bāṇāī) or devotees (the Hāṭkar Dhangars). He is hungry in the literal sense and eats voraciously, like any valiant folk hero or folk deity, beginning with Indra and well-known from folk tales ever since. In terms of the Vedic texts he could be compared with Rudra-Agni, who stands upon the altar in the form of the sacrificial flame "longing for food" (*annam ichamānas* *ŚB* 9.1.1.1, Long 1983: 115). But the physical hunger turns out to be the desire for an offering (*nived*, Skt. *naivedya*). Moreover, as other Dhangar stories tell us, the god is not just physically hungry, but hungry for a bhakta who would care for him in an untiring and selfless manner, showing true devotion (cp. Sontheimer 1977). Here, of course, we are informed by other traditions, namely by the uncompromising devotion of bhaktas and *vīras* (heroes) in folk religion in the Khaṇḍobā cult (Sontheimer 1985b) and the *niṣkāma* bhakti associated with the Viṭhobā cult of Paṇḍharpūr (Stanley 1987).

In our versions of the myth the Dhangars gradually realize the divinity of Khaṇḍobā. They advise Bāṇāī to offer him *nived* (647ff.), or the god on his own tells her that she should offer him *nived* (LS). But before she can do so, the events have already reached their dramatic climax. Khaṇḍobā has slaughtered all the 900,000 sheep and goats in a cathartic act of violence—a mythologem which appears in *all* the versions of the myth. On the condition that Bāṇāī marry him, or rather become his bhakta, he revives the sheep. Sacrifice creates life out of death, and we are told in another version of the myth that the 900,000 sheep miraculously doubled in number after the slaughter. Similarly to the way that the "sacrifice" to the wolves increases the herd, the sacrifice of sheep to Khaṇḍobā promises life. But now the "sacrifice" is no longer exclusively to the unbound, undomesticated powers of nature, that is, to the wolves, but is directed to the god in a regulated ritual, after which the Dhangars hold a communal dinner. Their old "tribal" belief in the efficacy of "sacrifice" to the wolves has not disappeared, but has been superseded by the worship of Khaṇḍobā. Consequently some Dhangars sacrifice sheep to Khaṇḍobā directly, at Khaṇḍobā cult centres in remote places. In Jejuri, however, the Dhangars no longer sacrifice to Khaṇḍobā, but to Bāṇāī or to the Daityas. Here other traditions, which the *Ovī* notices, take over, namely Liṅgāyat vegetarianism (771-8) and, in Sanskrit and Marathi texts, the trend towards vegetarianism. Though the *MM* (18.4,1) still speaks of non-vegetarian offerings to Mallāri (c. 13th cent.), a later text tells us that they are to be given to the Daityas as a special favour of the god (*MV* 33.5-7; in Marathi, c. 1823; Sontheimer 1987: 21). The Vaiṣṇava saint Rāmdās is believed to have contributed to this trend (Sontheimer 1987: 21). The singer is aware of the trend and knows, though not directly, the story of the Daitya in the texts. He links the Dhangars with the Daityas: both are devotees of Khaṇḍobā by "conversion".

The Dhangars have to offer non-vegetarian *nived* to the Daityas, a privilege (*mān*) given to the Daityas (and to the Dhangars) by Khaṇḍobā/Mallāri (761-78).

5.2.2 THE GAME OF DICE

A brief reference must be made here to the game of dice between Khaṇḍobā and Mhāḷsā. The theme of Śiva and Pārvatī playing dice is mainly found in Purāṇic sources (e.g. *Vāmanapurāṇa* 10.34-6: Sarkar 1974: 149ff.; Meyer 1937: 145ff.) and is not primarily Dhangar mythology. It is not clear what kind of dice game the narrator had in mind.[1] But, though the story may not provide any new information on the history or the rules of the game, the circumstances and consequences of the game in the two versions throw light on the background of the Khaṇḍobā cult. The explanation has to be based on the traditions embodied in B and D rather than those of A. We should start by pointing to the all-important presence of the "dog" in the mythology and ritual of Khaṇḍobā. In this connection another version is also helpful. It was told not by a Hāṭkar Dhangar, but by a member of a settled community.[2] According to his story Khaṇḍobā would forfeit his rule over the "Fort of Jejuri", would lose his dogs Gulhe and Mogare[3] to Mhāḷsā, would have to wear only sack-cloth and would have to leave Jejuri forever, *if he loses.*[4] Khaṇḍobā as a hunter without the company of his favourite dogs would be reduced to nothing—or, may we say, to a "dog"? In the *Ovī* (686f.; cp. 814) Khaṇḍobā turns up with a *koṭamā*—the rectangular, wooden begging bowl. In other words, he comes as the divine prototype of the Vāghyās, who act as the dogs of god (Sontheimer 1987: 163ff.). One might even compare them to the Vedic *sattrins* (cp. *Chāndogya-Upaniṣad* 1.12) and *vrātyas*, who went into the wilderness because of hunger (cp. Falk 1986: 36ff., 57f.). An old prayer to *koṭamā* (*koṭaṃ[b]yācī āratī*) sung by the Vāghyās refers to the "doghood" of the Vāghyās:

> He became the Vāgh[y]ā of the god
> Into his hand [the god] gave [him] a *koṭamā*
> Barking [like a dog] and roaring [like a tiger]
> He came to the door of Mallāri's bhakta...[5]

When, according to the story, he casts the dice three times, each throw amounts to "*sunā*" = "empty", "void", "zero" (Skt. *śūnya*). We suspect a folk etymology here which contaminates M *sunā* and Skt.

śvan/śunā/śūnya.[6] This speculation gains some plausibility if we view Khaṇḍobā's defeat at the game of dice and his exit to the forest once more against the pervasive continuity between Rudra and Khaṇḍobā/ Mallāri. We are guided here by a recent detailed study of the game of dice and ancient sodalities ("Bruderschaften") by H. Falk (1986: 109ff. *et passim*). Without going into the details of Falk's study, we can note that in the game of "dice", which was played with nuts, the loser rather than the winner became the leader of a group of youths. They wandered into the wilderness to seek their fortune. The loser who retained the last nut, called *kali*, was the "dog" and became "Rudra", who was associated with Death. In our versions of the myth Khaṇḍobā, left with nothing except his magical pouch, is relegated to the wilderness, which, though ambivalent, is on the surface charged with signs of danger and death. Nevertheless he is a leader of a "*sainya*" of 12,000 (LS). This recalls the *Akṣasūkta* of the *Ṛgveda* (see 10.34.12) and the "*senānī* of a great *gaṇa*", and "the king or the leader of the *vrāta*" (Falk 1986: 186).

The god's exit to the forest is also depicted in two ancient stone panels, probably of the Yādava period (13th cent.) which serve today as *mūrtis* in two villages near Jejuri. The god is locally called Vandev. He has a Bhairava halo and is armed with a bow and arrows. He hunts sambhar and wild boar (cp. SR of LS) and is followed by a queen wearing a crown who reminds us of Mhāḷsā anxious to protect the god. He is also accompanied by a host of demons who look like walking skeletons. According to LS the "army of 12,000" returns after the hunt rather exhausted and emaciated because of lack of water. Khaṇḍobā apparently nearly dies of thirst, but he is the god who cannot possibly die. Victoriously he cries "Yeḷkoṭ, Yeḷkoṭ" (696 and note). He returns from the slaughter of wild animals, from the slaughter of sheep and goats, and from the battle with the Daityas as if from a *raṇayajña*. In the case of Yāmū it is the unflinching devotion consisting of *tapas* and *pūjā* which makes him defeat death. Both of them return with a fortune from the wilderness, namely with Bāṇāī.

5.2.3 Conclusion

Thus the myth is full of meanings and possibilities for interpreting them. But one thing is certain: The myth binds the Hāṭkar Dhangars to Khaṇḍobā and it is this meaning which we want to emphasize here. It is the all-important turmeric powder (*bhaṇḍār*), a manifestation of the god's magical healing powers, which ends their quarrels and unites them (LS)—and all the other groups of devotees—in the worship of Khaṇḍobā. All the groups (except Brāhmaṇs) participate in the ritual hunt of the god in Jejuri on Somvatī Amāvāsyā (745ff., 799ff.). This is a new moon day on a Monday, which, according to the *Ovī* (799), comes generally twice a year. It is a day fraught with sinister forces which the god, however, masters and controls and turns into auspicious power (Stanley 1977). The myth is echoed in the rituals of this *jatrā* (799-801), which also assume a many-layered meaning emanating from other traditions. The Hāṭkar Dhangars join the "army of 12000", which nowadays may consist of ten times more pilgrims, and lead the great procession (or hunt). It starts from the "Fort" and ends at the river Karhā. The Hāṭkar Dhangars carry ceremonial spears. In the Karhā river they bathe jointly with the god at the end of the hunt. On that day they also bring their iron chains (*laṅgar*), which they break with the help of the power of Khaṇḍobā and in order to ascertain his existence (773-5). On other occasions they bring water from the river Karhā, which is "Gaṅgā", to bathe the god in the temple (cp. 95). This custom is also reflected in two versions of the myth: Bāṇāī, whom some would consider to be Gaṅgā, sends water for Khaṇḍobā, who thus becomes peaceful (*śānt*) (499ff.). The god sees her name written on the vessel (*jhārī*) filled with water, a little detail which registers the growing literacy in the environment of the *Ovī* singer. In LS, a version more "conservative" in the literal sense than the *Ovī*, it is a vessel inlaid with nine jewels which serves as a sign for the god to recognise Bāṇāī.

On account of Khaṇḍobā the Hāṭkar Dhangars also have the ritual of *jāgraṇ*—a folk-religious ritual combining a vigil with song and dance in honour of Khaṇḍobā (825). The Hāṭkar Dhangars also follow the general custom of making a vow to him in case of childlessness. The first-born child is dedicated to the god. If it is a boy, he becomes a Vāghyā, traditionally considered to be a "dog" of the god. If it is a girl, she is married to Khaṇḍobā as a Muraḷī, just as Raṃbhā, alias Bāṇāī, is married to Khaṇḍobā.[7] Both customs have, however, fallen into disrepute nowadays.

In conclusion we may say that the myth deals with the involvement of the god in the world of humans. It shows the horizontal extension of the realm of the god or "god as king on earth" into the territory of the pastoralist Hāṭkar Dhangars. He takes upon himself the life of a Dhangar and becomes a Dhangar himself. To establish the vertical, cosmic dimensions of the god and, consequently, his aloofness from the human world, is not what the myth wants primarily to convey. This would be focussed on in other traditions of the cults, as e.g. in the Skt. *Mallāri Māhātmya.* Yet the god's divinity is never in doubt, and we sense a certain detachment amidst all involvement. He has to be shaken into action by the minister (cp. Shulman 1985). It is the minister who performs all the errands, and only in his acts of sacrifice and "conversion" is the god really active.

The two versions of the myth, we would finally like to suggest, are not just of interest to folklorists or to the student of religion. They ramify into many versions all over India and are part of an all-Indian myth. Moreover, such folk sources are not detached from Sanskrit sources, but the two kinds of sources supplement each other. It is only the adequate consideration of both which will eventually enable us to see and understand Indian culture as a whole.

NOTES TO 5.2.2 AND 5.2.3

(1) The nearest parallel may be found in Lüders 1907: 29, who refers to the game of dice between Puṇṇaka, a *yakṣa,* and the king of the Kurus in the *Vidhurapaṇḍitajātaka* (VI, 280, 1ff.). Lüders writes: "Nach der Vorstellung der Jātaka gab es 24 verschiedenartige *āyas,* von denen jeder der beiden Spieler sich vor Beginn einen wählt. Wem es dann gelingt, den gewählten zu werfen, der hat gewonnen". Mr. R. Mühlhäuser has drawn my attention to this reference.

(2) Āṇṇā Khaṇḍu Aṅkus; his home village is Ghategari, in Usmanabad (Taluk and District). He gives his caste as "Marāṭhā" and is a *vārū,* that is, he has taken a vow to act as a "horse" of the god in the festival of Khaṇḍobā.

(3) The Dhangars would insist that these dogs belong to Bāṇāī (cp. 533ff.).

(4) We shall not go into a discussion here of the obvious parallels to the *Mahābhārata.*

(5) Collection of songs in the possession of Jānu Malhāri Kadam, Jejuri (old unpublished notebook, 47f.). Note that the dogs are sometimes compared with tigers (Sontheimer 1987: 166).

(6) The Marathi transcription of the passage is as follows:

mag pahilā ḍāv ṭāklā. ti sunāc gelā.
dusrā ṭāklā. tibī sunāc gelā
tisrā ṭāklā. tibī sunāc gelā...

Though the narrator does not explicitly identify the "zero" with the "dog", we would like to see a connection between them, especially in the context of Rudra and Khaṇḍobā. The matter is under scrutiny. So far I have come across only one study which deals with *śuna* and *śūnya*: Bhāgirath Prasād Tripāṭhī, "Śune kukkurāya hitaṃ śūnyam?" In: *Sārasvati-Suṣamā* (Sanskrit University, Varanasi), 24/2 (1969). The article was not available to me. I owe the reference to R.N. Dandekar.

(7) The connection between Raṃbhā and Bāṇāī is not insisted on in Jejuri. There Raṃbhā, who is married to Khaṇḍobā, is a Śiṃpīṇ, i.e. of the tailor caste. In all, Khaṇḍobā has five wives, though only Mhāḷsā and Bāṇāī are really of major importance.

ACKNOWLEDGEMENTS

This paper includes material which was collected in Maharashtra from August 1984 to April 1985 and during previous stays financed by the DFG (Deutsche Forschungsgemeinschaft). I gratefully acknowledge their help as well as that of Mr. Rajaram Zagade and Mr. Ramdas Atkar, who have helped in elucidating some obscure passages in the texts. I should like to dedicate this article to the late Limba Torve and to Sakharam Lakade. I also want to thank Mr. Aditya Malik for helping me bring the article into shape.

APPENDIX

TEXT OF LIṂBĀ'S STORY

।। लिंबाची गोष्ट ।।

तवा आसं काई झालं, महाराज । खंडुबनी म्हाळसानी काई केलं । म्हाळसान[1] खंडुबा आसी कुटं श्याजारी बसली व्हती । तवा रोज आपली आसी कुटं बसाइची। तवा हिगडीपरधान त्याचा म्याव्हना, "इजिमाइलासिका",[2] म्हंगाला,[3] "यांचा वाकुडपणा आणला पाइजे काइतरी" । तवा परधानानी काइ केलं । जे पळत जे सुटला ती भॉळ्यापसी ग्याला । भॉळा म्हणतो "आरे, आरे, परधाना का आलास"। "आता काइ सांगू, द्यावा, तुला। द्यावाजीनी सोगटयाचं डाव मागितलत"। "आसुं हे", म्हंगाला, "हा, हा, आसं हे"। म्हगाला, "आ ल्याका, कशाचं डाव," भॉळा म्हणतो। "हा भांडणं लावाइच्यामाघं आलाइ । ह्यो रे, कसलं सोगटयाचं डाव नेहतोय"। तवा मंग त्यानी काइ केलं । "बरं," महंगाला, "बरं, बबा,

आलास । जा सोगट्याचं तिथलं दोन डाव उचल आण जा घेवूनशनी"। आता त्यानी काइ केलं । दोन सोगट्यांच डाव उचाललं आण ग्याला घेवूनशानी। आता द्यावाजवळ जवळ ग्याला । "ये, द्यावाजी, द्यावाजी"। "आरे, काइ म्हनतो"। "आरे, ही तुला करमणुक आणली, हे बग" । "आरे, काइ"। "आरे, सोगट्याचं डाव उगाची उगाच बसतोस आण मुकाट्या बसतोस तं[4] हे खेळलं मजी करमणुक तरी व्हइल[5] तुला"। म्हंगाला, "बरी की आणलीस। आ ल्याका, बरं, का वाइट"। आता देव आंतरी म्हणतो "च्याइलासिका,[6] ह्यानी भांडान आणलं घरात। ह्यानि हे कशाचं डाव आणलत[7] । बरं आणलं हे बरं झालं"। आता महाराज काई झालं। त्यानी ते डाव न्याह्याल्यावर द्यावाजीच्या म्होरं टाकलं। आता द्यावाजीनी घेतलं गॉळा करुन। आता आसं काइ झालं । आंघुळआष्ट्यान किली आण द्यावाजी आता डाव खेळलं पाइजेत। आता देव आपला ग्याला डावाव, डावाव बसला। आता पहिला डाव बॉलला पाचाचा। डाव पडला आडचाचा । पुन्हा डाव बॉलला धाचा। डाव पडला पाचाचा। पुन्हा डाव बॉलला पंधराचा । डाव पडला धाचा । पुन्हा डाव बॉलला इसाचा[8]। डाव पडला पंधराचा। पुन्हा डाव बॉलला पंचविसाचा। डाव पडला इसाचा। झालं द्यावाचं डाव पुरं। आता म्हाळसाव डाव आलं। आता म्हाळसानी काई केलं। नाहून घुवून महाराज भांगटिळा करुन, रंगन वदून, पिवळं पाताळ निसून, उजवा पायी रंगनात टाकला आण डावावर बसली। पहिला डाव बुलली सवाचा। डाव पडला आडचाचा । पुन्हा डाव बुलली आडचाचा। डाव पडला पाचाचा। पुन्हा डाव बुलली पाचाचा। डाव पडला धाचा । पुन्हा डाव बुलली धाचा। डाव पडला पंधराचा। पुन्हा डाव बुलली पंधराचा। डाव पडला इसाचा । डाव बुलली इसाचा। डाव पडला पंचविसाचा। झालं डाव पुरं। "आता, द्यावाजी," म्हंगाली, "काई कराइचं। तर आता डाव आपूण खेळलो, याचा इसाब[9] कराइचा"। "आ ल्याका," म्हंगाला, "कशाचा इसाब आलाय। झालं आसतील कुणाचं तरी जास्ती, आता काइ कराइचय"। "छा छा," म्हंगाली, "द्यावा, रडीची खडी घिवू नकुस। खरं आसल ती खरं व्हइल। कुणाचं डाव जास्ती झालं ती इसाब कराई पाइजे। ती बघितलं पाइजे"। आता म्हंगाला, "तिच्याइला बघा, करा"। म्हंगाली, "माझं डाव जास्ती झालं तर तुम्ही सम्द[10] उतरून आंगावलं ठेवलं पाइजे। तुमचं जर जास्ती झालं तर कच्च्या घागरीनी पाणी मी तुमच्याहितं वाहीन"। "आंस हे," म्हंगाला। "हा हा," म्हंगाली, "आसं हे, आरे द्यावाजी, तुम्ही डाव क्यावढ्याचं बॉलला व्हता"। "इच्यामाइलासिका, मी बोललो व्हतो पाचाचा वाटतं"। "मंग क्यावढ्यावा डाव पडला"। "डाव पडला आडचाचा, वाटतं।" आण त्वा डाव क्यावढ्याचा बॉलला"। "डाव बोललो धाचा "। "डाव क्यावढ्याचा पडला"। "डाव पडला पाचाचा"। "पुन्हा डाव क्यावढ्याचा बॉलला"। "डाव बोललो पंधाराचा"। "डाव क्यावढ्याचा पडला"। "डाव पडला धाचा"। "पुन्हा डाव क्यावढ्याचा बॉलला"। "डाव बोललो,"। म्हंगाला, "इसाचा। डाव पडला पंधराचा । डाव बोललो पंचविसाचा आण डाव पडला इसाचा"। म्हंगाला, "झालं आमचं डाव पुरं"। म्हंगाली, "बरं, तुमचा इसाब झाला, आता आमचा करा बघू,"। म्हंगाला, "बरं, करा। तुम्ही डाव क्यावढ्याचा बोलला व्हता"। "आम्ही डाव बोललो व्हतो सवाचा। डाव पडला आडचाचा"। "द्यावा, डुकीला काइ हे ती खाली उतरुन

ठेव''।म्हंगाला, ''डुकीला मंदील हे''।''ठेव बघू उतरुन''।उतारला।''द्यावा,''म्हंगाली, ''डाव बुलली आडचाचा।डाव पडला पाचाचा।आंगामंदी काइ हे, उतरुन ठेव''।म्हंगाला, ''हाये कोट''।''उतरुन ठेव''। ट्यावला उतरुन ।''आता डाव क्यावढ्याचा बुलली''। ''डाब बुलली पाचाचा। डाव पडला धाचा''।''द्यावा, कंबरला काइ हे, उतरुन ठेव''। म्हंगाला, ''कबंरला करगुटा हे''। ''ठेव उतरुन । पुन्हा डाव क्यावढ्याचा बुलली''। ''पंधराचा।डाव पडला इसाचा''।म्हंगाली, ''द्यावा, हातात काइ हे''।म्हंगाला, ''सॉन्याची आंगठी हे''।''उतरुन ठेव खाली''। द्यावानी ठेवली।''पुन्हा डाव बुलली इसाचा। डाव पडला पंचविसाचा''। ''द्यावा,'' म्हंगाली, ''पायामंदी काइ हे''। ''तॉडा हे''। तॉडा ट्यावला काढून। आता म्हंगाली, ''द्यावा, जास्ती डाव कुणाचं झालं''।''डाव,'' म्हंगाला, ''तुमचंच जास्ती झालं''।''आमचं जास्ती झालं ना, द्यावा, सम्द उतरुन ठेवलस पण तेवडं गळ्यातलं कातोडं उतरुन ठेव''। ''छा छा छा छा,'' म्हंगाला, ''ते कातडं नाइ उतरून ट्यावायचो''।''का, आरे, द्यावा,''म्हंगाली, ''ते कातोडं तं तेवढं उतरुन ठेव''।''छा छा,'' म्हंगाला, ''तु काइ जरी केलस तरी ते काइ ट्यावायचो नाही । ते बॉटभर कातोडं मला पॉट भराइ पाहिजे''।तं म्हंगाली, ''त्या बॉटभर कातोड्यावर सारी रात वाघ्यामुरुळी उभी करशील। जागरान करशील, तुझ्या नावानी सारी रात गाणं गातील, जागरानं व्हतील''।मंग द्यावानी काइ कातोडं ठेवलं नाइ उतरुन ।झ्यांडा भंडारी घितली आण देव रुसूनशानी आसा कुंठ, महाराज, चावढीमंदी ग्याला।देव चावढीमंदी निजल्यागत झाला।आता ते निजल्यागत झाल्यावर सप्री बाणाई दिसली ।परधानाला काइ म्हणतो, ''आरे, आरे, परधाना, लवकर,''म्हंगाला, ''सुतार बोलव। हा चंदनखांब कोर। ह्या खांबामंदी मनुष्य शिरलय''। ''आरे, द्यावा,'' म्हंगाला, ''तुला का,''म्हंगाला, ''याड लागलं का काइ, आरे, ह्या खांबामंदी मनुष्य कुटं शिरतं व्हइ। आरे, तुझं मुतानी पॉट फुगलं आसल आण उताना निजला आसशील आण सपान पडलं आसल तुला, मनुष्य कुटं खांबात शिरतं व्हइ''। ''काइ जणू, तिच्याइलासिका,''म्हंगाला, ''पण मला सपान पडलय, तिच्याइलासिका, शिरलय''।''आरे, मुताबिताया ग्याला व्हतास का''। ''आरे,'' म्हंगाला, ''गेलो व्हतो। ग्याल्यावानी झालतो। एवडं एवडं याक डबार साटलं व्हतं याक घोडं पाणी प्याया सारकं''। ''आरे, खरं का खोटं''। आरे, खरच साचल्यावानी झालं व्हतं''।''बरं झालं, तिथली कर्तुक तिथं''। मंग काइ झालं, महाराज। देव आसा रुसून आता म्हंगाला, ''परधाना ह्या नगराला हाळी मार''।हाळी मारुनशानी आता म्हंगाला, ''शिकारीला जावू। चला रे, चला''। देव चालला शिकारीला। मंग काइ केलं। तॉफा बंदुक्याचं बार भरलं ।सबन[11] नगराला हाळी मारली।''चला, रे, चला, देव चालला शिकारीला''।द्यावाच्या माघं बारा हाजार सैना।निघूनशानी चालली।जिजुरगड सॉडला आण आशी कुटं चाललिया खालती। तवा जाता जाता पानपटी इसरुन राहिली । तवा हिगडी परधानाला काइ म्हणतो, ''आरे, आरे, परधाना, पानपटी घेवून ये आपल्याला''। परधान माघारा ग्याला पानपटी आणाइला। तिकून[12] म्हारनी आपल्या सरपानाच्या मॉळ्या घेवून आल्या। सरपानाच्या मॉळ्या घेवून आल्यावर म्हाळसा वरनं बगतिया।''आरे, आरे, देव

चालला रुसून । ह्या द्यावाला, रांडाहो, म्होरं," म्हंगाली, "सरपानाच्या मॉळ्या घेवून जा, पाच मॉकळ्या घागरी घेवून जा। देव माघारा फिरवा"। आता त्या म्हारनी काइ म्हणू लागल्या, "आगं, बया, देव चालला रुसून जाइना हालक्या उलासानी आण बाणाई इना चुडा भरुनशनी आमचं गं काइ जातय"। "बरं, रांडाहो, नाही ना तुम्ही जात," म्हंगाली, "तुम्हाला मिरच्याची धुरी दिती, तुमची कोपटं सम्दी जाळती आण तुम्हाला मिरच्याची धुरी दिवून जाळते"। आता एक म्हारीन व्हती म्हातारी। "आगं, रांडाहो," म्हंगाली, "यावडा देव लावला रुसूनशानी म्हाळसानी आण तुमची गं काइ किम्मत हे। चला की द्यावाला आडव्या जावू"। मंग काइ झालं, आशा कुटं त्या म्हारनीनी, बाबा, अशा घ्यातल्या गवर्याच्या पाट्या, कुणी घ्यातल्या सरपानाच्या मॉळ्या, कुणी घ्यातल्या मॉकळ्या घागरी आण द्यावाला आडव्या ग्याल्या। देव हिकून निघालाया। हिगडी परधानानी पाहिलं। "आरे, आरे, द्यावाजी, मॉठा," म्हंगाला, "आपल्याला आपसकून झाला"। "आरे, कशाचा"। "आ ल्याका," म्हंगाला, "मॉकळ्या घागरी आल्या। सरपानाच्या मॉळ्या आल्या आण गवर्याच्या पाट्या आल्या। आपल्याला मॉठा आपसकून झाला"। "आरे", म्हंगाला, "आपल्याला बूलीपरमान घेवून ये । मॉकळ्या घागरी व्हतील पाणी प्यायला । गवर्या व्हतील इस्तू प्याटवाइला आण सरपान व्हइल चुलीला लावाइला । घेवून ये दिलं तं त्यांनी"। ह्यानी काइ केलं, कुरकुरपचं भंडार, उधळलं आण त्या घागरी मधानी भरलीत। ह्या गवर्याचं झालं तळीव मळीव। सरपानाचं झालं ऊस आण ते परधान आसा जवळ जवळ ग्याल्यावर, "आगं ये, बायाहो, ह्या मॉळ्या द्यायायच्यात का" । "दियाचीत की, बाबा, झालं, बाबा"। खाली जु डुकीवनं टाकतीत तं त्याचं बनलीत ऊस । मंग म्हारनी फिरल्या । "बाबा," म्हंगाली, "काइ, रे, तु घ्याणार पडला, आरे, ह्या थळावनं त्या थळाव, त्या थळावनं त्या गुर्हाळाव, टिपरं टिपरं गॉळा करुन आणलं । ल्याकराबाळाला चालावलइ, आण तुला रे, कोण देतया[13]। झालं, बाबा, त्या बदालल्या । आता ग्याला गवर्यावाल्यापसी । "आगं, बायाहो, ह्या पाट्या द्याता का"। "आरे, बाबा," म्हंगाली, "घ्यातल्या तं दियाच्या हाइत की" । बाया आशा खाली उतरून बगतीत तं ते सम्द तळीव मळीव । "आरे, बाबा," म्हंगाली, "कसला रे, आलाइ तु घ्याणार । हे घर पीट, त्या घरी जा। त्या दारात उभी राहा। तिथनं योक निवद घे, हितनं योक निवद घे। आन ल्याकराबाळाला गॉळा करुन चालवलत, आण तुला, रे, कुटलं दियाचं"। आता ग्याला, बाबा, घागरीवं। "आगं, बायाहो, तुमच्या घागरी दियाचित का"। "व्हइ की, बाबा, दियाचित," म्हंगाली, "आता घागरी जु डुकीवनं खाली उतारतीत तं मदानी डबाबलीत। "आरे, बाबा, आमच्या घागरी भरलीत । ह्यो कडा उचकट, त्यो दगोड उचकट, ते झाडझुडूप, तिथं मद बघ हितं मद बघ । हितला वाइच, हितला वाइच, तिथला वाइच गॉळा क्याला। आण घागरी भरुनशानी चालावलीत पॉराबाळाला खायान तुला रे, कुटला दियाचा"। झालं, बाबा, त्या बी बदालल्या । मंग काई झालं । "आशा त्या घागरी," आता म्हंगाला, "गड्या बूलीपरमान एक एक घागर तरी द्या"। मंग एक घागर घितली । गवर्यावाल्याकं[14] ग्याला । म्हंगाला, "पाच गवर्या तरी द्या" । पाच गवर्या घ्यातल्या ऊसवाल्याकं ग्याला।

पाच ऊस घेतलं आण द्यावापसी ग्याला । "ये, द्यावाजी, द्यावाजी," आ, "टिकूरं खाता का टिकूरं"।"काइ म्हणतो," म्हंगाला, "लका आरे, टिकूरं खातो का," म्हंगाला, मनं काइ म्हणतो। आरे, ऊसाचं टिपरं खातो का टिपरं"।"उसाचं टिपरं म्हंगालास, व्हय," म्हंगाला आण हिकडं मंग ते घेतलं तवा, बाबा, आता काइ झालालं हे, जागरान सार्यारात चवक पुजूनशानी मधी घागर ठेवतो। चवकडं चार ऊस बांधतो। त्याला ती कडाकनी बांधतो । सार्यारात त्याचं जागरान घालतो। मंग हे जागरान हितं झालं। म्होरं कर्तुक काइ झाली त्याची। मंग देव आसा शिकारीला ग्याला। शिकार करु लागाला। पहिली हाळी मारली। गादगादा रान भेलं। दुसरी हाळी मारली । झाडं झुडं भिली । तिसरी हाळी मारली। कडाबाली सुटल्या। चवथी हाळी मारली। आशी कुठं खांडं पिटवून काडली । पाचवी हाळी मारल्यावर शिकार करु लागला। सहावी हाळी मारली। आसं कुटं मासाचं उडवं[15] घातलं। आशा कुटं शिकारीच्या सिराड्या रचल्या, आण देव शिकार करु लागला । तवा बारा हजार सैना आसी कुटं तान्ह्याली। जळसोस सॉधला। पाणी नाही कुटं आण बारा हजार सैना जिजुरगडाला आली। द्यावानी काइ केलं । आसा कुटं देव काळ्या कड्याला बसला । "आरे, आरे, परधाना," म्हंगाला, "गड्या, आता कंठास पराण आला। तहान तं लागली। पाणी तं नाही"। परधान मंग ही कडा सोधतोय, ही बारव सोधतोय। ती नदी सोधतोय । पाणी काइ कुठं नाही। मॉट्या कड्याव चढला तवा तिथं योक भुजंग म्यालाला व्हता। तवा त्या भुजंगाची लाळ बॉटावानी गळून आपली ती याक्या नळीतनं ती आपलं डबार साचलं व्हतं। "आईला," म्हंगाला, "तितं पाणी हे" । म्हणून बिगीबिगी ग्याला। पहिली झारी बुडावली। आता देव प्याल्याशिवाय आपूण कसं प्यायाचं। म्हणून द्यावाला भरून चालावली । आता ते इस चालावलं भरून। आंतरी म्हाळसाला कळलं ।"आरे, आरे, देव मराया करतो। आता हे इस पेवूनशानी जगदुनयाला आंधार पडल"। मंग काइ केलं म्हाळसानी, गरुड पक्षाची बाळं बॉलावली। "आरे, आरे, पक्षाच्या बाळाहो लवकर," म्हंगाली, "लगुलग मानंच्या[16] जॉरानी, पायाच्या न्याटानी, पखाच्या जॉरानी झारी पालथी करा। पालथी करुनशानी तेवडं इस[17] वतून द्या"।गरुड पक्षाची बाळं जी सुटली, जशी जशी गुंगाट्यानी गिली, तशी, पायाच्या न्याटानी, पखाच्या जॉरानी आन मानंच्या न्याटानी पालथी झारी किली। पालथी झारी क्याल्यावर बाणधनुष्या परधानानी जॉडला आण "आईलासिका," म्हंगाला, "देव तान्ह्यालाया[18] द्यावासाठी मी पाणी चालावलं। इजीमाइला पक्षानी पालथं केलं"। म्हणून बाणधनुष्या जॉडला । जे पक्षा जी निघाला ती कमळाच्या झाडाव[19] जावून बसला । कमळाच्या झाडाव बसल्यावर तिथं काइ केलं, बाणधनुष्या आसा जॉडावा त तिथं त्या भुजंगाव नदार गिली ।"आरे, रेरेरे, रे, रे," म्हंगाला, "च्याइलासिका मॉठा घात झाला। आईला, या गरुडपक्षानी हे जर इस नसतं वतलं तं देव प्याला आसता तं म्याला आसता"। मंग काय केलं, गरुडपक्षाची बाळं बॉलावली। त्यांच्या पाठीवनं हात फिरावला। त्यानला सुडून दिली। आता द्यावाला पाणी न्याहाइचं कुठलं । तवा, दादा, काइ केलं। मॉठा आघ्राळ्या योक वड व्हता । त्या वडावर चढला आण तिथनं, बाबा, वडाव चढूनशानी पाहिलं। तं या ल्यांड्याचं

धूर, सा सा महिन्याचं ढिग ही कुठं प्याटलालं त्याचा कुठं धूर निगत व्हता। "आईला," म्हंगाला, "त्यो धूर निघतोय त्या ठिकाण्याव," म्हंगाला, "पाणी आसल"। देव तं मुरुन बसलाई। लगे परधान ग्याला। आण म्हंगाला, "पाणी द्यावा," म्हंगाला, "धूर निघतोय तिथं पाणी आसल। मी घेवून येतो"। "बरं बरं," म्हंगाला। आता त्यो परधान जी निघाला तं, बाबा, ग्याला । आता ग्याल्याव आळशी कुंडी आण दुबळी धुंडी त्यांचं घर आसं नेमकं कॉपर्याव, त्यांनी याता याता पाहिलं। आता पाहिल्यावर मंग काइ इकीमिकीला[20] म्हणतीत, "आगं, बया, कोंडे, आगं," म्हंगाली, "ते काइ ग यतया"। "आगं," म्हगाली, "काइ आसल ति लेंडघार हे। आगं, आपल्या मिंढ्या ग्याल्या उठून आण ती लेंडघार नाइका आखराव इती ती आसल"। "आगं, नाही गं धोंडे," म्हंगाली, "आगं, माणुस दिसतय"। "आगं नाही नाही," म्हंगली, "लेंडघार आसल"। बरं, आसा जवळ जवळ ग्याला। तं ही माणुस दिसलं। "आगं," म्हंगाली, "बया, इना का आला तं कोण म्याला," म्हंगाली, "आपलं गं काइ न्याह्याचाइ। नेहलं तं," म्हंगाली, "बाणाईचं धनदिरव्य निहील। आपलं गं काइ न्याह्याचाइ गरिबाचं"। मगं, बाबा, आसा जवळ आला। आता जवळ आल्यावर आसा कुठं बाणाईनी पाहिला । सात रत्नाची झारी। आसी कुटं त्यानी पाहिली। सात रत्नाची झारी ठीविली आण नवू रत्नाची झारी द्यावाला भरुन दिली। नवू रत्नाची झारी भरुन दिल्यावर परधानानी कुटं घितली। आता देव पाणी प्याल्याशिवाय त्याला पाणी प्यायाचं नाही। आता, बाबा, त्या द्यावापसी ग्याला। देव काळ्या कड्याला चिपून बसलाइ। आता लांब जु हाये ह्या भिताडाइतका देव लागला हासाइला। आता देव हासाया लागल्यावर, "आ ल्याका," म्हंगाला, "द्यावा, तु खुशाल हासतोया आण मला पळून पळून नकोसी परान झाला। धर, पाणी पे"। "आता, लका, माझी गिली तहान। आता नाइ मला तहान"। "आ ल्याका," म्हंगाला, "काइ द्यावा तु"। तवा मंग काइ झालं। देव म्हंगाला, "माझी गिली तहान"। मगं आता तहान गिली म्हंगाल्यावर "काइ ल्याका," म्हंगाला, "द्यावा, मी पळून पळून कटाळलो। आण तु म्हणतो माझी तहान गिली"। "बरं," म्हंगाला, "परधान आता माझी गिली तहान। तु पे पाणी। आणा कुठनं आणलय पाणी तिथं जाऊ"। "आरे," म्हंगाला, "द्यावा, तिथं कसलं आलय। तिथं माइंदाळ्या बाया। उफारटी थानं टाकलीत माघं कुकरी करढं पितीत। काइ, रे, ती आपल्याला जगून दितीत। तु काइ बॉलला-बिललास तर मारतील, बाबा, आपल्याला"। "नाइ, नाइ," म्हंगाला, "काइ नाइ बॉलाइचो । तु सांगशील तसा मी काही बोलाइचो नाही। तु सांगशील तसा वागल[21]"। "आसा वागशील"। "हा," म्हंगाला, "आसा वागल"। आता, बाबा, देवन[22] दोघं निघालं। आता आसं निघल्यावर जवळ जवळ जु ग्याला तं आळशा कुंडीचन दुबळ्या धुंडीचं कॉपर्याव बिर्हाड। "आगं, कोंडे," म्हगाली, "काल योक आला व्हता। आज दोघं दिसतितय,[23] कोण गं, बया, हे"। "आगं नाही गं, धोंडे, त्या लेंडघारी हेता"। त्या म्हंगाली, "मिंढ्याच्या आखारव आल्या आसतील। त्या दुन्ही इतिताया"। "आगं नाही गं माणसावानी दिसताइन[24] आगं," म्हंगाली, "इना का आलं तं आपलं गं काइ न्याह्याचाइ। नेहलं तं, बाणाईचं निहीतील"। झालं, बाबा, आसं जवळ जवळ

आलं। साडंतिनशे सनगरनी, साडंतिनशे धनगरनी आशा कुटं उभ्या राहिलीत। उफारटी थानं टाकलीत। कुकरी करढं पितीत। आण माघं कुणी घेतलय मुसाळ, कुणी घ्यातला फाटा, कुणी घेतलं लाकुड, कुणी घ्यातलाइ पाटा, कुणी घ्यातलाइ वरुटा। आशा कुटं उभ्या राहिलीत। उभ्य राहिल्यावर बाणाई काइ म्हणती। "बरा बॉलाल तं बरा नाही तं भला, कुटून करा कनकीचा उंडा"। बरं हे । आता हे जवळ जवळ ग्याल्यावर, साडंसातशे उभ्या राहिलीत। तवा हा जवळ जवळ देव ग्याला। देव एकदम त्याततिका हे तं त्या भिताडावानी। "ये, बायाहो, आ ल्याका," म्हंगाला, "तुम्हाला काइ नवरंबिवरं हेत का नाही"। "आरे, तुझा मुढदा ग्याला तुझा यागदाचा, अमचं नवरंबिवरं लागला वानाइला"। जवा लागलीतइ कुटाइला तवा कुणी वरुट्यानी मारतय, कुणी पाट्यानी मारतय, कुणी लाकडानी मारतय। जे जे देव त्यातनं निसाटला, ल्यांड्याच्या ढिगाव जावून बसला। गबा गबा ल्यांड्या खाया लागला। मंग बाणाई आली। "आगं, रांडाहो," म्हंगाली, "ते याड्यावनं यडं आण गबा गबा ल्यांड्या खातय आण ल्याला ग काइ मारता"। झालं, बाबा, त्या घरुघर ग्याल्या। मंग त्यो देव तिथंच राहिला । परधान जेजुरगडाला पळून आला आण देव तिथंच राहिला। तिथं राहिल्याव साजंचा ग्याला। सांजचा ग्याल्याव मेंडकं शेळकं आपल्यावानी जमून आलं म आसा देव तिथं आला। "ये, ल्याका," म्हंगाला, "मला गडी ट्यावता का रे, कुणी"। "हा, हा, तुज्यासारका काइ म्हणतो। आ ल्याका, माझी हे तारमळ, तिज्याइला, राहा, म्हातार्या, राहा माज्याहितं। आता, बाबा, तु ट्यावलास, सकाळच्या पहारी तुज्या बाइकुनी भाकरी क्याल्या, दॉघाच्या आपल्या"। " दॉघाच्या भाकरी खावून ध्यातल्या। तरी म्हातार्याचं पॉट भराना। आता बाइकू सांजची म्हणू लागली, "बया, आपल्या दॉघाचं जेवान खाल्लं"। तरी म्हंगाली, "त्याचं पॉट भराना। नकू, बाबा, आपल्यात"। "ये बाबा, तु आलास," म्हंगाला, "म्हातार्या आपल्याला नकू, बाबा, तु आपलं हाये तिच बरं हे"। मगं, बाबा, त्यो म्हातारा तिथनं निघला। "आता," म्हगाला, "काइ इचार क्याला"। म्हंगाला, "हे आता बाणाईच्या हितं ट्यवा"। मंग बाणाईच्या हितं ट्यावला। मंग त्याला सवाखंडीचं आनपाणी, रांजणभरुन ताक मंग आसा देव खावू लागला। मंग फुगू लागला। दुइदुइ हातानी। दह्यादुधाचं फुरकं मारु लागला। मिशा वारु लागला। मंग देव चाकरी राहिला। द्यावाच्या चालल्या हिकडं मिंढ्या। दुनवीच्या[25] चालल्या हिकडं । द्यावाच्या मिंढ्या आल्या तट फुगून आण दुनवीच्या मिंढ्या लागल्या लाडलाड कराइला। "लका, म्हातारं, चांगलं मिंढ्या चारतइ। म्हातार्यानी मिंढ्या चारल्या"। म्हातार्याला बाणाई काइ म्हणती। "आरे, म्हातार्या, आरे, बसलाइस तं," म्हंगाली, "ते नवालाखाची गोधन हे ती कॉकर्याला वाइच लिंबाबिंबाचं ढाळ घालीनास"। म्हातारं, जी गेलं आण लिंब धर की टाक, आण बाभळ धर का टाक, ती नवालाखाची गोधन पार मारुन टाकली। ठार कुकरी मारली । आता ठार कुकरी मारल्यावर, बाणाई जु आली सांच्यापाहारी बघाइला तं ही कुकरी सबंधी मारुन टाकलीत । (मरुन पडलीत ।) मरुन पडलीत[27] । "आरे, आरे, वाटुळ्या," म्हंगाली, "सारी कुकरी मरुन पडलीत, आरे, चला ये, माझी बघाइला"। तवा आपलं गनगावडं बघाइला गेलं। पार कुकरी गड्यानी मारली। मंग आता

कुकरी जु बघाइ गेलं कुरंकुरपचं भंडार उधाळलं तं ती गडी बघाया ग्याल्यावर ती कुकरी गुचू गुचू गुचू गुचू गुचू पाला खातीत। "आ ल्याका, बाणाई, काइ ग लबाड हेस तु"। "आ ल्याका," म्हंगाला, "काइ कुकरी पाला खातीतइ आण काइ फुगलीतइ आण तु म्हणतीस की कुकरी मारली। लका, लबाड कशी बुललीस"। झालं, बाबा, बाणाईला लबाड किली। आता म्होरं काइ झालं, "आता मिंढ्या," म्हंगाली, "नान्हाइ जायाच्या"। म्हातारा ग्याला नान्हाइला। "बाणाई," म्हंगाला, "लवकर ये भाकर घेवून। सवा खंडीचं आणपाणी आण रांजण भरुन ताक"। बाणाईनी भाकरी क्याल्या। सवा खंडीचा घाटाघुटा क्याला। आण रांजण भरुन ताक घेतलं आण बाणाई भाकरी घेवून गिली। ह्यानी धर मिंढी आपट, धर मिंढी आपट। रक्ताचं पूर इकीकं, मिंढ्यच्या शिराड्या इकीकं, बाणाई जु तिथं गिली तं करुळं क्यास तुडू लागली"। "आरे, आरे, आरे, म्याल्या ही रे, काइ," म्हंगाली, "केलस। आरे," म्हंगाली, "सार्या मिंढ्या मारुन टाकल्यास। रक्ताचं पूर चाललत। मिंढ्याच्या शिराड्या रचलीत। आण कसल्या नान्हतोस"। "आ ल्याका, दम, बाणाई, मला जेबूंदे जरा, भूक लागली आधी"। "आरे, तुझी डुली गिली," म्हंगाली, "कसला जेवतोइस तु। आरे, सारं वाटूळं केलस जिनगानीचं"। "बरंबरं बरं," म्हंगाला, "म्होरं हो, म्होरं हो, म्होरं हो," ह्यानी कुरकुरपचं भंडार उधाळलं। जशी जशी जी मिंढ्यची म्होर लागली तशा बाणाईला कशाला आइकत्यात। बाणाई ह्यो पायी उच्यालती की त्यो पायी सराट्यानी भरतोइ। त्या पायातलं सराटं काढती की दुसरा पायी भरतोइ। आशी बाणाई तिथं कटळून गिली। जे जे मिंढ्या जी सुटल्या ती कुनब्याच्या जोंधळ्यात ग्याल्या। तरी बाणाई तिथंच चाललीया। ह्यानी काइ केलं। त्या दह्याचा ड्यारा घ्यातला वतून आण त्या दुइ दुइ हातानी वरबडू लागला। मिशा वारु लागला। दुइ दुइ हातानी वरबडून आसा तट फुगला। पाणीबिणी प्याला। आण मंग मिंढ्यच्या माघं ग्याला। तं त्या कुनब्याच्या सार्या जोंधळ्याला मिंढ्यानी याढा दिला। हा जावूनशानी तिथं एक कुळव पडला व्हता, तवा त्या कुळवाला उसं दिलं आण तिथं आपला निजला। पेशल निजला आण मिंढ्यानी पेशल जोंधळा खाल्ला। आता, बाबा, कुनबी आला याढ्यला तं जोंधळा पार वावरातला खाल्ला। "आ ल्याका, उन्हाळा क्याला"। म्हंगाला, "आ ल्याका, माझा जोंधळा पार खाल्ला। चला बघाइला माझा भरुन घ्यायाचाइ"। म्हणून आसं पाच पंच निघालं आण जोंधळा बघाया जु चाललं तं ह्यानी कुरकुरपचं भंडार उधाळलं, आगदी जोंधळा पण निस्ता दुइथड्या बसलाइ। सबन सारका आगदी। "आ, तुइया आइलासिका," म्हंगाला, "लबाड रे, काइ तु काइ बॉललास, आरे, जोंधळा दुइथड्या बसलाइ आण सबन सारका बसलाइ आण तू म्हणतोस की जोंधळा पार खाल्ला। म्हणून चार्ही कोपरं हिंडला ह्या कॉपर्याला ग्याला। त्या कॉपर्याला ग्याला। पंच म्हणू लागलं, "लका, आता आम्हाला बघाया आणल्यासारकं हुरड्याला चार कणसं तरी मोड"। म्हणून चार कॉपर्याव ग्याला। कनीस काइ मॉडाया जिव व्हइना। तवा तीन कॉपरं हिंडलान चवथ्या कॉपर्याव ग्याला। तिथं बॉंब ठुकली। ती, बघा, आता तीन कॉपरं इतीतन योक कॉपरा जातोय। तवा त्यानी कणीस नाही मोडलं। आण मंग काइ झालं, महाराज, तिथनं तथि कर्तुक झाली। आता सांजचा म्हातारा ग्याला, आता गनगावडं

बॉलावलं।"ये गनगावड्याहो,"म्हगांला, "हिकडं या काइ रे, म्हातार्या"।तं म्हंगाला, "ह्या बाणईचन माझं लग्न लावा आण ही ल्यांड्याची आक्षादा टाका दॉघावबी आण कॉकर्याची गोधन सुडून द्या। कुकरी ब्या ब्या कराइ लागली की आम्हाव आक्षादा टाका"। आसं हे म्हंगाले, "तं आसं हे"। मंग काइ झालं, बाबा, ते ठरावलं। मंग संध्याकाळी आसी सांजची नवलाख जानी चरुन आली। कॉकर्याची गोधन सुडली। आण मंग सामंधुमं ल्यांढ्याची आक्षादा टाकली। आण त्याची लग्न लागल्यावर लगेच त्यानी काइ केलं, बाणाई घातली घोड्यवरी।उधाळलं कुरंकुरपचं भंडार, बाणाई घातली घोड्यवर, आला जिजुरगडला निघून। बाणाई बघती माघारी। "आरे, आरे, द्यावा। गनगावड्याचं लागलं भांडण। धुल्यामोगर्याचं लागलं भांडण।जगदुनव्या लागली माझ्यासाठी मराइ।उधळ,"म्हंगाली, "कुरकुरपचं भंडार आन त्यांची भांडणं तोडव"। त्यांनी कुरकुरपचं उधाळलं भंडार आन त्यांची भांडणं तोडावली। त्यांनी जसं राज्य केलं तसं तुम्ही करा।।

LINGUISTIC NOTES TO THE APPENDIX

An attempt has been made here to transcribe an oral text into Devanāgarī to enable Marathi-knowing non-linguists who are not familiar with phonemic transcriptions to read the original. The oral text is in spoken rural Marathi. In the pronunciation of *written* Marathi, vowels are slurred over or rather silent in a sequence of VC(V)CV, but this is not indicated in the script. We have followed this convention here. Some of the most important linguistic characteristics of the oral text are noted below:

(a) The opposition between intervocalic aspirated and unaspirated consonants is absent in rapid speech, but is noted if the aspirant is distinctly audible.
(b) There is no opposition between /ś/ and /s/, between /ś/ and /ṣ/. Following written Marāṭhī /ṣ/ is, however, reproduced.
(c) There is no opposition between /i/ and /ī/, /u/ and /ū/, /u/ and /o/. Often /i/ ~ /e/.
(d) There is no opposition between initial /l/ and /n/, or medial /ṇ/ and /n/.
(e) Initial /o/ > /va/. Especially in the sequence /C/o/C/ā/ there is a tendency of /o/ > /ô/.
(f) In /C/e/C/a/ there is a palatalization of /C/, e.g. /gelā/ > /gyālā/ .
(g) There is frequent denasalization, e.g. SM soṃgṭā > sogṭā.

Annotations to the Text

1. *Mhāḷsā* + *n* (< SM *āṇi*).
2. < *yācyāmāīlāśikā.*
3. SM *mhaṇālā.*
4. SM *tar.*
5. SM *hoīl.*
6. *yācyāīlāśikā.*
7. SM *āṇle āhet.*
8. SM *viṣācā.*
9. SM *hiśob, hiśeb.*
10. SM *sabandha.*
11. SM *sabandha nagarālā.*
12. SM *tikaḍūn.*
13. SM *det āhe.*
14. SM *gavravālyākaḍeṃ.*
15. *uḍveṃ* is a Koṅkaṇī word and means "rice etc. (here: meat) kept on a wooden scaffold for drying".
16. SM *mānecyā.*
17. Written M *viṣ.*
18. SM *tānhyālā āhe.*
19. SM *jhāḍāvar.*
20. SM *ekāmekīlā.*
21. SM *distāt.*
22. *dev* + *an* (SM *āṇi*), cp. (1).
23. SM *distāt.*
24. *distāi* + *n*, cp. (22).
25. SM *duniyācyā.*
26. *lakā* ~ *lyākā* < SM *lekā.*
27. Interjection of listener, the *huṃkār deṇārā* (see 4.0).

God as the King for All: The Sanskrit *Mallāri Māhātmya* and its Context

1. INTRODUCTION: THE TEXT AND ITS CONTEXT

THE *Mallāri Māhātmya* (*MM*) claims to be a part of the *Kṣetrakhaṇḍa* of the *Brahmāṇḍapurāṇa*, but it is not included in the standard edition of the *Brahmāṇḍapurāṇa* of the Veṅkaṭeśvara press. It shares the characteristic feature of all successful Sanskrit *Māhātmyas*, especially *Sthala-Māhātmyas*, namely, a high level of abstraction from the context in which it originated. Such abstraction from transient reality reminds us of the classical *śrauta* ritual, which became a domain of a separate, transcendental world, detached from mundane reality. A tension between mundane and supramundane reality is also found in the Dharmaśāstra, where *mīmāṃsā*, the science of interpretation, required that all customs conflicting with *śruti* and *smṛti* should be treated as void. Thus *dharma* was put on a high level, with strong moral, supramundane sanctions. In practice, however, *custom* was followed even if it was repugnant to the *śāstra*. The *Purāṇas* could afford to locate their gods in heaven and thus make them nearly inaccessible, except perhaps with the help of Brāhmaṇs, who functioned as gods on earth. The author of a *Sthala-Māhātmya* was in a more difficult position. He had to deal with concrete places, pre-existing cults and the expectations of sometimes self-conscious devotees. He had to make a compromise between ultimately unrelated abstraction and too much involvement in particular details of time, place, historical persons and events, which would deprive the work of supramundane sanctions. Yet devotees wanted to recognize themselves in and identify themselves with the cult and derive favours from it to satisfy mundane as well as supramundane aspirations, or, as the *Māhātmyas* would say: to obtain *bhukti* and *mukti*.

The brahmanical author of the *MM* (assuming that there was indeed a single author) was facing, and perhaps even participating in, another religious current besides that of the śāstric tradition of the *Purāṇas:* folk religion. The cult of Mallāri was and is very widespread in the Deccan and is expressive of very self-conscious beliefs and attitudes of groups of people whom the Brāhmaṇs would classify as Śūdras, but who could not readily be subsumed under the hierarchical *varṇa* order headed by the Brāhmaṇ. According to the beliefs and attitudes of these groups Mallāri was on earth, accessible 'here and now', and not living in a distant purāṇic heaven. This is, in my view, one of the essential criteria of folk religion. Mallāri's predecessors were gods like the ancient Rudra, and by this we do not mean the Rudra of the Vedic *śrauta* ritual incorporated as Agni in the *agnicayana* ritual, but rather a deity with very personal characteristics and often personified by a leader of a group (or groups), e.g. the Ekavrātya or the *sthapati* of the Vrātyas.[1] The relationship between follower, leader as personified god, and god was characterized by mutual imitation and possession, affection and participation, which was the root of the later *bhakti* current. As Rudra was the leader of a motley assembly of groups, Mallāri was worshipped by tribals, "Untouchables", Brāhmaṇs, robbers, rising kings, thieves, pastoral castes, pastoral farmers, merchants, Jains, Liṅgāyats, and not least by Muslims. The cult of Mallāri can, therefore, not be comprehended by reference to the Sanskrit text alone. In fact the emphasis of research ought to be, at least in this case, on the folk-religious aspects of the cult, the oral traditions, inscriptions and references in traditional Kannada, Telugu, and Marathi sources. Moreover, the observation of separate or common rituals of various groups tends to explain the cult and throw light on the meaning of the text. Typical of the folk religion on the Deccan, the rituals of the cult do not just consist of symbolic, more or less mechanically performed acts and recitations, but enact the divine play of the god, whether it is e.g. by imitating the god or aspects of his court, or by participating in his royal hunt. After all, this god on earth is perceived as a king by his followers, especially by the medieval heroes and the Marāṭhās. Thus we may see aspects of an ancient notion of folk-religious kingship that are not generally emphasized in the śāstric texts, not even in the present *Māhātmya*.

2. THE SANSKRIT TEXT: ITS AGE AND PROVENANCE

The lithograph text of the Sanskrit *MM*, which is easily available in Maharashtra and is used here as a basis, has hardly any misprints and provides no philological errors. The few misprints and doubtful readings can be corrected and clarified by reference to just one ms, a photostat copy of which has been additionally used for the present purpose.[2] The original ms (B) belongs to the *Staatsbibliothek, Preuss. Kulturbesitz, Orientabteilung* (*Ms. or. oct.* 771), and is dated *saṃvat* 1842 or *śake* 1708, i.e. A.D. 1786. The colophon of the lithograph edition (A) is as follows:

iti Śrī-Brahmāṇḍapurāṇe kṣetrakhaṇḍe Śrī-Mallāri-prasāda-vākyaṃ nāma dvāviṃśatitamo 'dhyāyaḥ//

As neither a critical text nor a translation in a western language is published, a short synopsis of the text by means of a tentative translation or paraphrase of passages relevant for the context is given at the end of this essay.

The date and the authorship of the text cannot be exactly fixed. Presumably it was composed by Deśastha Brāhmaṇs. They were prominent devotees of Mallāri/Khaṇḍerāyā, who was their *kulasvāmin*. Deśastha Brāhmaṇs can be found not only in Maharashtra but also in Karnataka and other parts of the Deccan. For instance, it is known that the *kulasvāmin* of the saint-poet Dāsopanta (1551-1615) was the Mallāri of Premapura.[3] This is to the north of the city of Bidar, in the northern part of Karnataka, and the *MM* glorifies it as a *tīrtha-kṣetra* and the origin of Mallāri (see below). During the time of Dāsopanta, Bidar was the capital of the Muslim Bahāmani dynasty of Bidar.[4] The god of Prempura was also the family deity of the famous Deśastha Brāhmaṇ poet Śrīdhara, who composed a Marathi version of the *Malhāri* (sic) *Māhātmya* in the beginning of the 18th century and who says of his father:

The father's *bhakti* was marvellous, after he had seen the king of Premapuri.[5]

The first translation of the *MM* into Marathi is attributed to Siddhapāl Kesarī. He finished composing the work in the year 1585 and is said to have lived in Pāl-Peṃbereṃ, an important centre of the Khaṇḍobā cult in the Satara District of Maharashtra.[6] Peṃbereṃ or Pember is the Marathi version of Premapura, and it seems that, with the decay of the original *kṣetra* Premapura, Pāl or Pāli developed during the

Marāṭhā period and was to some extent identified with the original *kṣetra*. Marathi traditions are fairly unanimous that Mallāri or Khaṇḍobā originally came from Ādimailāra, which is alternately called Mailarpur/Premapuri or Pember, in Karnataka, from where he went to Naldurg in Usmanabad Dt., then to Pal, and then to Jejuri (Pune Dt.).

The Marathi version by Siddhapāl Kesarī follows more or less the Sanskrit original, which Siddhapāl Kesarī purported to translate. The *MM* states that the god in the form of a *svayambhū liṅga* appeared on Campāṣaṣṭhī, i.e. on the sixth day of the light half of the month of Mārgaśīrṣa (see below, *MM* 18.6). The Campāṣaṣṭhī *vrata* is mentioned in the *Vratakhaṇḍa* of the *Caturvargacintāmaṇi* (1260-71) by Hemādri, but with reference to Kumāra or Skanda. Though hundreds of *vratas* and works are listed, the *MM* is not mentioned. It is only in the *Nirṇayasindhu* (1612) by Kamalākarabhaṭṭa that Campāṣaṣṭhī is expressly connected with the *MM*. The story of Śiva killing the two demons Maṇi and Malla at the instance of the seven Ṛṣis is also mentioned in the *Yogavāsiṣṭha*, a Marathi work wrongly attributed to Jñāneśvara, which was composed according to A.K. Priyolkar some time before 1540. These dates have led R.C. Dhere to the conclusion that the Sanskrit *MM* must have been composed within 200 to 250 years after 1260.[7]

The cult is known of course much earlier than the twelfth century, especially from inscriptions and antagonistic references in Jaina sources and Liṅgāyat *vacanas*. But it was essentially a folk cult and had apparently not reached the level "worthy" of a Sanskrit *Māhātmya*. The folk origin of Mailāra seems to be reflected to some extent in the *Samayaparīkṣe* (2.71) of the Jain author Brahmaśiva (*c.* 1150-60) of Karnataka, who claims that a person of Jain faith who had died with obstinate valour on the battlefield, later on became known as Mailāra. On the whole the pre-13th century evidence suggests that Mallāri/Mailāra etc. was worshipped by simple folk, heroes, officers, and kings of minor dynasties, and Brāhmaṇs. In the 13th and 14th centuries we find that Mailāra, Mairāl[~ḷ]a etc. is increasingly mentioned in literary works. The advent of the Muslims seems to have facilitated the rise of folk deities concomitant with the ruin of the classical (Hemāḍpantī) temples of the Yādava period. In any case, Cakradhara (d. 1270), the famous "founder" of the Mahānubhāva "sect", while explaining the events to occur at the end of the Kaliyuga, said in the *Līḷācaritra:*

kāḷicāṃ aṃtīṃ sivāilemṃ [v.l.: *Śivālayeṃ*] *Vis*[sic] *ṇugraheṃ lopatī: Mairāḷa kṣetrapāḷa yeṃ sthāneṃ hotī* [v.l.: *Mairāḷa kṣetrapālāciyā sthāpanā hotī*].[8]

At the end of the Kaliyuga the Śiva and Viṣṇu temples disappear. The temples of Mairāḷa [and] *kṣetrapālas* exist [or: are established].

It is especially in the middle of the 14th century that references to Mailāra/Mairāḷa in inscriptions and literary works increasingly appear. In an inscription dated A.D.1369 on a pillar in the compound of the Malleśvara or Mailāradeva temple at Ainavolu near Warangal in northwestern Andhra Pradesh, the myth of Maillāri is mentioned.[9] About five stanzas (23-7) in this inscription, which is in Telugu and Sanskrit, narrate that god Śiva, in order to protect Arjuna, assumed the form of a Śabara, fought with the demon Malla, and killed him, thus acquiring the name Mallāri, which in the course of time became Mailāra. The goddess who accompanied the god in the form of a huntress is said to have been given the name Māḷācī. Unfortunately the inscription has not been published, and the details do not match with our *MM*, but at least we can say that different versions of the myth circulated in the 14th century Deccan. Ailōni was near the capital of the Kākatīya dynasty, Warangal, and the god Mailāra in the capital itself was said to be the *kulasvāmin* of the Kākatīyas. The *Krīḍābhirāmamu* from Orugallu (present Warangal) describes Mailāra and calls him "this village god worthy of receiving praise from noble people". It also describes the self-torturing feats of the followers of Mailāra, the Mailāra Vīrabhaṭṭas.[10] The successors of these *vīras* still exist today. The author lived in the early part of the 15th century, but the work is said to be a translation of an earlier Sanskrit work, entitled *Premābhirāma*, by Tippana, a contemporary of the Kākatīya king Pratāpa Rudra (1298-1323).[11] In about 1350 Vidyāraṇya, who was associated with the Vijayanagara kingdom, is supposed to have composed his famous work, the *Pañcadaśī*. He gives a list of deities as examples of lower manifestations of Īśvara, which are worshipped as granting fulfilment of wishes. Amongst them he mentions Mairāla (= Mailāra) (6.206-8):

vighna bhairava mairāla/mātrikā yakṣa rakṣasāṇ//

The tendency to classify Mairāla-Mailāra amongst the lower divinities continued throughout the literature of the Liṅgāyat and Maharashtrian *bhakti* saints. Vidyāraṇya's brother Sāyaṇa seems to allude to the Mallāri cult when he explains *mallāḥ* as *maṇilāḥ* (= with a dewlap) in his commentary on the *Taittirīya-Saṃhitā* 5.1.2. This may be a reference to Maṇi and Malha = Malla. Malhāri is a frequent variant of Mallāri. The enemy (*ari*) of Malha (he-goat; a name of Prajāpati) could allude to the mythological antagonism of Rudra and Prajāpati. But the question has to be pursued further. We should add here that we are confronted with constant punning and identifications on the basis of sound similarities, justified by a plausible context and purpose irrespective of a correct philological etymology. This occurs not only on the folk level, but also in Sanskrit texts, e.g. where the popular name "Mailāra" is identified with "Mallāri" and also with "Śambhu" (Śiva) and "Viṣṇu" in the same process (see below, *MM* 18.11-14).

The Mailāra cult and its centres were close to the Vijayanagara kingdom.[12] For instance, in the beginning of the 14th century a chief (*adhipa*) of Bhujaṅganagara (Havanur in the Haveri Tk. of Dharwad District) was a devotee of Mallāri and attended the car-festival of the god Vīrūpākṣa at Hampi along with other chiefs and kings.

In short, we may surmise that the most likely period during which the present Sanskrit text of the *MM* was composed must have been the 14th century.

3. THE LOCAL SETTING OF THE TEXT

The *MM* states that on Campāṣaṣṭhī of the month of Mārgaśīrṣa, Śiva and his Śakti manifested themselves under a tree (*MM* 18.5) and that Premapura, the capital of the enemy of Maṇi, came into being (*MM* 18.9,1). Premapura—nobody doubts—is the present Pember, Mailarpur or Khanapur near Bidar in northern Karnataka. The Maharashtrians call it Ādimailār, that is, the place from where, as we have said above, the Mallāri cult spread to some major, and hundreds of minor, places in Maharashtra. There it must have coalesced with the pre-existing cult of Khaṇḍaka (the patron *yakṣa* of Paithan, i.e. Pratiṣṭhāna), Khaṇḍunāth alias Khaṇḍobā, and acquired its characteristic regional Maharashtrian timbre. Marathi oral and written texts agree that the god is Kānaḍyā Khaṇḍerāyā—"the Khaṇḍerāyā from Karnataka".[13] Whether Premapura is actually the historical *mūlasthāna* may be doubted. The most important centres of the Mailāra cult in Karnataka are further south, namely Mailar or Manmailar in Hadagalli Tk. of Bellary Dt., and Devaragudda in Dharwad Dt. between Dharwad and Hubli, near Ranebennur. But in any case there is no doubt that the *MM* is connected with Premapura. Premapura = Pember is situated 22 km. to the north of Bidar. The temple complex is situated in a large grove. The area around the temple looks deserted, though there are enough traces to show that there must have been a considerable settlement formerly. No archaeological report on the place exists and no inscriptions are reported, as far as I know. It is here that three regions—Karnataka, Andhra, and Maharashtra—meet and Mallāri is also readily and spontaneously known by his other names: Mallanna (Ka. Mallaṇṇa), Mailāra, Mairāḷa, Mallu Khān, Khaṇḍerāyā, etc. Pember comes to full life during the *yātrā,* which begins on the first day of the bright half of Mārgaśīrṣa. The most important day is Campāṣaṣṭhī. But the *yātrā* lasts till *amāvāsyā* and Sundays are specially observed. The *yātrā,* or, as it is popularly called, the *jatrā,* is connected with a large cattle market. The road which passes Pember leads via Udgir to another famous Khaṇḍobā cult at Malegaon and from there to the Godavari valley. In Malegaon the *jatrā* takes place in the month of Pauṣa (December/January) and is again connected with a large cattle market, where horses, camels, elephants, and especially donkeys are traded. In fact, Malegaon and Pember were situated on an old trade route which connected the north with the kingdoms of the south, whether Hindu or Muslim. The nearest capital was Bidar. Merchants, such as the early Jains, the Banajigas, the Lingāyat *vāṇīs,* or itinerant merchants like Gone Perikes of Andhra, who are all in one way or the other connected with the cult of Mallanna/Mailāra/Khaṇḍobā, must have travelled this route. Thus Khaṇḍobā or Mallanna of Malegaon is said to have been brought by Banjārī traders travelling to Bidar with their pack oxen loaded with rice. Even today many traders with large herds of donkeys come from as far as Kathiawar to sell their animals at Malegaon, Pember and Jejuri. We do not know the motives of the author of the *MM* when he chose the myth of Kṣatrī Mahābāhu for the glorification of one of the eight *tīrthas* of the *kṣetra* (*MM* 19.29ff.). In any case, the story fits the context well. Mahābāhu is a highway robber who is condemned to be reborn as a donkey. The road from Bidar to Udgir had until some years ago a reputation of being unsafe for travellers because of robbers, and this reputation was probably not newly earned. The impoverished Mahābāhu is said to have killed ten Brāhmaṇs. This seems not to be too far-fetched a possibility, considering the unsettled areas of the Deccan between the major kingdoms in the south and the north, and if we keep in mind that the occasion of the *MM* is the rescue of the *dharmaputras,* i.e. Brāhmaṇs, from the depredations of Maṇi and Malla. One

Marathi version of the myth describes Maṇi and Malla as *mārgaghna*, i.e. 'waylayers'.[14] The mention of the bridal couples in the myth of Mahābāhu (*MM* 19.30) may appear strange if we do not know that it is a special custom throughout the cult of Mallanna/Mailāra/ Khaṇḍobā that newly-wed couples have to show themselves to their *kulasvāmin*. Even today in Pember the newly-weds of the Gavḷī pastoral caste come with the ends of their *dhotar* and sari tied together and untie them after *darśana*. The custom is widespread in the cult of Mallanna/Mailāra/Khaṇḍobā.

The identification of the eight *tīrthas* described in chapter 19 of the *MM* presents difficulties. The present main temple of Mailāra was built or rebuilt under Muslim or Marāṭhā influence and the whole complex needs systematic exploration. There are enough sculptural and architectural remains in the *kṣetra* to show that it existed *before* the Muslims. To the west, behind the temple of Mailāra, which faces east, there are a small and a large *kuṇḍa*. The latter is called (Ma.) Gāymukh or Gaṅgākuṇḍ. As it is an old tank, it may be identical to the Gayatīrtha mentioned in the *MM*. The Gaṅgākuṇḍa and the Ghṛtamārīkuṇḍa mentioned in the *MM* are still shown, but their situation does not accord with the directions given in the *MM*.

The *MM* tries to combine the "northern" tendency, emphasizing the purifying effect of *snāna* as regards sins, and the "southern" preoccupation with *bhakti* and *darśana* of a particular god at a particular place. The obsession with the purifying effect of water and *kuṇḍas* in the *MM* is not noticeable today. *Snāna* is considered as a part of the worship of the god or goddess and is performed at the beginning of the fulfilment of a vow to the god or goddess. We may say that folk religion is primarily observed. Thus e.g. in Pember in fulfilment of vows to the goddess little children are put on rafts (Ma. *tāphā*) or, rather, on the big blades of the Ambāḍī plant (*Hibiscus cannabinus*) and floated on the water of the Gaṅgā Kuṇḍ(?).[15]

4. THE BACKGROUND OF MAṆI, THE *DAITYA*

The *MM* emphasizes the association of the *daitya* Maṇi rather than Malla with Premapura. After Mārtaṇḍa Bhairava had manifested himself, the city of Premapura came into existence; it is also called the capital of Maṇi-dviṣa = "the enemy of Maṇi" (*MM* 18.9,1). On his death Maṇi specifically requests Mārtaṇḍa Bhairava to allow him to stay with his horse near Mārtaṇḍa Bhairava (13.57). In other words, the *daitya* becomes not only a *bhakta*, but also a guardian of Mārtaṇḍa Bhairava. But why Maṇi? The myth of Malla, the *daitya*, occurs without Maṇi in some versions and there seems to be no need to introduce Maṇi. Maṇi also does not seem to take part in the raid on the *āśrama* of the Ṛṣis and appears later in the myth (*MM* 2.20).

Another remarkable feature of the *MM* in this connection is the repeated reference to the *mūrti* of Mārtaṇḍa Bhairava as being "made of earth" or "clay" (see below *MM* 18.10: *mūrti mahīmayī*, 18.13: *pārthiva deva*, 18.25: *mṛṇmaya*). Now in Mailar, Hadagalli Tk., Bellary Dt., according to oral traditions, Mārtaṇḍa Bhairava is said to have been living in a termite mound which a certain Gomuni (we would suggest: a cowherd) transformed into a *mūrti* of Mārtaṇḍa Bhairava, using the clay of the mound (Ka. *maṇṇu* = clay). Mailāra is thus called Maṇṇumailāra—"the earthen Mailāra". The present *mūrti* of Mārtaṇḍa Bhairava in the temple actually consists of petrified clay from a termite mound covered with layers of soot and oil. Mārtaṇḍa Bhairava holds *ḍamaru*, *triśūla*, *bhaṇḍāra* (turmeric powder) *pātra* and *khaḍga* in his four hands. According to the *temple* version of the myth, Gomuni once saw one of his cows shedding milk into the termite mound. After digging it up he found Kapilamuni (cp. *MM* 19.22-4, where the effects of bathing in the Kapilatīrtha are described), who had attained his salvation and, pleased, ordered Gomuni to spread the fame of Mārtaṇḍa Bhairava.[16] Other oral versions from Andhra tell us that Mārtaṇḍa Bhairava or Mallanna was found in an anthill along with sheep and dogs. In fact, we also learn from local oral traditions at Pember/Premapura that Mārtaṇḍa Bhairava originated in a termite mound. We may follow R.C. Dhere and question whether Maṇi is not a "sanskritized" version of *maṇṇu*. In other words, we may wonder whether the low (or folk) origin of the god is not retained, living on in the demon who simultaneously is his own original lower self or *alter ego* of folk origin and becomes his guardian and *bhakta*. Mārtaṇḍa Bhairava, the *avatāra* of the purāṇic Śiva on earth, incorporates many features of the demons, as I have tried to show elsewhere.[17]

But there may be another background to the meaning of Maṇi. In many places of the cult of Mallāri/Mailāra there is a pervasive and consistent Jain background. For instance, at Maṇmailār the present temple is said to have been a Jain Basadi. In Pember there is a small shrine with an old *mūrti* of a Jain *tīrthaṅkara*. Thus it is also possible to see a Jain background in Maṇi, who may actually be Maṇibhadra. The *yakṣa* Maṇibhadra was popular among Jain merchants and was the tutelary deity of merchants and travellers. Maṇibhadra is often mentioned in mythology in connection with cobras. These features fit well in the historical context of Pember. The Jain influence was strong in this part of the Deccan and was superseded in many places by Śaivite—in the case of the Liṅgāyats violent—reactions. We should note that the famous town of Kalyāṇī, associated with Basavaṇṇa, is not situated very far from Bidar. The emphasis on Maṇi in the *MM* may reflect the fact that the Jain tutelary god Maṇi was subordinated to Mallāri and became his guardian and *bhakta*.

The strange insistence in the text on Mārtaṇḍa Bhairava being *mṛṇmaya* may, as we have said, reflect the folk origin of Mārtaṇḍa Bhairava. Typically of the purāṇic aloofness of the text the termite mound, a very frequent if not stereotypical origin of folk cults on the Deccan, is not mentioned. The connection with Maṇi and the serpents believed to live in termite mounds may also be seen in the huge serpent facing the god in the temple at Pember. At this spot we would expect the converted demon to be represented as a *bhakta*. The serpent may, however, be reminiscent of Maṇi, or the god living amongst the serpents in a termite mound who becomes Śiva/ Mārtaṇḍa Bhairava by a purāṇic metamorphosis.

5. THE CASE OF MALLA

The word Malla and its meaning have an old ancestry reaching back to the Vedic *mārya* = "ein junger Mann in der Blüte seiner Kraft" (Grassmann). The term is used in the *Ṛgveda* especially of the Maruts, Indra and Agni. Old Indian *mārya* (*-ry-*) changed into Middle Indian *malla* (*-ll-*), and we have, for instance, the statement of Manu that the Mallas were Kṣatriya Vrātyas (*Manusmṛti* 6.22).[18] Many medieval kings of the Deccan, but also chieftains or headmen of villages, especially among the agricultural and pastoral castes, have *malla* and variants of it as their *biruda* or part of their name. As I have tried to show elsewhere, Malla is a mythic epitome of the upstart king or rising robber king, *maṇḍaleśvara* or *daṇḍanāyaka*, usurping or threatening the centre of the world and the brāhmaṇical dharmic order (Sontheimer 1984: 155-70). The Ṛṣis or *dharmaputras* complain to Śiva that Maṇi and Malla, staying on the mountain (which tends to symbolize the centre in myths) Maṇiśaila, performed *tapas* and received a boon from Brahmā making them invincible, and also that they uprooted *liṅgas*, and even had themselves worshipped by Indra! (*MM* 7.13-36).[19] This rising king, who was himself god rather than enacting god, did not necessarily subscribe to the *varṇāśrama* ideology of the Brāhmaṇ. Cattle-lifting, capturing women and even attacking *agrahāras* were not considered unethical, but rather seen as expressions of the values of prowess and bravery. The *MM* repeatedly stresses the bravery (*śaurya*) of the *daityas*.

Like the king such a god was in need of loyal followers (Ma. *dev bhakticā bhūkelā*), who in turn received loyalty from him. His followers emulated him and were as if a part of him. The *MM* seems to utilize these sentiments: Śiva becomes Mārtaṇḍa Bhairava, the king on earth, and replaces, so to say, the rule of the demons by the overlordship of Śiva/Mārtaṇḍa Bhairava. The sentiment of loyalty or *bhakti* is made full use of: the *daityas* realize their blindness (*MM* 16.52) and request Śiva to grant *sāyujya* or *sannidhi*. After all, the world is pervaded by Śiva; how can the *daityas* then be separate? This is the argument of Malla (*MM* 17.4). Malla merges in Śiva's Name and obtains *vilaya* (*MM* 17.42), and Maṇi remains close by in his equestrian form (*MM* 18.10). Malla is not keen on going to heaven, as he has "seen the god" who includes everything (17.34; *parāvara*). In a way this also indicates that Śiva has become a god on earth, who, like the ancient Rudra, is a real folk deity and thus accessible to all *jātis* and *varṇas*. He appears as a *svayambhū liṅga*, which has to be distinguished from the "regular" śāstric installation (*prāṇapratiṣṭhā*) of a *liṅga* in a classical Śivālaya.

6. THE TRANSFORMATION OF ŚIVA, MAṆI AND MALLA AND OTHER INCIDENTS OF THE CULT AS REFLECTED IN THE *MALLĀRI MĀHĀTMYA*

According to the *MM* (8.2) the purāṇic Śiva takes the form of Mārtaṇḍa Bhairava on earth (*MM* 8.2). But Mārtaṇḍa Bhairava is not the usual purāṇic Bhairava, created by Śiva in order to represent him on earth, nor is he a partial manifestation. It is made clear that it is Śiva *himself* who assumes another form. Mārtaṇḍa is a name of the sun, and Mārtaṇḍa Bhairava is considered to be a combination of Śiva and Sūrya. For instance, Mārtaṇḍa Bhairava's ear-ring (one? Siddhapāl Kesari translates: his earrings sparkle like the sun and the moon) is like the burning sun. This is the only reference where the text overtly suggests that Mārtaṇḍa Bhairava is a combination of Śiva and Sūrya. Temples of Sūrya or Āditya were quite frequent during the time of the Yādavas of Devagiri as e.g. the *Līḷācaritra* indicates. They may have been superseded or absorbed by folk cults, as in the village of Nandūr, Ahmednagar District, where the Āditya temple mentioned in the *Līḷācaritra* "degenerated" into the worship of Nimbādaitya, who is said to have been a *bhakta* of Rāma. A Mārtaṇḍeśvara temple dedicated to Śiva is known from the Kanigiri Tk. in the Nellore Dt. In the Khaṇḍobā cult the worship of the sun and the moon finds various forms of expression. Sunday and Monday, especially Somvatī Amāvāsyā (the conjunction of the sun and the moon on a Monday) are most important days. It is also said that Mārtaṇḍa Bhairava manifested himself on a Sunday (*MM* 18.6). The moon and the sun also decorate the door of Khaṇḍobā's temple at Jejuri.

The sun, turmeric powder and gold are very often linked in ritual and myth. Plaques for the worship of Khaṇḍobā in house shrines should be preferably made of *gold*. Turmeric powder (Ma. *bhaṇḍār*, Skt. *haridrācūrṇa*) is an important ingredient in the rituals and festivals of Mallanna/Mailāra/Khaṇḍobā (*MM* 18.15; 21.70). It has healing properties and Mallanna/Mailāra/Khaṇḍobā may also be compared in this respect to Sūrya, the great healer. Mārtaṇḍa Bhairava is not only identified with the sun, but both may also be identifiable with the termite mound. We have seen that Mārtaṇḍa Bhairava is connected with or lives in the termite mound. According to a Vedic text Agni stays in it during the night to emerge as the sun at daybreak. There is widespread worship (Sontheimer 1989, *passim*) of the termite mound as the sun and for fertility in marriages. Mallanna/Mailāra/Khaṇḍobā also plays an important role in the blessing and fertility of marriages (cp. *MM* 21.57-8).

Mārtaṇḍa Bhairava is listed in another Sanskrit text as one of the 64 Bhairavas. R.C. Dhere has suggested that it seems far-fetched to explain Mārtaṇḍa Bhairava's name solely on the basis of Sanskrit sources like the list of names in this text, and he has instead proposed that Mārtaṇḍa consists of a bilingual word derived from Ka. *mari* and Ma. *toṇḍ*—both meaning "head", "face". "*Maritoṇḍ*" was then sanskritized into Mārtaṇḍa (Dhere 1962, 40). According to Dhere, the god might have been originally worshipped in the form of heads made of cloth (*mukhavṭā*); he refers to the medieval Muslim *bhakti* poet Shekh Mahaṃmad, who speaks adversely about this god whose *mukhavṭās* were "made of rags" (Dhere 1962: 41f.). We cannot exclude this additional "etymology" of Mārtaṇḍa, given the fondness for punning, which we have already mentioned, and the popularity of bilingual words from Kannada and Marathi in the cult, e.g. Heggade (Ka.)-Pradhān (Ma.) (the minister of god), *cāṅg-bhalā* (Ka.

cāṅgu, Ma. *bhalā*: both mean "good"). The point is that we cannot question the validity of such religious, though popular, "etymologies" if they prove to be acceptable to devotees.

Whereas the *daityas* accept the overlordship of Mārtaṇḍa Bhairava, the god for his part absorbs more and more the qualities and attributes of his royal opponents. We may also say that the *daityas* resemble more the ancient folk god Rudra and his followers than the purāṇic Śiva. This existence of folk elements, especially in the conception of royalty, is expressed in the dramatic performance of rituals and in oral literature, and it is much more explicit in the Marathi versions of the *MM* than in the Sanskrit *MM*. Some examples may demonstrate this: The dog plays an important role in the cult, because it is important for the pastoral groups, for itinerant merchants, for the hunting king and hunters in general, hunting being an important occupation of some groups connected with the cult. But in the text the dog is mentioned just in passing, in connection with Śiva assuming the form of Mārtaṇḍa Bhairava (*MM* 8.2-7). This reticence in the text also does not reflect the most important devotees of the cult of Mallanna/Mailāra/Khaṇḍobā, namely the Vaggayyas (Ka.), Oggus (Tel.) and Vāghyās (Ma.), and their dog rituals. In view of their dress and habits, these devotees may be traced back to the Vrātyas, the special followers of the folk-religious Rudra.

Or: the *MM* speaks of the horse only in connection with Maṇi (*MM* 13.9, 2; 57, 1). Śiva himself is seated on his bull (*MM* 8.11, 1). This does not sufficiently account for the tremendous importance of the horse in the cult of Mallanna/Mailāra/Khaṇḍobā, where especially Khaṇḍobā himself is mostly depicted as seated on the horse, though the Nandin is also his *vāhana*. There is no house shrine of a Khaṇḍobā devotee which does not contain a *mūrti* or a plaque showing Khaṇḍobā seated on a horse together with his wife Mhāḷsā. This indicates that in folk religion the *rūpa* of the *daitya* devotee was transposed to Mārtaṇḍa Bhairava.

The context of the cult is often betrayed by the text when it lays particular or even peculiar emphasis on an aspect which may or may not be a standard purāṇic incident. Thus, when the great serpent of Śiva, which serves as his apparel (*MM* 13.7), is mentioned, we may still think of a poetical, purāṇic description, but when it is told that the *daitya* cuts asunder the serpent with one stroke of his sword (*MM* 13.30-1) and again it is mentioned that he cuts the snakes (*bhujaṅga*) with his arrows (13.37), we feel reminded of the chain-breaking rituals in the cult of Mallanna/Mailāra/Khaṇḍobā: heavy iron chains have to be broken with one jerk in fulfilment of vows to Mallanna/ Mailāra/Khaṇḍobā. Different explanations of the meaning of the chain and its breaking are given by informants; not all of these explanations can be discussed here. But we are often told by informants that the chain represents the snake of Śiva. In Mailār (Hadagalli Tk.) it is said that Mārtaṇḍa Bhairava changed his snake into a chain (Ka. *sarapali*, Ma. *langar*) and tied it around his neck while fighting with the demons. The demons broke that chain into pieces, but Śiva made it whole. In memory of this the "ritual of the chain" (Ka. *sarapali kāyaka*) is performed. Two observations have to be made: first, the *bhakta* can identify himself with the *daitya* and his actions by breaking the chain. After all, the *daitya* is a *bhakta*, though he expresses his *bhakti* by *vaira* (*MM* 13.43; Cintāmaṇi in his *MM* of 1818: 3.71 calls it *virodha bhakti*). For the ordinary devotee, on the other hand, there is no feeling of *vaira*, and the chain-breaking has only positive connotations, namely, the fulfilment of a vow or the performance of a regular annual family rite.

Another conspicuous feature in the *MM* is the request of Malla to fulfil the wishes of those devotees "who cut themselves etc." (*MM* 17.37). This refers to the mortifications of devotees in the Mallanna/ Mailāra/Khaṇḍobā cult. The rituals occasionally involved suicide. The *MM* sounds as if Malla pleads on behalf of his own followers, that is to say, the followers of the pre-existing folk cult of Mailāra-Mairāḷa, which the *MM* attempts to ethicize while at the same time acknowledging rituals which could not just be overlooked. Obviously the god also received non-vegetarian sacrifices (*MM* 18.4,1), which nowadays are given, at the most, to the *daityas* or to Mallanna/ Mailāra/Khaṇḍobā's second wife, who comes from a tribal or pastoral community. Though extremely important, she is not mentioned in the text, but she is often identified with Gaṅgā, who does occur in the text.

The quarrel between the two wives of Śiva, well-known from purāṇic sources, is intensely mirrored in oral traditions describing the quarrel between Mhāḷsā (= Pārvatī), who comes from the Liṅgāyat *vāṇīs*, and Bāṇāī (= Gaṅgā), who is a cowherd (Gavḷī) or shepherd woman. According to the *MM* (20.23,1), Gaṅgā angrily went "to the earth", which Siddhapāl Kesarī translates "to the underworld" (20.26: *patāḷaprati gelī*). The *MM* seems to attempt to end the quarrel of the co-wives by suggesting that they are one (*MM* 20.24). In folk myths the beautiful Gaṅgā, alias Bāṇāī or Bālāi, is said to live in the underworld. From there the god abducts and marries her, and she becomes Yogeśvarī (Sontheimer 1976: 62). In other words, the *kāminī* Bāṇāī becomes a *yoginī* on her marriage with the god. The two wives are both *yoginīs*, especially when they accompany the warrior Mārtaṇḍa Bhairava. This may explain the two identical *mūrtis* of the two goddesses flanking the *ugra-mūrti* of Mārtaṇḍa Bhairava in the temple of Jejuri. Both are called Jogeśvarī. It is in Mailār (Hadagalli Tk.) that Gaṅgā and Gaurī are said to have become Gaṅgimālavva and to have accompanied the god in his fight against Maṇi and Malla. Mhāḷsā/Mallavva etc. was an independent *śakti* cult which seems to have been incorporated in the cult of Mallanna/Mailāra/Khaṇḍobā and is sometimes identified with the ferocious goddess Ghṛtamārī (Ka. Tuppada Mālavva). Bāṇāī is the erotic goddess coming from the forest and the "forest tribe" and reflects the ancient Vaḷḷi, the beloved of Murukaṉ.

One of the important institutions—considering that it is a cult where the god is taken as a king on earth—is mentioned rather in passing. *MM* 18.16 mentions the "festival of girls" (or "festive girls") or celestial harlots like Rambhā, etc. (18.7-8); this refers to the *devadāsīs*, who are called *muraḷīs* in Marathi (cp. Ka. *maruḷī* = "madly devoted woman"). The social catholicity of the cult is reflected in the statement that even Muslims (*mlecchas*) are *bhaktas* of the god (*MM* 21.7), a phenomenon which has lived on in the cult. In Pember even today Mailāra or Khaṇḍobā is called Mallukhān or Mallukā Paṭhān. Perhaps this is why Premapura is also called Khanapur.

Thus we may say that the *MM* records in its own purāṇic *kāvya* style a very popular, widespread, and ancient, even Vedic, cult of a folk deity which flourished especially in the Deccan from medieval times. This cult lives on today and presents a self-conscious folk culture which uses the *Māhātmya* at its convenience and without assigning to it any authority. The mutual interaction and reflection between the *Māhātmya* and this folk culture with its non-classical or "non-standard" *bhakti* requires not only acquaintance with the Sanskrit text but the study of its complex context.

7. A SYNOPSIS OF THE *MALLĀRI MĀHĀTMYA*

Chapter 1: The Raiding of the Āśram (*āśrama-pīḍana*).

At the instance of Pārvatī, Śiva tells her what Sanatkumāra related to him about the *kṣetra-tīrtha*, i.e. Premapura, which Śiva established out of com-passion for humans. He also tells her which *vratas* can be performed in this *kṣetra-tīrtha* of Śiva where one can obtain *bhukti* and *mukti*.

In the Kṛtyayuga the Seven Ṛṣis or seven *dharmaputras* were practising *tapas* on the mountain Maṇicūl. One day Malla, the king of the *daityas*, along with his *rākṣasas*, while on a hunt, raided their *āśrama*. The *āśrama* was devastated, the trees were uprooted (1.15), the equipment for pulling water from the wells was demolished, the sons of Malla urinated in the fire of the sacrificial pit (1.16), the blossoms of trees meant for the worship of the gods were destroyed (1.17), and Malla frolicked and drank on the very sacrificial grounds (*vedis*) which were meant for the *pūjā* of the gods. Cows were killed (1.20), the wives of the Ṛṣis were molested and some of the Ṛṣis were tied with ropes around their necks and pushed into the wells (1.21). After Malla had disappeared, the maltreated and grieving *dharmaputras* hid their families and sacrificial fires (*kutumbyāny agnihotrāṇi*) in safe mountain places (1.23). They went to Indra appealing for help against the *daityas*. Maṇi, the brother of Malla, is mentioned for the first time in 2.20.

Chapter 2: The Appeal to Indra (*Śakrābhigamana*).

When the Ṛṣis explained their grievance to Indra he declared his inability to help them against Maṇi and Malla or to grant them *abhaya*, as the two *daityas* had performed *tapas* and had obtained a boon from Brahmā (2.21) and were therefore of invincible bravery (2.21: *parākramadurādharṣau*) and intoxicated by their strength gained through *tapas* (2.22: *tapo-vīrya-madoddhatau*). Thus he sent them on to Viṣṇu.

Chapter 3: The Appeal to Viṣṇu (Vaikuṇṭhābhigamana).

After Viṣṇu declared his inability to help, the Ṛṣis were advised to go to Kailāsa and ask for redress from Śiva.

Chapter 4: Description of Kailāsa (*Kailāsa-varṇana*).

Chapter 5: Description of Śiva's Court (*Candracūḍa-sabhā-varṇana*).

Chapter 6: Description of Śiva (*Śiva-varṇana*).

Chapter 7: The Request Addressed to Śiva (*Śiva-vijñāpana*).

The Ṛṣis told Śiva the story of the *daityas* who were intoxicated by their power. Śiva in great anger said he would swallow these lowest of the *daityas* and hit the earth with his matted hair like a snake with its hood (7.39):

daityādhamam grasāmīti sāttahāsam samutthitaḥ//
jaṭāḥ samtrāsayāmāsa phaṭāṭopāhinā bhuvi //39//,

wherepon "*Mahāmārī*" arose from the earth shining like the blaze of a forest fire. The Ṛṣis sprinkled ghee over her, who was in the *agnikuṇḍa*, whence she is called "Ghṛtamārī" (7.41).

Chapter 8: The Description of Śiva's Army (*Śiva-sainya-varṇana*).

Śiva assumed the form of Mārtaṇḍa Bhairava (8.2). The great serpent (*mahāhi*) served as an upper garment, the burning sun as an earring. He held *ḍamaru, triśūla, khaḍga*, and *pātra*, and was adorned with a garland which appeared like heated gold, a row of teeth which looked like a string of jewels, and on the forehead the crescent moon and three eyes. He was wearing a crown, was covered all over with turmeric powder, and was accompanied by a dog (*sārameya*) and seven crores of *gaṇas* (*sapta-koṭi-gaṇāḥ*) (8.2-7).

Chapter 9: Description of the Army of the Daityas (*Daitya-sainya-varṇana*).

Chapter 10: The Destruction of Mallāsura's Army (*Mallāsura-sainya-vadha*).

Chapter 11: The Killing of Khaḍga-draṃṣṭra (*Khaḍga-draṃṣṭra-vadha*).

Kārttikasvāmī/Skanda/Ṣaḍānana killed the general of the demon.

Chapter 12: The killing of Ulkāmukha and Kuntalaloma (*Ulkāmukha-Kuntalaloma-vadha*).

These two generals of the demons were killed by Gaṇeśa and Nandin respectively.

Chapter 13: The Killing of Maṇikāsura (Maṇi) (*Maṇikāsura-vadha*).

Maṇikāsura's war-cry (*siṃhanādana*) resounded in the three worlds and the summit of Kailāsa trembled (17.6). He taunted Mārtaṇḍa Bhairava: "By whom are you deceived? Go begging! That is preferable for mendicants! What use is there for a battle?" (13.15). Mārtaṇḍa

Bhairava's anger was aroused and a furious battle followed. It is noteworthy that in the course of the battle Maṇi turned into a *śarabha* and bit Mārtaṇḍa Bhairava on the arm (13.24), whereas Śambhu used the Kṛttikās (sometimes said to resemble a knife, Siddhapāl Kesarī: *kartari* = scissors), which Maṇi swallowed like a pebble (13.25). When Śambhu hit him on the chest and the back with his trident, Maṇi changed into a horse of tremendous size, neighing so that the three worlds trembled (13.27). Mārtaṇḍa Bhairava cut off Maṇi's head, and Maṇi replaced it with the head of an elephant (13.28). Mārtaṇḍa Bhairava thereupon cut off that head with an axe (13.29, 1). After this the *daitya* changed into a rider on a horse (13.29, 2). With his sword he hit Śaṅkara on the arm (13.30). With one stroke he cut asunder the serpent which was the ornament of Girijāpati, who in turn released the fire weapon (13.31). When it hit him (Siddhapāl Kesarī: his tongue was singed), Maṇi, along with his horse, fell into water, whence the *tīrtha* called "Horse-Tīrtha" (Turuṅgatīrtha) came into being at this spot. The serpents which are the ornaments of Śiva were cut by the arrows of Maṇi. They became furious and, as if consecrated by the *daitya*, shone with their hoods like Kāla, Death (13.37). Eventually the *daitya* lost consciousness and fell on the ground, rolling his eyeballs (13.41). Śambhu placed his foot on the head. With great *bhakti* the *daitya* held the foot and kept it on his head (13.42). He asked: "Where do you go after I have pleased you with my enmity (*vaireṇa*). You have been seen by me (= I had *darśana*) at the end as Death on the battlefield. I won't ever leave you" (13.43). He bowed to Jagadīśvara, who had become pleased with his bravery. Having seen the god himself, the *daitya* chief became a vessel of grace (*kṛpā-pātra*) (13.44). Maṇi praised Mārtaṇḍa Bhairava in a *stotra*, calling him Bhūtanātha, Rudra, Dānavāri, Saptakoṭigaṇasainya—"the leader of the seven crores of *gaṇas*", etc. (13.45-52). Finally Mārtaṇḍa Bhairava, pleased by Maṇi's simple-minded, perfect *bhakti*, granted a boon. Maṇi desired that the readers of this *stotra* should get Lakṣmi, that is wealth, to do *upakāra*, and wealth which provides enjoyable things like sons, horses, and elephants (13.55). They should get *mokṣa* on the battlefield, bravery (*śaurya*) and speech full of nine kinds of *rasa* (13.56). And: "May my head be always at your feet" (13.56, 2). "May my form connected with the horse always be near you" (13.57, 1).

Chapter 14: The Appeal to the Daitya (*Daityābhigamana*).
Mārtaṇḍa Bhairava, who was pleased about the *bhakti* of Maṇi,

decided to spare the life of Malla, and sent Viṣṇu as a mediator to persuade Malla to abstain from battle. Malla should request Mārtaṇḍa Bhairava to forgive him and should live with the remaining *daityas* in the Pātāla. Malla was born in the Prahlādakula, and Viṣṇu, therefore, is kindly disposed towards him. Malla, however, remained adamant and Viṣṇu's attempt was fruitless.

Chapter 15: The Description of the Battle with Ghṛtamārī (*Ghṛtamārī-yuddha-varṇana*).

The appearance of the furious *daitya*, the warrior Mahākāla, the Mahāvīra, on the battlefield made Kailāsa lose its crown, mountains tremble, and *siddhas* give up the embraces of their loves.

Mārtaṇḍa Bhairava first sent Ghṛtamārī into the battle. She began to swallow the army of the *daitya*. She cut off the arm of the *daitya* and a flow of blood emerged from his shoulder (the origin of the Soṇatīrtha) (15.21-2). Finally Ghṛtamārī was killed by innumerable arrows (15.28).

Chapter 16: The Battle between Malla, the *asura*, and Mārtaṇḍa Bhairava (*Mallāsura-Mārtaṇḍa Bhairava-yuddha*).

Malla, intoxicated by his bravery and strength (*śauryasattva-pramattaḥ*), insulted Mārtaṇḍa Bhairava:

> Return to your mountain (16.1). Compare your and my fortune, Śiva. You are seated on a single bull, I am accompanied by elephants (16.2). I have celestial clothes, you have a skin besmeared with blood; I have golden ornaments, you, instead, have serpents (16.3). I am anointed with sandal paste mixed with gold dust, you have ash from the burning ground mixed with dust of bone-ash (16.4). You have only one old woman, I have thousands of beautiful young women. Now, if it is so, who is higher than me, the Lord of the three worlds? (16.5: Tribhuvaneśvara). Are you not ashamed to say: I want to fight with you? Who with childish pranks competes with drunken elephants? (16.6). Is it possible for a fly, even if it were thirsty, to drink the ocean? Can a butterfly extinguish the tremendous blaze of the fire of the *pralaya*? (16.7). Is wind from a fan suited to drive away the cloud of the end of the Kalpa? What mouse, even if it is big, will make an effort to uproot mount Meru? (*kiṃ kalpa-megha-nāśāya kalpate vyajanānilaḥ // meror unmīlano* [B: *unmūlano*] *dyogaṃ kurute kiṃ mahonduruḥ //8//*).

Śiva answered the insults with arrows from his bows. Malla parried them with his spear and in turn attacked Śiva with his sword. A tremendous battle developed which had the dimensions of a *pralaya*. The combatants used various weapons. Malla turned into an elephant whose size reached the sky (16.16). Finally Śiva = Śambhu hit Malla with his *triśūla,* which was consecrated with the Pāśupata *mantra* (16.47). Malla intended to avoid the stroke with his various weapons and with the power (*śakti*) granted by Brahmā (16.49). With disk, axe, ploughshares, and sword Śiva hit upon the heart of Malla. Malla ran away and fell down on the earth (16.50). "You want to fight with me", Hara said, bursting into laughter, and he placed his foot on the head of the *daitya* in the battle (16.51). By the touch of his lotuslike foot the evil mind (*durmati*) of Malla came to an end (*śānta*) (16.52). Tearful, he placed his head on the feet of Śambhu (16.53). And, his hair erect (because of fear or joy), Malla praised Śambhu (16.53).

Chapter 17: The *Stuti* made by Mallāsura in Praise of Sadāśiva (*Mallāsura-kṛtā sadāśiva-stuti*).

On the battlefield the dying *daitya* enveloped by the grace of Pareśa composed a *stotra* (17.1). In this Malla cited a famous passage:

pāpo'haṃ pāpakarmāhaṃ pāpātmā pāpa-saṃbhavaḥ //

and continued:

magnaṃ durmati-paṅkābdhau māṃ samuddhara śaṅkara//2//

Then he continued:

Independent are the *jīvas* because of their deeds, O Śambhu; you are the *sūtradhāra* in respect of good and bad deeds (17.3).

Somewhat reproachfully Malla said:

You are the creator of the world, the universe is pervaded by you. Are, therefore, the *daityas* separated [from you]? You only know this, O Pareśa (17.4).

As you, in the form of will (*buddhi-rūpa*), impel with your *līlā*, so this movable and immovable world is produced (17.5).

The god who is in all beings in the form of *buddhi*, to him I bow, to him I bow . . . (17.6).

The god who is . . . in the form of *moha* . . . [many forms are enumerated].

Sadāśiva was pleased by the *stotra* of the *daitya* Malla and granted a wish to him (17.33.1). Malla answered:

With great courage I led Indra to dependence. Without doubt I have attained happiness and enjoyment, which is unattainable even by the gods. Why should I think of heaven when I have seen you, O All-embracing (17.34)?

I have attained fame in the world by death on the battlefield from you, O Lord of the World. What else could I wish for? Nevertheless I pray, O Śiva (17.35), that my name should be before your name, O Sureśvara (17.36, 1). My head and corpse should be forever under your feet (17.36, 2). Fulfil promptly the wishes of those *bhaktas* who worship you by cutting themselves etc., if you are satisfied with them (17.37). Grant *siddhi* to those who daily read the *stotra* composed by me for you at the time of death (17.38). There should never be disease, or poverty, greed, impure thought, or unhappiness or envy for these (17.39). And be Lakṣmī in their homes and delightful speech in their mouths (17.30, 1). Those who worship you with intense *bhakti* (17.40, 2) should have [endless] pleasure, having reached you easily (17.41, 1).

Śrī Mārtaṇḍa Bhairava said: "I am pleased by your battle and your perfect *bhakti*. What is desired by you, Malla, shall be, by my order (*śāsanāt*)" (17.41).

After Malla had attained absorption (*vilaya*), the five sons of Malla came to fight in a boisterous mood. Śiva, not taking them seriously, condemned them to be five mountains (17.42-4).

Chapter 18: The Granting of the Wish of the Gods and Ṛṣis (*surarṣi-vara-pradāna*).

Candraśekhara called the seven *dharmaputras* or *munis* and, honouring them, told them of the death of the Mahādaitya and said that they should enjoy through his *līlā* their desired happiness (*sukham īpsitam*) (18.1-2). They requested him to stay as *svayambhū* for the happiness of those who are afflicted by mistakes committed in the Kali time (18.4). Śiva consented and two *liṅgas*, Śiva being connected with Śakti, appeared under a tree (18.5).

The day of the appearance of the *liṅgam* (sing.) was on Sunday, the sixth day, in the Amalapakṣa, in the month of Mārgaśīrṣa, when the moon was in the Śatatāra *nakṣatra* (18.6). On this day the gods with their wives and sons, the *munis* with their families, the *nāgas* with their *nāginīs*, the serpents, the *siddhas* with their beautiful women, *gandharvas, kinnaras, yakṣas,* and celestial harlots beginning with Menakā (18.7-8) came for the *yātrā.* The city of Premapura came into being, the capital of *Maṇidviṣa* (18.9,1): *tatra premapuraṃ jātaṃ rājadhānī maṇi-dviṣaḥ* / / 18.9, 1 / /. The gods made it accessible for all *varṇas* and *jātis* through meditation: *sarvāsāṃ varṇa-jātināṃ dhyāna-gamyā suraiḥ kṛtā* / / 18.9, 2 / /.

The *mūrti* of Śambhu as well as that of Mārtaṇḍa Bhairavī was made of clay. It is combined with Maṇi, who is on the side seated on a horse (18.10): *mūrtir mahīmayī śambhor yathā mārtaṇḍa bhairavī // aśvena-*

sādinā-pārśva-vartinā-maṇinā yutā //10//. The syllable *ma* means Śambhu, the syllable *a* Viṣṇu; if these two [gods] are on earth (*ila*), the word *mela* (*ma* + *a* + *ila*) comes into existence. He is an enemy (*ārātiti*) to this *melā*. On account of this word analysis Mallāri's name has become Mailāra. The syllables *ra* and *lā*, it is said, are homophones: from this Mairāla comes into existence (18.11-14).

maḥ śambhur aś ca viṣṇuś ca tāv ilāyāṃ yadā sthitau//
tadā melāpadaṃ jātaṃ tām ārātiti vigrahāt//11//
mailāra iti mallārer nāmadheyam abhūt tadā//
sāvarṇyaṃ ra-la-yor [abhedaḥ] proktaṃ mairāla iti tena vā //12//.

"Salutation to this god Mairāla", said the gods. This god made of clay was worshipped by gods with flowers from Indra's garden (18.13). With incense, lights and betel, and plates full of meat... (18.14). But he should also be worshipped with enjoyable songs and dances (18.14), with mirrors and flywhisks, . . . with turmeric powder (*haridrācūrṇa*) and sandalwood paste (18.15) . . . with bunches of peacock feathers and festivals of girls (*taruṇīnāṃ-mahotsavaiḥ*) (18.16). After this the gods praised Mallāri. Amongst his epithets the following are conspicuous (18.17-24): "The one with great swinging sword" (*lola-mahākhaḍga*), "the husband of Mhālasā" (*śrī-mhālasā-kānta*), "the spreader of valour" (*pratāpa-vistārin*), "the killer of Mallāsura" (*mallāsurāntaka*), "the hero of battle" (*saṅgaravīra*), "Rudra, who holds the spear" (*rudrāya śūline*), "who loves the *bhaktas*" (*bhakta-priya*), "for whom destruction is a play" (*saṃhāra-kelaye*).

Though he was made of clay he was endowed with consciousness and he gave a boon to *munis* and gods (18.25): *mṛṇmayo 'pi ca mallāreś cetanātmābhavat tadā// uvāca sa munīn devān vṛṇudhvam iti satvaram* //25//. The gods said:

By the god everything has been made agreeable for the world. The earth is free of its burden, the *daitya* and his army are done with (18.26). Yet what ought to be done, O God, for those in whose mind you are, that is: be the giver of unequalled prosperity in their houses, of relinquishment (*tyāga*) and enjoyment (*bhoga*) (18.27), of much cattle, sons, horses, and the desired happiness. To kings a giver of a kingdom without enemies, full of horses and elephants (18.28), treasure, land, army, beautiful women. To wives great happiness and sons who become a hundred years of age (18.29). Continuous recognition by the king, always victory in the battlefield. In disputes victory against those who speak wrongly (18.30). Their fame should spread in all parts of the world (*brahmāṇḍa-khaṇḍa*). At the end give a place of *mokṣa*, protect us, Mallamardana (18.31). Be a giver of boons for those who daily read for you this *Māhātmya* which contains 700 *ślokas,* O Śaṅkara (18.32). Those who worship this written book (*likhitaṃ pustakam*) shall obtain perpetual happiness, richness, money, heaven, success, welfare, glory, victory, good fortune (18.33). For them there shall be sons learned in the sciences. The enemies shall perish. The house may always be happy (18.34). *Grahas, bhūtas, piśācas* shall not afflict (*bādhā na kurvantu*) him, as well as *ḍākinīs, yakṣas* and *rākṣasas.* Serpents shall not bite him (18.35). Immovable and movable, artificially produced poisons do not affect him. *Mantras, yantras, abhicāra,* etc. shall become blunt where the book is worshipped (18.36).

Mallāri replied: "What has been requested by you, gods and *munis,* that shall by my grace (*anugrahāt*) forever be for humans" (18.37).

Chapter 19: The Description of the Eight Tīrthas (*aṣṭa-tīrtha-varṇana*).

There are three-and-a-half crores of *tīrthas* in Premapura, but Sanatkumāra restricts his description to the eight most important of them, to the auspicious date and to the *phalaśruti* of bathing in them, that is, *siddhi* and purification from all sorts of sins. (1) To the north of the god is the Śaktikuṇḍa, where Ghṛtamārī was worshipped by the gods (19.7). (2) To the southeast is the Gayātīrtha; there are the footprints of Mallāri and the *tīrtha* is especially suited for *piṇḍadāna* (19.16). (3) To the north of the god is the Kapilatīrtha. (4) To the northeast of Mallāri is the Vāpitīrtha and the Gupta Malleśvar. If one sips the water of the *tīrtha* one is freed from all sins and obtains an excellent rebirth (*parāṃ gati*). (5) To the south of Mallāri is a *tīrtha* called Pāpavināśa. Having taken a bath there and having embraced (*āliṅgya;* Siddhapāl Kesarī: *pradakṣiṇa*) Bhairava in the form of an Aśvattha tree, one should see Mallāri in order to be free from all sins (19.39-41). (6) Next to the Pāpavināśa Tirtha is the Nandīkuṇḍa (19.42-5), where one should give cows along with horns of gold worth one lakh wrapped in red cloth to Brāhmaṇs learned in the Veda. If one sees Mallāri after that the greatness (*māhātmyam*) of one's *puṇya* cannot be comprehended even by Brahmā. (7) To the northeast at a distance of a hundred bow lengths there is the Rudrakuṇḍa, the Mahātīrtha, and its merits are difficult to obtain even for *yogīs.* If one bathes there one will not be reborn, one will obtain *jñāna,* but one may also gain enjoyment (*bhoga*). (8) To the north of the Śivālaya is the Ambudhārā Tīrtha, where one can have a bath and then see Mallāri to obtain liberation and go to the world of the thirty-three gods.

Chapter 20: The Description of the sixty *tīrthas* (*ṣaṣṭi-tīrtha-varṇana*).

The description of the *tīrthas* is given along with their *phalas* of bath and worship. The list of the *tīrthas* is as follows: Rāmatīrtha (20.3), Malleśvāratīrtha (20.4): absolves from *brahmahatyā*. Sūryakuṇḍa (20.5-6): heals eighteen types of leprosy. Śoṇatīrtha, Vaitaraṇi, Paraśurāmatīrtha, Śivatīrtha, Aśvatīrtha, Śaktikuṇḍa, Ugrakuṇḍa, Gaṇapatitīrtha, Varuṇatīrtha, Pārvatītīrtha,'where Gaṅgā became angry with Bhairava and went to Patālā, whereupon Pārvatī started quarrelling with Śiva. After this Śiva made Gaṅgā and Pārvatī one. Assuming a beautiful form, she became half the body of Mārtaṇḍa Bhairava. Mhālasā is called *ādiśakti* (20.22-4). Hearing of the *avatāra* of Mārtaṇḍa Bhairava, many Ṛṣis came. At the places where they performed *tapas* many *tīrthas* originated, e.g. Agastitīrtha, Gautamītīrtha. In this way thirty-five *tīrthas* came into existence.

Chapter 21: The worship of Mallāri (*śiva-pūjā-vidhi-nirūpaṇa*).

Sanatkumāra tells the Ṛṣis the various kinds of *bhakti* and expounds the eightfold *bhakti* as told by Mallāri (21.4). The ninefold *bhakti* consists of: *bhakti, prīti,* desire to hear the story of Mallāri (*kathākāṅkṣā*), *dhyāna, japa,* recitation of *stotra,* and living on getting possessed (*āveśenopajīvanam*) [by *Mallāri*] (21.5). This eightfold *bhakti* is even practised by the Mlecchas. The *bhakta* is not afflicted by *grahas, bhūtas, piśācas, ḍākinīs* like Pūtanā, etc. (21.7). Nor is he troubled by thieves, snakes, elephants, or tigers. Kings are his friends and even if he is dumb he is speaking (21.8). Calamity, enemies, diseases, poison administered by slaves (*cetako'pi viṣāṇi ca*), black magic (*abhicāra*), and evil *yantras* will not touch this man.

I am not fond of learned Caturvedī *vipras* and sacrificial priests (*yājñikaḥ śrotriyo*). Any *bhakta* of mine who is a worshipper of this *avatāra* shall be dear to me, even if he were one who cooks dogs (*śvapaco'pi vā,* i.e. a Caṇḍāla). Having given to him and thereupon having taken he should be worshipped as if he were me (21.10-11). (*tasmai deyaṃ yato grāhyaṃ sa ca pūjyo yathā hy aham //*). The one who sees me in everything and sees everything located in me, in his body I stay forever (21.12) (*yo māṃ sarvagataṃ paśyet sarvaṃ ca mayi saṃsthitam // tasyāham nityam ātmasthas taraṅgaiḥ salilaṃ yathā//*).

The Ācārya is to be worshipped according to one's means with gold, clothes, and ornaments (21.14). From him one obtains the Mallāri *mantra*. He who recites the *mantra* with meditation will obtain the fruit of eightfold *bhakti*, if he observes *sadācāra* and *śuci*, in a pure *pūjā* shrine.

On the 14th of the month of Caitra [full-moon day] or any other such day (i.e. *pūrṇimā* [full-moon day]) Mallāri's *mahotsava* shall be observed with one's property.[20] The devotees will have all sorts of temporary enjoyments and will reach the highest state in the next world; they will conquer their enemy as told by Śiva (21.46).

Vasantakeli-līlā: from the third of the light half of the month of Caitra, Mhālasākānt (the husband of Mhālasā), Mallārideva, the Bhūpati, is worshipped by bright-faced women (*kāminī*) with fans, by the brave ones who are like kings, in the form of a *mūrti* of Kandarpa.

The dear wife of him who worships Mallāri together with Mhālasā on Mahānavamī with love and hears his *Māhātmya* will be a vessel of love (21.59-60), and he will obtain *mokṣa*, if he wants *mokṣa*, otherwise heaven. From the first of the bright half of Mārgaśīrṣa till the 6th he should feed a Brāhmaṇ, increasing the daily number by one or, according to his desire for greatness and power (*vaibhavecchayā*), many Brāhmaṇs, in whose house and *kula* Lakṣmī constantly resides with pleasure (21.61). On the sixth of Mārgaśīrṣa (i.e. on Campāṣaṣṭhī) those who do the *yātrā* of Mallārideva will have the fruits of one *yajña* for each step.

Chapter 22: The Statement of Prasāda by Mallāri (*Mallāri-prasāda-vākyam*).

Mairāla tells in his own words the difficult *bhakti* which men get with effort—without having done good acts previously (22, 1):

Those who always worship my *pratimā* in their houses stay with gods and Ṛṣis (22.2). Those who keep the written book won't be affected by *grahas* etc. In the house of that person Lakṣmī as well as progeny will stay till the end of the *kalpa*, and there is no need to say that I protect his *kula* (22.9). The one who listens to this *Māhātmya* of mine will rejoice in heaven as many years as there are letters in it (22.10). The one who commits fraud or cheats and uses force, and who hears or recites it is even as dear to me as Svāmī (Kārttikeya), Lambodara (Gaṇeśa), and Gauri are to me (22.18-21). I destroy the accumulated heap of sins of the one who from birth is with full faith devoted to me in every respect (22.22). In short he is my eternal *bhakta* who just says without doubt, "I am he" (22.25).

(Sanatkumāra:) After that Mallāri dismissed everybody and they went to their homes looking pleased (22.26). 188,000 years ago the lord of Kailāsa came, therefore, in the Kaliyuga. He offered *bhukti* and *mukti*, and *siddhi*. Therefore in the Kaliyuga no other power (*prabhāva*) exists (22.26-8).

(Śiva:) Having then praised the Mahātma (i.e. Sanatkumāra), the ancient Munis went to their *aśramas* and all performed *japa, yajña,* and *mahotsavās* (22.33).

(Śiva tells Pārvatī): Therefore, I am the bestower of *siddhi* for men in the Kaliyuga. This *kṣetra-tīrtha* which gives the fruit of *bhukti* and *mukti* has been established by me and you out of mercy for the mortals. Whosoever with faith wishes something will get everything without consideration of his motives. Therefore, in every way, with all devotion I am always worshipped by the wise, (who say): "there is no other" (22.34-7, 1).

8. CONCLUSION

The *MM* records a very popular, widespread and ancient cult of a folk deity and casts it in purāṇic terms and mythology. This cult flourished from medieval times and contributed to the rise of the Khaṇḍobā cult of Maharashtra. The god is represented as a king on earth and the *Māhātmya* shifts the preoccupation of folk religion with deified kings, represented by the demon kings Maṇi and Malla, to the worship of god as king in a *kṣetra*. It is Śiva who takes the position of a king. The *Māhātmya* depicts the anomaly of kings claiming to be "the ruler of the three worlds". It stresses repeatedly the profit of reading and hearing the book and shows that the unbridled power of the *daityas* must fail, as it is misdirected against Brāhmaṇs in particular and the dharmic order in general. For that matter, anyone who thinks he must emulate their "folly" must fail. The *stotras* of Malla make it clear that hearing his praise of Śiva grants freedom from disease, poverty, and inhibiting character blemishes (17.39). In fact, Malla, as before him Maṇi (ch. 13), has become the perfect *bhakta*, with whom the devotee can identify. Though Brāhmaṇs, *ṛṣis*, and gods have been restored to their position and the all-embracing, beneficial effects of reading and hearing the *Māhātmya* have been described in glowing terms, the folk religious ingredients of the cult are reflected in non-classical, non-standard forms of *bhakti*. Even self-mortifications and non-vegetarian offerings to the god are mentioned which nowadays are hardly ever offered to the gods directly, but are given rather to the demon or to the goddess Bāṇāī.

The wide range of effects of worship reach from mundane

enjoyment (*bhukti*) to superior powers (*siddhi*), merging into salvation (*mukti*). This seems to be rather a continuous and overlapping scale of values, reaching from physical well-being and immortality (through progeny) up to spiritual immortality through salvation. There is, however, no reference to the religious suicides of the medieval heroes who by their act achieved salvation, that is, heaven, or awareness of or merger with God. The royal element of the cult is also reflected in many rituals in various places in Karnataka and Maharashtra. For instance, in Mailar (Karnataka) the battle against the demon is enacted. Here the god is personified by a *svāmin*, a member of the Wodeyar (*Kṣatriya*) family. The Somvatī Amāvāsyā festival in Jejuri (Maharashtra) has strong resemblences with a royal hunt and shows clear vestiges of the ancient Aśvamedha ritual. There are many features in this cult which especially inspired kings and those who would be kings. There is no reference to such old rituals in the text. The acceptability of Mlecchas, i.e. Muslims, as *bhaktas* shows the "secular" approach of the medieval Indian king, e.g. Kṛṣṇadēvarāyā of Vijayanagara.

The text and its context represent two streams which occasionally converge and again part from each other: the purāṇic-śāstric *Māhātmya* tradition and the folk tradition. The self-conscious folk culture uses the *Māhātmya* at its convenience and without assigning it the sole authority. A full picture of the cult cannot be drawn on the basis of the text alone, and the meaning of the cult is unintelligible (even to devotees) without persistent reference to the contextual sources, of whatever provenance, especially folk literature and folk rituals.

NOTES

Further documents and reference to aspects of this paper may be found in previous articles of the author listed in the bibliography.

1. Sontheimer 1987, 1f.; idem [1988], *passim*.
2. An edition on the basis of several mss is in progress.
3. Dhere 1961: 144.
4. Founded in 1526 or 1547, merged into Bijapur in 1618.
5. Dhere 1975: 6 (*MM* 2.153).
6. Bhāve 1975: 243.
7. Dhere 1961: 8.
8. Kolte 1978: 616 (*Pūrvārdha* 436).
9. Sircar 1971: 8-9, 21.
10. *Kriḍābhirāmamu* 141-2.

11. Sastry 1978: 9; cp. Rao 1973: 6.
12. Sontheimer 1985: 144ff.
13. E.g. Ekanāth (*Abhaṅg* 3730.3), see Sontheimer 1985: 149 and n. 32.
14. *MM* by Rāmdās, "Sadāśiva's servant", 1857: 2.28; Sontheimer 1984: 157.
15. Khare 1958: 124f.
16. Kāṭṭi 1966: *passim.*
17. Sontheimer 1987: 16ff., 19.
18. Bollée 1981: 180-8.
19. Maṇi and Malla behave like the mythical being Bali, who ordered his subjects to sacrifice to him rather than to Indra. *Mahābhārata, Śanti* 218.13, 14. Crit. edn. Tripati 1968: 48f. There is also the legend of king Raji, who acquired such excessive power that he won Indra's kingdom, deprived him of his share in the Vedic sacrifice and disregarded dharma and the Vedic way. *Viṣṇupurāṇa* IV.9.8.
20. Siddhapāl Kesarī smuggles in *davaṇā: davaṇā* is Southernwood, *Artemisia abrotanum.* Ma. *davṇīpunav, davṇipūrṇimā* is the full-moon day in Caitra, during which sprigs of the shrub *davṇā* are placed on an idol. Davṇā is a very popular offering to Khaṇḍobā.

Bhakti in the Khaṇḍobā Cult

BHAKTI IN FOLK RELIGION

THE INQUIRY into the complex and manifold expressions of bhakti in the cult of the most popular folk god of Maharashtra, Khaṇḍobā, may throw light on aspects of bhakti which are generally not central in the poetry of the bhakti saints or in "purāṇic" and "sectarian" literature. There can be no doubt that the bhakti saints and the bhakti movements initiated by them owe much to folk life and its deities, its oral genres and its folk metres, even while more or less vehemently rejecting folk religion and its deities.[1] The old Tamil (Caṅkam) literature e.g. reflects a development in which the god of the hills and hunters, Murukaṉ, becomes a god of bhakti and in the process 'bards are replaced by saints and the chieftains by gods' (Ramanujan 1989: 200). In Maharashtra the reinterpretation of folk-religious elements in bhakti literature can also be found, e.g. in the *Bhāruḍe* of the saint Eknāth or in saint Rāmdās's identification of Khaṇḍobā with Rāma. We should, therefore, not preclude from our purview possible forms of bhakti merely because they are found in folk religion and cannot be traced in "standard" Vaiṣṇava and Śaiva bhakti literature except as reflections of folk religion.

An observer of the fervent attachment of the devotees to Khaṇḍobā can have no doubt that he is a deity to whom one resorts not just in fear and/or with a utilitarian purpose. These are generally said to be the motives in the worship of folk deities (cp. Stanley 1986: 51-67). Whether a particular act of devotion in the Khaṇḍobā cult, like bringing water from the river in a *kāvaḍī* (a water vessel and the ritual), has practical (*bhukti*) or transcendental (*mukti*) results depends on whether it is practised *sakāma* or *niṣkāma*, according to the *Mārtaṇḍa Vijaya* (32.34ff.). This is the high-level nomenclature in a text composed by a Brāhmaṇ devotee, yet it acknowledges that folk rituals may be done without practical purposes. Folk religion does not explain itself. It does not supply theological reasons and thus we are left to speculate whether perhaps much in folk religion reflects an organic world view and the relationship between devotee and environment, e.g. the mountain, to which the devotee wishes periodically, if not constantly, to be realigned, e.g. by bringing the water of the river to the mountain god Khaṇḍobā. Nor is devotion to Khaṇḍobā a simple question of a kind of Śaivite bhakti as practised by Śaivite "sects" like the Pāśupatas, Kāpālikas, Nāths, etc., with their own peculiar rituals and philosophy. The folk notion of Khaṇḍobā as a personal god reflects rather a deity who is basically a hunter, a chieftain, a great merchant, the master of the robbers, a hero, and a king of all these groups. He is "hungry" (*bhūkelā*) for loyal followers and sometimes literally *hungry* for food.[2] Khaṇḍobā is actually not primarily like the Śiva of the Purāṇas or of the "sectarians", but like the Rudra of the Vedic texts. I have tried to show elsewhere that we can directly link Khaṇḍobā with Rudra without the benefit of the epics or the purāṇic and later "sectarian" Śaivite versions of Rudra (Sontheimer 1986: 1-36). There is not only a coincidental or structural identity between the two gods but a basic identity. Nearly all the references to Rudra in Vedic literature can be traced as incidents of the Khaṇḍobā cult if we consider Rudra not only in the context of the *śrauta* ritual and from the point of view of the Brāhmaṇical specialist of the Vedic *śrauta* ritual, but first of all as a folk deity.

As such he is the lord and, in fact, a mirror—as the famous *Śatarudrīya* hymn of the *Taittirīya Saṃhitā* testifies—of all types of folk, including tribals, hunters, heroes, horsemen, cowherds, thieves, robbers, and artisans, who all recur as devotees in the Khaṇḍobā cult. All the epithets and attributes of Rudra match the description of Khaṇḍobā. Just to cite one example: the *Śatarudrīya* (TS iv.5.2.k) praises the *vanija*—the merchant par excellence, while Khaṇḍobā in folk literature is the great merchant of Jejuri (*Jejuricā vāṇī*) (Ahire 1964: 50f.). Rudra is also the chief deity of the Vrātyas, as they appear e.g. in the *Atharvaveda* (ch. XV). In their rituals, which are alien to the *śrauta* ritual, they attempt to emulate Rudra, whether these rituals are cosmogonic, as in chapter XV of the *Atharvaveda,* or whether they relate to dress and outfit and the imitation of dogs (Sontheimer 1986: 3ff.). These incidents are reflected in detail in the Khaṇḍobā cult, especially in the equivalent Mailāra cult at Devaraguḍḍa and Mailār in Karnataka (Sontheimer 1986: 3ff.; 1989a: 299-337, 314ff.). In bhakti literature the imitation of animals like dogs represents the self-humiliation of the "dog-like" self before God, as expressed e.g. by Māṇikkavācakar.[3] The Vaggayyas of Mailāra and the Vāghyās of Khaṇḍobā, however, take pride (at least traditionally) in being the dogs of the god, and they accompany him on his hunt. After all, the God may appear himself as a dog and this is one reason why dogs are worshipped. Moreover, for the hunter, the shepherd, the itinerant merchant and the Marāṭhā king, the dog is not a "messenger of death" or an impure creature, but an embodiment of bravery and faithfulness.[4]

Rudra, unlike the other Vedic gods, is also a very personal god. Though he has the malevolent features met with in any folk deity, he is nevertheless immediately accessible to his followers, "easily to be pleased" and "excessively bountiful".[5] His ubiquity and omnipresence, which are said to ultimately culminate in the philosophical universality of the *Śvetāśvataropaniṣad* (III.2), are shared by many folk deities like Khaṇḍobā and Murukaṉ, as is his personal presence "here and now". It is surprising that these features have been viewed with some uncertainty by classical Indologists who stress his malevolence. R.N. Dandekar, following R.G. Bhandarkar, rightly emphasized the ambivalence of Rudra and his personal characteristics, which distinguish him from other Vedic gods. Dandekar says:

> . . . the worshippers think of the god in terms of his immediate presence—they always look upon him as being very close to them, as directly influencing their lives. The fact that Śiva is not generally taking *avatāras* is very significant in this context. (Dandekar 1979: 199-277, 275 fn. 241)

The distinct physical appearance of Rudra in the *Śatarudrīya* has recently made one author wonder why Rudra was never represented in iconographic form during the Vedic period (Long 1983, 109) After all, a god of bhakti seems to presume a visible, iconic form associated with a place, as in the henolocotheism of Tamilnadu (Zvelebil 1973: 201, 206), the association of Kṛṣṇa's deeds with definite spots in Braj, or the tremendous importance of the *mūrti* of Viṭhobā in Pandharpur. But in the cases of Rudra, Khaṇḍobā, Mallanna, Mailāra, Murukaṉ and the pastoral Kṛṣṇa of the *Harivaṃśa,* we find—to use a generic term—a *sthapati,* or chieftain, who is human in appearance but who represents or incorporates divine powers. These make him superior to his followers. They in turn emulate him in an *imitatio dei* as regards his appearance and actions. Thus the Vrātyas of the Vedic texts are clad like their *sthapati,* who in turn looks like Rudra. Kṛṣṇa of the *Harivaṃśa* and the *Viṣṇupurāṇa* is—if we ignore the later Vaiṣṇavization—a *gopā*, a tribal hero and leader. He is a cowherd like his companions, ascending the mountain with them to worship his "other self" or what must have been originally a mountain spirit (Vaudeville 1980: 4f.). He surpasses the others by his prowess, which sometimes suggests the "unethical" ambivalence met with in folk deities. There is another tradition which says that Kṛṣṇa belonged to and was worshipped by the Satvatas, who, according to the *Manusmṛti* (10.23), were Vrātyas (Hauer 1927: 227). Kṛṣṇa was also the *Mahāmalla*—the great wrestler who defeated the two *mallas* (wrestlers) Cāṇura and Muṣṭika and acquired the epithet "Mallāri" = "the enemy of (the) Malla(s)" (Bollée 1981: 183). Mallāri is actually also an epithet of Khaṇḍobā which he acquires after defeating the two demons Maṇi and Malla. Often Maṇimalla is considered to be one, that is, he is "Mani, the Malla". The Mallas are also related to the Ṛgvedic *máryas*, who were a kind of brotherhood. The term *márya* is also applied to the Maruts. Rudra was the father of the Maruts (Bollée 1981: 80).

Imitation, nearness, possession, and identity mark the mutual relationship between the god, whether Rudra or Khaṇḍobā, and his followers. It is the same with the original Murukaṉ. He is the god of the mountainous area and lives among the community of tribal men and women. The chief dancer is called *vēlaṉ* after Murukaṉ's weapon, the spear. *Vēlaṉ* is also another name of Murukaṉ. The possessed dancer does not simply worship or adore the god; he invokes the god by representing him. He dances the god's dance, he wears the Red One's robes and insignia, carries his spear or lance (*vel̤*), imitating the god till he becomes Him, simulating Him until he is assimilated. The *vēlaṉ* becomes the *Vēlaṉ* (Ramanujan 1981: 115).

In the case of Khaṇḍobā we find the same mutual mirroring of bhakta and God. For the merchants he is the Merchant; for the hunters he is the Hunter; animal imitations of the devotees reflect the manifestation of the god as an animal or as his favourite animal; for the hero he is the divine Hero. This mutual intimate relationship is reflected in folk literature as well as in folk rituals. For instance, it can be observed during the Dhangar shepherds' annual festival (*kheḷ* = "play"). This festival in honour of ancestors and gods takes place before the shepherds leave their monsoon camp for the annual migration (Sontheimer 1988: 109-30). At the end of the dance which brings ancestors and gods to life, the young Dhangar *devruṣi* ("shaman") becomes possessed by Khaṇḍobā. He holds a spear—one of the characteristic weapons of Khaṇḍobā—, carries a heavy chain and rides on the shoulders of a friend as if he were a horse. The young man is an accepted *devruṣi* who has been tested to see if the god truly takes possession of him. But before this test a special relationship had been formed between him and Khaṇḍobā. The Dhangar had broken his arm in an accident and during this liminal stage he had a vision of Khaṇḍobā. This is not just a case of somebody choosing a deity as his *iṣṭadevatā*, but the encounter was spontaneous and caused by a physically and emotionally painful experience. The individual relationship between devotee and god was later supplemented by the relationship between the Dhangar group and the god; the god became a *kuldaivat* after his "genuineness" and "presence" were tested by his taking possession of the Dhangar.

Another case involved a young Dhangar from an outlying area who visited the temple of Khaṇḍobā at Jejuri in the company of his parents, wife, brothers, and others. He tried to enter the temple with his pointed, sharp spear. Dhangars often carry a spear, which nowadays has its tip blunted into a knob. Again and again he was repelled by the invisible power of the god, staggered backwards out of the temple, and then tried to reenter. Finally he managed to enter the inner shrine and collapsed in front of the gods. He would have fallen over the *svayaṃbhū piṇḍs* of Khaṇḍobā and his wife, the goddess Mhāḷsā, had not the *pūjārīs* prevented him from doing so, lest he hurt the god (or himself) with his spear. This example shows again that within a group of devotees who worship their *kuldaivat* there can be individual expressions of bhakti, and yet this bhakti need not transgress the borders of family and kinship group.

The god who is the Lord of the hunters still goes on a hunting excursion on Somvatī Amāvāsyā, a new moon day which falls on a Monday. Dhangars with their spears accompany the palanquin of the god, which is carried to the Karhā river. Other devotees become possessed by the wind of the god and act like horses in the *svārī*, the procession of the Lord. At the end of the hunt devotees participate in the bath of the god in the river, and everybody becomes as if one with the god.

The extreme example is the devotion of the *vīras*, the heroes. In the past the *vīras* played a considerable role in the cult of Khaṇḍobā, Mailāra and Mallanna. Khaṇḍobā is himself the great *vīra*. The euhemeristic explanation of the Jainas was that he was originally a hero who died in battle.[6] The hero's devotion was expressed by bravery. Even today we can witness the self-tortures of the Vaggayyas (also called Kañcavīras) at Devaraguḍḍa, who, by their act of bravery called *pavāḍā* (in Ka.), show their loyalty to their god and force his appearance. This kind of devotion of the Kañcavīras is as old as the 13th century *Krīḍābhirāmamu* (Sontheimer 1981: 13f.). In the case of these folk deities it is not primarily Śiva's heaven which is the main goal of the hero, but closeness to one's divine master, who is "here and now". Causing pain by striking oneself with a staff or sword is quite frequent in the cults of Khaṇḍobā, Mhaskobā, Birobā and other folk deities. It is motivated by the desire to urge the deity to appear and to take an interest in the life of the devotees. The breaking of chains which is done during the festivals of Khaṇḍobā and Mailāra testifies to the existence and presence of the god, which is often called *sattva* (Sontheimer 1977: 116, 124; 1984: 156). This devotion often takes the form of ritualized play and assumes an element of violence, e.g. in the ritual of hookswinging (*bagāḍ*)—to add one more example. This play does not exactly correspond to the divine play, which is expressed by the term *līlā* and is enacted e.g. by Śiva, because it is the devotees who persuade and even coerce the god to participate in the play. The ritualized play (*kheḷ*) is enacted by the devotees for the gods and the devotees, rather than by gods who—like Māṇikkavācakar's Śiva—somewhat arbitrarily manifest their *līlā* (cp. Yocum 1977: 40f.).

The element of violence and play may be characteristic of this devotion, but memorials consisting of *pādukās* of Khaṇḍobā in Khaṇḍobā temples, as well as *pādukās* in Karnataka, show that there once existed an even stronger kind of devotion, namely ritual suicide. The *pādukās* are surrounded by human heads and the heads of rams. From Kannada inscriptions we know that these memorials refer to self-sacrifices offered in order to achieve union with god. This god is, as we said, not primarily the purāṇic Śiva, but a very earthbound god, or he was a divine leader if not a divine king. "For the *vīra* the king is god", the *Mārtaṇḍa Vijaya* describes this relationship (16.20).

The aim of the relationship is clear: it may be expressed in the classical terms of *sārūpya, sāmīpya,* and *sāyujya* practised in folk religion. It may be called *ugra bhakti,* but the devotees do not know this, and for those who know the term it bears no negative connotation.

To describe the devotion as a case of *sakhya bhakti* or *dāsya bhakti* may not be fully apt, because of the impetuous and violent urge toward identity with and merging into the god.

Tukārām often bases his poetry on images from real situations in folk life and folk religion, and then turns them, with the masterly twist of any good bhakti poet, into metaphors of his own bhakti religion. As already Kabīr before him (Vaudeville 1974: 146), he used the example of the hero (Ma. *pāīk, sūr*) as a literally not very far-fetched example of "true" bhakti. The hero is the *pāīk*, a lowly armed attendant according to Molesworth (1857: 498). Here are some excerpts from Tukārām's *abhangs*:

॥... ॥१॥
पाइकावांचुन नव्हे कधिं सुख।
प्रजांमधें दुःख न सरे पीदा ॥ २ ॥
तरि व्हावें पाईक जिवाचे उदार ।
सकळ त्यांचा भार स्वामी वाहे ॥ ३ ॥
पाइकीचें सुख जयां नाहीं ठावें ।
धिग त्यांनीं ज्यावें वांयांविण ॥ ४ ॥
तुका म्हणे एका क्षणांचा करार।
पाईक अपार सुख भोगी ॥ ५ ॥ अभंग १०६२.

पाइकीचें सुख पाइकासी ठवें।

म्हनोणियां जीवें केली साटीं ॥ अभंग १०६३.
[...]

Without the heroism of a *pāīk*,
There is never any happiness.
The harassment and distress of the people never go.
Thus a *pāīk* should be ready to sacrifice his life.
All his burden is carried by the Lord.
Those who do not know the service of a *pāīk*,
Fie upon them! They live their life in vain.
Tuka says, Striking a deal in a moment
The *pāīk* enjoys endless bliss. *(abhaṃga)* 1062.

The happiness of soldiery only a true *pāīk* knows
Therefore he exchanges his life for this happiness.
(*abhaṃga*) 1063.

This bravery and uncompromising devotion are also attested by the vow of medieval heroes "to win or die" in battle. The vow is documented by numerous hero stones without or, in Karnataka, with inscriptions. Vows were not only given to one's human master, but also to the divine king, in our case, Khaṇḍobā. Made with the offering of *bhaṇḍār* (turmeric powder), such vows were and still are absolutely binding. As a typical illustration of the close bond of Marāṭhā warriors and Khaṇḍobā we may cite an incident related by Grant Duff:

> Pāli [a famous centre of Khaṇḍobā between Satara and Karad] village and temple are closely connected with a celebrated exploit of Chitursingh in February 1799 in revenge for the defeat of his brother Shāhū, the Sātārā Rājā. He had heard that Rāste was encamped near Sātārā fort with a force of 2000 or 3000 men on behalf of the Peshvā. He accordingly led 600 infantry through the hills and valleys till opposite Pāl where he remained till night. He then repaired to the celebrated temple, performed the usual worship, and the whole party solemnly invoked the deity, stained their clothes with yellow dye,[7] rubbed their hands and faces with turmeric in token of a vow to win or die, and issued forth to the attack. The enemy was not unprepared but had only time to fire a few rounds when they were furiously charged sword in hand, their guns taken, and the whole body dispersed in a few minutes.... (Duff 1963, 858f.)

BHAKTI IN THE FOLK (ORAL) LITERATURE OF KHAṆḌOBĀ

Khaṇḍobā's bards are the Vāghyās. A Vāghyā is a lifelong devotee dedicated to the god by his parents in fulfilment of a vow. Besides the Vāghyās there are the Muraḷīs, who are (now no longer, it is said) "married" to the god, or rather to his sword. Vāghyās and Muraḷīs perform for their patrons the *jāgraṇ*, a nightlong vigil during which the Muraḷīs and a Vāghyā dance. Other Vāghyās accompany them with instruments and sing the *padeṃ* of Khaṇḍobā. We are reminded of the ancient *sūta* (court bard) or the *magadha* ("wandering bard") who accompanies the Vrātya along with the *puṃścalī* (a kind of sacred prostitute) (Sontheimer 1986: 9f.). The Vāghyās sing of the prowess of Khaṇḍobā and of his adventures as a hunter, lover, and king. Khaṇḍobā is god as king for many devotees. He rules on the hill fort (*gaḍkoṭ*) of Jejuri, which is his capital (*rājdhānī*). He rides a horse or an elephant and has an entourage of followers. He goes for a hunt with his followers, amongst them the shepherds with their spears. He has one regular wife, who is a Liṅgāyat, and another wife who is married to him in a totally unsanskritic marriage. She is Bāṇāī, the rich and beautiful but dirty shepherdess with whom Khaṇḍobā/ Malhāri has incurably fallen in love. Mhāḷsā complains to Bāṇāī, who has made Khaṇḍobā go crazy. We could say that this is only the theme of Śiva and Pārvatī quarrelling because of Gaṅgā which is duplicated on the folk level. But who can say what came first: the folk story of the folk god or the story of Śiva according to the Purāṇas. Besides, folk versions assume their own vividness and spontaneity, e.g. in the following old Vāghyā song:

"My Malhārī has gone crazy, dear me, how!"
Mhāḷsā pines in her heart,
"Whom should I blame?"
//jī jī//
My rival, his wife, bosses over me,
she flirts as she flatters him,
she moves around with the god, never leaving him.
Bānu has forcibly invaded my house//
Raṃbhāī has also seduced him,
he has gifted her his silken shawl.
And he even goes to bed with Phulābāī//
The mud clings to the water, and the water, too, won't
leave the mud!
Let's see the god and worship Mālu, the king of the earth//
Śaṅkar Viṭṭhal [the poet] says to Rāma, to Janārdan, to
Sonā Mhāḷsā:
"Let's look at the god."
Tatyābā sings the same tune:
"Let's see the god."[8]

In any case the theme of the tribal woman beloved by the god is as old as the Caṅkam literature, where Murukaṉ falls in love with Vaḷḷi of the Kuruvar tribe (Zvelebil 1977: 227-46; 1974, 188f.). It is an ubiquitous theme in the folklore of south India and the Deccan and is probably prior to the Purāṇas. Khaṇḍobā has five wives in all: Mhāḷsā, the Liṅgāyat; Bāṇāī, the Dhangar shepherdess; Phūlāī, a woman of the Māḷī caste; Raṃbhāī, a woman of the Śimpī (tailor) caste; and Candāī Bhagvanīṇ, a Muslim woman.

The contents of the songs of Khaṇḍobā deal with a god who exists "here and now". A real presence of a localized god is felt and the contents of the songs are often enacted in rituals which can hardly pass muster as "sanskritic". The content of the *Māhātmya* plays only a marginal role. The *padeṃ* are replete with vibrant folk religion. The Vāghyā reminds us in a way of the bard in the Caṅkam literature who is described as praising the deeds of a slain hero on the request of a cowherd, as benefit will accrue from it (*Puṟaṉāṉūṟu* 263). But the bard of Khaṇḍobā is more than a bard. He is also a bhakta. Many of the *padeṃ* reflect a tender, deep bond of affection for the god, a mutual relationship. The picture of an almost corporeal, vivid folk deity and of real things, places, and people is blended with bhakti and notions of *mukti*. The borderline between, on the one hand, ordinary human love and emotions amongst humans, and, on the other hand, divine love between the god and the devotee is fluid and permeable, just as, in the case of the god-king and the *devadāsī*, love may be sexual *and* divine (Marglin 1985). Surely, the bhakta bard does not just take his images as metaphors, the way the bhakti saint Tukārām took the *pāīk* as a metaphor for real bhakti.

Unfortunately the *padeṃ* of Khaṇḍobā have nowhere been systematically collected, let alone critically edited. Especially the *old* songs are dying out, because in today's Maharashtra, where more than ever before a drastic social transformation is being experienced, the outlook of the patrons is changing. It is the fate of the highly concrete and historical contents of the songs to become outdated in view of the modern, fundamental changes. Thus the old songs are decaying and are being replaced by modern tunes and simplified contents. Besides several old notebooks, including one from an old Vāghyā and another from a famous Muraḷī, I came across a booklet of *Khaṇḍobāciṃ padeṃ* with 45 *padeṃ* (Bhāūmahārāja 1961). The text is extremely valuable, even though it is corrupt and has to be restored with the help of old informants who might still know the songs in question. But even they often do not know the correct texts, and at times we get a plausible reading only by a close and repeated observation of the devotees while they perform their rites and celebrate their festivals.

Thus the correct reading and meaning of *pad* 22 on the Somvatī Amāvāsyā festival, a complex, essentially non-sanskritic festival, cannot be explained if one has not seen the festival several times. Just to question the participants about the festival is not always of help. The meaning of the rite is not generally present in the minds of the participants. Ritual for them is something to be *done*, not something to be explained. One example of the *padeṃ* may illus-trate the kind of bhakti in these folk songs. The song deals with Raṃbhāī, Khaṇḍobā's Śiṃpī wife, who is an example of spontaneous bhakti.

Khaṇḍobā is addressed as Mālu in the *pad*:

Song 19:

Wearing a pyjama laced with golden and silver threads,
a long gown, a turban tied around his head/
around his neck a *liṅg*, swaggering like a Paṭhāṇ, ...//

In his ears, pendants with four pearls,
a diamond ring sparkled on his finger/
He wore a bright red shawl
a crest of pearls [on his turban]
Like the wind he circled with a horse
on the earth, the eight-petalled lotus//

The lustre of his *svarūpa* spreads like stars// *Main tune*//

When, O Mālu, mounted on a blue horse,
he saw the town [of Jejuri],
he, Mallāri, descended there// *Together*//

The women of the town told Raṃbāī, the Śimpīṇ:
"A stranger, a most shrewd fellow [has come]."

He roars before us Vāghyās, the flag flutters,
he rides a horse called Turanga,
fast as the wind of the mind,
wields a Frank sword/
He roars before us Vāghyās,
the flag flutters in the wind//1//

"He spoke in Kannada, asked for the *vāḍā* [of Raṃbhāī]
and went straight there."

Raṃbhāī saw the God, the King, Nīlakaṃṭha,
came with an *ārati* of her five *prāṇas* lights
on a golden platter and kept it
on the pride [reduced to] *raṅgoḷi* lines,
on the seat of yoga// *Main tune*//

She anointed him with various unctions
with oil containing camphor, O Mālu,

She kept excellent *abīr*-powder from Vijyapur, O Mālu,
filled with affection, fragrant musk// *Together*//

Śrīraṅg bathed on the square platform
with water stored in a silver vessel
[pouring it from] a round pot,

He roars before us Vāghyās, the flag flutters
[seated] on a horse called Turaṅga,
swift as the wind of the mind,
he roars before us Vāghyās,
wielding a Frank sword,
the flag flutters in the wind//2//

"A fine cloth it is, wipe your body with it,
wear a silken garment with embroidered borders."
The body decorated with *bhaṇḍār,*
a holy mark on the forehead.
She made an offering of herself
[placing] on both his sides delicacies,
a curry of brinjal, millet bread
with ghee—for the day and the night meal—
capātīs with ghee, fragrant unhusked rice, lentil soup
// *Main tune*//

Sixty vegetables and salads, Mālu,
pickles on both sides, O Mālu, fried cakes,
cakes made of pulse, crisp, O Mālu//*Together*//

Various kinds of porridge [she served],
with sugar from Rāypūr,
maṇḍa[9] mixed in milk . . .
He roars before us Vāghyās, the flag flutters,
his horse Turaṅga, swift as the wind of the mind,
he wields the sword, the flag flutters/

He rinsed his mouth, took betel leaves,
on the silver platter a bundle of leaves,
she adorned him with a garland of flowers,
bedecked he was with ornaments inset with gems,
the mansion is resplendent red,
the wall was gravelled with rubies.

She arranged a bed inside, with four lampstands.
When the god saw the faith of Raṃbhāī,

he became pleased. She called [him].
God has tender feelings for his bhakta,
he is an ocean of mercy//3//

He brought her, the Beauty,
O Mālu, [and] kept her [Raṃbhābāī]
on the bank of the Karhā River, Oh Mālu.
Every six months, on Monday,
the god goes to her temple//*Together*//

Guru Mukīnda[10] was satisfied,
bathed in a sea of love,
in the city flooded by affection,[11]
Bāṇū Vāghyā is firmly at his feet,
a stone to step on . . .

His horse called Turaṅga, swift as the wind of the mind,
he wields a Frank sword,
roars before us Vāghyās, the flag flutters//4//

Mallāri, alias Khaṇḍobā, is viewed as an intruder, a Paṭhāṇ. The Pāthāṇs were actually Muslims, considered to be audacious warriors and of ferocious temper. Mallāri is an outsider who speaks Kannada. He descends from the sky with his horse, an event which in folk belief frequently indicates the arrival of a god before he settles at a particular place. In another text, the *Khaṇḍerāyācī Ādi* (*ovī* 67), Khaṇḍobā appears as a *yogī* who rides a bull (*ḍhor*) and is clad in skins. He is not immediately admitted into the village, so he stays in the *smaśān*. It seems to be a common motif in folk religion that a powerful god appears from outside or resides in the forested area, as in the case of Viṭhobā, the Gavḷī, who emerged from the once forested pastoral area of Pandharpur and hailed from Karnataka. It is the true bhakta who first recognizes the intruder as the god, as Bāṇāī, the Dhangar shepherdess, eventually recognizes the true god in the stranger who serves in her shepherd camp (Sontheimer 1989b: 7-62). In the case of Bāṇāī the position is initially reversed: the god has to leave the town, where life has become stagnant and intolerable, in order to find a true bhakta outside, in the wilderness. From the Dhangars' point of view, Khaṇḍobā, in the guise of an old, leprous man, is an intruder in their camp. They attempt to beat him up, but Bāṇāī intervenes.

In the present case it is Raṃbhāī who unhesitatingly receives the stranger from outside and serves him as a Muraḷī or *devadāsī*. Like the true folk deity, he devours huge quantities of food. But human love and the offering of food subtly shift to seemingly spiritual meanings. The text (see Appendix) falters and becomes "corrupt": instead of *ātma niṣada,* a proper reading could be *ātmaniveda*—while serving an enormous number of dishes she makes an offering of herself. *Ātmaniveda* could be *ātmanivedana,* that is, one of the nine modes of bhakti according to the *Bhāgavata Purāṇa.* But we could also simply read *ātmaniveda. Nived* is a popular corruption of Skt. *naivedya,* that is, an offering to a god. In folk poetry such ambiguities cannot always be resolved by a settled and final meaning.

Rambhāī might have been historically a *devadāsī,* though she is now worshipped as a *devī* on the bank of the river Karhā near Jejuri. There the god visits her at the Somvatī Amāvāsyā festival after his hunt and ritual bath in the river. The "circling with a horse like a wind on the earth" and "the horse as swift as the wind of the mind" may evoke yogic associations, but may also allude to the horse of the *aśvamedha* ritual, which circles the earth. An allusion to the horse traversing the earth on behalf of the conquering king seems also to be reflected in the Somvatī Amāvāsyā ritual. During the festival the horse of the god is led at a fast pace to the river in advance of the hunting procession. The horse is an object of eager worship on this day and especially while it moves towards the river. Horse and sword are aspects highlighted in the Khaṇḍobā cult. In folk epics, like that of Lorik, they are the divine aids of human, sometimes deified heroes (Flueckinger 1989: 45). King Malla, the great but demonic hero, resembles the folk hero and is the martial, mundane model of the *avatār* of Śiva. Malla rides a horse and wields a sword which "even cuts the wind" (*MMRā* 1.79f.).

THE VAIṢṆAVA ATTITUDE TOWARDS KHAṆḌOBĀ

It would be interesting to trace in detail the reaction of Vaiṣṇava authors of purāṇic and bhakti works in Marathi. A few illustrations, however, must suffice here. In Nāmdev's *Gāthā* we find an *abhaṅg* which is perhaps wrongly attributed to him.[12] *Abhaṅg* 82 tells us that in Nanda's house the Campāṣaṣṭhī ritual in honour of the *kulasvāmī* Mārtaṇḍa was observed. Kṛṣṇa, the child, acts as if mad when Vāghyās are invited and food is spread out by Yaśodā before the gods as an offering. Yaśodā believes him to be possessed by the fierce (*duraḷa*) family god. Even a *devṛṣi* is called to free Kṛṣṇa from the possession, though the *devṛṣi's* efforts are of no avail. Finally the mother realizes that it was she who was caught in a net of illusion and that an offering to the *kulasvāmī* is an offering to Kṛṣṇa. Śrīdhara, the author of the *Harivijaya*, deals with the same theme.[13] Kṛṣṇa drinks the milk meant for Mallāri and acts as if he were mad. Yaśodā prays to Mallāri, because she thinks that Kṛṣṇa is possessed by him. "Mārtaṇḍa Khaṇḍerāyā" appears and tells the mother that all the gods are contained in Kṛṣṇa's body. Both possession and the existence of a *devṛṣi* represent folk religious elements which are deprecated by the Vaiṣṇava authors. The folk deity Mallāri is subordinated to the purāṇic Kṛṣṇa. Here *māyā* is not the power of a folk deity to assume different forms and play tricks (Mar. *māv*), but the philosophical concept of illusion which keeps the devotee from discerning Kṛṣṇa as the universal God. In the Sanskrit *Jayādrimāhātmya*, a *Māhātmya* which is related to Jejuri (17th cent.), the story is told differently. Kṛṣṇa actually *does* get possessed and becomes a mad dog; only after going on a *yātrā* to the *kulasvāmī* in Jejuri and having *darśana* of Mārtaṇḍa Bhairava does he regain his old form.[14] Here the power of the famous folk deity is accepted in a brahmanical text which had to admit his importance even at the cost of subordinating Kṛṣṇa.

The attitude of the bhakti saint Tukārām differs from the approach of Śrīdhara, the author in the purāṇic narrative style. In Tukārām's famous *abhaṅg, anaṃta jugācā devhārā* (466), the Khaṇḍobā cult with its rituals, ritual implements and devotees becomes a metaphor for "inner religion."

It is a shrine of endless *yugas*/
Where the humming [of the possessed]
    is of the knowledge of the self//
The wind of possession/
    Oh this god Mallāri has captured me//1//

The cowrie is of pure *sattva*/
And the necklace is of knowledge//
Round the neck is the collar of non-attachment/
I shall show the ways of bhakti//2//

The heart is the (wooden) begging bowl/
The *ghoḷ*[15] strikes the unstruck sound//
The bag [of a Vāghyā] is full of the *bhaṇḍār* [turmeric powder] of knowledge/
And is not empty even at the end of the *kalpa*//3//

84 lakhs of births at our houses/

He [the Vāghyā] has begged for alms//
The god Mallāri is pleased/
I remain becoming Him//4//

The "wind' of the god fills him/
The body shakes with fits of love//
Just as a mad dog growls/
God has made Tukā bark//5//

BHAKTI IN THE *MALLĀRI MĀHĀTMYA* AND IN THE *MĀRTAṆḌA VIJAYA*

Especially in the Purāṇas we notice that Rudra, the "demonic" folk deity of the Vedic texts, is split into two manifestations. On the one hand, there is the more or less benign (*saumya*) Śiva living in heaven on Kailās, married to Pārvatī, and his pure manifestation on earth hedged in in temples in the form of an installed *liṅgam*. On the other hand, there is the *ugra* form, Bhairava, often the deity of Śaivite sects, who takes upon himself some of the functions of Rudra. A similar process of splitting appears with respect to the folk deity Khaṇḍobā in the brāhmaṇical *Mallāri Māhātmya*. The *Māhātmya* is said to belong to the *Brahmāṇḍa Purāṇa*. We must emphasize that the full contents of the *Māhātmya* are as yet hardly known amongst most of the groups involved in the worship of Khaṇḍobā, though the first Marathi version was already composed in the year 1585 by Siddhapāl Kesarī.[16] In agreement with the *Māhātmya* it is acknowledged that Śaṅkar/Śiva became an *avatār* to save his *bhaktas* from the oppression of the demons Maṇi and Malla. Folk religion has very often no difficulty in linking itself to the Sanskritic tradition of the Brāhmaṇs and then proceeding to make its own points. According to the *Māhātmya*, however, it was in order to save the Ṛṣis or Brāhmaṇs and their *āśrama* from the depredations of the demon kings Maṇi and Malla that Śiva became Mārtaṇḍa Bhairava.

Even at the time of the great saint Rāmdās the synthesis or merger between the Khaṇḍobā of the folk (who resembles Rudra) and the Śiva of the Purāṇas was apparently not yet complete. Rāmdās says:

The god is an *avatāra* of Śiva. He has settled on the hill-fort (of Jejuri). One [Khaṇḍobā] is seated on a blue horse. The other is on a white bull. One [Śiva] has white ash as his ornament. The other [Khaṇḍobā] has turmeric powder (Ma. *bhaṇḍār*). For Rāmdās they became one. He does not distinguish between the two.[17]

In fact, Khaṇḍobā has never received total recognition as a "respectable" deity, that is, as a classical god like Śiva served by Brāhmaṇs in a respectable *kṣetra* like, for instance, Tryambakeśvar near Nasik (Sontheimer 1989a: 299-337). In the *Māhātmya* Khaṇḍobā, the *avatāra* of Śiva, takes over many of the attributes, paraphernalia, and characteristics of the great demon kings, who are famous heroes and robbers. In fact, the basic, original folk deity Khaṇḍobā as he is worshipped even today by some groups in outlying areas, e.g. with non-vegetarian offerings, resembles much more the "demonic" folk deity Rudra than the Śiva of the *Purāṇas*. One might say that what the *Māhātmya* purports is to demonize some characteristics of the folk deity and to upgrade others, identifying them with those of the classical Śiva. Or we might say that now the folk deity sheds his asuric form and acquires brāhmaṇical sanction as Śiva who is the saviour of the Brāhmaṇs and the restorer of *yajña* and *dharma*. The demons have to be sacrificed in a great sacrificial battle (*raṇa-yajña*) to restore the original dharmic order. They have been blind, full of *ahaṃkār*, but on their death realize their original unity with the god, become his bhaktas, and attain *sāyujyatā* or *mukti*, or, according to one version, Śiva's heaven.[18] Their misdirected heroism is now turned to rightful purposes. They become *dvārapālas*. Malla at his own request has merged into Khaṇḍobā's name and that is why Khaṇḍobā is called Mallāri.

According to most versions of the *Māhātmya* it is the tremendous bravery of the heroic demons which pleases the god, who turns them into bhaktas.[19] One author[20] considers the fight of Maṇi as a case of *virodhabhakti*. Śiva is happy with Maṇi's war and grants *sārūpyatā*. He warns Malla by telling him that their friendship will be in *paraloka* (4.35). He makes a divine body for him and sends him to Kailās (5.21).

The trend to *ethicize* bhakti with the help of texts composed by Brāhmaṇs is also visible in the "codification" of bhakti. The *Mārtaṇḍa Vijaya* of Gaṅgādhara classifies bhakti within the usual framework of the ninefold division, but the types of bhakti differ substantially from the contents in the classical Vaiṣṇava scheme. After all, the forms of bhakti in the worship of the folk Khaṇḍobā were and still are strong and could not just be explained away with the help of a Vaiṣṇava Bhāgavata scheme. The list of the forms of bhakti in the *Mārtaṇḍa Vijaya* is as follows (35.45-8):

1. *Daivī* Bhakti

If the worshippers practise *mantrajapa,* they obtain *siddhi.* By this practise they obtain full enjoyment (*sampūrṇa bhoga*) in Śiva's heaven forever. They do not follow other modes of worship. They will reside endlessly near Śiva.

2. *Mānuṣī* Bhakti

This is characterized by worshipping a *pratimā* in human form with great faith and joy. The worshippers obtain full enjoyment in this world and on their death attain *svārūpyatā mukti* near Śiva, to whom they are very dear.

3. *Rākṣasī* Bhakti

This is characterized by the rite of hook-swinging (*bagāḍa*).

4. *Piśācī* Bhakti

This form of bhakti is characterized by devotees who invoke and get possessed by god in the form of the "wind" (*vāyu.* Khāḍe 1924: 73).

5. *Āsurī* Bhakti

This is like *rākṣasī* bhakti. Those who practise *rākṣasī, piśācī,* or *āsurī* bhakti will get happiness and material benefits in this world. They will attain Śiva's world on their death, but will sit there bewildered and will never obtain enjoyment.

6. *Kaumārī* Bhakti

The devotee offers *pūjā* pleasing the inner self (*antaḥkaraṇa*). He will gain a seat in Śiva's *sabhā* and supreme bliss there (*paramānanda*).

7. *Yoginī* Bhakti

The devotee recalls the *mūrti* resembling the god (*sādṛśya mūrti*) and performs *pūjā* mentally. Those who worship in this manner obtain happiness in this world and in the end will sit near Śiva in his court enjoying endless bliss.

8. *Rājasī* Bhakti

This is the worship of the deity with honours and services due to a king. The devotees will enjoy happiness in this world and will sit after their life near Śiva.

9. *Sāttvikī* Bhakti

This mode of bhakti is the feeding of a Brāhmaṇ, who is to be imagined as a form of Mārtaṇḍa.

This list of different modes of bhakti does not apparently present a strict hierarchical sequence from *daivī* bhakti to *sāttvikī* bhakti. *Daivī* bhakti seems to be placed in opposition to *mānuṣī* (human). *Daivī* bhakti does not require acts of worship which need a *pratimā*, but can be performed quietly and without the hustle and bustle which other forms of bhakti entail. (35.61: *varakaḍa na karitī sādhana/ khaṭapatī bahueka*). What is common to *rākṣasī, piśācī,* and *āsurī* bhakti is that they are incidents of folk religion: animal sacrifice (*paśuvadha*), hook-swinging (*bagāḍa*), and possession (*aṃgī aveśe aṇūn ...*). *Rākṣasī* and *āsurī* bhakti are practised on account of vows (*navasa*) to the god. They are *ugra* and have their origin in the mythological event in which the dying demon (*rākṣasa, daitya* or *asura*) Malla requested Mārtaṇḍa Bhairava (MV 19.65-8; 35.5) that his followers be allowed to enjoy the fruit of their ferocious bhakti. The classification of this bhakti as *rākṣasī* or *āsurī* seems to equate these bhaktas to the "demon devotee" Malla (cp. Shulman 1980: ch. V). Their worship yields transcendent results and they do attain Śiva's heaven at the end of their life, yet they are clearly not worthy of enjoyment in heaven. Gaṅgādhara, the author of the MV, does not disjoin the rites of folk religion incidental to the Khaṇḍobā cult from respectable and acknowledged *saumya* forms of worship, but subordinates them to an inherently lower position.

It is similar with *piśācī* bhakti. To get possessed by the god in the form of the wind (*vāyu*), which traditionally is another form of Rudra, is deprecated, as it is used as a means of subsistence. In the state of possession the Vāghyā (or perhaps the *devruṣī*) treats afflictions and solves problems of his clients (*lokāṃcī koḍī sāṃgatī/mājhe aṃgī*

Mārtaṃḍa ālā mhaṇona) on a particular day (33.50-1). In the name of god he receives food as alms (*vārī*). This possession is called an illusionary idea (35.52: *māyika vicāra*), and the author thus takes the position of a Vedāntist like Vidyāraṇya, who, in his *Pañcadaśī* (6.206-8), relegated Mairāla = Mailāra to the position of a lower manifestation of Īśvara. Such lower divinities could grant the fulfilment of wishes, but were part of the illusionary world. Gaṅgādhara thus devalues possession by a deity, which is one of the basic experiences of bhakti in folk religion.

Rājasī bhakti is appropriately associated with heat, that is, the ritual of firewalking (33.11-20). It is said to be practised by all castes (*jātī*) including Brāhmaṇs on account of a vow (*navasa*). Accordingly we have a rather long description of the rite, which includes the worship of the fire pit (*hāḷa*) with the "sixteen modes of worship" (33.16: *hāḷācem ṣoḍaśopacārem karāvem pūjana*).

The scheme seems to be informed by classical precedents. The following categories emerge and partially overlap:

a. divine, human, and demonic (*daivī, māṇuśī, āsurī*) bhakti;
b. tantric forms of worship: *kaumārī, yoginī* bhakti;
c. *tāmasī, rājasī* and *sāttvikī* bhakti.

The term *tamoguṇī navasa* appears at MV 19.66 and refers to the vow to perform animal sacrifice. But whatever the basis of the scheme may be, it seems doubtful whether the majority of the devotees are aware of or are directly affected by this attempt to interpret and "codify" the modes of bhakti.

CONCLUSION

In conclusion we may say that folk bhakti has to be considered on its own within the realm of folk religion and not as a degenerate or aberrant version of the "classical" bhakti of the *Purāṇas* and *Māhātmyas* or of the saint poets. In response to folk bhakti the *Purāṇas* or *Māhātmyas* mày codify and ethicize bhakti from the Brāhmaṇ's point of view. The saint poets may turn bhakti incidents into metaphors of "inner religion". The awareness and study of folk devotion and its expression by folk genres will thus help us to understand and to trace the emergence, formation and nature of other forms of bhakti in which folk bhakti is reinterpreted or simply dismissed.

APPENDIX

Mallāri and Raṃbhāī, the Muraḷī

॥ पद १९ ॥

भरगच्ची पायजमा अंगामधि झगा बांधला चिरा । लिंगकार गळ्यामधी डौल[1] पठार[2] लिग[3] मोहरा ॥ बिगबाळी[4] कानी चौकडा, मुदीवर खडा चमकतो हिरा । लालीलाल अंगावर शाल, मोत्याचा तुरा । घोड्यानी धरते[5] मण्डळ अष्ट[6] कमळ फिरतो वारा ॥ स्वरूपाच्या फाकल्या प्रभा जशा काय तारा ॥ चाल ॥ देखली[7] नाम नगरी आरे मालु निळ्या घोड्यावर आहे स्वारी आरे मालु तेथे उतरले मल्हारी अरे मालु ॥ मिळवणी ॥ नगर नारी[8] संगती तिला रंभाई शिंपिणीला मुशाकर[9] गुंडाजी जी आम्हा वाघापुढें गरजतो भडकतो झेंडा मन पवन वारु तो रंग[10] नाम फीरंग हातामध्ये खंडा जी । आम्हा वाघा पुढें गरजतो भडकतो झेंडा ॥ १ ॥ बोली बोलतो कानडा पुसतो बागा[11] चालला नीट जी जी । रंभाईने पाहिला देव राजे निळकट[12] पांची प्राणांची आरती घेऊन राव हातीं सोन्याचें ताट अभिमान रांगोळ्यावर योगाचे पाट जी ॥ चाल ॥ लावी उटने नानापरी आरे मालू तेल अत्तरमय लावी गिरी[13] आरे मालु ॥ उंच आबीर विज्यापुरी आरे मालु प्रेमळ सुगंधी कस्तुरी आरे मालु ॥ मिळवणी ॥ घंगाळी पाणी चौरंग न्हाती श्रीरंग चांदीचा हांडा आम्हां वाघापुढें गरजतो भडकतो झेंडा । मन पाहून[14] वारु तो रंग[15] नाम फी रंग[16] हातामध्ये खंडा आम्हां बाधापुढें गरजतो भडकतो झेंडा ॥ २ ॥ सुकुमार वस्त्र अंग पुसा[17] पितांबर नेसा[18] भडक जरी काठींअंगीं[19] भंडाराचें भूषण टिळा ललाटी जी हा आत्म निषद[20] हारु हार नाजुक प्रकार भरीत तूप रोटी आहो रोटी तूप[21] पोळ्या साळीचा भात सुगंधीत आमटी जी ॥ चाल ॥ सात भाज्या कोशींबरी आरे मालु लोण्याच्या[22] चटण्या हारो हारी आरे मालु घारगे वडे अरे कुरकुरीत अरे मालु ॥ मिळवणी ॥ परोपरी वाढिल्या खिरी साखर नाहीं पुरी[23] दुधामधि मांडा आम्हां वाघ्यापुढें गरजतो भडकतो झेंडा मन पावन[24] वारु तो रंग[25] फी रंग[26] हातामध्यें खंडा ॥ ३ ॥ आधां[27] वाघापुढें गरजतो भडकतो झेंडा अचवून[28] घेतला विडा तबकामध्यें पुडा फुलांचा हार पोशाख केला देवाला जडित सिनगार लालीलाल चमकतो माहाल कोंदणें लाल हिरे कंकर आंत टाकला पलंग समया चार रंभाइच्या पाहुनी भाव प्रसन्न झाले देव । आवई दिलीवर[29] देव भक्ताच कनवाळु कृपासागर ॥ चाल ॥ घेऊन आला सुन्दरी आरे मालु ठेवली करेच्या[30] तिरिं आरे मालु सहा महिन्या सोमवारीं आरे मालु देव जाती तिच्या मंदिरी आरे मालु ॥ मिळवणी ॥ गुरु मुकींद मनामध्यें घाले सागरी न्हाले प्रेमपुरि लोंढा बाणु वाघा चरणीं स्थरी[31] पायरीचा घोंडा मन पावन[32] वारु तो फी रंग[33] हातामध्ये खंडा आम्हां वाघापुढें गरजतो भडकतो झेंडा ॥ ४ ॥

1. डुल । 2. Cp. *Khaṃḍobācīṃ padeṃ, pad* 42: . . . डौल पठाण घाट 3. लिंग । 4. भीकबाळी । 5. धरले । 6. ०दल । 7. Read जेजुरी after देखली (*Khaṃḍobācīṃ*

pad 25.4: ...जेजुरी नाम नगरी). 8. नगरनारी। 9. मुशाफर। 10. तुरंग। 11. वाडा। 12. निलकंठ। 13. शिरी। 14. पवन । 15. See fn. 10. 16. फिरंग। 17. पुसी। 18. नेसी। 19. जरीकाठीं अंगी। 20. आत्म-निवेद (Skt. नैवेद्य or निवेदन). 21. तूप रोटी। 22. लोणच्याच्या। 23. रायपुरी। 24. पवन। 25. See fn. 10. 26. See fn. 16. 27. आम्हां। 28. आंचवून। 29. दिल्यावर। 30. कर्हेच्या। 31. स्थिर। 32. See fn. 24. 33. See fn. 16.

NOTES

1. Perhaps the success of southern *viraha bhakti* in northern India was enhanced by a pre-existing substratum of the theme of *viraha* in the oral folk literature of Rajasthan and elsewhere. Cp. Hardy 1983.
2. MV 5.12: *bhaktīcā bhūkelā*. Khaṇḍobā devours huge amounts of millet bread, porridge, and buttermilk in the shepherds' camp (Sontheimer 1989b: 32f.). Rudra, too, is "longing for food" (Sontheimer 1989b: 43). We are, of course, reminded of another mountain deity, namely, Śrī Girirāj, who is Kṛṣṇa-Gopāl or Kṛṣṇa-Govardhan. He is feasted by cowherds with much food in the Annakūṭ festival. See Vaudeville 1980: 1ff.
3. *Tiruvācakam*, e.g. 1.60; 4.214; 5.2.13; 4.37 and 39; etc.
4. The case of King Śāhū's dog Khaṇḍya is a famous example. He saved the life of the king from a tiger and received honours normally bestowed on a Sardār (Chitnis 1924: 121).
5. TS IV.5.2.n; *mīḍhuṣṭama*. E.g., *Śivapurāṇa* IV 6.5: *kṣipraprasāda*.
6. *Samayaparīkṣe* of Brahmaśiva 2.71 (A.D. 1112). After the battle against Mārtaṇḍa Bhairava/Khaṇḍobā, the demon Malla addresses the god as the "hero of the battle" (MM 18.27: the *saṃgrāma vīra*) and "great hero" (MM 18.30: *mahāvīra*).
7. In Jejuri yellow handprints on the shirt of the worshipping devotee are called the "seal" (*śikkā*) of Khaṇḍobā. The seal is proof that the devotee has been to Khaṇḍobā's temple and met the god. It is impressed on the shirt by a *pūjārī* (of the Gurav caste) who has dipped his hands into the mixture of turmeric and water (besides other offerings like bananas and milk) in the rectangular pit which is the seat of the *svayambhū piṇḍs* of Khaṇḍobā and Mhāḷsā.
8. Translation of a *pad* from the notebook of Māṇikbāī Bhagvān Reṇke, Pune, a Muraḷī and a famous performer in *jāgraṇs*. The translation is by the author and Dilip Chitre.
9. A certain preparation like dumplings, made of wheat flour.
10. Bāṇū Vāghyā or Vāghā is the bard, whereas Guru Mukīnda seems to have been his guru. Guru Mukīnda is said to have lived in the first quarter of the 19th century.
11. *nhāle premapurī loṃḍhā*. Prempur or modern Pember is said to be the original place of Khaṇḍobā/Mailāra, but the name can also refer to Jejuri (Sontheimer 1990). Pember is situated 22 kms to the north of Bidar.
12. *Śrīnāmadeva Gāthā*, 1970: 33 (no. 82). The *abhaṅg* may be spurious.
13. Śrīdhara 1975: ch. ix, 92-218. According to Tulpule 1979: 406, the *Harivijaya* was written in 1702.
14. Available in Marathi in Khāḍe 1924: 1-5.

15. A short bar of iron with chains attached to it; used by the Vāghyā people (according to Molesworth 1857: 265). Instead of it a cloth handle with a little bell at each end (*ghāṭi*) is used by some Vāghyās.
16. See Ḍhere 1961: 8.
17. *Śrīsamarthāṃcī Gāthā, abhaṃg* 70.
18. Ciṃtāmaṇi, *Mallāri-Māhātmya*, 5.21. Ms., Marathi, dated A.D. 1818.
19. See Vināyaka: 14.3.
20. Ciṃtāmaṇi: 3.71.

All the God's Wives

VĀGHYĀS AND Muraḷīs sing and play the deeds of the god who is variously called Khaṇḍobā, Khaṇḍerāyā, Mallu Khān, Mārtaṇḍa (-Bhairava), Mhāḷsākānt, Mallāri, Malhārī, Khaṇḍu Gāvḍā, and Jejurīcā Vāṇī. The Vāghyās are, so to speak, the bards of the god, and the Muraḷīs are his courtesans. Often called *devāṅganās*, the Muraḷīs are also married to the god.

This paper is based mainly on *padeṃ* (the plural of *pada*), or songs, of the Vāghyās and Muraḷīs.[1] The *padeṃ* contain a good deal of historical information, and, in some cases, they cannot be understood—or rather, reconstructed—without a knowledge of the context. These *padeṃ* are generally sung during a *jāgraṇ*, or "vigil". Khaṇḍobā loves these *jāgraṇs,* and they are often arranged in fulfilment of a vow—for example, a vow made for the birth of children—or as atonement for some misconduct. For this paper I have chosen some *padeṃ* that deal with the relationships among Khaṇḍobā's wives and between Khaṇḍobā and his wives. Khaṇḍobā's wives represent the position of women in Maharashtrian culture, and reflect views on divine and human femininity within that culture. As far as possible, I want to let the sources speak for themselves in translation.

Much of folk religion in Maharashtra is traditionally interwoven with elements of kingship. Khaṇḍobā is God Śiva, who has (con)descended to become King on earth. He rules in his fort (*khillā* or *gaḍkoṭ*), at his capital in Jejuri. He holds court, liberally giving away gold. He has a Minister, Hegaḍe Pradhān, who plays an important role in the life of the court. As so often happens in traditional accounts about kings, King Khaṇḍobā goes on a hunting expedition that shades into an erotic adventure.[2] Classical Sanskrit traditions relating to royalty also come into play. The story of Bāṇu, Khaṇḍobā's second wife, resembles in its basic outlines the story of Śakuntalā and King Duḥśānta, as told, for example, in the *Mahābhārata* (1.63-7). Śakuntalā was the daughter of Menakā, one of the *apsarās* in Indra's court. As a folk god, Khaṇḍobā also resembles Indra, and his court is compared to Indra's.

Khaṇḍobā has five wives. Two of them, Mhāḷsā and Bāṇu/Bāṇāī/Bāṇubāī, are the most important. The story of the king or god and his two wives is one that is found with many variations all over India. In Tamil Nadu, the god Murukaṉ has the two wives Devasenā and Vaḷḷi. Veṅkaṭeśvar, at Tirupati, has Lakṣmī and Padmāvatī; Viṭhobā, at Pandharpur, has Rukmiṇī and Padubāī. At Pushkar, in Rajasthan, the god Brahmā has the two wives Sarasvatī and Gāyatrī. Mallikārjuna at Śrīśailam has Pārvatī and a Ceñcu wife; Narasiṃha has both Lakṣmī and Ceñcu-Lakṣmī. There are also examples in Bihar, Bengal, and Uttar Pradesh, and the Purāṇas include stories of the rivalry between Śiva's wives Pārvatī and Gaṅgā.[3]

Mhāḷsā, the primordial *śakti*, is probably a manifestation of an old, independent goddess (*devī*) who has been subordinated to the male Śaivite Khaṇḍobā cult as the god's wife. In the *Mallāri Māhātmya* she is Pārvatī, the wife of Śiva. The *Mallāri Māhātmya* does not mention Bāṇāī as such. Instead (20.23.1), the text states that Gaṅgā came down angrily to earth. The Māhātmya also cuts short the notorious quarrel between Mhāḷsā (Pārvati)) and Bāṇāī (Gaṅgā) by suggesting that they are one (*Mallāri Māhātmya* 20.24). In the *padeṃ*, there are occasional allusions to the Purāṇic version of the myth in the Māhātmya, and to iconography. But these features do not dominate. They are subordinated to folk themes; they are transformed; they are given a new twist. The genre of the *padeṃ* thus presents "another harmony".[4]

Classical, Purāṇic, and scriptural literature and religion have a cosmology that is vertical in time and space. The events in the stories are separated from the present by *yugas*. The gods are in heaven, and life on earth is hierarchical, organized according to the *varṇāśrama* system. The *padeṃ*, like folk literature and folk religion in general, have a *horizontal* cosmology. Satyayuga and Kaliyuga merge, and Jejuri is the heaven Kailāsa itself. The borderline between divine and human is very thin, as is the borderline between divine love and human erotic love. There is an atmosphere of equality among people, and between humans and gods.

The horizontal cosmos of folk literature and folk religion is divided into two realms: the inside and the outside. For instance, the fort, which is inside, is contrasted with the forest, which is outside but is also a very important area for the king. In Sanskrit terms, the inside is the *kṣetra*; the outside, the *vana* or *araṇya*.[5] In Marathi, the pastoral area, the *rān* or *māḷ*, stands for separation (*viraha*), as the *mullai* does in classical Tamil literature. The contrast between the two realms is not a strict dichotomy. The *kṣetra* and the forest are interdependent, and there is a good deal of interaction between them.

From this contrast emanates the contrast between the two wives. The first wife, Mhāḷsā, has a regular marriage with Khaṇḍobā; Bāṇāī's is a marriage by capture—basically, a love marriage. Mhāḷsā, as a member of the Liṅgāyat merchant caste (a Liṅgāyat Vāṇī), comes from a respectable, high-caste family; Bāṇāī, as a Dhangar, comes from among people who live in the forest, outside—the Dhangars, the Gavḷis, and the Gāvḍās.[6] She is a shepherdess from the wilderness out there.

The characterization of the two wives in the *padeṃ* conforms to the basic contrast between inside and outside. Mhāḷsā is domestic: she cooks well, and the god praises her cooking. Bāṇāī doesn't know how to cook. Mhāḷsā is depicted as cantankerous and jealous, Bāṇāī as headstrong and resolute, and only occasionally as jealous or mean. Sometimes Mhāḷsā is portrayed as ugly; Bāṇāī is invariably beautiful and erotic. Whereas Mhāḷsā is "pure as gold", Bāṇāī is impure. Mhāḷsā is married to the god in a ritualistically proper ceremony; Bāṇāī's marriage rituals are more than questionable. In short, Mhāḷsā represents "culture" and Bāṇāī "nature"; God, the king, stands between them.

But the god has more than two wives. After all, he is a king, and by his marriage alliances he keeps contact with different communities. Khaṇḍobā's third wife is Raṃbhāī Śimpīn, the tailor woman. Raṃbhāī is a heavenly nymph and dancer (*devāṅganā*), and is sometimes identified with Bāṇāī. On the divine but mundane level, she is the prototype of the Muraḷī, the temple dancer, devoted to the royal god Khaṇḍobā, whose court is compared with Indra's. Raṃbhāī is worshipped as a goddess whom the god visits after his hunt. She is also localized, being said to come from the village of Belsare, near Jejuri.

Khaṇḍobā's fourth wife is Phulāī Māḷīn, a woman of the Gardener caste. She was a particular Muraḷī and is thus a deified devotee of Khaṇḍobā. The god visits her, during his hunting expedition, at Davṇā Māḷ, the "Field of Southernwood"—a herb which is specially dear to Khaṇḍobā. Through her, Māḷī women have a special right (*mān*) to sell southernwood and marigolds at a conspicuous place in Jejuri.

The fifth wife is Candāī Bhagvanīn. She is a Muslim woman, or sometimes a Telīn, a woman of the Oilpresser caste. Khaṇḍobā himself is also sometimes a Muslim; as such he is called Mallu Khān or simply Mālu. But the emphasis in the songs is chiefly on Mhāḷsā and Bāṇāī, to some extent on Raṃbhāī, and to a lesser degree on Phulāī Māḷīn. I have not been able to find any songs about Candāī Bhagvanīn.

Many of the *padeṃ* deal with the quarrel between Mhāḷsā and Bāṇāī. But first, there is a quarrel between Khaṇḍobā and Mhāḷsā. What is the deeper reason for *this* quarrel? A story told by a Dhangar explains quite clearly: Mhāḷsā and Khaṇḍobā were just sitting there side by side, doing nothing for days and days. The world came to a standstill. The minister got really worried; he brought the game of chess from Bhoḷā Śaṅkar. Mhāḷsā and Khaṇḍobā played, and Khaṇḍobā lost everything to Mhāḷsā except his loincloth, his *jheṇḍā* (banner), his wand, and his *bhaṇḍārī*, the magic bag filled with his all-powerful *bhaṇḍār* (turmeric powder). He even lost his two dogs to Mhāḷsā. During the night, Khaṇḍobā had a dream. He saw Bāṇāī in the dream, and he decided to leave town to go hunting in the wilderness. He evaded his army, stayed twelve years with Bāṇāī, and married her in a totally unsanskritic form of marriage ritual.

One of the *padeṃ*—in fact, the longest of them—describes Khaṇḍobā's exit

Song 48

One

The Mahāraj of Fort Jejuri, Savāī Malukhān
Leads a hunting expedition to the forest,
He rides a horse, the Minister by his side
Among his retinue of titled nobles (*mānkarīs*),
    [and] strong heroes (*vīr baḷivān*) is
Yeśvant Rāv with his flame-red banner in front.
Battle music sounds, the hunting pack growls,
The god hunts and plays among the shadows of the forest.
Surrounded by mountains and cliffs the thirsty Malhār
Searches rivers and lakes. And he finds Cannāpur,
The shepherds' town with nine lakh sheep.
He asks for water, and Bān[ṇ]āī comes out.
And looking at Bāṇu, he loses his mind.
Says the graceful Mhāḷsā: "Listen, oh Raṃbhāī,
The Lord has gone for a hunt,

why isn't he back yet?"
Said Mhāḷsā: "Listen, O Raṃbhāī,..."

In another *pad*, the angry Mhāḷsā describes her own marriage with Khaṇḍobā and his fascination with Bāṇāī. Somewhat like the classical Śiva who marries Satī, Khaṇḍobā is a loafer; he is not really "respectable":

Song 33

Lady Mhāḷsā spoke in utter fury:
Do you mean I am a thief, O Malurāyā?
Says Mhāḷsā: Nevāsā is my parental home.
What do you think, Mister! My father Tamśeṭ
is a merchant prince.
This is no marriage of equals.
Your grotesque, howling horde of 900,000 followers!
The wedding was set up, I was placed on the
marriage platform.
Five Brahmans acted as Parameśvar.
You brought me back to Jejuri
Again going around on the Nine Continents.
Lady Mhāḷsā spoke in utter fury.

Were we pitted against each other in a previous life
That you should bring Bāṇu as my rival wife?
Sharing a husband is too much pain
I want my whole millet bread, you gave half of it to her.
Boiled water will never taste the same again.
You are too easy to cheat, my Lord, how do you expect me
to share you?
It's vile to think of becoming someone's second wife.
Just to look at her makes me burn.
Lady Mhāḷsā spoke in utter fury.
Surely you don't need two knives in one hand.
How far can I teach you, have some sense! Our fight
will come before the people's court
And you will have to hang your head in shame.
Says Hegaḍe: O Lord!
Because of Bāṇu you have to swallow this bitter pill.
Lady Mhāḷsā spoke in utter fury.

Four lamps burnt at your bedside

as you dreamt of Bāṇu, the Shepherdess.
He got up, Lord Malhārī,
Brought her and kept her in a cave.
As people loudly cheer to celebrate
  the fullmoon of Chaitra
He stealthily throws some turmeric dust on Bāṇu.
Malla, the Vāghyā, rolls at his feet
Beholding them, wearing a *ling* and a bag of turmeric
  dust around his neck.
Lady Mhāḷsā spoke in utter fury.

Two *padeṃ* tell how Khaṇḍobā met Bāṇāī or Bāṇu, how he dreamed of her:

Song 13

Let me go, O Mallukhān,
  have you gone crazy?
You dwell at a great *tīrtha,* O Resident of Pember
You are of royal blood,
  you abide in the three worlds
The black powder of *abīr* is your signature,
  have you gone crazy?

I am now on my way to Pember
  to smell milk and curds
My mother-in-law is wicked, she awaits
  me at home, don't stop me
My ornaments are broken,
Why have you gone crazy?

Let go of my sari,
  You have torn off my fine *cunaḍī*
You have broken my nine-stringed necklace
  and crushed my bangles
Go and pick up the scattered pearls from the courtyard,
  have you gone crazy?
Mahipati says in conclusion:
This bold, shameless fellow
  is none other than Mallukhān,
The ruler of the Deccan
Oh hear the drums beating in the Nagarkhāna,
  have you gone crazy?

Song 30

All dressed-up Bāṇu
Pots of milk of her head
She was on her way to the weekly market
When she met the Lord.
You are holding the loose end of my sari,
Says Bāṇu, Get out of my way
The Dhangars are ruffians
They will pick a fight with you.
Bāṇu pushes the king away
Hands off my sari, let me go home.

Hearing Bāṇu's rebuff
Says God Malhār,
I charm you with a pinch of turmeric dust
And carry you off on my horse.
At this the beautiful Bāṇu
Began to tremble
I report all this at home
Hands off my sari, let me go home.

In any case, the Lord goes to Candanpur to find Bāṇu:

Song 37a

The Lord just had to go to Candanpūr
He took his Minister along
Blistering heat
The Minister held the royal parasol to shade the Lord
To shade the Lord—*O Mālu!*
No water to drink
No water to drink—*O Mālu!*
The Lady Bāṇu is of the shepherd caste
She has nine hundred thousand sheep
My Lord, Bāṇu—
Made you work hard
Made you sweep the sheep pen
Bāṇu got furious
She pounded together sheep droppings and wool—*O Mālu!*
Mixed it and made a watery gruel
And served it as a meal—*O Mālu!*
Mhāḷsā, *O Lord Malhārī,*

Was watching from a distance
From the fort of the Nine Hundred Thousand Steps
Bhikājī stands in the court.
Inspire my song!
She made you work hard—*O Mālu!*

The Lord is fascinated by Bāṇu:

Song 44

Bāṇu sat down to beautify her head
She put turmeric dust in the part of her hair—
a flawless hairdo:
To each hair she tied a pearl
She fastened ornaments to her pigtail.
From the centre of her head she wears a string of flowers.
Ah Bāṇu! Like a lance in the shape of a woman
Holding a mirror in her hand the amorous one looked at
her own face
She quickly chewed a betel leaf roll to redden her mouth
The Lord found Bāṇu fascinating
As she stood amidst the pillars of Light.
She was wearing a gold on white sari
Beneath the curls *kuṃkuṃ* traced across the forehead
Her beautiful skin glowed like gold.
His attention wandered from her sari to her tender lips
And the necklace of the nine gems she wore.

Malhārī is her husband
He mounted a horse
'Nagadhim' the drums beat,
He holds a golden shield
The Lord is fascinated by Bāṇu
Bāṇu, the bride, is fully adorned
As the flames of torches dance around
And cries of victory rise
The followers cannot control their delight
They are the favourites of Malu Sāheb
Who even makes Death tremble in fear
says Bhikar Khaṇḍubā
The blazing red flag flutters in the wind.
The Lord is fascinated by Bāṇu.

Another song describes the situation from the point of view of the Vāghyā and his audience:

Song 29

What made him crave for Bāṇu and Mhāḷsā?
Oh, the Lord has really gone crazy
Oh, the Lord has really gone crazy.
O Bāṇu the Lord went to Candanpūr
Bravo! Bravo! O Bāṇu!
He became her man-servant
Became a herdsman of her sheep and goats.
See, my Lord, I lie at your feet
I have come to sing.
Oh, the Lord has really gone crazy.

The Lady Bāṇu makes him lose his head
Bravo! Bravo! O Bāṇu!
She is beautiful as the Crescent Moon
She makes Lord Malhār crazy.
See, my Lord, I lie at your feet
I have come to sing
Oh, the Lord has really gone crazy.

The Lord has really mounted his horse
Bravo! Bravo! O Bāṇu! Bravo!
He took the beautiful Bāṇu along
Brought her half-way up the Fort.
A stealthy shower of turmeric dust for her
See, my Lord, I lie at your feet
I have come to sing
Oh, the Lord has really gone crazy.

Mhāḷsā gets sad about the absence of her husband:

Song 37b

"My Malhārī has gone crazy, dear me, how,"
Mhāḷsā pines in her heart,
"Whom should I blame?"
My rival, his wife, bosses over me,
  she flirts as she flatters him,
  she moves around with the god never leaving him.

Bānū has forcibly invaded my house
Raṃbhāī has also seduced him,
he has gifted her his silken shawl.
And he even goes to bed with Phulābāī
The mud clings to the water, and the water, too, won't
leave the mud!
Let's see the god and worship Mālu, the king of the earth
Śaṅkar Viṭṭhal [the poet] says to Rāma, to Janārdan, to
Sonā Mhāḷsā:
"Let's look at the god."
Tatyābā sings the same tune:
"Let's see the god."

Mhāḷsā pleads with god, and describes her advantages in comparison to Bāṇu:[7]

Song 6

Mhāḷsā says to the Lord: Believe me, my Master,
O believe me
I swear by your life, I have no quarrel with you
I am your proper wife and queen,
O I am the queen.
Tell me: who has done injustice to me?
If you weigh it in the balance, I am the purest kind of gold.
Why are you indifferent, why has your mind become distracted?
I have decorated my hair with *jāī, juī,* and
śevantī-flowers
I have lit fragrant joss-sticks
Come, O Lord of the Three Worlds, and take your seat
I swear by your life, I have no quarrel with you
Mhāḷsā says to the Lord: Believe me, my Master,
O believe me
Arise to enjoy your feast, O Lord and King
The water for your bath is ready
I have rolled *boṭave* with my own fingers and *śevaya* with
my own hands
Sit down and have a hearty meal, O Lord and King
Why do you take away my only shelter on earth,
my only shelter on earth
I have no one other than you, my Saviour
Who except you is there to love me

Someone else poisoned your ear, and you started off to the forest
I swear by your life, I have no quarrel with you.

Just think of Bāṇu's place
She is from the black bank of the river in Bāglaṇ, in Khāndeś
You brought her and fulfilled your desire
Why did you bring Bāṇu and keep her in the palace of pleasures?
On her forehead she wore *mūdrakhaḍī,*
  the gossip spread in the town
From all four sides crowds thronged to see her.
  There was such a jam!
Bālakṛṣṇa with folded hands enjoys the fun.
I swear by your life, I have no quarrel with you.

Now Mhāḷsā quarrels with Bāṇu:

Song 14

We are Liṅgāyat Vāṇīs
We are Liṅgāyat Vāṇīs
We follow the Śiva-*dharma,* O Woman,
We follow the Śiva-*dharma,*
We constantly contemplate Śiva,
  We keep our food and water covered.

There are mirrors inlaid in our courtyard walls,
  where we count our diamonds and precious stones
After bathing with Gaṅgā water
After bathing with Gaṅgā water, we worship the Tuḷsī plant,
  smearing ashes on the forehead.
Your entry
  has polluted our house,
  has polluted our house,
  has polluted our house.
Oh my, oh my, what a spell you have cast on the Lord.
O Woman, you have made Mallāri crazy,
  Mhāḷsā said: O Bāṇu, O Woman
  You have made Mallāri crazy

Mhāḷsā lashed out:
You vulgar shepherdesses, your bodies stink
Your place is in the wilderness
You luckless wretches don't belong to palaces and temples

The very sight of the god
Made you drool.
You clung to his feet,
To Mālu's feet.
How did you lure him away, O Woman,
  how did you lure the god,
How did you make Malhārī crazy.
  Mhāḷsā said: O Bāṇu, O Woman
  You have made Mallāri crazy.

Song 39

Oh! In the house of the King of Gods Bāṇu and Mhāḷsā quarrel
What a stunning sight! They tear each other's hair apart!
Mhāḷsā asks the Minister to report to the Lord:
I can't get on with this one, keep her elsewhere
Her manners are bad, she constantly quarrels
What more shall I tell you, O king of the Gods:
  You set up a house with her in the forest.
As though you have gone broke
A Threepenny Opera! What treasures to show?
My mansion is worth lakhs, the whole world knows
Each wall studded with mirrors, lit with lamps everywhere.
Oh! In such a place of the Lord Bāṇu and Mhāḷsā quarrel.

The following quarrel song is sung by a Vāghyā from among the Khutekar Dhangars; for him, Bāṇāī is Pārvatī.

Song 7

Says Mhāḷsā to Bāṇū:
"What spell have you cast on Malhārī?
How did Malhārī get carried away?
He has brought back a piece of cowdung
At her home he washed her goats and sheep,
and I can still smell the stink."
Says Mhāḷsā to Bāṇū:
"What spell have you cast...?"

Says Bāṇū to Mhāḷsā: "Don't run me down, please!
  The god came by himself to my palace and said:
  'Let me be your servant.'
    And so he became a Dhangar."

The "cowdung" now becomes Pārvatī and
Lives on the Fort of Jejuri.
Rām Hoḷkar respectfully touches her feet.

If the quarrel between Mhāḷsā and Bāṇāī gets too serious, there is sometimes an appeal to a higher authority:

Song 37c

One

Bāṇu and Mhāḷsā, both were quarrelling in the open court.
Malhārī laughs behind his sleeve
Mhāḷsā pleads her own case before the god:
"You have tortured me for nothing,
constantly you are in the company of that shepherdess.
A rival wife is like a phial of poison, like a knife she stabs the heart.
She burns my life like a fire, she is like thunder and lightning."
"Oh wonder of wonder," the god is given the news,
"The filthy shepherdess speaks dirty words.
But you like whatever she says.
I speak the truth, but you find Bāṇū's words truer."
Mhāḷsā says, mark these words:
"My body, speech and mind belong to Mālu.
He is the *piṇḍi* in the Brahmāṇḍa
On the top there is the thousand-petalled lotus.
He is Śiva with a half syllable above him.
How shall I convince my rival,
it's like trying to pour water into an upside down pot."
Malhārī laughs behind his sleeve.

Two

"You have listened to her, now hear me out,
You eight ministers, sitting in the court.
Give your verdict on this dispute between us two,
Life will be too short for me to describe my own reputation."
"Listen, Mhāḷsā, I tell you how to clear the problem,"
Says Siddha Pātakeśvar [Siddhapāl Kesarī],
"accept what the *Mallāri Māhātmya* says,
Forget this rival wife, forget your bias
(*yā savatīcī karā nivṛtti, āḍhī manātīl kāḍhā*)."

Sometimes the quarrel is not only between Mhāḷsā and Bāṇāī but among three of Khaṇḍobā's wives—Mhāḷsā, Bāṇāī, and Raṃbhāī as well. In a song about a shawl, Raṃbhāī comes to the rescue. Can you imagine a king without an embroidered shawl?

Song 39a

The Quarrel between Bāṇu and Mhāḷsā

One

Jamnāmīya, the washerman
Washed the shawl
And took it to Mhāḷsā
Get up, O Lady Mhāḷsā, the Lord has sent the shawl
Embroider its ends
No sooner had Mhāḷsā seen the shawl than she flew into a rage
She threw it into the washroom sink
Lord Malhārī huffs and puffs, he doesn't speak to me
Why did he marry me?
He loves the shepherdess Bāṇu and brought her home.
Go! She will embroider it.
Bāṇu and Mhāḷsā have quarrelled and now they sit sulking
Neither of them would embroider the shawl.
Bāṇu and Mhāḷsā have quarrelled and now they sit sulking

Two

Jamnāmīya, the washerman, went back quickly
Picking up the shawl from the sink
He washed the shawl of the Lord with soap
And took it to Bāṇāī
Get up, Bāṇu, the Lord has sent the shawl
Embroider its ends
No sooner had Bāṇāī seen the shawl than she flew into a rage
She threw it on a thorny bush.
The Lord Malhārī huffs and puffs, he doesn't speak to me
Why did he bring me here?
He married Madam Mhāḷsā. Be she [Let her be?] his mistress!
Go! She will embroider it.
Bāṇu and Mhāḷsā have quarrelled and now they sit sulking

Three

Jamnāmīya, the washerman, feeling very bad

Went to the Lord's court.
Listen, O Lord! Why do you call yourself great?
Nobody embroiders your shawl.
Now it was Mallukhān's turn to fly into a rage
Near him was Hegaḍe Pradhān.
Hegaḍe Pradhān! Saddle my horse
I will throw out Bāṇu and Mhāḷsā
In person did Lord Mallukhān ride to Dahīṭhaṇ
His eyes fell on Raṃbhāī, the tailor woman
Raṃbhāī, the tailor woman, recognized the Lord
and touched his feet
And after she made him sit on the bedstead
Raṃbhāī took needle and thread
And embroidered the shawl
She embroidered the picture of Bāṇu on one side
and of Mhāḷsā on the other.
Such was the consummate skill of the tailor woman!
Cover her eyes, O Hegaḍe Pradhān,
And let's ride away with her on the horse.
Bāṇu and Mhāḷsā have quarrelled and now they sit sulking

Ultimately, however, everybody has to cooperate. This is especially true during festivals, when the lord is on duty, so to speak, in his temple. Bāṇāī and Mhāḷsā join together in unison to celebrate the festival; the *kāminīs* (erotic women) become *yoginīs* (female *yogīs*). A representation of Khaṇḍobā on the back wall of the sanctuary of the temple in Jejuri shows the Lord as Mārtaṇḍa Bhairava, the form he assumed when he battled the demons. On each side he is flanked by a goddess. Both of the goddesses look exactly alike. They should be Bāṇāī and Mhāḷsā, but whenever one asks who they are, the invariable answer is that both are called Yogeśvarī.

Song 40

Comes the Festival of Divālī

One

Parrots chatter on the cluster of trees
Crows caw, sparrows twitter at the doorstep
Herons at the reservoir, kokilas in the mango grove
High on the tree blue jays and little spotted owls.

The peacock's cries!
The celestial maidens go to fetch water with their pots.
Jejuri, the city of birds, where the water of the River Karhā
is like nectar.
Bāṇu and Mhāḷsā anoint the Lord with fragrant pastes
Seated on a square wooden platform the Lord bathes
with hot water from the two-handled vessel.
He wears a silken, yellow dhoti, a musk mark
on his forehead
Phulāī, the gardener woman, garlands him
Raṃbhāī, the tailor woman, embroiders his shawl.
In a chamber a Muraḷī lovingly sings his praise.
His ornaments are golden, golden is his silken upper garment.
He is offered a seat of sandalwood, with coloured powders
they draw decorative patterns in front of him.
Wake up, quick! It's Divālī, says Mhāḷsā to Lord Mālu
Wake up, let me put collyrium into your eyes
Divālī has come.

Two

The hall festooned with fresh flowers
Screens of flowers in the palace.
Joss-sticks burn everywhere, everything becomes diffused
with fragrance.
Torches burn in broad daylight casting their glow upon the Great
Gate.
The sprinkled courtyard, fully drawn figure, wooden seats
Row of lampstands lit, the Seers seated in a line
for a splendid feast.
Bāṇu and Mhāḷsā serve them on golden plates.
Fruits of *amṛt*, oranges, sweet grapes, figs and bananas
Muraḷīs serve in silver trays in the Mahāl.
Wake up, quick, it's Divālī, says Mhāḷsā to Lord Mālu.

Three

As they chew scented betel-leaf rolls, their lips flash like rubies.
One could not take stock of the richly brocaded garments
They bring forth the neatly folded garments in silver trays.
Garlands in their hands, the headmen of the servants stand
awaiting orders.

A fully-adorned Mhāḷsā watches from behind a curtain
And Bāṇāī, too, is bejewelled
As though from her beauty sparks are flying.
Cling to his feet in the crescendo of drums
This sound seizes the wind in his grip again and again
In the golden, broidered silk sari with gold and
silver threads, her yellow blouse
Mhāḷsā looks fresh like the core of a banana plant,
or the petal of a flower.
Wake up quickly! It's Divālī, says Mhāḷsā to Lord Mālu.

Four

Thirty-three crores of gods crowd the Court of the Three Worlds.
Enter Nārad and Tumbar to narrate the news
Vāghyās and Muraḷīs sing their songs, ringing their
hand-bells.
The unstruck sound resounds in heaven. There is a crowd to meet
the Lord.
Hearing the sweet name in Bāpu's voice Mukundagīr is pleased.
Haribhāū's female companion sings the heavenly tune.
Good deeds of the past have borne fruit at last
Mālu's name is written on the forehead
Forgive me, O Lord, my thousand lapses.
Keep me under your merciful shadow, give me a place
under your feet.
This is what I beg forever.
Wake up, quick! It's Divālī, says Mhāḷsā to Lord Mālu.

NOTES

Professor Sontheimer presented this paper at the Fourth International Conference on Maharashtra: Culture and Society at Arizona State University. He died, on 1 June 1992, without having prepared a written version of the paper. The present paper has been reconstructed by Anne Feldhaus from Professor Sontheimer's notes. The translations are the product of the collaborative effort of Professor Sontheimer and Dilip Chitre. The article was first published in *Images of Women in Maharashtrian Literature and Religion*, edited by Anne Feldhaus (Albany: State University of New York Press, 1996), and is reprinted here by permission of the State University of New York Press.

1. The songs are drawn from the following sources:
—*Śrī Khaṇḍobācaṃ padeṃ. Śrī Sadguru Bhāūmahārāj yāṃcyā saṃgrahāṃtūl.* Puṇeṃ:

Vā. Dā. Gokhale, Śake 1883 [1967]. [Caste: Parīṭ].
—Notebook of Maṇikbāī Bhagvān Reṇusā, Puṇeṃ [Muraḷī], (photocopy).
—Notebook of Janu Kadam, Jejuri [Caste: Vīr].
—Manuscript (*vahī*) of Nāmā bīn Dhanājī Parīṭ Jaktāp [Jagtāp], Kesanaṃd, Havelī Tālukā, Jilhā Puṇeṃ, dated Śake 1798 [1876]. (Ms. in the collection of Rā. Ciṃ Ḍhere). [Caste: Parīṭ].
—Śrī Gabājī Kisan Saḷūṅke, Śivatakrār Mahāḷuṅgī, Śirūr Tālukā, Jilhā Puṇeṃ [Mairāḷ Vāghe].
—Renubāī Mahātu Bhembe, Khāmgāv Dahiṭhān, Tālukā Dauṇḍ, Jilhā Puṇeṃ [Muraḷī].
—Śāntabāī Khaṇḍu Jādhav, Śeguḍ, Tālukā Karjat, Jilhā Raigaḍ [Muraḷī].
The numbers of the songs are those in a forthcoming collection of translations by Günther Sontheimer and Dilip Chitre.

2. See Günther Sontheimer, "King Khaṇḍobā's Hunting Expedition", in *Flags of Fame,* edited by Heidrun Brückner, Lothar Lutze, and Aditya Malik (New Delhi: Manohar, 1994), pp. 19-80. See also the 1992 film "King Khandoba's Hunting Expedition" by Henning Stegmüller and Günther Sontheimer.
3. In addition, the *Vāmanapurāṇa* tells of Śiva and Pārvatī quarrelling over their game of dice, as Khaṇḍobā and Mhāḷsā quarrel over a game in the story narrated below.
4. See *Another Harmony: New Essays on the Folklore of India,* edited by Stuart H. Blackburn and A.K. Ramanujan (Berkeley: University of California Press, 1986).
5. For a more detailed discussion of this distinction, see G.D. Sontheimer, "The *Vana* and the *Kṣetra*: The Tribal Background of Some Famous Cults", in *Eschmann Memorial Lectures,* edited by G.C. Tripathi and Hermann Kulke (Bhubaneswar, 1987), pp. 117-64.
6. In Karnataka, Mallavvā comes from the Gāvḍās, people who have large herds of cattle.
7. See also Song 26:

   O Lord, speak gently to me
   You seem to be under the spell of Bāṇu.
   Mallāri
   Until now we were full of Love
   We found everything in each other
   Mallāri
   Suddenly you betrayed me
   Your heart has turned to stone
   Mallāri
   How that wicked Bāṇu has cast a spell on you
   You have left our Fort Jejuri
   Mallāri
   O Lord, speak gently to me.

   Bāṇu says: "Hey, Lord, Mallāri
   Why have you come to my house?"
   Mallāri
   He ran around like a slave to sweep
   the sheep-pen

Mallāri
See how he slurps buttermilk gruel
With both hands he wipes his moustache
Mallāri
How Bāṇu has cast her spell on you
She is a nuisance in our midst
Mallāri
O Lord, speak gently to me.

King Khaṇḍobā's Hunt and His Encounter with Bāṇāī, the Shepherdess

I. THE SOMVATĪ AMĀVĀSYĀ FESTIVAL IN THE KHAṆḌOBĀ CULT: TWO STRANDS

ONE OF THE most important festivals in the Khaṇḍobā cult of Maharashtra is observed on Somvatī Amāvāsyā, that is, on a new moon day which falls on a Monday. The major centre of the cult is Jejurī in the Pune district and it is here that the festival is observed most conspicuously and elaborately. The festival is also observed in other places where Khaṇḍobā and similar Śaivite folk deities are worshipped, but at such places it is of only local importance.[1] There are many dimensions of this festival (see Stanley 1977), but we shall emphasize here the hunting excursion of the Lord, and the folk-religious and royal character of this day. Though outwardly there is little to show that the royal god actually goes for a hunt, this is a frequent explanation given by participants in the festival.

Before we proceed, it is necessary to point out that the festival incorporates two main religious orientations, which at times coalesce and at other times stand apart, maintaining more or less a dynamically fluctuating relationship. From the point of view of the brahmanical texts, though not one which is necessarily shared by all Brāhmaṇs who are also devotees of Khaṇḍobā, the essence of the festival would be that it is a purifying ritual at an inauspicious point of time, namely the conjunction of the sun and the moon on a Monday. Terms like *snāna, śuddhi* and *pāpa* are used in expressing this attitude. The other orientation belongs to the realm of folk religion. The god's exit into the "forest" is dramatically performed and the devotees participate in the royal "hunt", which culminates in a common bath of the god and his devotees in the Karhā river.

The motives of the devotees who participate in the festival are variously expressed, but can be summarized by the desire to secure "life and prosperity" (Heesterman 1985: 31), or to seek the values of "bodily existence and well-being" or "auspiciousness" or "higher quality of life" (Marriott 1976: 194). Both orientations, the brahmanical and the folk, and the rites connected with them are, of course, pervaded by the peculiar sacredness of Somvatī Amāvāsyā, a day on which the "fluidity of power" (Stanley 1977: 30) is "unambivalently auspicious" (Stanley 1977: 42) in the Khaṇḍobā cult. In the following article we shall also try to explore some of the dimensions of these attitudes and their mutual interaction, as they are expressed in oral folk myths, in scriptural brahmanical texts, and in the dramatic performances and rituals of the festival. We shall spread our net rather wide, to draw together scattered and variegated materials which may eventually provide the background to the festival, especially the hunting excursion of the god. In passing, we should like to point out the pervasiveness and spatial spread of the incidents of the Khaṇḍobā cult and its relationships and/or indebtedness to similar cults, especially in Tamilnadu, Karnataka, and Andhra Pradesh. Future research will probably have to concentrate on parallels between similar folk cults in different regions: too often the local or regional data are taken to be unique, without comparative scrutiny to show whether this is true or not.

II. SOMVATĪ AMĀVĀSYĀ IN THE *JAYĀDRI MĀHĀTMYA*, *MĀRTAṆḌAVIJAYA* AND OTHER SCRIPTURAL SOURCES

The *Jayādri Māhātmya* is an unpublished Sanskrit text which describes literally "the Greatness of Jejurī". It links the Jejurī (*Jayādri*) cult firmly to the *Mahābhārata* and to purāṇic precedents while heavily aetiologizing local events and incidents pertaining to Jejurī and to another important place of the cult, namely Naḷdurg, in the Usmanabad district. The oldest ms. is dated *śake* 1678 (A.D. 1756).[2] It was around this time, namely between A.D. 1635-1790, that increased building activity is recorded in inscriptions in the temple complex of Jejurī (Potdar 1914: 265-72, Khare 1958: 91-3). Other scriptural sources are the *Mārtaṇḍavijaya* (A.D. 1823)[3] and the *Śrīkṣetra-Jejurī-Māhātmya* (1925),[4] both in Marathi.

The *JM* basically relates a conversation between the five Pāṇḍavas and Śiva. The Pāṇḍavas have arrived at Jejurī and Dharmarāja asks a host of questions which are mostly answered by Śiva or Vaiśampāyana.

The questions resemble a checklist of the mythical and ritual constituents of the cult of Jejurī. It appears that Jejurī as a *kṣetra* was given its scriptural sanction in the 17th and 18th centuries, though the *JM* presupposes an earlier cult, and the earliest inscribed reference to the deity at Jejurī probably dates to the 13th century (Potdār 1933: 265; Sontheimer 1987: 13). Dharmarāja enquires about the cause of the important festivals (*utsava*) of Campāṣaṣṭhī and the full moon (*pūrṇimā*) festivals in the months of Pauṣa (Dec.-Jan.), Māgha (Jan.-Feb.), and Caitra (Mar.-Apr.), but the equally important Somvatī Amāvāsyā is not included in his questionnaire. The *JM* makes him ask about the origin (*utpatti*) of the river Karhā and why a particular spot on the bank is called "Ghoḍe-uḍḍān". While answering these questions, Śiva also narrates the aetiology of Somvatī Amāvāsyā. The question about the origin of the Karhā seems somewhat inconsistent and illogical when we come to know that the Pāṇḍavas have been the cause of the origin of the river. We summarize the passage (Khāḍe 1925: 16):

At the time when the Pāṇḍavas were to perform their sacrifice (*yajña*), there was no water for the sacred bath of Brāhmaṇs, and water is necessary for a *yajña*. Bhīma managed to topple over the *kamaṇḍalū* of Brahmadeva, who was engaged in meditation.[5] From the enraged Brahmadeva's pot flowed the river. Brahmadeva eventually came from the (Mountain) Brahmādri to Pāṇḍeśvar (a village near the Karhā river), where the *yajña* was to be performed. He was reconciled with Bhīma because it was for the sake of *yajña* that Bhīma had committed a mistake (*aparādha*). This happened in the month of Phālgun (Feb.-Mar.) on Somvatī Amāvāsyā. When Mārtaṇḍa Bhairava saw the river "flow like the Gaṅgā" he went to have purifying bath (*snāna*). Brahmadeva and Nārada also came for a bath. The spot where they bathed is also known as Ghoḍe-uḍḍān.[6] It was at this spot that "the *tīrtha* which destroys sins" (*pāpa-nāśana-tīrtha*) originated. Ever since, when there is Amāvāsyā on a Monday, Mārtaṇḍa Bhairava (*alias* Khaṇḍobā) comes for a purifying bath (*snāna*) from the Jayādri Mountain.

The *MV* (28, 76-95) tells us very much the same myth in Marathi and adds:

Brahmadeva was reconciled to the idea that the water was needed to perform the *yajña* with the connivance of Mhāḷsākānt ("the husband of Mhāḷsā"). Mhāḷsākānt, alias Khaṇḍobā, came on horseback and had a bath in the river. The gods followed him and became purified by the water of his feet (*śrīcaraṇodakeṃ*). They threw turmeric dust (Ma. *bhaṇḍār*) on the Lord. The site where Nārada bathed is called Ghoḍe-uḍān [*sic*]. It is the "sin-destroying *tīrtha*". Ever since that day, known as Somvatī Amāvāsyā *parva*, Mhāḷsākānt comes from the Jayādri Mountain. The river was called Mandākinī or "Brahmā's vessel" by gods and Ṛṣis, which changed into "Karhā" in Prākṛt (*Karhā nāṃva Prākṛta jāṇa bolīṃ*). Somvatī Amāvāsyā is an auspicious day and extremely pure (*paramapāvana*); it increases *puṇya* (*puṇyavardhana*) and is suitable for *snāna* and *dāna.*

Thus we have a myth which proposes to serve as an epic and purāṇic "pretext" for the Somvatī Amāvāsyā festival. The Vedic *yajña* is replaced by the *yātrā* or *utsava* during which Mārtaṇḍa Bhairava has a ritual bath, *snāna,* in the Karhā river. The day is also said to be fit for making donations (*dāna*). Besides Somvatī Amāvāsyā, the four annual festivals in the months of Pauṣ, Māgh, and Caitra, and at Caṃpāṣaṣṭhi in the month of Mārgaśīrṣa (Nov.-Dec.) are mentioned. In the *JM* or *MV* we do not find a particular emphasis on Mārtaṇḍa Bhairava in his capacity as a king, let alone as a hunter, nor is the hunt mentioned. The only passages in which a hunter is mentioned are found in the *MV* and the *MM.* Here Malla, the Daitya, goes on a hunt which turns into a raid on the *āśrama* of the Seven Ṛṣis.[7] Those Brāhmaṇs and others who believe in the efficacy of the scriptures would be satisfied with reading or listening to them, even if they are in Marathi, because they promise to yield the desired *phala.* This may include enjoyment of life as well as the goods of life (*bhukti*), the acquisition of "super-natural" worldly power (*siddhi*), and even final salvation (*mukti*).

We could have let the matter rest at this point and concluded that the scriptural aetiology is firmly entrenched and the festival has its brahmanical sanction. But, in fact, the participants in the festival never refer to this aetiology, nor do they refer to the *JM* or *MV* in the way one would refer to the Veda (or *śruti*) as an authority, even if its contents are not known. Even the Brāhmaṇs do not refer to it; they participate in the festival during the moments where their ritual expertise is needed—e.g. to fix the exact astrological time for the conjunction of the sun and the moon—though they abstain from the tumultuous, playful performance of the festival.

III. KHAṆḌOBĀ AS A FOLK DEITY, KING AND HUNTER

In folk perception Khaṇḍobā reflects the traditional king, though this image may have become elusive in modern times. He is responsible for the welfare of the people and is endowed with divine powers to bestow fertility on his realm and to redistribute "the goods of life" which he obtains through the efforts of his followers. There is some reason to hold that one of the origins of the Khaṇḍobā cult is found in the charismatic heroic chieftain or *rājā* or local potentate, who was believed to be divine by his followers because of his prowess and resourcefulness. An early inscription of the last quarter of the 7th cent. A.D. from Ajaṇṭā mentions a certain ruler Khaṇḍeśvara ("the lord of the sword"), and calls him Mallayeśa-kārttānta, "the destroyer of Mallayeśa" (Chabra 1955: 124; Malandra 1982). It is characteristic of the folk attitude to deify successful living heroes or heroes who died a violent death. Heroes who performed a heroic feat and survived could become local rulers as a next step in their career and were considered divine by their folk. The beginning of the dynasties of the Hoysalas and the Yādavas of Devgiri are attributed to legendary heroic feats of the founders of these dynasties—the killing of tigers (Derrett 1957: 7) and the defence of village cattle (Verma 1970: 14). In the early medieval period heroes died for their master or king, who was considered divine, if not *quasi* a deity. In other words, loyalty to the king or chieftain was expressed by unflinching bhakti leading to self-immolation at times (Sontheimer 1991b: 23). This bhakti was eventually directed towards a god like Mallanna, Mailāra or Khaṇḍobā, or a goddess, worshipped in a temple. These deities were also *quasi* royal masters. Self-immolation became a sacrifice, an extreme form of bhakti, which was now directed to the god as king on earth. Memorials depicting heads of heroes and oral myths in the Khaṇḍobā-Mailāra cult still testify to these acts of bravery and the defiance of death. Perhaps this is what the *MV* means when it says: "For the hero god is king".[8]

The objection of the *MM* and *MV* to the demon kings Malla and Maṇi was not so much directed to their bravery and heroism—their tremendous prowess, though unethical as it were, is stressed—but to the fact that they would let themselves be worshipped as gods (*MM* 7.13-36). The *MM* and the *MV* emphasize the point that it is a purāṇic deity, namely Śiva, who descends to become an *avatāra* and even "condescends" to become a king on earth. The historical elevation of a hero and local ruler to a god, who would eventually attain the status of Indra, Śiva or Viṣṇu, was ignored. Folk deities who were claimed to be Śiva by their followers and had, for example, a historical root—like in the death of a hero in a battle—could be ridiculed, especially by sectarians. Followers of Mailāra, for instance, when challenged by the Liṅgāyat saint Dāsimayya, claimed that the deity was none other than Śiva himself. But in this they were rebuked by the saint, who argued that Mailāra was a warrior killed by hunters

(Sontheimer 1987: 14). The attitude in the *MM* and *MV* seems to have been to assimilate the local or regional folk cult of the king by splitting it into halves which were then hierarchized: the local king was demonized and the demon was defeated by an *avatāra* of Viṣṇu or Śiva. The purāṇic deity now became god as king on earth and he assumed the court and regalia of his mundane, demonized predecessor, who would become his demon devotee, his flunkey, or a subordinate deity. The local folk cult, whether it was related to a living royal master or to a hero deified after his death, as some opponents of folk deities would claim was the case with Mailāra (Sontheimer 1987: 13) or even Viṭhobā (for instance, Sontheimer 1989c: 70), acquired a new vertical, even transcendent, purāṇic or "sectarian" dimension. The god was now worshipped as Śiva or Viṣṇu or a form of them. He could grant not only *bhukti*, but also *mukti*, which otherwise had been possible only by violent self-immolation. As in the scriptural texts relating to the Khaṇḍobā cult, *bhukti* and *mukti* were values which were not delinked from each other, but constituted a continuum. *Bhukti* implies mundane values like prosperity, which we have referred to above. Though the two values are not delinked from each other, there is an emphasis on reading and listening to scriptures, and individual worship through *pūjā*, in the brahmanical attitude. However, the folk traditions and the oral texts about Khaṇḍobā, for example, emphasize the dramatic rather than the scriptural and ritual enactment of bhakti.

In folk perception Khaṇḍobā, Khaṇḍerāyā or Khaṇḍerāv, as these popular appellations indicate, is not just viewed as an *avatār*, but he is Śiva himself as king on earth—"here and now"—in order to look after the welfare of his followers or devotees. It is pre-eminently a cult of folk bhakti and therefore we have to shift into the realm of folk culture with its dramatic performances and oral literature. Again, however, we do not want to postulate a dichotomy between the scriptural texts and oral folk literature, or between ritual emphasized in the brahmanical sphere and dramatic folk performances. There is a constant interaction between these two realms. It may be advisable not to generalize about the cult on the basis of either point of view, but to try to inquire contextually when, how, and where one or the other realm stands forth. For instance, one of the tasks of the scriptural text of the local *Māhātmya* is to explain the existence of the typical dramatically performed folk rites and oral myths, to devalue them by hierarchization within the framework of the brahmanical system, or even to ignore them. Hookswinging, possession, walking on fire, breaking of chains, etc. are thus hierarchized by being classified as *rākṣasī*, *piśācī* or *rājasī* rather than *sāttvikī* bhakti.[9] In folk bhakti, however, such rites are considered to be *sāttvikī*. *Sattva* is often taken to mean *sattā*, which, essentially, means "power". This power is often gained by acts of violent, vehement, and insistent bhakti. Such bhakti provokes the *sattva* of the god, his powerful presence which lends strength and renewal to the devotee as well as to the god. For instance, the Vāghyās, who are the "dog-men" or "tiger-men" of Khaṇḍobā, and also the Dhangar shepherds, break their iron chains on Somvatī Amāvāsyā. The breaking is a sure sign that they are infused with Khaṇḍobā's *sattva* and that he will remove all obstacles. Hook-swinging (Ma. *bagāḍ*), which exists now only in a mild form at some places, shows the serious will of the devotee to honour his pledges (Ma. *navas*) and to elicit Khaṇḍobā's *sattva*. In an old song of the Vāghyās we hear (*pad* 8):[10]

The Lord of the earth is the ruling force in the Deccan
The thunder of King Malhār resounds all over the world.
Great noblemen come.
The devotees wear *bhaṇḍār* (turmeric dust) on their forehead and
show their fierce will by circling
in the air suspended by a hook.
His *sattva* is great
They raise cries of "Yeḷkoṭ" ("Seven Crores"),
And sins and faults are removed.

In the *MM*, on the other hand, Śiva is seated on the distant Kailāsa, looking from far away on his *kṣetra* on earth. The primordial events which led to its establishment are also far removed in time. His other self, so to say, rules as Mārtaṇḍa Bhairava on Earth. In folk perception, Jejurī is the very Kailās on earth and it is Śaṅkar who rules there as King Khaṇḍobā. Thus we hear in another Vāghyā song (*pad* 24):

He is the Lord of the Three Worlds
He resides in happiness
Have faith in him
Malhārī (Khaṇḍobā)
will fulfil your wishes.
Jejurī is Kailās.

An oral legend tells how one devotee, who belonged to the Māṅg caste, prompted Śiva to stay on earth by sacrificing himself after Śiva had defeated the demons Maṇi and Malla (Sontheimer 1989b: 313). Characteristic of folk religion, this violent act of suicidal self-sacrifice leads to the deification of the devotee. He did not even have to travel to Kailāsa and get his celestial legitimation to return as a deified hero to earth, as is sometimes required in folk religion (Blackburn 1985). Today he is known as Yeśvant Rāv and he is said to be the Havaldār[11] of the temple fort in Jejurī. He has his shrine near the main entrance of the fort (Gaḍkoṭ). Such devotees are said to practise *ugra bhakti*. The term *ugra* lends itself to negative interpretations and may mean "terrible", "wrathful", "hideous", in the view of the brahmanical scripture and ritual, or from a modern reformist perspective. But *ugra* for the bhakta, who may even call his god or goddess *ugra*, has no negative connotations and means "fearful", "powerful", "mighty", "strong", "high", and "noble".[12] This epithet was even shared by a king who was not yet hedged in by brahmanical norms. Thus Mārtaṇḍa Bhairava is *ugra* when he battles the demons Maṇi and Malla, and he also appears in his *ugra* form when he goes on a hunt.

In the past at least Khaṇḍobā was involved in all spheres of the life of his devotees, for example, in legal, social, psychological, medical, artistic, entertaining, or soteriological matters. Khaṇḍobā is the family deity of groups ranging from the (formerly untouchable) Māṅgs to the Brāhmaṇs, and the spectrum included nobles, warriors, robbers, merchants, nomads, forest dwellers, farmers, pastoralists, Muslims and so on. As a family god he has assumed all the characteristics of most of his followers and their caste professions.

The immanence of the divine in the world of humans, according to folk religion, is also reflected in the cosmology and the experience of time which prevailed in folk belief. The classical theory of four *yugas* of long duration is replaced by the simple notion of the Satyayuga ("the *yuga* of truth") and the Kaliyuga ("the *yuga* of vice") in the folk religious experience. Moreover, there is still co-inherence of the Satyayuga in the Kaliyuga. The Satyayuga prevails on certain occasions, for instance, on Somvatī Amāvāsyā. The qualities of both ages mingle the further we turn away from the influence of the brahmanical ritual and text. A Dhangar shepherd and devotee of Khaṇḍobā can still say about Somvatī Amāvāsyā:

> On that day we go to Jejurī. If there were no Satyayuga we would not go to Jejurī.

Because the cosmos of folk religion is preponderantly horizontal, and god is immanent in this world, oral literature tends to reflect life on earth and its environment. The songs of the bards of Khaṇḍobā or the myths (*ovīs*) sung by the Dhangar shepherds reflect an enchanted and yet often realistic, intimate view of their traditional life. Oral literature may use images and ideas from scriptural texts in Sanskrit and Marathi, or from the bhakti literature of the Maharashtrian saints, but such borrowings are marginal, often transformed and interpreted in the context of folk culture. In the songs of the Vāghyās, who are the bards of Khaṇḍobā and sing his miraculous deeds, the Lord is a king who goes on a hunt on Somvatī Amāvāsyā day.

IV. THE HISTORICAL BACKGROUND OF THE HUNTING EXCURSION

Thus in the matrix of the festival we find the idea that Khaṇḍobā goes on a hunt. Nowadays this idea may become disfunctional and evanescent. There is no game to be hunted by hunters and food gatherers, or by sedentary communities who enrich their settled life and supplement their food by hunting in the wilderness. There are no kings or princes who practise the royal pastime of hunting. Yet the old notion that hunting involves excitement or even eroticism, besides food, and the generation of life out of death, is still reflected in oral literature and in casual statements made on Somvatī Amāvāsyā, when it is said that the Lord "goes for a hunt" or "plays at hunting". Folk religion is more sensitive to the environmental, social, historical, and local context than the written brahmanical text, which tries to disentangle the cult from the phenomenal world. One may ask why Khaṇḍobā's hunt is traditionally emphasized. And we may answer that he is, like Rudra, the "Lord of the hunters" and, like Mallanna in Warangal (Sontheimer 1985: 148), "the Lord of the those who hunt with spears", and that this was instrumental in celebrating a common epithet or mythologeme in the festival. Or we may say: after all Khaṇḍobā is a king, and kings must go hunting according to their dharma and have erotic adventures in the forest. It seems, however, that such traditions are not observed for these reasons alone, but go back to an environmental core and to ancient, if not prehistoric, roots which have survived. In fact, the whole cult is a mirror of survivals. For example, if Khaṇḍobā is (or rather was) the "Lord of Robbers", i.e. of the Rāmośīs, the environmental and historical core is the fact that robber chieftains and heroes like Umājī Naik would raid merchant caravans passing Jejurī, which was situated at a crossroad. The legend of Vālmīki, "the robber", could be localized near Jejurī for the same reason (Sontheimer 1989: 174-6).

Hunting wild boars was quite common amongst the villagers around Jejurī. A 52-year-old member of the Māḷi ("gardener") caste tells how his father used to go hunting near his village, Sākurḍe, close to Jejurī. He would use a spear or an axe to hunt wild boars. Not only was the "mutton" a dietary supplement, but oil extracted while cooking the meat had medicinal properties against rheumatism etc. Within living memory the Karhā valley and, in particular, the eastern part of it up to Bārāmatī was covered with trees and bushes typical of the pastoral area in Maharashtra. They are all mentioned in the songs of the Vāghyās, in the description of the forest(s) which Khaṇḍobā traverses while on the hunt: the Bābhūḷ (*Acacia Arabica*), the Nīm (*Azadirachta Indica*), the Bor or Jujube (*Zyzyphus Jujuba*), the Khair (*Acacia catechu*), the Hivar (*Mimosa* or *Acacia Tomentosa*), the Murmuti (?; a bush), the Nivaḍuṅg (Prickly Pear; *Cactus Indicus*), the Tarvaḍ (a bush; *Cassia Auriculata*), and so on.[13] In prehistoric times hunting and fishing communities must have frequented the area. Microliths can be found along the banks of the eastern part of the river, mostly on its northern bank. D.D. Kosambi, in his study of the microlithic tracks in Poona District, mentions: "The finest technique belongs to the Karhā track, and may be seen at its highest development in Deuḷgav-Gāḍā" (Kosambi 1962: 128). Subsequently, a rather casual search at the spot (Ghoḍe-uḍḍān) where Khaṇḍobā terminates his hunt with a bath in the river, again yielded microliths of the finest quality. Formerly, according to oral sources, the hunt would lead across the river up to the northern margin of the valley and the ancient Yādava temple of Bhuleśvar. This is an area where many Dhangars still have their seasonal monsoon camps.

Today the god still crosses the Karhā river after his bath and visits the village of Dhālavḍi. Here he is "shown" *nived* (= Skt. *naivedya*) consisting mainly of millet bread, and his entourage is given a meal by the villagers at the shrine of the god Bābīr. This shrine is flanked by ancestor stones, each showing a warrior and his wife seated on a horse, in imitation of the popular representations of Khaṇḍobā and his wife Mhāḷsā (or Bāṇāī, his second wife, from the Dhangar shepherd community). Bābīr was originally a deity of the Gavḷīs, a widespread community of keepers of buffaloes and large cattle in the semi-arid southern parts of Maharashtra. Because of deteriorating pastures they were replaced by the sheep-breeding Dhangars. Bābīr himself was a cowherd boy. He was slain by Rāmośīs who protected standing crops in the fields belonging to the farmers. After his death he was deified. A major shrine with a festival (*jatrā*) for this god is found at Nhāī Rūī between Indāpūr and Bārāmati (Sontheimer 1989: 87). The survival of the "tribal" element may be seen in the Mahādev Koḷīs. They were the traditional hunters and, when forced by circumstances, the traditional robbers of Maharashtra, before they were absorbed by the rural populace as a caste of boatmen and water carriers, or survived as "tribes" in the forested parts of the Western Ghats.

The tradition of the "God as King" going on a hunt is also attested to by two stone panels which are found in the village of Sākurḍe, to which we have already referred, and in the village of Mūrti Moḍhve, situated about 5 km. to the east of Jejurī. The panels show a hunter with a bow who wears large earrings and a halo typical of Bhairava. He is followed by a woman who wears a crown (*kirīṭa,* in Mūrti Moḍhve) or a halo similar to Bhairava's (in Sākurḍe). She may be his *śakti.* In front of the hunter, who holds a raised bow, wild boars and antelopes are in flight, pursued by dogs. Several emaciated followers are indicated. The god is now locally called *Vandev* (the god of the forest) or Bhairava. The sculptures are characteristic of the Yādava period (*c.* 13th or 14th cent.). In Mūrti Moḍhve hero-stones of the same period also exist in considerable numbers. Some of them depict the defence of cattle and the death of the hero. Wild cows or *vangāys* were still plentiful around Mūrti Moḍhve a few decades ago. At the instance of the villagers, members of an itinerant hunter caste, the Rās Phāse Pārḍhīs, had to chase them away, because they damaged the standing crops. Now only an occasional pack of wolves or rabbits can be met in this area. Amongst the famous royal devotees of the Khaṇḍobā of Jejurī were King Śāhū (1709-49), who was an "avid hunter" (Sontheimer 1989c: 217), and Malhārrāv Hoḷkar (Sontheimer 1989a: 308).

Thus the excursion on Somvatī Amāvāsyā may be a reflection of this situational core of hunting, which is deeply embedded in the natural environment and the local hunting traditions.

V. KHAṆḌOBĀ'S HUNT IN THE ORAL TRADITIONS OF THE VĀGHYĀS AND DHANGARS

In an old Vāghyā song called the *Somvatī pad* (*pad* 22) we have the description of the hunting procession of the Lord.[14] The song is at least as old as 1823.

> ...I see the splendid procession going to the Karhā river
> The sparkling vanguard at the Wednesday Bazaar
> The Lord goes to meet the Hoḷkar
> They run, push, jostle, choke the whole road
> What crowds! What throngs!
> It's a glorious multitude
> *Breaking away the king flashes and vanishes*
> *eluding all his horsemen*
> Nīlgāy, spotted deer, sāṃbar take flight in fear
> The hunting dogs are unleashed
> Antelopes, leopards, sāṃbars, deer stampede away
> Enjoying his hunting game the Lord
> arrives at the Karhā river.
> (Emphasis added).

The longest song of the Vāghyās (*pad* 48) describes the exit of Khaṇḍobā alias Malukhān into the forest, his hunt, and his stay at Bāṇāī's shepherd camp. It is again a song at least as old as 1823.
Here is the beginning:

> The Mahārāj of Fort Jejurī, Savāī Malukhān,
> Leads a hunting expedition to the forest,
> He rides a horse, the Minister by his side
> Among his retinue of titled nobles (*mānkarīs*)
> [and] strong heroes (*vīr baḷivān*) is
> Yeśvant Rāv with his flame-red banner in front.
> Battle music sounds, the hunting pack growls,
> The god hunts and plays among the shadows of the forest.
> Surrounded by mountains and cliffs the thirsty Malhār
> Searches for river and lakes. And he finds Cannāpur
> The shepherds' town with nine lakh sheep.

The are many versions of the story of Bāṇāī, the shepherdess whom Khaṇḍobā meets and marries after he has traversed the forest. The parallels to the story of Śakuntalā, according to the *Mahābhārata*, are evident. We shall give a representative excerpt from a long version of the myth told by a Dhangar informant, the late Limba Torve:

What happened now while the god was sulking? He said: "Pārdhān (Minister), call the people of the town. After calling them we shall go hunting. Let's go hunting". Then what did the Pārdhān do? He loaded the cannons and guns. He called the people of the town: "Come, the god is going to go hunting". There was an army of 12,000 men. The god was on his way. He left the fort of Jejurī. And the army came down . . . .

The god started hunting. The first time he shouted. His shouting made the forest tremble. The second time he shouted. Trees and bushes were shaken. The third time he shouted. Cliffs and rocks loosened. The fourth time he shouted [in a retold version: he rounded up the herds of game: sāṃbar, spotted deer, and wild boar] and began to hunt. The sixth time he shouted. He made heaps of the hunted animals. He piled the meat on a wooden scaffold. The god started hunting. The army of 12,000 became thirsty. The 12,000 became very thirsty. Nowhere was there water. And thus the army of 12,000 went back to the fort of Jejurī . . . .[15]

Khaṇḍobā has to cross five or more different "frightful" forests. Finally even his Minister (Heggaḍe-Pradhān) is sent back before they arrive at Bāṇāī's shepherds' camp or settlement (Ma. *vāḍā*). According to the *Mahābhārata*, King Duḥṣanta [sic] has to cross several forests during his hunt, makes a virtual slaughter of the animals of the forest and finally reaches the *āśrama* of the Ṛṣi Kaṇva (1.63-7, crit. edn.). During his march he is accompanied by his army, the people of the town, the ministers (*āmātya*) and his "chaplain" (*purohita*). Like Khaṇḍobā he leaves them behind one by one, and when he reaches Kaṇva's hermitage within the *āśrama* (similar to Bāṇāī's *vāḍā* in the encampment or settlement of the Dhangars) he meets Śakuntalā, who was abandoned by Menakā (of Indra's heaven) in the forest. Bāṇāī or Raṃbhāī (one of Indra's daughters, see below) was similarly "abandoned" in the forest, according to Dhangar stories (Sontheimer 1989a).

But, independent of the similarity of incidents in the Śakuntalā story and the myth of Bāṇāī, we find a basic structure wherever we look in our materials, and we obtain what could perhaps be called the meta-contextual text of the king's hunt and the encounter with the girl from the wilderness. The components of the text would be: crossing the threshold—hunting (which merges into cattle raids, capture of women, and conquests)—snatching life out of the jaws of death—eroticism—*vanvās*—winning life and the goods of life (e.g.

the prey, which is hunted for food, *vīrya*, fertility, etc.)—the extension or restoration of *sva* or the renewal of life—triumphant return.

VI. HUNTING AND EROTICISM IN THE FOREST

Wilderness, its dangers and ambivalence, hunting, the passion and excitement of hunting, death and fertility, eroticism and the adventures of the hero, king, or god are all invariably linked in actual hunting practices, ritual hunts, and literature. These pervasive themes occur *mutatis mutandis* in hunting practices of "tribals" and in their oral literature, in temple rituals and temple legends, in the two epics, in purāṇic and poetic Sanskrit literature,[16] in classical Tamil literature, and in medieval south Indian literature. A few examples may illustrate this point.

In the eastern Ghats in Andhra Pradesh shifting cultivators like the Koṇḍu Reḍḍis associate hunting with eroticism. In their hunting practices, herbal juices, expressly called "love potions" (Tel. *valapu mandu*) are used while tracing the footprints of the wild boar (Tel. *aḍavi pandi*). The hunter sprinkles the herbal juice on its footprints and waits for the prey to return. The beast is attracted by the love potion and returns to the hunter, who kills it with bow and arrow. The Koṇḍu Reḍḍis make it explicit that the wild boar develops love (Tel. *valapu*) for the hunter and comes towards him, thereby facing death.[17]

The ritual hunt of the goddess Bharāḍī in the village Angevadi (Malvan taluka) in the Sindhudurg district of Maharashtra is an example of an event which in other places now lives only in memory. Annually, the young male population of the village has to go on a wild boar hunt. The actual village festival (*jatrā*) cannot begin unless a boar is shot. Some of the hunters are equipped with guns and are, as it were, led and inspired by the goddess. That is, if no beast can be tracked down, one of the hunters will be possessed by the goddess and she will direct the way through her medium. The whole hunt—which may take several days—is felt as fraught with horripilation, especially if a whole troop of wild boars turns up "like an avalanche of stones". The stay in the jungle (Ma. *rān*), the communal meals, and drinking the water of the forest is an experience which transcends the normal flow of village life. The hunter who first sights a boar receives special honours. The women of the village, meanwhile, prepare garlands of flowers. When the wild boar or "he who presides over the village border" (Ma. *sīmecā adhikārī*) is carried into the village—tied upside down to a pole—he is garlanded by the villagers. The young women of the village perform the ceremony of lights (*ārati*) by waving lights around the beast. The "hero" who has sighted the boar first will get the best piece of the meat, whereas the other parts will be distributed amongst all the households. The "hero" is asked to give a common dinner for the small village community (Sāvant 1985: 77-80). The goddess Bharāḍī is identified with "Jagadambā Māyabhavānī", the Maharashtrian Durgāmahiṣāsuramardinī, who has her centre in Tuljapur in the Osmanabad district. An erotic relationship between the Devī and the buffalo demon is suggested in Sanskrit texts (Shulman 1980: 178), in the desire of Mahiṣa to marry the goddess. A similar relationship is continued on the level of south Indian village religion, where the goddess's desire for her lover, the buffalo victim, provides a pervasive theme in ritual and legend (Brubaker 1978; Shulman 1980). Bharāḍī is a village goddess who annually goes on a hunt and possesses the hunters before and during the hunt. Her dead prey is received and worshipped by the festive women of the village, who seem to represent the goddess. Though there is no marriage between the two, the case reminds us of the intruding god Mhasobā/Mhaskobā of Vīr (Purandar taluka, Pune district), who is first killed by the goddess at the border of the village and then married to the village goddess (Kosambi 1962: 122; Shulman 1980: 178; Sontheimer 1989: 57). The goddess, and the village represented by her, need the stimulus of the outsider who comes from the wilderness. In the context of agriculture the fertility of the fields increases. The success or failure of crops depends on hunting, as amongst the Murias of Bastar (Elwin 1947: 204), who also enact a communal hunt which precedes the ceremonial eating of the first mangoes of the year (Elwin 1947: 214). The nature of the wild boar is thus frequently seen as ambivalent: he destroys crops, but he also ploughs (for example, Gonda 1954: 128ff.; Oppitz 1983).

The hunting in the wilderness usually ends with an erotic adventure for the hunter, hero, king, or god who meets the beautiful girl in the forest and falls in love with her. The most famous example in south India is, of course, Murukaṉ's courtship of Vaḷḷi. The earliest reference to Murukaṉ and Vaḷḷi in personified form is found in an early poem of the Caṅkam period (*naṟṟiṇai* 82.4; Zvelebil 1977: 233). Ever since, the theme has been perpetuated in Tamil culture and has its climax in the Kantapurāṇam of Kaciyappa Civācāriyar (see e.g. Zvelebil 1977: 288-46; Shulman 1980: ch.8)—composed around A.D.1550 (Zvelebil 1974: 186). According to the Kantapurāṇam, two daughters of Viṣṇu performed *tapas* near Caravaṇappokai to be wed to Murukaṉ. By the grace of Murukaṉ, one of them was born as the daughter of Indra and was raised by his white elephant; hence she was named Teyvayāṉai [...] The second daughter of Viṣṇu was born to a deer which had been impregnated by the lustful glance of the sage Civamuṉi. The deer abandoned her in a pit, where she was found by Nampi, the lord of the Kuṟuvai hunters, who longed for a daughter. The hunter chief adopted her and named her Vaḷḷi, since she was born in a pit from which old men scrape the roots of the Vaḷḷi [...] Eventually, after many obstacles and mutual lovesickness, Murukaṉ married Vaḷḷi (Shulman 1980: 275).

Arjuna, during his sojourn in the forest, is known for four encounters with women: with Ulūpī, a Nāga princess; with Citrāṅgadā; with five Apsarases; and with Kṛṣṇa's sister Subhadrā, whom he fell in love with (Ruben 1962: 7). Bhīma marries the demoness Hiḍimbā, who fell in love with him. His reputation has spread far amongst the tribes. Amongst the Koyi tribe in Andhra Pradesh there is a tradition that Bhīma, while hunting in the jungle, met a tribal woman and married her. The Koyis trace their ancestry to this liaison (Thurston 1909: Vol. IV, 56, 71). In the myth of Ceñcūlakṣmī and Narasiṃha, the heroine is the daughter of a Ceñcū "chief" or "king". She was a huntress and when she saw a lion in the forest of the Eastern Ghats, she shot him with a bow and arrow. From the dead lion the handsome Narasiṃha arose and they fell in love with each other (Sontheimer 1985: 146). The story of Narasiṃha and Ceñcūlakṣmī is associated, for instance, with Ahobilam, an important centre of the Narasiṃha cult in Andhra Pradesh. Here, in the heavily forested upper part of Ahobilam, Narasiṃha is said to be *ugra*, whereas in the temple complex of the *kṣetra* in the valley he is said to be *saumya*. A vivid panel in one of the shrines shows a huge Ceñcūlakṣmī with a leaf skirt, who leans on her bow. A miniature Narasiṃha kneels before her and removes a thorn from her foot.

The myth of the god or king and his two wives is one of the most widespread in India; its most famous example is Murukaṉ, Teyvayāṉai and Vaḷḷi, who belongs to the tribal Kuṟuvars. In Tirupati Veṅkaṭeśvar fell in love with Padmāvatī while on a hunt in the forest, according to the temple *Māhātmya* (*Śrī Venkateshwara Leela Mahatmyamu,* ch. XVI). In every cult of a folk deity similar to that of Khaṇḍobā—in the Mallanna cult (Andhra Pradesh), the Mailāra cult (Karnataka), etc.—the oral myth of the second "wife" is very elaborate. The second wife comes from or is brought up amongst forest tribals, fisherfolk, hunters, pastoralists, or even itinerant merchants: Khaṇḍobā's second wife in Malegaon (Nanded district) comes from the once itinerant merchant groups of the Bañjāras. As we move away from folk traditions into a structured, stratified, or hierarchized context, the first wife is assigned a vertical, celestial, scriptural-purāṇic background. She is a manifestation of Pārvatī and at the same time belongs to a dominant caste. Thus Mhāḷsā, the first wife of Khaṇḍobā, is said to belong to the once influential caste of the Liṅgāyat merchants (Liṅgāyat Vāṇīs), and she is brought up by the rich merchant prince Timmāśeṭ of Nevāsā. The second "wife" becomes a manifestation of another celestial female—for example, of the heavenly courtesan Raṃbhā of Indra's court, or of Gaṅgā, who is assigned a place in the forest or in the underworld (as Pātālagaṅgā). Thus Gaṅgā is often said to be "reborn" on earth as Bāṇāī.

Inevitably the hunt of the god leads to the encounter with Bāṇāī and their subsequent "marriage", which causes a sustained tension and open quarrel between the wives.[18] Apparently, the second wife is given a lower status in the *kṣetra* of the god. For instance, Bāṇāī is assigned a place in a temple which has been built over what is actually a little "cave". It is situated outside the temple fort, halfway up the stairs leading to the hill fort. But this does not reflect the importance of Bāṇāī in the Khaṇḍobā cult. It seems that—as has also been demonstrated in the context of other royal cults and ritual kingship—the values of eroticism and fertility which Bāṇāī stands for are given a higher rank than ritual purity.[19] These values account also for the reproach which is sometimes levelled at the "rustic" (Kosambi 1962: 86) Khaṇḍobā cult, in which—as a Maharashtrian Brāhmaṇ noted at the end of the last century—non-brahmanical priests "were *pūjārīs* and ritual purity was very little respected" (Sontheimer 1989b: 333). Modern authorities like the historian G.H. Khare could, moreover, categorically hold that it is only a cult of *sakāma bhakti* (Khare 1958: 88). Thus, in certain contexts, the status of the two women seems to be equal, and at times the status of the resolute, "rustic" Bāṇāī seems to be even higher. It is Bāṇāī, besides Khaṇḍobā, to whom wishes for cattle and fertility of crops are directed, rather than to Mhāḷsā, and nonvegetarian offerings are sent to Bāṇāī. The purity of the *kṣetra* is represented by Mhāḷsā, and Bāṇāī introduces the pollution of the wilderness. Thus a Vāghyā song (*pad* 14) describes the anger of Mhāḷsā:

We are Liṅgāyat Vāṇīs
We are Liṅgāyat Vāṇīs
We follow the Śiva-Dharma, O Woman,
We follow the Śiva-Dharma,
We constantly contemplate Śiva,
  We keep our food and water covered .

There are mirrors inlaid in our courtyard walls,
  where we count our diamonds and precious stones
After bathing with Gaṅgā water
After bathing with Gaṅgā water, we worship the Tuḷsi plant,
  smearing ashes on the forehead.
Your entry
  has polluted our house,
  has polluted our house,
  has polluted our house,
Oh my, oh my, what spell you have cast on the Lord.
O Woman, how did you make Mallāri crazy,
  Mhāḷsā said: O Bāṇu, O Woman,
  You have made Mallāri crazy

Yet, in other contexts, as we have said, the two women are equal, stand in a complementary relationship, and even cooperate in ritual contexts, for example during Divālī. In fact, all the king's wives and courtesans (the Muraḷīs) cooperate in perfect harmony. We quote the first stanza of a Vāghyā song (*pad* 40):

Parrots chatter among the trees
Crows caw, sparrows twitter at the doorstep
Herons at the reservoir, Kokilas in the mango grove
High on the tree Blue Jays and Little Spotted Owls
The peacock's cries!
The celestial maidens go to fetch water with their pots.
Jejurī, the city of birds, where the water of the River
  Karhā is like nectar.
Bāṇu and Mhāḷsā anoint the Lord with fragrant pastes
Seated on a square wooden platform the Lord bathes
  with hot water from the two-handled vessel.

He wears a silken, yellow dhoti, a musk mark
 on his forehead
Phulāī, the gardener woman, garlands him
Raṃbhāī, the tailor woman, embroiders his shawl.
In a chamber a Muraḷī lovingly sings his praise.
His ornaments are golden, golden is his silken upper garment.
He is offered a seat of sandalwood, with coloured
 powders they draw decorative
 patterns in front of him.
Wake up, quick! It's Divālī, says Mhāḷsā to Lord Mālu
Wake up, let me put collyrium into your eyes
Divālī has come.

At times the "vegetarian" Mhāḷsā catches fish, while Bāṇāī watches this reversal of roles. At other times Bāṇāī and Mhāḷsā even eat from the same plate, a scene which can otherwise be seen only amongst "uncouth" Dhangar children.

Thus the hunt leads to the encounter with Bāṇāī, which can be viewed from various related points of view. The fixed settlement, the village or the *kṣetra* needs the complementarity of the forest. The king has to dominate the forest as part of his kingdom or extend his kingdom into it. The sacrifice of the animals (which may merge into a battle against enemies or demons) may amount to the assimilation of powers of the wild animals to the personal powers of the king, but hunting is also a sacrifice to enhance the fertility of the fields —and often, incidentally, fields are temporarily turned into a forest for the purposes of the hunt (see below and cp. Höfer 1968: 74). After the hunt follows the erotic adventure or even direct love relationship by which the king or god binds to himself the powers and riches of the forest, or, in the case of Bāṇāī, of her habitat, the pastoral area. Bāṇāī is often the rich, beautiful "Mirdhīn" (Head) of twelve Dhangar *vāḍās* or settlements, who owns 900,000 sheep. From another point of view the erotic relationship turns into emotional *bhakti*. Bāṇāī is the epitome of that emotional love which drives the Lord "crazy" Along with her come her followers, the Dhangars, who become the most faithful bhaktas of the Lord and would not miss attending a single Somvatī Amāvāsyā. We might also conclude that Khaṇḍobā now dominates the forest and the pastoral world and has become the Lord of the pastoralists, whereas he has converted the pastoralists into "hunters", if only in the ritual drama of the Somvatī Amāvāsyā festival.

Mhāḷsā—in the songs of the Vāghyās—insists in vain on her prior, "legal", and superior rights and status, her domestic qualities, her excellent food, and her intrinsic love for her protector. From her point of view, Mhāḷsā cannot resign herself to the fact that Khaṇḍobā goes on a hunt. At times she seems to accompany him, because on the level of the *Māhātmya* and in certain ritual contexts she can also be called the *ardhāṅgiṇī* of Śiva. Or she actively helps him as his *śakti*, according to the more *śākticversions* of the myth of his battle against the demon kings Maṇi and Malla.[20] But in the story of the hunt and the encounter with Bāṇāī, she remains at home, trying to put obstacles in his way by magical means—which could kill him, or so it seems. She is sorry to have caused the exit of the Lord into the wilderness and she experiences a kind of *viraha*, a separation from the distant hunter traversing the five forests and the pastoral area. In the song which narrates the sojourn of the Lord in the wilderness Mhāḷsā expresses her anxiety to her female confidante. It is a constant refrain at the end of each stanza (*pad* 48):

> Says the graceful Mhāḷsā: "Listen, oh Raṃbhāī,
> The Lord has gone on a hunt,
> why isn't he back yet?"

Yet it is not just Mhāḷsā who drives him out into the wilderness. Actually it is the standstill of the world, the stagnation of life. Life has become insipid in the *kṣetra* and this leads to Khaṇḍobā's exit. Thus, in the version of the Bāṇāī legend told by Limba Torve (see above), we hear (in short):

> Khaṇḍobā and his wife Mhāḷsā: What did they do? They were sitting side by side—somewhere. At that time they used to sit like this some-where every day . . . .
>
> The Minister was worried by their idleness and brought the game of chess in order to create a quarrel between the two. Khaṇḍobā lost and had to surrender all his clothes, his ornaments, and even his dogs to Mhāḷsā. He retained only his pouch containing magical turmeric dust (*bhaṇḍār*) and his spear (*jheṇḍā*). Sulking, he ordered his minister to call the 12,000 inhabitants of the town and went with them on a hunt in the wilderness (cited above).

In another version he loses not only his crown "worked with golden threads", but also his kingdom, including Pāli (Pāli-Peṃber), Naḷdurg, and Jejurī.[21]

VII. THE ENCOUNTER WITH BĀṆĀĪ

1. THE ORIGINS OF BĀṆĀĪ

About Mhāḷsā's purāṇic background there is unanimity in the scriptural and oral texts in Maharashtra: Pārvatī is "born" as Mhāḷsā on earth. The sources also basically agree that Mhāḷsā was brought up by her foster father Timmaśeṭ at Nevāsā (Aurangabad district) and married at Pāli (Satara district) where her marriage to Khaṇḍobā is celebrated annually on the 15th of the light half of the month of Pauṣ (Dec.-Jan.). This is also told in the *JM* (Khāḍe 1925: 44). Historically, Mhāḷsā seems to have been an independent goddess who had her own cult before it was absorbed by the Khaṇḍobā cult by identifying her with Pārvatī and naming Khaṇḍobā Mhāḷsākānt, "the husband of Mhāḷsā". In the *Līḷācaritra* (13th cent.), which records the life of Cakradhara, the "founder" of the Mahānubhāva sect, Mhāḷsā is an independent goddess at Nevāsā (*Uttarārdha* 331; Ḍhere 1961: 74), and even today separate temples for her continue to exist (Ḍhere 1961: 67).

The sources on Bāṇāī's background tell a much more chequered story. Whereas one would think that the dominant view, in *all* the oral versions we have come across so far, makes Bāṇāī the *second* wife of Khaṇḍobā, the *JM* and the *MV* strike a discordant note. Here Bāṇāī is the *third* wife of Mārtaṇḍa Bhairava. She was Jayā, a friend or *dāsī* of Pārvatī. We shall give a summary of the version in the *MV* (27.35ff):

Pārvatī promised Jayā, her favourite friend (*sakhī*), who is like a "creeper of beauty" (*lāvaṇyalatikā*) and has "eyes like a doe" (*mṛgākṣī*), that she would also become Paśupati's husband (*bhartā*) on earth. Śiva warns that another wife will cause her great difficulties. He forecasts that after he has despatched Maṇi and Malla and is known as Mallāri she (Jayā) will be born as a daughter of the demon Bāṇā (Bāṇāsura) and thus will be called Bāṇā. When Malla was slain by Malhārī, Bāṇā was born after some time. She insisted on marrying nobody except Hara. Seeing his daughter's obstinacy, Bāṇāsura consulted Nārada, who said that she would become Śiva's wife after performing *tapas*. When Nārada saw the *bhakti* of Bāṇā he taught her the Malhāri-mantra. Bāṇā retired to the frightful forest equipped with the mantra. She practised excessively harsh *tapas* without avail. Thus she left the place and came to a village called Candanpur. There, on the bank of the river, she practised austere *tapas* with pleasure. She stood on the river bank under the Candana tree and recited the mantra, remembering Nārada's feet. Mārtaṇḍa remembered the boon granted to Jayā. In the forest there was a shepherds' *vāḍā* (encampment) which was inhabited by Dhangars. Their headman was Ajāmeḷ, who was very rich and a great bhakta of Śiva. Mārtaṇḍa called the Minister and both speedily rode to Bāṇā. Malhārī swooned (*dehabhāna gelā visaroni*). Then he ordered the Pradhān to tell her that the aim of her *tapas* had been accomplished and that he whom she had seen in her mind was present in person. When Bāṇā saw Malhārī, her mind was shaken and she was overpowered by the eight feelings (*aṣṭabhāva*) of *bhakti* and her eyes filled with tears. On her request Ajāmeḷ, her foster father, was to come along for the marriage. Immediately elephants, horses, and palanquins appeared in the forest. Ajāmeḷ and all the Dhangars took a seat on the elephants etc. Malhārī took Bāṇā along on his horse and, full of joy, they all quickly reached Naḷdurg. There, after an auspicious time (*muhūrta*) had been fixed, the marriage with Bāṇā was performed (*Bāṇesī lāvileṃ lagna*). After 16 days the festival (*utsāha*) came to an end.

Jayā/Bāṇāī as the "third wife" of Mārtaṇḍa and daughter of Bāṇa seems to be an exceptional solution which just serves as an etymological aetiology for "Jayādri/Jayā", which is Jejurī. Bāṇāsura, however, himself figures occasionally in oral stories when Gaṅgā is to be "born" on earth as Bāṇāī. It is left to Bāṇāsura to deposit the little girl in the middle of the forest:

Gaṅgā had fallen out of Śiva's matted hair during the war with demons and had become a rock. She had fallen near the place where the demons had turned into rocks after their defeat. Thus she had to be salvaged. Viṣṇu, Brahmā, and Maheś turned her into a three-month-old girl. They made a box and kept her in it. They fixed on it a chain made out of nine jewels. They asked Bāṇāsura to place the box in the thick forest near Candanpur, where it was found by the Dhangars. Because the box had been taken there by Bāṇāsura and she was Gaṅgā from Śiva's matted hair, the little girl was called Bāngaṅgā. Her father was a great bhakta of Śaṅkar, and worshipped him on the bank of the river. The girl would always follow her father rather than do her work at home. When she was 15 or 16 years old she would go with her father—where? To the Karhā-Gaṅgā. He had his bath (Ma. *aṃghol*) and then went ahead to visit the temple [of Khaṇḍobā in Jejurī]. She entered the Gaṅgā. Then she also [like her father] made 21 *liṅgs* of sand on the river bank.[22]

Some folk traditions make Bāṇāī one of the seven daughters of Indra.[23] She was expelled by Indra and left as a little girl in a box in the forest of Candanpur. There she was found by the Dhangars. When she grew up she became a worshipper of Śiva, alias Khaṇḍobā, and eventually married him after staying with him in the forest for twelve years (Ḍhere 1961: 52). According to another elaborate version, a childless, rich Dhangar called Khyāmū practised *tapas* in the forest for twelve years and worshipped Indra. Finally Indra sent the heavenly courtesan Rambhā in the shape of a net of flowers to the earth. Khyāmū had to retrieve it from the ocean and was nearly drowned. When he unfolded the net a little girl emerged, who was eventually called Bāṇāī.

She grew up and became the head of twelve Dhangar settlements. There is never any mention in this long and detailed version that Bāṇāī worshipped Khaṇḍobā before he appeared in the *vāḍā* (Sontheimer 1989: 7-62).

Another story told by a Vāghyā shows how aspects of Bāṇāī proliferate, but also how she assumes the characteristics of her social and natural environment:

A girl was born of Puṣpavantī and turmeric dust given to her by Nārada. She was called Bāṇu, that is, Bāngaṅgā. She was put into a box and the box was immersed in the Gaṅgā. The box fell into the net of fishermen (Bhoīs). They tried to pull it out, but it was too heavy and they pushed it again into the river. Twelve boys of twelve castes were playing the stick game (*iṭhidaṇḍī*). The stick fell into the river. They jumped into the river. The box came floating down the river. They pulled it out, but it smelled of *davṇā*.[24] "Damned", they said, "it stinks", and they threw it back. Meanwhile a Dhangar came with his flock to the bank of the river. He jumped into the river and pulled out the box. He tied it to the neck of his favourite sheep. It became the *ghāṭī* [the handbell of the Muraḷīs which they ring during their dances]. The sheep went into the field of the Māḷīs [traditionally "gardeners" and agriculturists], [the boys] untied the bell and put it in a large sack. Her light spread from it. The light went to the field of the Māḷīs. The Māḷī women were stringing flowers. The light became Bāṇu. The Māḷī women put a flower garland around her neck. She went from the field of the Māḷīs to the Karhā river. She had a bath. She became Pāngaṅgā [*sic*].[25]

In most stories Bāṇāī begins her career on earth in a river—for example, in the Bāṇgaṅgā, which may be the tributary of the Godāvarī in the Nasik district or e.g. the Bāṇgaṅgā at Phaltan (Satara district). At times she is found in a hole or deep part of the river (Ma. *ḍoha*) where water stays even in the dry season, as e.g. Indra's eldest daughter was found by Gāvḍās in a deep part of the River Girṇā (Nasik district).[26] Most of the sources make her a devotee of Śiva, and sometimes of the Sun and the Tuḷśī bush.[27] These twin traditions of the worship of Sūrya and Śiva in separate cults have their confluence in the Mārtaṇḍa-Bhairava cult. Sometimes the two are even taken as separate, and it is Bhairava and not Mārtaṇḍa who marries the Śaivite

Liṅgāyat Mhāḷsā. The "identification" of the sun and the moon with Khaṇḍobā (according to Stanley 1977 *passim*) probably amounts rather to a subordination of the sun and moon cult to the Khaṇḍobā cult. The *MM* (by Siddhapāl Kesarī) clearly states that Sūrya serves Śiva (5.30-1) and in the *MV* it is said that Mārtaṇḍa is of the *light* of the sun (28.138).

Bāṇāī's connection with water and fertility is pervasive. Not only is she connected with the river, but, as we have seen, she is also retrieved from the *ocean* by the Dhangar Khyāmū. When Khaṇḍobā goes on a hunt he invariably gets thirsty, according to all versions known to us. Though probably the great magician could have quenched his thirst by flinging a handful of *bhaṇḍār* and thereby magically producing water, the oral sources agree that it is Bāṇāī who quenched his thirst. Thus we hear in a Dhangar epic (*ovī*):

> "At Candanpur is Bāṇāī's *vāḍā*./ There you will get water"./ Hegaḍe Pardhān [*sic*]/ Took a pot/ Went off/ To Bānubāī's *vāḍā*./ "Please give us water/ The god is thirsty/ The god's throat is dry/ He is very thirsty"./ Hastily Bānubāī got up/ Her own pot/ She cleaned and/ Filled with water./ "Hegaḍe Pardhān/ Go to the god/ Give him water"./ "Hegaḍe Pardhān/ Took to the pot/ Went to the god/ The god drank the water/ Became peaceful/ The god looked at the pot/ On the pot/ Bānubāī's name/ The god said: / "Alone I will go ahead."/ [28]

Under Bāṇāī's leadership the herds of the Dhangars thrived. She herself is the owner of "900,000 sheep and goats". Her connection with fertility, vegetation and music is reflected in the strong fragrance of the *davṇā* plant which the boys of the twelve castes notice, in the flower garlands of the Māḷī women, and in the handbell of the Muraḷīs. She also provides food which is typical of the pastoral area: at her *vāḍā* the disguised Lord is served tremendous amounts of millet bread and buttermilk, and twenty-five maunds of millet porridge (Sontheimer 1989a: 33). Bāṇāī, though an *avatār* of Gaṅgā, is basically a goddess of pastoral groups like the Gavḷīs and Dhangars, and of the millet-growing pastoral farmers. Her status is somewhat more stable than it seems to be in Andhra Pradesh, where the traditionally pastoral Gollas worship the goddess Gaṅgā as the second wife of Śiva (Narayana Rao 1989: 114). Bāṇāī's quarrels with Mhāḷsā are notorious, but her credentials as the "second wife" have become fully accepted, and on the level of the scriptural *Māhātmya* (*MV* 27.121) the unity of the two is even proclaimed. What Bāṇāī and the Gaṅgā of the Gollas have in common is their "watery nature"

(Narayana Rao 1989: 114). Besides, Khaṇḍoba's connection with the sun, which Bāṇāī worships, and her riverine and oceanic background suggest that she has some affiliation with the moon. For some ancient commentators on the Caṅkam literature Vaḷḷi is the lunar and female principle, closely connected with Murukaṉ, the sun (Zvelebil 1977: 242). But we can suggest nothing except a vague possibility. At times the beautiful Bāṇāī reflects the beauty of the moon (*pad* 48):

> . . . Her forehead glowed like the Full Moon's light
> Making the rising stars fade

Or (*pad* 29):

> . . . She is beautiful as the Crescent Moon
> She makes Lord Malhār crazy.

And when Bāṇāī had to show herself to Mhāḷsā and to the whole court on the insistence of Mhāḷsā, the Vāghyā sings of it (*pad* 48):

> With hands joined in salutation Bāṇāī stood before them
> It was as though the Full Moon's light spread out
> When Mhāḷsā saw Bāṇāī she felt a stab of a
> dagger in her heart.

From a Vāghyā song recorded very recently we may cite two lines:

> The gem Bāṇāī is born
> As though the moon has risen.[29]

2. Khaṇḍobā's Stay with the Dhangars and His Marriage with Bāṇāī

The scriptural sources like the *MV* and some of the oral traditions influenced by them clearly point to a celestial prehistory of Bāṇāī and trace her origin to Gaṅgā or Indra's daughter. Moreover they often suggest that she performed *tapas* to obtain a husband who is equivalent to Śiva. Sometimes we hear that she wants a husband (*bhratār* = *bhartā*) who

> does not drown if he is thrown into water,
> who does not burn if he is thrown into fire,
> and who does not get hurt by a stroke of an axe.[30]

As the seventh daughter of Indra she is relegated to the world of the mortals by a "curse" (Ma. *śāp*) which is countered by a boon (Ma. *uśāp*):

"It is very well that you leave me in the world of the mortals,
but add a boon to the curse".
"There is the King of Jejurī. He will take you as a spouse
and you will be his Queen of equal rank".[31]

Most versions of Bāṇāī's myth forego the "pretext" of the celestial credential, or her purāṇic background is reduced at the most to epithets. They concentrate on events on the earth. The horizontal cosmos on earth is divided into inside and outside, the *kṣetra* and the *vana*. Khaṇḍobā's encounter is then a thinly veiled love story at times. Bāṇāī has come into his dream and, maddened by love, he leaves the town on a hunt and finds her in the forest. There are songs which describe him as a bully and a trickster, "a proud Paṭhāṇ" who resembles his royal demon predecessor with his waylaying habits and his sexual prowess. For example, we hear (*pad* 30):

All dressed-up Bāṇu
Pots of milk on her head
She was on her way to the weekly market
When she met the Lord.
"You are holding the loose end of my sari",
Says Bāṇu, "Get out of my way
The Dhangars are ruffians
They will pick a fight with you".
Bāṇu pushes the king away
Bāṇu pushes Mallāri away
"Hands off my sari, let me go home".

Hearing Bāṇu's rebuff
Says God Malhār,
"I will charm you with a pinch of turmeric dust
And carry you off on my horse".
At this the beautiful Bāṇu
Began to tremble
"I will report all this at home
Hands off my sari, let me go home".

But the core of many versions about his stay in Bāṇāī's town or camp is essentially the same. It is striking that now it is not Bāṇāī who is practising *tapas* but it is the Lord who degrades himself and serves Bāṇāī in the disguise of an "old man". Some would tell us that Khaṇḍobā spent twelve years of *tapas* or *vanvās* (an unsettled life) in the *vāḍā* of Bāṇāī. We are reminded of Narasiṃha serving Ceñcūlakṣmī, and of Murukaṉ, "who walks on the thorns and rocks of Vaḷḷimallai seeking the golden hunter girl, massages her feet and brings sheaves of leaves for the royal hunter woman to fashion a dress for her" (Zvelebil 1977: 244). Khaṇḍobā becomes Khaṇḍu Gāvḍā from Jejurī. Gāvḍās were (as in Karnataka) farmers of the pastoral area who owned cattle. Thus we hear (*pad* 45):

> They call me Khaṇḍu Gāvḍā of Jejurī
> Give me a chance to serve
> So the Lord was employed as a servant in Bāṇu's house
> Then in Bāṇu's house
> He was given regular duties:
> He grazed the 900,000 sheep
> Just imagine—the Lord a herdsman!
> He took the kids and lambs to suckle.
> In the buttermilk gruel
> The beautiful Bāṇāī served him some wool.

During his stay the Lord performed several seemingly impossible tasks. The narrators and singers revel in describing the different miracles he performed and the final cathartic transformative sacrifice of the sheep. All versions nearly agree on the events described, for example, in a song (*pad* 48):

> "Hey, you servant", said Bāṇu.
> "Go, wash my sheep in the 'Five Gaṅgās'".
> The disguised Lord, hearing Bāṇu's words,
> Took charge of the nine lakh sheep
> "I need no herdsman [to go] with me.
> Just bring me my millet bread for the midday meal".
> He drowned the nine lakh of sheep in the darkest
>   pool of the river deeps.
> A bunch at a time he grabbed them by their hind legs
>   and smashed them on the rock.
> The bank of the Gaṅgā was flooded with blood.
> Their heads floating like lotuses.
> The Gaṅgā rose wave after wave
> Bursting into a bloody flow, rocks tumbled down.
> There were mountainous heaps of sheep skin,
> The god played his magic.
> The god performed his tricks.

"Listen, O judges of merit! Nine lakh of sheep he slaughtered, not one was left".

But Khaṇḍobā is ready to revive the sheep on the condition that Bāṇāī "first serve him food" (*pad* 48). Revealing his true nature, he elopes with her on his horse to Jejurī. But that seems not to have been all that easy, as we learn from the continuation of *pad* 48:

"A soldier had lifted Bāṇu".
They heard of the astounding deed.
Confounded, all the Dhangars gathered.
Their slings were ready for use, they wielded sticks.
There was a hail of stones which came down like a rainfall.
The god flung [turmeric dust], threw them into confusion.
They were beating each other [and] one another.
The son would not recognize his father and beat him with his stick,
The brother would not recognize his brother and hit him on the neck.
One would roll on the ground, shouting wildly.
Another would lisp or stammer in fear:
"Enough of punishment, now be merciful.
Let the birds of the forest live as their nature is".

A straightforward case of a marriage of elopement or, as the Dharmaśāstra would teach us, a mixture of a *gāndharva* and a *rākṣasa* marriage befitting royalty (Kane 1974: Vol. II, pt.1, 522f.), is found in the traditions of the Māṅgs or Mātaṅgs. They are ardent devotees of the Khaṇḍobā of Pāli (Satara district) and attend the *jatrā* in the month of Pauṣ (Dec.-Jan.) on the Mṛganakṣatra after the full moon. On that day the marriage of Khaṇḍobā to Mhāḷsā is celebrated by large numbers of devotees. A Mātaṅga devotee tells us:

The Lord escaped with Goddess Bāṇu and came into this village. He had brought her from a Dhangar family. He stayed with her in the jungle on the bank of the river Tāraḷī near the little village of Pāli. Goddess Bāṇu had gone with her father into the *jungle* to graze the sheep. While the Lord was wandering in the forest on a hunt, he and the goddess met. He was attracted by the girl, but her father objected and so the Lord took her on his horse and eloped with her. All the Dhangars disliked the outrageous behaviour of the Lord. They pursued him in the narrow valley of the Tāraḷī river. He was hiding in the forest looking for a chance to escape with Bāṇu.

At that time the Lord enlisted the help of the heroic and predatory Mātaṅgas and Rāmośīs, who keep their word once it is given. They supported the Lord.

All of them took up their sticks and axes and told him: "Even if it means our life, we will not let a hair of your head be touched". Thus, at that time, the Māṅg and Rāmośī people helped the Lord. For the sake of the Lord, they took up their sticks and axes and fought with the Dhangars. Therefore, to remember the bravery of that time, the Māṅgs and Rāmośīs take part with sticks in the marriage procession as the vanguard, and only after them follow the other privileged notables (*mānkarīs*).[32]

Most sources would say that before this happened Bāṇāī insisted on an actual marriage being performed at the Dhangar *vāḍā*. It was done in a rather rustic manner (Sontheimer 1989: 20,34). The *MV*, however, suggests that there was a respectable *brāhmavivāha*, and that *Bāṇāī*, in the form of a *liṅg*, was married to the Lord Mārtaṇḍa on the 15th of the light half of the month of Śrāvaṇ (July-Aug.) (Khāḍe 1925: 53). The whole affair retains the relished element of a scandal: Khaṇḍobā in Jejurī is said to visit Bāṇāī stealthily every midnight, or, as we hear in a song (*pad* 29):

The Lord had really mounted his horse
Bravo! Bravo, O Bāṇu! Bravo!
He took the beautiful Bāṇu along
Brought her halfway up the Fort.
A stealthy shower of turmeric dust for her
See, my Lord, I lie at your feet
I have come to sing
Oh, the Lord has really gone crazy.

The scandal is cherished in the songs and narrations as if it were of a high value. The structured life in the settlement, in the pure *kṣetra*, has become barren and stagnant and needs the fresh wilderness. The story of Bāṇāī transgresses the regular bounds of society, but is a necessary complement to them. Bāṇāī's story is not only of entertainment value, because Bāṇāī also stands for fertility and beauty. The king or the royal god who goes on the hunt in the wilderness and meets the beautiful girl from the forest absorbs something of the nature and environment of the people she represents. Now Khaṇḍobā has become a Dhangar, too. He has enriched, so to say, his *sva*—his own self and properties. The myth of Bāṇāī binds the Dhangars to the Lord.

It is noteworthy how frequently the theme of the king and/or god, his hunt and the encounter with the girl from the "tribe" can be found in literature, myth, and temple rituals, sometimes with detailed parallels (cp., for example, Obeyesekere 1978: 470; L'Hernauld 1984: 257ff.).

VIII. A COMMENTATED DESCRIPTION OF THE SOMVATĪ AMĀVĀSYĀ FESTIVAL

The festival, which occurs twice or thrice a year depending on when there is conjunction of the sun and moon on a Monday (see further Stanley 1977), attracts devotees from all over Maharashtra. Many devotees make vows which involve a promise for a request to be granted (Ma. *navas*), or they make an offering in return for a request that has been granted (Ma. *navas pheḍṇe*)—for instance, by unloading sizeable sacks of turmeric dust (Ma. *bhaṇḍār*) on the *svāyaṃbhu piṇḍs* of Khaṇḍobā and Mhāḷsā in the temple of the Gaḍkoṭ. Many devotees come without a particular request to the god and simply feel that the participation in the festival lends strength, confidence and success (Ma. *yaś*) to their domestic and professional activities. Khaṇḍobā is primarily a family god (Ma. *kulsvāmī*) who looks after their life in the world (Ma. *prapañca*). Many will feel a sense of deprivation if they do not visit their god on this day suffused with the powers of the god. The *darśan,* the vision of Khaṇḍobā, and a previous bath in the river Karhā are the standard ritual expressions of this feeling and faith (Ma. *bhāv*). After the *darśan,* many devotees throw handfuls of turmeric powder mixed with coconut kernels, on behalf of the Lord, onto the huge platform in front of the temple. Here Muraḷīs and Vāghyās might perform, devotees get possessed by the Lord, prostrate themselves, and many children try to catch the coconut kernels, which are coloured yellow with turmeric dust. The coconut kernels are sometimes said to be the gold coins which King Mārtaṇḍa threw amongst the devotees, alas, in the Satyayuga. The importance of turmeric dust and the "swinging" of the world in contradistinction to its standstill are demonstrated in another song of the Vāghyās (*pad* 32, 1st stanza):

See! The whole world is swinging
There is a scramble for turmeric dust
The magnanimous Mallukhān
Is giving away mountains of gold.
See! The whole world is swinging
There is a scramble for turmeric dust

The song expresses the turbulence throughout the festival, but the actual event starts with the preparation of the palanquin in the temple courtyard, which is thronged by crowds. At a certain moment determined by a Brāhmaṇ, who belongs to the "eight ministers" (Ma. *aṣṭa pradhān*) of Khaṇḍobā, the sign is given for the departure of the huge palanquin. The family name of the Brāhmaṇ is Peśve, which suggests that it was originally a title, and that they are "ministers" of the King Khaṇḍobā (similar to the Peśvās, who were prime ministers of the Marāṭhā kings before rising to *de facto* rulers). We notice that the royal folk deity does not want to dispense with the Brāhmaṇ's high—even if only marginal—knowledge of astrology and ritual. On the other hand, the Brāhmaṇ, who, from an "orthodox" point of view, ought not to participate in folk festivals (Heesterman 1985: 39) or get involved in the world, does not want to forego a limited but important role in this festival. Not only he, but each of the "eighteen castes" has an honorary right or privilege (Ma. *mān*) which was acquired at one time by some ancestor on account of some special *bhakti* or heroic act and/or because of his occupation. Each caste has the privilege of performing certain functions and assignments during this festival (and in the cult in general). The performance of these functions gives a structure to the festival, which at first glance seems to be chaotic and uncontrolled.

Now the palanquin procession starts. The palanquin is carried by Rāmośīs and Kolhāṭīs at the rear, and by Marāṭhās in front. The Rāmośīs were a robber caste. One of them was the famous Sardār Umājī Nāīk, who was defeated and hanged by the British in 1831. The privilege of the Rāmośīs to carry the palanquin at the rear is traced to this ancestor at times, but may, in fact, be older. The front of the palanquin faces east, like the god in the temple. The palanquin has to be turned 180 degrees so that the *pradakṣiṇā* around the temple complex can be correctly carried out. The turn causes tremendous "chaos", which is enacted anew precisely the same way each time the festival takes place. The turn, as well as the whole procession around the temple, down the temple stairs and through the lanes of the town, resembles an antagonistic game or a "tug-of-war" (Stanley 1977: 36) between the two groups of palanquin bearers, the Marāṭhās and Rāmośīs, or so it seems. There is incredible pushing and jostling. The swinging of the palanquin forward and backward, the semicircular turns at critical points, and the swaying descent down the "900,000" steps from the fort is said to be the

"Lord's play". It is an expression of a folk-religious phenomenon which is, of course, not confined to the Khaṇḍobā cult. It is found in all such festivals. It reminds us of the "assault on the sense of equilibrium" of Bastar Muriyā youths when they dance with their (wooden) clan deity Aṅga.[33] The vehement movements initiated by the bearers of Khaṇḍobā's palanquin are multiplied by the inertial properties of the heavy wooden load. The movements seem to go counter to the intentionality of the individual bearers, and a rhythm is established which is partially unwilled and originates in the inanimate mass of the palanquin. In other words the bearers are "outside themselves", because their physical equilibrium, the centre of gravity, is now lodged in the ponderous but at the same time sensitive palanquin of the Lord. Or, we may say, the Lord "asserts his will" and generates his own forces (Gell 1980: 222-4).

The extraordinary, "liminal" state of affairs is intensified, because the air is pervaded by *bhaṇḍār* (turmeric dust) and, at times, by clumps of wool thrown by Dhangars from the high wall surrounding the temple complex. Loud shouts resound in which all the devotees join: "Victory to King Khaṇḍobā, the leader of [or victor over] seven crores (*Khaṇḍerāyācā Yeḷkoṭ*)" or "The Seven Crores of eternal happiness (*Sadānandācā Yeḷkoṭ*)". The procession circumambulating the temple complex is led by musicians or Ghaḍśīs, who were formerly untouchables. The banner carriers are of the formerly untouchable Māṅg caste, who claim the hero Yeśvant Rāv, the *havildār* of the *khillā*, as their legendary ancestor. Now the "Hall of the Twelve Doors" or "Durbar Hall" has been reached. So far the god and his wife or *śakti* Mhāḷsā have been invisibly present in the palanquin. Now the *utsav-mūrtis*, which embody the two deities in visible form, are carried from the "Treasury" to the Durbar Hall and are placed in the palanquin. The *mūrtis* of Khaṇḍobā and Mhāḷsā are carried by members of two different families of Guravs, the (non-brāhmaṇical) *pūjārīs* of Khaṇḍobā. In the mêlée inside the Durbar Hall a member of the barber caste manages to hold a mirror in front of the god. The palanquin leaves the Durbar Hall and is pushed through the two narrow gates of the wall of the fort which are connected by a steep staircase. The crowd, by now thoroughly coloured by *bhaṇḍār*, pushes down the "900,000" steps from the temple to the town. One wonders whether at times the individual bearer's feet have anything else than a fleeting contact with the ground. After a *pradakṣiṇā* of the cave temple of Bāṇāī, the procession arrives at the foot of the hill and rolls through the narrow lanes of the town. The procession moves to a Śaivite *maṭh* and then proceeds for a halt at the Śiva temple built by Malhārāv Hoḷkar, a member of the blanket weaver subcaste (Khuṭekar) of the Dhangars. He rose to the position of a general of the Peśvās in the 18th cent. and founded the dynasty of the Mahārājās of Indore. His family god was Khaṇḍobā. Now the procession crosses the border of the town, beyond the town gate, and moves in front of the goddess Marīāī, the cholera goddess. Here, as at other places, devotees break heavy iron chains. At the border numerous nomadic Hāṭkar Dhangars (Shepherds) wait for the Lord. They wear red turbans and iron chains and carry "spears" which now have only ceremonial purposes. The spear (Ma. *jheṇḍā*) is also one of the many manifestations of Khaṇḍobā. He is said to have taken it along when he left for the forest after he had lost his kingdom to Mhāḷsā in a game of dice. The Dhangars also carry heavy iron chains over their shoulders. The god heads for the "wilderness", accompanied by his "hunters". A Marāṭhā tells about the hunt:

> After the chain is broken, the palanquin proceeds. From ancient times the *pālkhī* goes over the field of Sakhārām Thorat. The crop in the field will be extremely good. In former times the Lord would go for a good hunt on this path. They went hunting and hunting up to the foot of the Bhuleśvar temple [at the other side of the valley]. The god would hunt gazelles and tigers. But now the jungle has decreased, and so he will just hunt down a rabbit. Because of the *sattva* of the Lord (*devāce sattva*) they will hunt down a rabbit somewhere after he has left the Marīāī temple and before he reaches the Karhā river.

A Māḷī tells us in a similar vein:

> During the Somvatī Amāvāsyā which comes in the month of Śrāvaṇ, the Lord comes to the Karhā. But when there is a hunt towards the river, it is excellent. So, if one comes across a rabbit or deer, a full-fledged hunt is on.

Other informants remember that a few drops of blood of the kill used to be offered to the palanquin of the Lord.

Meanwhile, the horse has left the Marīāī temple and is led far ahead of the procession. Some Dhangars try to touch his hooves. The horse is led by a member of the Muslim family which has been in charge of the care of the god's horses for many generations. The distance between the horse of the god and its invisible rider is striking, and may re-enact "the king breaking away . . . eluding all his horsemen" (See above, *pad* 22). It also reminds us of the Vedic *aśvamedha*. The presence of the horse and the dramatic performances connected with the horse are ubiquitous in the Khaṇḍobā cult of Maharashtra and the Mailāra cult of Karnataka, in which festivals are called "festivals of horses" (Ka. *kudureya habba*; Sontheimer 1989a: 330). In the *aśvamedha* the horse of the king, embodying royal powers, roams through the "world", which is then claimed by the conquering king. Though the Vedic *aśvamedha* ritual is said to have become extinct, it was transformed and continued in the rituals of the traditional kingdoms, especially in the Durgā festival (Stein 1980: 384ff; Sontheimer 1985: 150ff.). In the Khaṇḍobā cult, devotees who beat themselves with special whips get possessed by "the wind of the god", and trot like horses, or rather move up and down like riders on horses. These devotees appear in large numbers at the festival in Naḷdurg from the 1st to the 12th of the light half of the month of Pauṣ (Dec.-Jan.). Some of the "horses" (Ma. *vāru*) also turn up during the Somvatī excursion near the river, as we shall see.

Meanwhile, before the palanquin arrives, many families worship their ancestors, besides Khaṇḍobā and perhaps the Bhavānī of Tuljāpur, on the river bank. The gods and ancestors are mostly represented by small plaques (Ma. *ṭāk*) which are otherwise enshrined at home. Khaṇḍobā, who is also represented by brass masks or brass figures showing him seated on a horse with Mhāḷsā, and the ancestors, who are depicted as heroes (Ma. *vīras*) on the plaques, are bathed in the river and worshipped. This is a ceremony of folk religion and not a *śrāddha* as prescribed in śāstric texts. In fact the *MV*, following the *JM*, is explicit that there can be no *śrāddha*, because Jejurī is the capital of the Lord.[34] The descendants eat together with the ancestors and engage the services of the Muraḷīs, who dance for the ancestors, and the Vāghyās, who play and sing for them the deeds of the god and his wives. On this occasion songs are not coherent narratives and the lines are eclectic, but they probably reflect what spontaneously comes into the mind of the singer in the context of the Somvatī Amāvāsyā festival. For instance:

> Bāṇu Mhāḷsā are the wives of the Lord
> The Lord went to Candanpur
> To the house of Bāṇu, the Shepherdess
> He became thirsty in the wild forest
> On the sixth month's Somvatī
> The Lord came to the Lady Karhā.[35]

Some worshippers get possessed by the ancestors and Khaṇḍobā as soon as they hear the songs, the sound of the tabors played by the Vāghyās, and the handbells rung by the Muraḷīs. The devotees leave no doubt that participation in the Somvatī Festival in this way ensures the support of the ancestors and the Lord for their domestic and professional life or for the coming months. Besides, the ancestors and the gods of the household shrines have been endowed with new powers.

The whole day, but especially before the procession arrives at the river, the Dhangars break their heavy chains. The chain is fixed in a hole in a boulder near the shrine of Raṃbhāī on the river bank. A pinch of *bhaṇḍār* is thrown on the chain and, calling upon the Lord, the devotees break it with a jerk. If the chain breaks, the *sattva*, the existence, nearness of the Lord is confirmed. It does not harm the credibility of the "miracle" if the chain, which on a superficial look appears to be unbreakable, has some thin places here and there. These may be treated with a hammer to make them even thinner, if the chain does not break at a second or third attempt.

The site on the river bank resembles a temporary encampment with small tea-shops and stalls where turmeric dust, coconut-kernel (Ma. *khobareṃ)*, bananas, etc., are sold. The Somvatī song of the Vāghyās describes the scene eloquently (*pad* 22):

> . . . Yellow tents pitched all over the place
> The shrines cannot be counted
> Holy men crowd around them
> At this fascinating centre there are
> Shops set up in every direction
> The bazaar arrests the eye with its display
> One forgets hunger and thirst here
> Oh what a joyous *yātrā*!

Thus the family gods have left their domestic shrines and receive temporary shrines in the wilderness: they are worshipped on a strip of red cloth which is placed on a woolen blanket. The scene and the incidents of the festival (*jatrā*) at the river also suggest the temporary "city" which comes into existence at the time of the *aśvamedha*, according to the classical epics (Raghavan 1979: 26ff.). There are the makeshift tents, the music and the dance of the Muraḷīs and Vāghyās, their narration of the deeds of the god, the mention of the presence of the Ṛṣis, etc. (cp. Raghavan 1979: 26ff.). The *jatrā* on the river may actually also be an echo of the ancient *sattra* which was performed by

Ṛṣis in the wilderness (Falk 1986: 34). Meanwhile, most of the Dhangar "hunters" running far ahead of the palanquin have arrived, have planted their *jhenḍās* into the earth and wait like everybody else for the entry of the Lord. That the Lord is a "hunter" accompanied by "hunters" is also indicated by the fact that occasionally devotees bring a dog with a garland of marigolds around its neck and its forehead heavily coated with *bhanḍār*. The Lord's arrival is announced by the sudden appearance of the horse. Then the palanquin of Khaṇḍobā arrives and before it dozens of devotees dance and trot as if they embodied the "horses" of the god. They are seized by his power and have become as if a part of him. Like the Nandī and the horses made of stone facing the god as his *vāhanas* in the temple, the devotees as horses now face the palanquin of the Lord. The day is, as Stanley (1976) has shown, full of the fluidity of the powers of the Lord. We may say that the motionless equine *vāhana* in the temple is now alive not only in the form of an actual horse, but also in the form of the devotees who act like live horses. The dogs of the Lord are worshipped and heavily coated with *bhanḍār*, and the human dog devotees of the god, the Vāghyās, who are the bards of the Lord, sing but are said to have growled and barked in a not-so-far-away past.

The palanquin is placed on a pedestal near the river.[36] With deafening shouts of "Sadānandācā Yeḷkoṭ", the Lord and his *śakti* (Mhāḷsā) are taken out of the palanquin and bathed briefly with the five nectarous substances (*pañcāmṛta*)—that is, milk, curds, etc.—a rite which is performed by Brāhmaṇs "and all".[37] Within seconds the *mūrtis* are carried into the river while the shouts praising the Lord continue. Numerous Dhangars carrying chains over their shoulders stand in the water and throw water on the Lord. That it is a privilege (*mān*) of the Dhangars to perform this chaotic play is spontaneously acknowledged by members of different castes, including Brāhmaṇs.[38] But there are also numerous Son-Koḷīs, the sea-fishermen from Bombay, who participate in the common bath, and other devotees as well, especially the "horses". After a few moments the *mūrtis* are carried back to the pedestal and placed in the palanquin. The Lord receives new clothes and a new turban brought by a washerman (*parīṭ*). The new clothes are traditionally contributed by the Brāhmaṇ Peśve family and a member of that family dresses the Lord. After this the Lord may look at himself in a mirror held by a member of the barber (Nhāvī) caste.

The folk-religious mythological background of the cult and the observation of the dramatic performance of the ritual of the Somvatī Amāvāsyā festival let us discern more than just an astrological event and its polluting effects which are averted and turned into something "unambivalently auspicious" (Stanley 1977: 42). The preponderantly horizontal view of the cosmos in folk religion leads to the enactment of the astrological event under the aegis of Khaṇḍobā. Rather than Khaṇḍobā being identified with the sun, the powers of the sun are reflected in his *mūrti* and become manifest in turmeric dust. On this day the fertile powers of the moon are said to dwell, or rather are absorbed, in the vegetative and aqueous female nature, including forests; rivers, which are part of the forests (Feldhaus 1990: 92); the deer of the forest; and the wealth of the pastoral area in the form of sheep. Thus the *Śatapatha-brāhmaṇa* (1,6,4,5) declares, for example: "When the moon is not seen either in the east or in the west, then he visits this world, and here he enters the waters and the plants".[39] By his action the Lord reabsorbs these powers of the sun and the moon and his powers become comparable to theirs. As King on earth, Śiva has a role to play, and he needs the loyalty, assistance or *bhakti* of his followers, whereas they are in need of protection and deflect renewed strength from him. The followers are associated with either the *kṣetra* or the *vana*. The claim to belong to the sun's powers or to him who conveys them may even be seen as being dramatized by the antagonistic struggle of the palanquin bearers.[40] Others serve the Lord by showering cascades of turmeric dust. The people of the forest, or of the moon's powers, present themselves as "hunters", pastoralist Dhangars and ocean fishermen. The mingling of the substances of power may already be seen to begin when the Dhangars, in fulfilment of vows, rain flocks of sheep wool,[41] which mixes with the clouds of turmeric dust, on the Lord in the courtyard at the beginning of the excursion. But the climax is the throwing of turmeric dust and water in the ritual at the river. The mingling of the powers of the sun and the moon, during which the Lord takes his bath in the river, is also echoed in the Somvatī song (*pad* 22), when it is said:

> When the Lord is bathed in milk
> It is as if the Karhā becomes as luminous as the sun
>   pure as the Bhāgirathī
> The source of the Karhā is higher than the twenty-one heavens
> The pure water of the seventeenth part of the moon
> [or: The pure water of the glowing and blooming life].[42]

It would be tempting to straightaway identify the river Karhā, which is the Bhāgirathī (= Gaṅgā), with Bāṇāī. Gaṅgā is reborn as Bāṇāī on earth according to most versions of her origin, or she is found in the ocean. But there is no confirmation that the Karhā is Bāṇāī. On the contrary: it is frequently said that the Lord crossed the Karhā during his hunt on his way to Bāṇāī's Candanpur, which is now normally located in Khāndesh (Malegaon district). The Dhangar informants, however, stress that it is because of Bāṇāī that they came into contact with Khaṇḍobā and received the privilege of participating in the bath in the river and throwing water on the god. No informant from another caste would dispute this. Bāṇāī, as the goddess from the forest, has, as we have seen, riverine and pastoral associations. Like the Dhangars, their predecessors, the Gavḷīs, were frequently "discoverers" of a Śiva *liṅg* in forests and on mountains at the origin of a Śaivite cult. A Gavḷī and a Koḷī are often said to have been the first to worship a Śiva *liṅg* with the water of a river. Today Dhangars bring water from far away rivers to their male gods. The static temple custom in the *kṣetra* is to bring water from a local tank and let it drip from a pot (*gaṅgājaḷī*) suspended over the *ling*. This is thus supplemented by the (earlier) folk custom of bringing water from beyond the *kṣetra*. On certain occasions, however, the god—tired of ritual routine—goes himself into the forest, and in folk myths it is often a Dhangar who directs him to Bāṇāī. She sends the pot of water to the thirsty god. In rituals, and especially in the context of the Somvatī Amāvāsyā festival, the Dhangars are the mediators between the river goddess and the Lord, who on this day comes, as if mobilized, from the mountain. On this day the Dhangars lead the Lord to the water and provide a cooling bath for him.

After he has received the five nectarous substances, his bath in the river, and his investiture with new clothes, the Lord moves in his palanquin to the goddess Raṃbhāī. She resides in a rough, unhewn *mūrti* covered with red lead (Ma. *śendūr*) on a high platform covered with a tin roof, but open on all sides. It looks like a temporary *maṇḍap* rather than a full-fledged temple. The Lord stays for a few moments with Raṃbhāī, who had once come from Indra's heaven as a Devāṅganā (heavenly courtesan), but has become a deified Muraḷī of the Śimpī (tailor) caste. In the songs of the Vāghyās she is famous for her spontaneous love for the Lord when for the first time he came circling in the air on his horse and descended on Jejurī. The gracious Lord settled her outside the town on the river Karhā and ever since visits her on Somvatī Amāvāsyā (Sontheimer 1991: 24; *pad* 19):

... He brought her, the Beauty
Kept her, "O Mālu!"
On the bank of the Karhā River, "O Mālu!"
Once every sixth month, on Monday
The Lord goes to her temple.

In another song (*pad* 2) the scene after the bath is described:

The Lord put on [new] clothes,
Came to Raṃbhāī's palace.
When he saw Raṃbhāī's faith,
Khaṇḍerāv was pleased
Accepting spontaneous faith,
He gave her a place at his feet.

The fleeting though riotous halt at Raṃbhāī's shrine, which includes an *āratī* ceremony for the Lord, does not suggest that, according to oral traditions (*Somvatī pad* 22):

The God holds court in Raṃbhā's palace
Among those seated is Indra himself
Sakhyā, the barber, holding the mirror
Stands in front of the god
His mirror reflecting the dazzling sun
Anointed with fragrant Mailagiri sandalwood paste
A dot of musk on the forehead
On the decorated floor his ruby-encrusted plate is laid
With shining silver bowls inside
Ṛddhi and Siddhi in person serve sweet rice porridge
Ṛṣis eat Amboḷī[43]
As soon as they finish and rinse their mouth,
  Raṃbhā offers them *pān*
It is a joyous *yātrā*.

After this halt the procession moves to the village Dhālavḍī. Some would say that the Lord continues his hunt. Formerly, according to the Somvatī song (*pad* 22), horse races seem to have taken place on the way to Dhālavḍī. Today the palanquin proceeds to Bābīr, the Gavḷī-Dhangar god in Dhālavḍī, and the palanquin bearers are given a meal of millet bread by the villagers. Then the Lord returns. The procession stops at a hamlet inhabited by Māḷīs. From there the Lord proceeds to visit another "wife" or Muraḷī, Phulāī Māḷīṇ of the Māḷī (gardener) caste, at the outskirts of the town, in the Davṇe Māḷ (Southernwood Field). Here the palanquin is kept for five minutes on the stone pedestal of Phulāī Māḷīṇ to allow the devotees to have a vision of the Lord. Because of Phulāī Māḷīṇ, reputed to be the first Muraḷī, the Māḷī women have the special privilege of selling *davṇā* (Southernwood), *jhenḍū* (marigold), and *bel* (Skt. *bilvā*) leaves at the Nandi Chowk in Jejurī. Here the "900,000" steps leading to the temple begin.

Then the Lord makes a triumphant entry into the town, according to the *pads* describing the return from his sojourn in the wilderness. The epic song, especially, on the encounter with Bāṇāī (*pad* 49) gives a vivid picture of the huge army of the Lord as it arrives in Jejurī. The Lord is followed by Bāṇāī in her "green" chariot. We may wonder from where the huge army is supposed to come after the king has "eluded his horsemen" and stayed in the wilderness separated from his retinue. However, the song shows that he emerges enriched and powerful from the wilderness. Today the palanquin moves to the goddess Janāī, who is supposed to be the Lord's sister and senior to him. At this spot the women perform the *ārati* ceremony to the palanquin, welcoming the returning Lord. After a rest of one and a half hours the palanquin is carried up the hill with a display of competitive sport similar to, but less violent than, that at the beginning of the excursion. Finally the palanquin is placed in the "Hall of the Twelve Doors". The Peśve, "one of the eight ministers", distributes what is called *rojmarā* (P. "wages") or *muśārā* (A. "pay" or "wages") to all devotees who served the Lord in this ritual, especially the musicians and the palanquin bearers. The *rojmarā* consists of *bhaṇḍār* and millet (*jovārī*) grains which have a special power and are sown into fields for a good crop or kept in the house shrine or "near one's business". The palanquin may return at any time of day or night, depending on the time of conjunction of the sun and the moon. If the palanquin returns in the night, the description of the procession in the *Somvatī pad* (*pad* 48) is vivid, but these days perhaps no longer a reality:

When the sun sets and there is the dark night of new moon then see!
The torches, the rockets, the red display of fireworks
As the king's procession meanders to the fort [*killā*],
the Assembly is seated in the
"Hall of the Twelve Gates".

IX. CONCLUSION

The Khaṇḍobā cult has its mythical background in scriptural and oral traditions. Today oral texts and their interaction with ritual expressions and scriptural texts tend to become evanescent; as literacy increases, proliferation of temple pamphlets and booklets is widespread, and generally modern change has an accelerating effect. The oral myths of the King's hunt and the myth of Bāṇāī are not found in the scriptural texts (*MM, JM*, and *MV*), but they had an important place in the cult and are complementary to the scriptural texts. The pervasive function of oral texts is seen in the Somvatī Amāvāsyā festival, where they contribute to the mythical background of the festival. On the surface the festival may look like a simple ritual event just consisting of a purifying *snāna* of the god in the river Karhā, and this is also suggested by the texts (*JM, MV*). This strand may even survive in a modernized world where the powers and goods of life will be sought elsewhere. Today the festival is still celebrated in a dramatic way which reflects a playful, folk-religious worship (Ma. *kheḷ*) of the Lord. According to this strand of expression Khaṇḍobā, who is King as God on earth, is on a hunt in the wilderness. The important role of the pastoralist Dhangars, who accompany the Lord on his hunt and throw water on him, is mythically connected with the story of Bāṇāī, the shepherdess. The royal Khaṇḍobā, with the help of his followers, negotiates a dramatic ritual (Ma./[Ṣkt.] *utsāh[a], utsava[a]*) which leads to the renewal of his reign and holds out the promise of renewal of life and success in the domestic affairs of all his followers participating in the festival. The festival also enlists the good will of the ancestors. With the help of his followers, who have to perform different, actual or potential functions, Khaṇḍobā dramatically re-enacts the conjunction of the sun and the moon on a Monday by conjoining the moon's and the sun's powers, which are subordinated to the Śaivite cult. The festival also echoes the ancient *aśvamedha* and *rājasūya* sacrifices in their non-classical (rather than "pre-classical"; Heesterman 1985: 5f. *et passim*) form, whereby the ultimate authority and legitimacy of the royal god may presumably be seen in the fact that Khaṇḍobā is also identical with Śiva. The festival also reflects the need for the periodical, dynamic interaction between "inside" *and* "outside"; the static *and* the mobile; the settlement *and* the forest, or the *kṣetra and* the *vana* (Ma. *rāṇ* < Skt. *araṇya*); the daily temple ritual routine *and* the dramatic, playful performance of the ritual; the hierarchized, vertical cosmos *and* the earthbound, horizontal cosmos of the cult. The Somvatī Amāvāsyā festival, its mythology and performance, then, suggest many identifiable meanings. This complex cult reflects many traditions, which co-exist simultaneously and present an open network. To assign one meaning to these traditions instead of leaving the question of their meanings in abeyance might please the argumentative scholar, but may inadvertently amount to a reductionist, if not a fundamentalist, approach.

NOTES

This paper draws on material collected during two stays in India which were respectively financed by the German Research Association (DFG; 1985/86) and the Volkswagen-Stiftung e.V. (1990/91). I am grateful to both institutions.

1. For instance in the cases of Mhaskobā (Vir, Purandar taluka, Pune district), Siddhanāth (Javali, Phaltan taluka, Satara district), Dhuḷobā (Vidhni, near Phaltan), Khaṇḍobā (Budh, Khatav taluka, Satara district). Whereas in these places the god is taken to the river, in Dhok Sangli, Shirur taluka, Ahmadnagar district, we have the widespread custom that water is *brought* to Khaṇḍobā from the (Bhimā) river in order to bathe the god.
2. A photocopy was obtained of the ms. in the possession of R.C. Dhere, to whom I am most grateful. The *Jayādri Māhātmya* purports to belong to the *Pātālakhaṇḍa* of the *Padmapurāṇa*.
3. The *MV* by Gaṅgādhara is a reworking of the *MM* and the *JM* and has important addi-tional information.
4. This work gathers all the important mythological and ritual matters from the *MM*, the *JM*, and the *MV*. See Khāḍe 1925.
5. This is according to *MV* 27.85. The *JM* says that he poured the water over Brahmadeva's head (Khāḍe 1925: 28).
6. Lit.: "the place where the god's horse 'pranced' or 'rose', or 'landed after having flown through the air'". For the first time Khaṇḍobā arrives on horseback at the mountain plateau (Kaḍe Paṭhār), which is situated higher up, about three miles beyond the main temple, called Gaḍkot or Khillā (both meaning "fort"). This spot, marked by "hoof-prints" in the rock, is also called Ghoḍe Uḍḍān. The second Ghoḍe Uḍḍān on the river bank is probably the spot where he lands with his horse starting off from the Gaḍkoṭ. Khaṇḍobā is often said to fly with his horse, which is called "wind" (Ma. *vāru*).
7. *MV* 1.88: under "the pretext of hunting" the *daitya* Malla left with his army. Observing the rite of hunting (*mṛgayāvidhī saṃpādūn*) he came to the *āśram* of the Ṛṣis.
8. *MV* 16.30:
   pāhā rājyanīti / vīrāsa īśvara bhūpati/
   svāmikāryāta sanmāna pāhatī/
   te dhanya hotī trijagīṃ/
   The phrase could possibly also be inverted and translated: "For the hero the king is god". Following Stein (1983: 88) one could say: Kingship and "sovereignty"

were transferred to the deity Khaṇḍobā and shared by powerful devotees like King Śāhū Mahārāj of Satara, Brāhmaṇ Sardārs, and rulers like the Hoḷkars and the Gāykvāḍs and many Marāṭhā *śiledārs*. The relationship between Khaṇḍobā as the divine king and his powerful devotees is reflected, in the cult, in the relationship between Khaṇḍobā and Heggaḍe Pradhān (Ka. = "Headman" and Skt. = "Minister"). The main cult at Jejurī was often duplicated by bhaktas, including headmen, in their villages.

9. See the discussion in Sontheimer 1991a.
10. Here the songs are numbered according to the collection *Khaṇḍobācīṃ padeṃ* by Śrī Sadguru Bhāūmahārāj. My translations were revised with the help of the eminent Marathi and English poet Dilip Chitre.
11. An officer attached to a fort. His duty was to arrange for the guards etc.
12. Cp., in early Tamil literature, the parallel concept of *maṟam*, which can mean "heroism, bravery (usually with the added connotation of fierceness or even cruelty)" (Shulman 1980: 288f.; 1985: 350).
13. For instance in a performance of a *jāgraṇ* ("vigil") by Shankar Dhondiba Jadhav, a famous Vāghyā (Marāṭhā) from Dhāmni (Khed taluka, Pune district.).
14. I generally prefer to use the term "Lord" for Ma. *dev*, rather than "the god" or "God". Khaṇḍobā has many names—for example, Mārt(t)aṇḍa Bhairava, Khaṇḍerāv/Khaṇḍerāyā, Mallāri, Malhār(ī), Mālu, Mallukhān—which are all used in different contexts by different people.
15. For text and translation of the full story see Sontheimer (1989a: 7-62).
16. For a highly informative paper on the evidence in Sanskrit literature, see Friedrich Wilhelm (1991: 7-16). Daśratha's addiction to hunting and his passion for a lovely woman were comparable appetites for Kālidāsa in his *Raghuvaṃśa* (IX.69) (Wilhelm 1991: 10). For the theme of hunting and eroticism see also Hofstetter (1980: 130ff.). Another reference may serve for many: In the *Vetālapañcaviṃśatikā* (XIX, 51ff.) King Rūpasena forgoes hunting and receives the daughter of the Ṛṣi in return. He marries her according to the Gāndharva rites.
17. Information received from Prof. M.L.K. Murty (Hyderabad).
18. For the popularity of the *ēcal* genre in Tamilnadu, a genre which deals with the quarrels of the co-wives of the god, see Shulman 1980a: 294f.
19. See Marglin 1985 and the essays in Carman 1985.
20. The myth is reflected visually in the ubiquitous depiction of Mallāri: Khaṇḍobā and Mhāḷsā seated on a horse defeating the demons Maṇi and Malla. It is Mhāḷsā who is shown shedding the blood of the demons.
21. Nāmdev Vāghe Śingṇāpūrkar, caste: Gopāl.
22. Malhārī Sakhārām Vāḷke, Dhangar.
23. In the *Bṛhatsaṃhitā* of Varāhamihira (42.39-40), Jayā and Vijayā are amongst the seven or five daughters of Indra (Raghavan 1979: 142).
24. Southernwood; it is a plant with a strong smell.
25. Bābū Bhaṃḍalkar, Vāghyā, caste: Dhangar.
26. Mārtaṇḍa Candrabhān Thorve, caste: Vanjāri.
27. For instance, in the story of Nāmdev Vāghe: *Sūryācī ārādhiṇ, tuḷśicī mahāpujā*.
28. Sakhārām Bābū Lakaḍe, caste: Hāṭkar Dhangar. For the translation of the whole epic, see Sontheimer (1989a).

29. Baban Bhāgujī Dheraṅge, caste: Marāṭhā.
30. For instance, in the story of Nāmdev Vāghe, above.
31. Mārtaṇḍa Candrabhān Thorve.
32. Pataṅgrāv Bhāū Avghaḍe.
33. Gell 1980: 219-48. I have adopted some of the observations and wordings of this author, but cannot dwell on his ideas because of the lack of space. Suffice it to say that his ideas correspond to my own experience of the festivals in Bastar. Note the description of the world as "swinging" during a Khaṇḍobā festival in *pad* 32, above.
34. MV 36.62-63: Everywhere else in other *kṣetras* [the rituals of] *śrāddha-tīrtha, upavāsa,* and *muṇḍana* are performed. But this is not so in the *rājadhānī* of the Lord, famous in the three worlds by the name Jayā. There is no *tīrthaśrāddha, upavāsa* (fasting) or *muṇḍana* (tonsure) here.
35. Khaṇḍu Vāghyā Jādhav.
36. The venue has shifted several times since a new dam was built down the river. Today the regular spot of the bath has to be shifted if the river is flooded.
37. This is the view of a Dhangar informant. Śāmkākā Peśve, a Deśastha Brāhmaṇ, said that it was the privilege of the Peśves of Jejurī and was ceded to the Belsare family, who are also Deśastha Brāhmaṇs. Note that *amṛta* is distributed by the moon through his rays (Enthoven 1924: 52; Gonda 1965: 58). *Amṛta* consists of the milk of the cow, etc., and rain (Gonda 1965: 62).
38. Everybody seems to agree: *Dhangar lok pāṇyāt ubhe rāhūn pāṇī siṃpadūn devālā āṅghoḷ ghāltāt.* (Śāmkākā Peśve).
39. Gonda 1965: 45. The moon directs and governs the waters which sponsor the growth of living beings; Soma expresses or is in these waters: *Aitareya-brāhmaṇa* 1, 7, 10. Gonda *ibidem,* 48. On the relationship between the moon, *soma,* and *amṛta* see Gonda *ibidem,* 38ff.
40. Cp. the famous passage in the *Kaṭhā-saṃhitā* 34.5 and elsewhere, where in the Mahāvrata ritual an Ārya and a Śūdra fight for a skin representing the sun. Sontheimer 1981: 2 and fn. 5.
41. The woolen wreath at the base of the blade of the *jhenḍā* or spear made of wool and the sheep and cattle herds are called *Lakṣumi* (Standard Ma. *Lakṣmī*). One may observe Dhangars who mix a little bit of wool in their food offerings during *jatrās* and afterwards eat these as *prasād.* See also *pad* 45, where Bāṇāī mixes some wool into the food of Khaṇḍobā.
42. *pad* 22: . . .

dudhī snāna hotī āṃgoḷa
ase suryāce teja karhe jaḷa
śuddha bhāgirathīcī kevaḷa
ekavisa svargāvara karhece mūḷa
śuddha satarāvīceṃ [sattravīceṃ] jaḷa.

The seventeenth digit of the moon is the root digit in which the sixteen digits inhere. It is called *jīvabalā,* that is, "blooming and beaming of life" (See *Mahārāṣṭra Śabdakośa,* pt. 7, p. 3007). The new moon enters the plants and the waters with the moon's last, sixteenth part (*kalā*) (Meyer 1937: 230 [part II]). According to the *Bṛhadāraṇyaka-upaniṣad* (1,5,14), it is Prajāpati who enters as the moon with his sixteenth *kalā* into everything which has life, and nothing should be injured on that day (Meyer 1937: *ibidem*). The prohibition against injuring anything on this day would contradict Khaṇḍobā's violent hunt and the subsequent mythical slaughter of the sheep. But it may be that the killing of the *mṛgas* and boars may also echo the famous killing of Prajāpati disguised as a *mṛga* by Rudra (who is *mṛgavyādha*). *Aitareya-brāhmaṇa* III.3.; Deppert 1977: 90ff., 100; Hofstetter 1980: 22ff.

The term *sattrāvi* also reveals the Vāghyā's (Mukindagiri's) acquaintance with the yoga of the Nāths. In fact, the sacred geography of Jejurī can also be expressed in yogic cosmology. This is another component in the cult which cannot be pursued here.

43. Flour soured by exposure to the air and slightly parched upon a baking-plate (Molesworth 1857: 37).

Bibliography

Ahire, Vā. Su. 1964. "Vāghyā muraḷicī gāṇī." In *Ek Hotā Rājā*, edited by Sarojinī Bābar. Mahārāṣṭra Rājya Lokasāhitya Mālā, Puṣpa 10. Bombay, pp. 50f.

Allchin, F.R. 1963. *Neolithic Cattle-Keepers of South India*. Cambridge.

Appasamy, Java. 1980. *Indian Paintings on Glass*. New Delhi: Indian Council for Cultural Relations.

Bābar, Sarojinī. 1976. *Lokasāhityaḥ Śabdakośa* Mumbaī: Mahārāṣṭra Rājya Lokasāhitya Mālā, Puṣpa 18ve.

Beals, Alan R. 1964. "Conflict and Interlocal Festivals in a South Indian Region." In *Religion in South Asia*, edited by Edward B. Harper. Seattle. pp. 99-113.

Bhāūmahārāj. 1961. See *Śrī Khaṇḍobācīṃ padeṃ*.

Bhāve, Vināyaka Lakṣmaṇ, and Śaṃ. Go. Tuḷpuḷe. 1973. *Mahārāṣṭra-Sārasvat*. 5th edition, Muṃbaī (revised by S.G. Tulpule).

Biardeau, Madeleine. 1972. *Clefs pour la pensée hindou*. Paris.

Blackburn, Stuart H. 1985. "Death and Deification: Folk Cults in Hinduism." *History of Religions* 24: 255-74.

Bollée, Willem B. 1977. "A Note on Evil and Its Conquest from Indra to Buddha." *Berkeley Buddhist Studies Series*. pp. 371-81.

———1981. "The Indo-European Sodalities in Ancient India." *Zeitschrift der Deutschen Morgenländischen Gesellschaft* 131/1: 172-91.

Brubaker, Richard. 1977. *The Ambivalent Mistress: A Study of South Indian Village Goddesses and their Meaning*. Ph.D. dissertation, University of Chicago.

Burrow, Thomas (comp.), and Emeneau, Murray B. 1961-68. *Dravidian Etymological Dictionary*. Oxford: Clarendon Press. [DED]

Bussaberger, Robert V., and Betty Dashew Robins. 1968. *The Everyday Art of India*. New York.

Caland, W. 1970. *Das Jaiminīya Brāhmaṇa in Auswahl*. Reprint, Wiesbaden.

Carman, John B., and F. A. Marglin, editors. 1985. *Purity and Auspiciousness in Indian Society*. In *Journal of Developing Societies* 1.1.

Chhabra, B. 1955. "The Incised Inscriptions." In *Ajanta*, edited by G. Yazdani. Volume IV, pp. 121-4. London: Oxford University Press.

Cidānandamūrti, M. 1966. "Kannada Kāvya, Śasanagaḷalli Mailāra mattu Māḷaci". In *Prabuddha Karnāṭake* 48.3: 41-62.

Cintāmaṇi. 1818. *Mallārī Māhātmya*, ms., Marathi, dated 1818.

Ciṭṇīs, Ma. Ra. 1924. *Malhāra Rāmarāva Ciṭaṇīsvaricita Thorale Śāhū Mahārāja hyāṃcem Caritra*, edited by R.B. Kashinath Narayan Sane. 3rd edition. Puṇe.

Clothey, Fred W. 1978. *The Many Faces of Murukaṉ*. The Hague.

Crooke, W. 1968. *The Popular Religion and Folk-Lore of Northern India*. 2 volumes. Delhi.

Dandekar, R. N. 1979. *Vedic Mythological Tracts*. Delhi.

Dāte, Ya. Rā., and Ciṃ. Ga. Karve. 1942, 1947. *Mahārāṣṭra Vākyasaṃpradāya Kośa*. 2 volumes. Puṇeṃ.

Deppert, Joachim. 1977. *Rudras Geburt*. Wiesbaden.

Derrett, J. Duncan M. 1957. *The Hoysaḷas: A Medieval Indian Royal Family*. London: Oxford University Press.

Dhavlikar, M.K. 1979. "Daimabad Bronzes." In *Harappan Civilization*, edited by Gregory L. Possehl. New Delhi: Oxford University Press, pp. 361-6.

Ḍhere, Rā. Ciṃ. 1961. *Khaṇḍobā*. Puṇeṃ: Deśmukh āṇi kampanī.

———1975. *Śrīdharasvāmī Nājharekara-viracita Śrīmalhāri Māhātmya*. Muṃbaī (5th edition).

Duff, Grant. 1963. *History of the Marathas*. Volume II (as cited in *Maharashtra State Gazetteer*, Volume xiv, Satara District, Bombay, 1963).

Dumont, Louis. 1959. "On the Different Aspects or Levels in Hinduism." *Contributions to Indian Sociology* 3.

Eberhard, Wolfram. 1978. *China und seine westlichen Nachbarn. Beiträge zur mittelalterlichen und neueren Geschichte Zentralasiens*. Darmstadt.

Eliade, M. 1977a. *Yoga* (German translation). Zürich.

———1977b. *Myths, Dreams and Mysteries* (English translation). Glasgow: Collins, The Fontana Library of Theology and Philosophy.

Elmore, Wilber Theodore. 1925. *Dravidian Gods in Modern Hinduism*. Madras etc.

Elwin, Verrier. 1947. *The Murias and their Ghotul*. London: Oxford University Press.

Enthoven, R.E. 1924. *The Folklore of Bombay*. Oxford.

Falk, Harry. 1987. *Bruderschaft und Würfelspiel. Untersuchungen und Entwicklungsgeschichte des vedischen Opfers*. Freiburg.

Feldhaus, A. 1990. "The Image of the Forest in the Māhātmyas of the Rivers of the Deccan." In *The History of Sacred Places in India as Reflected in Traditional Literature*, edited by H. Bakker. Leiden: E.J. Brill, pp. 90-102.

Filliozat, J. 1964. *The Classical Doctrine of Indian Medicine* (English translation). Delhi.

Flueckinger, Joyce B. 1989. "Caste and Regional Variants in an Oral Epic Tradition." In *Oral Epics in India*, edited by H. S. Blackburn, P.J. Claus, J.B. Flueckinger, and S.S. Wadley. Berkeley: University of California Press.

Franz, Albrecht, and P. Nagarajan, translators. 1977. *Das Tiruvasagam von Maṉikkavasagar.* Kaikudi.

Gail, A. 1969. *Bhakti im Bhāgavatapurāṇa.* Wiesbaden.

Gazetteer of the Bombay Presidency. 1884. Volume XXII, Dharwar. Bombay.

Gazetteer of Bombay State. 1953. *Botany,* Part I. Bombay.

Gell, A. 1980. "The Gods at Play: Vertigo and Possession in Muria Religion." *Man* 15: 218-48.

Gonda, Jan. 1943. "Zur Frage nach dem Ursprung und Wesen des indischen Dramas." *Acta Orientalia* 12: 329ff.

———1954. *Aspects of Early Viṣṇuism.* Den Haag: Oriental Bookshop.

———1965. *Change and Continuity in Indian Religion.* The Hague: Mouton.

———1978. *Die Religionen Indiens.* Volume I. Stuttgart (2nd edition).

Hardy, Friedhelm. 1983. *Viraha Bhakti. The Early History of Kṛṣṇa Devotion in South India.* Delhi. Oxford Uniyersity Press.

Hassan, Syed Siraj ul. 1920. *The Castes and Tribes of H.E.H. The Nizam's Dominions.* Bombay.

Hauer, J.W. 1927. *Der Vrātya. Untersuchungen über die nichtbrahmanische Religion Altindiens.* Stuttgart.

Heesterman, J.C. 1957. *The Ancient Indian Royal Consecration.* 's-Gravenhage: Mouton.

———1962. "Vrātya and Sacrifice." *Indo-Iranian Journal* 6: 1-37.

———1964. "Brahmin, Ritual and Renouncer." In *Wiener Zeitschrift der Kunde von Süd- und Ost-Asiens* 8: 1ff.

———1967. "The Case of the Severed Head." *Wiener Zeitschrift der Kunde von Süd-und Ost-Asiens* 11: 22-43.

———1981. "Veda and Society. Some Remarks à Propos of the Film 'Altar of Fire'." In *Proceedings of the Nordic South Asia Conference,* edited by Asko Parpola. Helsinki, pp. 51ff.

———1985. *The Inner Conflict of Tradition. Essays in Indian Ritual, Kingship, and Society.* Chicago and London: The University of Chicago Press.

Hiltebeitel, Alf. 1978. "The Indus Valley 'Proto-Śiva,' Reexamined through Reflections on the Goddess, the Buffalo, and the Symbolism of *vāhanas.*" *Anthropos* 73: 769-97.

Hiltebeitel, Alf, editor. 1989. *Criminal Gods and Demon Devotees. Essays on the Guardians of Popular Hinduism.* Albany: State University of New York Press.

Höfer, Andras. 1968. "Randbemerkungen über die Jagdriten im nordwestlichen Hinterindien." *Arehiv für Völkerkunde* 22: 67-89.

Höfer, Andras, and Bishnu P. Shrestha. 1973. "Ghost Exorcism among the Brahmans of Central Nepal." In *Religious Symbols and Their Functions,* edited by Haralds Biezais. Stockholm: Scripta Instituti Donneriani Aboensis, pp. 143f.

Hofstetter, Erich. 1980. *Der Herr der Tiere im alten Indien.* (Freiburger Beiträge zur Indologie, 14). Wiesbaden.

Huizinga, Johan. 1958. *Homo Ludens. Vom Ursprung der Kultur im Spiel.* Hamburg.

Ingalls, Daniel H. H. 1962. "Cynics and Pāśupatas: The Seeking of Dishonor." *Harvard Theological Review* 55: 281-98.

Israel, Milton, and N.K. Wagle, editors. 1987. *Religion and Society in Maharashtra.* (South Asian Studies Papers, 1). Toronto: University of Toronto.

Jayādri Māhātmya. Sanskrit ms., dated Śake 1678 (A.D. 1756), in the possession of R.C. Dhere, Puṇe.

Jettmar, Karl. 1975. *Die Religionen des Hindukusch.* Stuttgart.

Kane, P.V. 1974. *History of Dharmaśāstra.* Vol. V, Part 1. Poona: Bhaṇḍārkar Oriental Research Institute.

Kapp, Dieter B. 1977. *Ein Menschenschöpfungsmythos der Mundas und seine Parallelen.* (Abhandlungen für die Kunde des Morgenlandes, 43/2). Wiesbaden.

Kāṭṭi, L.S. 1966. *Mailāra Kṣetradarśana.* Haveri: Galaganath Mudralaya.

Khāḍe, Rā. Rā. Bāpūrāv Khaṇḍerāv. 1924. *Śrīkṣetra Jejurī-Māhātmya.* Puṇeṃ: Law Printing Press.

Khaṇḍerāyāci Ādi. Author: Jagjīvan. Xeroxed ms.

Khaṇḍobāciṃ Padeṃ. Śrī Sadguru Bhāūmahārāja yāṃcyā Saṃgrahāṃtīl Śrī Khaṇḍobāciṃ Padeṃ. Puṇeṃ, 1963.

Khare, Ga. Ha. 1958. *Mahārāṣṭraciṃ Cāra Daivateṃ.* Puṇeṃ.

Kittel, F. 1968. *Kannaḍa-English Dictionary.* Revised and enlarged edition. Madras.

Kolte, Vi. Bhi., editor. 1978. *Līḷācaritra.* Muṃbaī: Mahārāṣṭra Rājya Sāhitya Saṃskṛti Maṃḍaḷ.

Kosambi, D.D. 1958. *Myth and Reality. Studies in the Formation of Indian Culture.* Bombay.

Kramrisch, Stella. 1968. "Indian Varieties of Art Ritual." In *Myth and Symbols. Studies in Honour of Mircea Eliade,* edited by J. Kitagawa and Charles L. Long. Chicago: The University of Chicago Press.

Krīḍābhirāmamu. 1972. Vallabharāyadu, Vinukoṇḍa. Krīḍābhirāmamu. Secundarabad: Andhra Pradesh Book Distributors.

Law, Bimala Churn. 1973. *Tribes in Ancient India.* Poona (2nd edition).

L'Hernauld, Francoise. 1984. "Subrahmaṇya as a Supreme Deity." In *Discourses on Śiva: Proceedings of a Symposium on the Nature of Religious Imagery,* edited by Michael W. Meister. Bombay: Vakils, Feffer and Simons Ltd., pp. 257-70.

Long, J. Bruce. 1972. "Festival of Repentence: A Study of Mahāśivarātri." *Journal of the Oriental Institute, Baroda* 22: 15ff.

———1983. "Rudra as an Embodiment of Divine Ambivalence in the Śatarudrīya-Stotram." In *Experiencing Śiva,* edited by F.W. Clothey and J.B. Long. Delhi, pp. 104-8.

Lorenzen, David N. 1972. *The Kāpālikas and Kālāmukhas.* New Delhi.

Lüders, Heinrich. 1907. Das Würfelspiel in alten Indien. Berlin: Weidmann'sche Buchhandlung.

Maharashtra State Gazetteer. 1967. *History.* Part I, *Ancient Period.* Bombay.

Macdonell, A.A. 1974. *Vedic Mythology.* Reprint, Delhi.

Majumdar, R.C. 1960. *The Classical Accounts of India.* Calcutta.

Malandra, Geri H. 1982. "The Date of the Ajaṇṭā Cave 27 Inscription." In *Wiener Zeitschrift für die Kunde Südasiens* 26: 37-46.

Malhāri Māhātmya. 1975. *Kavi Śrīdhara Nājharekara kṛta Malhāri Māhātmya,* edited by R.C. Dhere. Puṇe.

Mallāri Māhātmya. Author: Rāmdās, "Disciple of Sadāśiva." Photocopied ms. composed in 1857 (obtained from Dr. S.G. Tulpule).

Mallāri Māhātmya. Author: Siddhapāl Kesarī. Marathi *pothī.*

Malik Aditya. 1993. *Das Puṣkara-Māhātmya: ein religionswissenschaftlicher Beitrag zum Wallfahrtsbegriff in Indien.* Stuttgart: Franz Steiner Verlag.

Manikavacakar. See Franz, Albrecht, and P. Nagarajan, translators.

Marglin, Frédérique A. 1985. *Wives of the God-King. The Rituals of the Devadasis of Puri.* Delhi: Oxford University Press.

Marriott, McKim. 1976. "Interpreting Indian Society: A Monistic Alternative to Dumont's Dualism." *Journal of Asian Studies* 36.1: 189-95.

Mārtaṇḍa Vijaya. Gaṅgādhara kaviviracita Mārtaṇḍavijaya. Edited by Rā. Ciṃ. Ḍhere. Puṇe: Varadā Buks, 1975.

Meyer, J.J. 1937 *Trilogie altindischer Mächte und Feste der Vegetation.* Zürich/ Leipzig.

Misra, P.K. *et al.* 1971. *Nomads in the Mysore City.* Calcutta: Anthropological Survey of India, Government of India.

Moeller, V. 1966. *Die Mythologie der vedischen Religion und des Hinduismus.* Stuttgart.

Molesworth, J.T. 1857. *A Dictionary, Marāṭhī and English.* Bombay.

———1975. *A Marathi-English Dictionary.* Reprint, Poona: Shubhada Saraswat.

Monier-Williams, Monier (compiler). 1970. *A Sanskrit-English Dictionary.* Delhi. Motilal Banarsidass (reprint).

Murty, M.L.K., and Günther D. Sontheimer. 1981. "Prehistoric Background to Pastoralism in the Southern Deccan in the Light of Oral Traditions and Cults of Some Pastoral Communites." *Anthropos* 75: 163-84.

Nāmdev Gāthā. 1970. Government of Maharashtra edition. Bombay.

Narayan Rao, Velcheru. 1989. "Tricking the Goddess: Cowherd Kāṭamarāju and Goddess Gaṅgā in the Telugu Folk Epic." In Hiltebeitel, editor 1989: 105-21.

Obeyesekere, Gananath. 1978. "The Fire-Walkers of Kataragama: The Rise of Bhakti Religiosity in Buddhist Sri Lanka." *Journal of Asian Studies* 37.3: 457-76.

O'Flaherty, Wendy Doniger. 1975. *Hindu Myths.* Penguin Books.

———1981. *Sexual Metaphors and Animal Symbols in Indian Mythology.* Delhi etc.

Oppitz, Michael. 1983. "The Wild Boar as a Plough." *Kailash* 10.3-4: 187-226.

Östor, Akos. 1980. *The Play of the Gods.* Chicago and London.

Paṇasikara, N. V., editor. 1968. *Ekanāthakṛta Āṭha Grantha.* Poona.

Pandey, Shyam Manohar. 1982. *The Hindi Oral Epic Canainī (The Tale of Lorik and Candā)*. (Instituto Universitario Orientale, Naples, Italy). Allahabad: Sahitya Bhawan Private Ltd.

Parpola, Asko. 1973. *Arguments for an Aryan Origin of the South Indian Megaliths*. Madras: State Department of Archaeology, Govt. of Tamilnadu.

———1979. "On the Symbol Concepts of the Vedic Rituals." In *Religious Symbols and Their Functions*, edited by Haralds Biezais. Stockholm: Scripta Instituti Donneriani Aboensis. pp. 143f.

———1983. "Pre-Vedic Indian Background of the Śrauta Ritual." In Frits Staal. *Agni: The Vedic Ritual of the Fire Altar*, Volume II. Berkeley: University of California Press.

———n.d. "The Epic Bard and the Early History of Indian Religions." Unpublished paper.

Pauly. 1925. *Paulys Real-Encyclopädie der classischen Altertumswissenschaft*. 12 volumes. Stuttgart.

Potdār, Da. Vā. 1913. "Jejurī yethīl Śilālekh." *Bhārat Itihās Saṃśodhak Maṇḍal Vārṣik Itivṛtta*, 235-71.

Raghavan, V. 1979. *Festivals, Sports and Pastimes in India*. Ahmedabad: B.J. Institute of Learing and Research.

Ramanujan, A.K. 1973. *Speaking of Śiva*. Baltimore: Penguin Books.

———1981. *Hymns for the Drowning. Poems for Viṣṇu by Nammāḻvār* Princeton: Princeton University Press.

———1989. "Where Mirrors are Windows: Towards an Anthology of Reflections." *History of Religions* 28.3: 187-216.

Rāmdās, "disciple of Sadāśiva". See *Mallāri Māhātmya*.

Rāmdāsi, Anantadās, editor. 1928, 1961, 1968. *Śrīsamarthāñcī/āṃcā Gāthā*. Puṇeṃ.

Rao, B.S.L. Hanumantha. 1973. *Religion in Andhra*. (Karnatak University Ph.D. thesis, 1969-70). Tripurasundari.

Ruben, Walter. 1962. *Waldabenteuer des indischen Helden*. Berlin: Akademie Verlag.

Russell and Hiralal. 1916. *The Castes and Tribes of the Central Provinces of India*. Volume III. Reprint, Delhi: Cosmo Publications, 1975.

Saletore, B.A. 1935. *The Wild Tribes in Indian History*. Lahore: Motilal Banarsi Das.

Samarthāñcī Gāthā. See Rāmdāsī, Anantadās, editor.

Sastry, P.V. Parabrahma. 1978. *The Kākatīyas*. (Arch. Series No. 52). Hyderabad.

Sāvant, Kṛ. Rā. 1985. "Āṅgaṇevāḍīcī Jatrā." In *Utsava, Dīpāvaḷī*. Mumbāī, Dādar: Śrīgaṅgādhar Printing Press, 77-80.

Settar, S. 1961. "The Brahmadeva Pillars." *Artibus Asiae* 33, No. 1/2.

———1975. *Hoysaḷa Sculptures in the National Museum Copenhagen*. Copenhagen.

———1982. "Memorial Stones in South India." In *The Memorial Stones of India*, edited by S. Settar and G.D. Sontheimer. Dharwad/Delhi. pp. 183-97.

Settar, S., and G.D. Sontheimer, editors. 1982. *The Memorial Stones of India* Dharwad/Delhi.

Sharma, B.R., editor. 1966. *Jaiminīya-Upaniṣad Brāhmaṇa*. Tirupati.

Shastri, D.R. 1963. *Origin and Development of the Rituals of Ancestor Worship in India*. Calcutta.

Shulman, David. 1979. "Murukaṉ, the Mango and Ekambareśvara-Śiva." *Indo-Iranian Journal* 21: 27-40.

———1980a. *Tamil Temple Myths: Sacrifice and Divine Marriage in the South Indian Śaiva Tradition*. Princeton: Princeton Universtiy Press.

———1980b. "On South Indian Bandits and Kings." *The Indian Economic and Social History Review* 17.3: 283-306.

———1985. *The King and the Clown in South Indian Myth and Poetry*. Princeton: Princeton University Press.

Sircar, D.C. 1971. "The Nāgas and the Yakṣas." In *Studies in the Religious Life of Ancient and Medieval India*, pp. 133ff. Delhi.

Sircar, D.C., editor. 1961. *Annual Report on Indian Epigraphy for 1957-58*. Delhi: Government of India Press.

Sontheimer, Günther-Dietz. 1976. *Birobā, Mhaskobā und Khaṇḍobā. Ursprung, Geschichte und Umwelt von pastoralen Gottheiten in Mahārāṣṭra*. (Schriftenreihe des Südasien-Instituts der Universität Heidelberg, 27) Wiesbaden. (English translation: 1989c).

———1977. "King Vikrama and Kamaḷu Śinḍe, the Shepherd: Bhakti Episodes from an Oral Epic of the Dhangars in Maharashtra." *South Asian Digest of Regional Writing* 6: 97-128.

———1978. "Some Incidents in the History of the God Khaṇḍobā." In *Asie du Sud. Traditions et Changements. VIth European Conference on Modern South Asian Studies*, edited by Marc Gaborieau and Alice Thorner, pp. 111-17. Paris. (See also this volume.)

———1981. "Dasarā at Devaraguḍḍa. Ritual and play in the Cult of Mailār/Khaṇḍobā." *South Asian Digest of Regional Writing* 10: 1-28. (See also this volume.)

———1982. "The Hero- and Sati-Stones of Mahārāṣṭra." In *The Memorial Stones of India*, edited by S. Settar and G.D. Sontheimer. Dharwad/Delhi, pp. 261-81.

———1983. "The Dasarā Festival at Devaraguḍḍa (Karnāṭaka): Ritual and Dramatic Performance in the Cult of Mailār." In *Procceedings of the VIIIth European Conference on Modern South Asian Studies*.

———1984. "The Mallāri/Khaṇḍobā Myth as Reflected in Folk Art and Ritual." *Anthropos* 79: 155-70. (See also this volume.)

———1985. "Folk Deities in the Vijayanagara Empire: Narasiṃha and Mallaṇṇa/Mailār." In *Vijayanagara—City and Empire: New Currents of*

Research, edited by Anna Libera Dallapiccola in collaboration with S. Zingel-Ave Lallemant. Wiesbaden, pp. 144-58.

———1986. "Bhakti in the Khaṇḍobā Cult." Paper read at the Third Conference on Early Devotional Literature in New Indo Aryan Languages, Leiden, 1985. (See also this volume.)

———1987. "Rudra and Khaṇḍobā: Continuity in Folk Religion." In *Religion and Society in Maharashtra*, edited by Milton Israel and N.K. Wagle. Toronto: University of Toronto, Centre for South Asian Studies, pp. 1-31. (See also this volume.)

———1989a. "Between Ghost and God: A Folk Deity of the Deccan." In *Criminal Gods and Demon Devotees: Essays on the Guardians of Popular Hinduism*, edited by Alf Hiltebeitel. Albany: SUNY Press, pp. 299-337. (See also this volume.)

———1989b. "The Myth of the God and His Two Wives: Two Pastoral Versions from Maharashtra." In *Living Texts from India*, edited by R. Barz and M. Thiel-Horstmann. Wiesbaden, pp. 7-62. (See also this volume.)

———1989c. *Pastoral Deities in Western India*, translated by Anne Feldhaus. New York: Oxford University Press.

———1990. "God as the King for All: The Sanskrit *Mallāri Māhātmya* and its Context." (See also this volume.)

———1991a. "The Ramāyāṇa in Contemporary Folk Traditions of Maharashtra." In *Ramāyāṇa and Ramāyāṇas*, edited by M. Thiel-Horstmann. Wiesbaden, pp. 115-37.

———1991b. "Bhakti in the Khaṇḍobā cult." In *Devotion Divine. Bhakti Traditions from the Regions of India*. Studies in Honour of Charlotte Vaudeville (Groningen Oriental Studies, 8). Groningen/Paris. pp. 231-53. (See also this volume.)

Sprockhoff, J.F. 1981. "Āraṇyaka and Vānaprastha in der vedischen Literatur." *WZKS* 25: 19-90.

Śrīdhara. 1975. *Śrī Harivijaya*. Puṇeṃ: Yaśavanta Prakāśan.

Śrīkṣetra-Jejurī-Māhātmya. See Khāḍe 1925.

Sri Venkateswara Leela Mahathyamu. See Subrahmanyam, N.

Stanley, John M. 1977. "Special Time, Special Power: The Fluidity of Power in a Popular Hindu Festival." *Journal of Asian Studies* 37.1: 27-43.

———1987. "Niṣkāma and Sakāma Bhakti: Pandharpur and Jejuri." In *Religion and Society in Maharashtra*, edited by M. Israel and N.K. Wagle. Toronto: University of Toronto, Centre for South Asian Studies, pp. 1-36.

Stein, Burton. 1969. "Integration of the Agrarian System of South India." In *Land Control and Social Structure in Indian History*, edited by R.E. Frykenberg. Madison.

——— 1983. "Mahāṇavamī: Medieval and Modern Kingly Ritual." In *Essays on Gupta Culture*, edited by Bardwell L. Smith. Delhi: Motilal Banarsidass, 67-90.

Stietencron, Heinrich von. 1966. *Indische Sonnenpriester. Sāmba und die Sākadvipiya-Brāhmaṇa*. Wiesbaden.

Subrahmanyam, N. 1962. *Sri Venkateswara Leela Mahathmyamu*. (English translation) *The Glories and Mysteries of Lord Venkateswara*. Tirumalai Hills.

Thakur, Upendra. 1963. *A History of Suicide in India*. Delhi.

Thurston, Edgar. 1909. *Castes and Tribes of Southern India*, Volume IV. Reprint, Delhi: Cosmo Publications, 1975.

Tripathi, Gaya Charan. 1968. *Der Ursprung und die Entwicklung der Vāmana-Legende in der indischen Literatur*. Wiesbaden.

Tripāṭhī, Bhāgirath Prasād. 1969. "Śune kukkurāya hitaṃ śūnyam?" *Sārasvati-Suṣamā* (Sanskrit University, Varanasi) 24.2.

Tukārām. 1972. *Tukārām-Gāthā*, edited by Pāṃgārkar. 2nd edition?, Puṇeṃ.

———1973. *Tukārāmabāvāñcyā Abhaṅgācī Gāthā*. Government of Maharashtra edition. Mumbaī.

Tulpule, Shankar Gopal. 1979. *Classical Marāṭhī Literature*. Wiesbaden.

Turner, R.L. 1966, 1969, 1971. *A Comparative Dictionary of the Indo-Aryan Languages*. London, New York, and Toronto: Oxford University Press.

Turner, Victor. 1977. "Sacrifice as Quintessential Process, Prophylaxis or Abandonment." *History of Religions* 16.3: 198-215.

Vallabharāyadu, Vinukoṇḍa. See *Krīḍābhirāmamu*.

Vaudeville, Charlotte. 1974. *Kabīr*. Oxford: Oxford University Press.

———1980. "The Govardhana Myth in Northern India." *Indo-Iranian Journal* 22: 1-24.

Veezhinathan, N., editor. 1976. *Śrīśaṅkaravijaya of Anantānandagiri*. Madras: Centre of Advanced Study in Philosophy, University of Madras.

Verma, Onkar P. 1970. *The Yādavas and Their Times*. Nagpur: Vidarbha Samshodhan Mandal.

Vinayaka. 1872. *Mallāri Māhātmya*. Marathi. Bombay, 1872 (composed in 1871).

Whitney, W.D., translator. 1905. *Atharva-Veda Saṃhitā*. Harvard Oriental Series, VIII. Cambridge.

Wilhelm, Friedrich. 1991. "Hunting and the Concept of Dharma." In *Rules and Remedies in Classical Indian Law*, edited by Julia Leslie. Leiden: E.J. Brill, pp. 7-16.

Yocum, Glenn E. 1977. "Mānikkavācakar's Image of Śiva." *History of Religions* 17: 20-41.

———1982. *Hymns to the Dancing Śiva*. New Delhi.

Zvelebil, Kamil Veith. 1973 *The Smile of Murugan*. Leiden.

———1974. *Tamil Literature*. Wiesbaden.

———1977a. "The Beginnings of *bhakti* in South India." *Temenos* 13: 223ff.

———1977b. "A Guide to Murukaṉ." *Journal of Tamil Studies* 11: 82-105.

———1977c. "Vaḷḷi and Murugan—A Dravidian Myth." *Indo-Iranian Journal* 19: 227-46.

Index